The Power of the People

Following the collapse of the Ottoman Empire and the founding of the Republic in 1923 under the rule of Atatürk and his Republican People's Party, Turkey embarked on extensive social, economic, cultural and administrative modernization programs which would lay the foundations for modern day Turkey. *The Power of the People* shows that the ordinary people shaped the social and political change of Turkey as much as Atatürk's strong spurt of modernization. Adopting a broader conception of politics, focusing on daily interactions between the state and society and using untapped archival sources, Murat Metinsoy reveals how rural and urban people coped with the state policies, local oppression, exploitation, and adverse conditions wrought by the Great Depression through diverse everyday survival and resistance strategies. Showing how the people's daily practices and beliefs survived and outweighed the modernizing elite's projects, this book gives new insights into the social and historical origins of Turkey's backslide to conservative and Islamist politics, demonstrating that the making of modern Turkey was an outcome of intersection between the modernization and the people's responses to it.

Murat Metinsoy is Professor of History and Political Science in the Faculty of Economics, at Istanbul University. His research interests include the history and politics of modern Turkey and popular politics under authoritarian regimes. As the author of *Turkey in World War II: State and Society in Everyday Life* (Third edition, 2020) he was awarded the Best Young Social Scientist Award by The Turkish Social Science Association and the Best Book Award by the Ottoman Bank Archives and Research Center. He is a member of the Middle East Studies Association, the Turkish Social Science Association, and the History Foundation of Turkey.

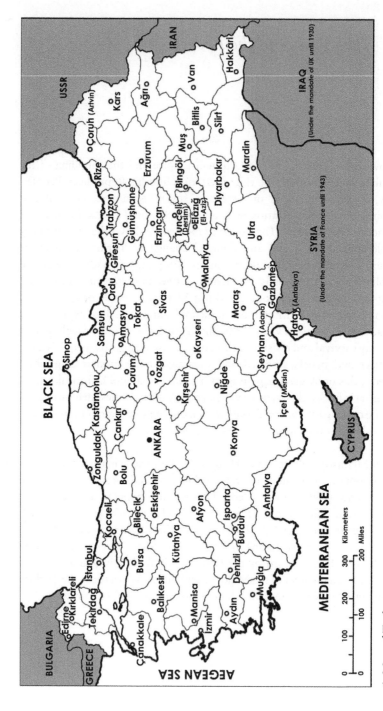

1 Map of Turkey

The Power of the People

Everyday Resistance and Dissent in the
Making of Modern Turkey, 1923–38

MURAT METİNSOY
Istanbul University

CAMBRIDGE
UNIVERSITY PRESS

University Printing House, Cambridge CB2 8BS, United Kingdom

One Liberty Plaza, 20th Floor, New York, NY 10006, USA

477 Williamstown Road, Port Melbourne, VIC 3207, Australia

314–321, 3rd Floor, Plot 3, Splendor Forum, Jasola District Centre, New Delhi – 110025, India

103 Penang Road, #05–06/07, Visioncrest Commercial, Singapore 238467

Cambridge University Press is part of the University of Cambridge.

It furthers the University's mission by disseminating knowledge in the pursuit of education, learning, and research at the highest international levels of excellence.

www.cambridge.org
Information on this title: www.cambridge.org/9781316515464
DOI: 10.1017/9781009025775

First published 2021

Printed in the United Kingdom by TJ Books Limited, Padstow Cornwall

A catalogue record for this publication is available from the British Library.

ISBN 978-1-316-51546-4 Hardback

Contents

Figures

Illustrations

Graphs

Tables

Acknowledgments

This book is the culmination of fifteen years of intense research. Many people and institutions have contributed to its fruition. I owe a debt of gratitude to them all. My greatest debt is to Asım Karaömerlioğlu, Şevket Pamuk, Zafer Toprak, Çağlar Keyder, Ayşe Buğra, Cengiz Kırlı and late Yavuz Selim Karakışla at Boğaziçi University; Ferdan Ergut at the Middle East Technical University (ODTÜ); and Levent Ürer, Namık S. Turan, Burak Gülboy, Ayşegül Komsuoğlu and Haluk Alkan at İstanbul University. They shared with me their time, energy, wisdom and knowledge, which shaped my understanding of history and politics. I am lucky to have developed my academic skills as a teaching assistant at the Atatürk Institute of Boğaziçi University and as a postdoctoral researcher at the History Department of ODTÜ. This book would not be possible without the academic freedom and pluralism of these institutions.

Many distinguished institutions and people also helped me generously. I would like to thank the American Research Institute in Turkey for the ARIT Doctoral Fellowship and the Boğaziçi University Foundation for the Ayşe-Zeynep Birkan Doctoral Fellowship. The Turkish Social Science Association and the Ottoman Bank Archive and Research Center that awarded my previous book in 2007 encouraged and enabled me to immerse myself in my studies. Ohio State University offered me the opportunity to carry out doctoral research in the United States. Carter Findley and Jane Hathaway at OSU shaped my views about Turkish history and helped me graciously during my stay in Columbus. The Turkish Academy of Science and the Scientific and Technological Research Council of Turkey financially supported my postdoctoral research. I feel very fortunate to be a postdoctoral fellow at ODTÜ and owe thanks to Seçil Akgün, Akile Zorlu-Durukan, Attila Aytekin and Agah Hazır. Many other people enriched this work by encouraging, guiding and critiquing me over the years. I am grateful to Stephanie Cronin, who organized the conferences at Oxford University where I received insightful commentaries. Our warm discussions with Paul Dumont in Strasbourg, where we visited for my wife's doctoral studies, provided me invaluable ideas I incorporated into my work. Kathryn Kranzler, Marta Tanrıkulu, Ami Naramor and Charlotte Weber had their touch on this book by editing its different parts. I am thankful to three respected publishers, Ahmet Salcan, Tanıl Bora and Kerem Ünüvar, who always trusted and encouraged me. I am grateful to the whole team at Cambridge University Press, especially my editor, Maria Marsh, Atifa Jiwa and Daniel Brown who perfectly and patiently guided me throughout the publication process. I also thank Thomas Haynes and Vigneswaran Viswanathan for their supportive efforts during production process. Undoubtedly I owe great debt to three anonymous reviewers. They meticulously examined the manuscript and offered constructive and vital comments. Özgün Emre Koç, Burak Hacıoğlu and Ahmet Köroğlu contributed to the preparation of illustrative materials. Nejat Akar, Cantürk Gümüş and İsmail Kara shared special images with me. I am thankful to them all.

For this research, I made countless forays into a number of archives and libraries. While I combed through the rich archives, roaming from library to library, leafing through the numerous volumes of old newspapers and journals, many archivists and librarians not only helped me but also turned into good companions. Particularly my extremely supportive friends Kamber Yılmaz and Seyfi Berk at the Boğaziçi University Aptullah Kuran Library supplied me with crucial sources at crucial moments. I also thank the whole staff at the Republican Archive, the General Directorate of Security Archive, the Interior Ministry Archive, the Turkish Historical Society Archive, the Library and Archive of the Grand National Assembly of Turkey, İstanbul University Library, Taksim Atatürk Library, Beyazıt State Library, the National Library and the William Oxley Thompson Library at OSU.

On the personal front, many people made my life easier and more cheerful. I will always remember the friendly assistance of Emre Sencer, Vefa Erginbaş, Tugan Eritenel and Sevay Atılgan. I would also like to express my gratitude to a history lover as well as one of the best physicians of Turkey, Tayyar Sarıoğlu. My brother Yılmaz Metinsoy and my friends Mustafa Eroğlu, Caner Sancaktar and Murat Çekem have my thanks for their good cheer and assistance during difficult times.

Last but certainly not least, I am grateful to my father, İbrahim Metinsoy, and my mother, Behiye Metinsoy. They taught me above all to be a good person. This book never would have happened without their unconditional love and support. My mother-in-law, Banu Mahir, and father-in-law, Mehmet Mahir, deserve my thanks for their support and kindness. I feel my deepest gratitude to my wife, Elif Mahir Metinsoy, and my little daughter, İpek Metinsoy. Elif juggled family life and her own academic studies to give me her time, and always supported me with her optimism and patience; İpek gave me most of her playing time, albeit reluctantly. Finally, this book is dedicated to my father, my source of inspiration, who stands out as a model for me with his adventurous life full of struggle against poverty and injustice, but without losing hope, just like most people featured in this book.

Introduction

Toward an Infrahistory of Republican Turkey

Taş olsam yandım idi	If I was stone I was burned
Toprak oldum da dayandım	I endured by becoming soil

Thus wrote Aşık Veysel, the greatest folk poet of the Turkish republic, eighty years ago. These verses powerfully suggest the subtlety with which the Anatolian people endured the challenges and shocking upheavals of the twentieth century. Indeed, this period – experienced in much of the world as an age of extremes – was by all measures an extraordinary one for Turkey's inhabitants too. The collapse of the Ottoman Empire through devastating wars created upheaval throughout the Anatolian peninsula. Modern Turkey arose from the ashes of the empire, but the fighting did not end with the establishment of the Republic of Turkey in 1923. The first two decades of the republic that elapsed after the wars were crucial in the making of modern Turkey. The citizens of the new state were exposed to yet another battle, this one for "progress." This battle poured salt into the wounds of war by creating social, political and cultural turbulence.

In 1923, Mustafa Kemal Atatürk, leader of the Independence War and founder of republican Turkey, established a modernizing dictatorship dominated by his Republican People's Party (Cumhuriyet Halk Partisi) (RPP). He assumed the presidency of both the Republic of Turkey and the RPP. Under his presidency from 1923 to 1938, the young republic witnessed spectacular schemes intended to catapult Turkey into modernity. The creation of a Turkish nation modeled on Western secular nations, a state-building process under an authoritarian system, the commercialization and commodification of the economy and state-led industrialization gained momentum. The world's most ruinous economic crisis, which depleted the country's resources and energy further, coincided with this period and helped consolidate authoritarianism. The costs of political and economic modernization

1

loomed in social problems. The rulers of the new Turkey, particularly Atatürk, sincerely desired to promote welfare by changing their society profoundly. However, this process created its own problems such as new hierarchies, privileges, burdens, grievances and conflicts, which reshaped the republican modernization in turn.

Despite the radical modernization schemes to achieve nation-state building, economic development and social and cultural renewal, many features of Turkish society changed little. The durability of the peasantry was so visible by the 1980s that it led famous historian Eric Hobsbawm to write about Turkey in his magnum opus *Age of Extremes*: "Only one peasant stronghold remained in or around the neighborhood of Europe and the Middle East – Turkey, where the peasantry declined but in the mid-1980s, still remained an absolute majority."[1] Not only the peasantry but also its culture would continue to live and even permeate urban areas. Secular reforms did not extinguish the people's religious and traditional way of life except for a tiny coterie of the ruling elite and educated urbanite middle class.

On one level, this persistence points to the early republican state's failure to transform the Turkish society from a rural, traditional one to an urban, modern one – that is, to the structural limits of Turkish modernization. However, as this book reveals, another important but unacknowledged reason is the everyday politics of ordinary people: the people's coping strategies, which Aşık Veysel expresses succinctly in his verse above. This politics revealed itself through everyday, mostly informal forms of resistance, which found its best expression in James C. Scott's notion of "weapons of the weak."[2] Anatolian people generally coped with the hardships they encountered through these weapons.

The proclamation of the republic and the abolition of the caliphate culminated in the formation of the first opposition political party, the Progressive Republican Party (Terakkiperver Cumhuriyet Fırkası) (PRP), in 1924 and the Sheikh Sait Rebellion with Kurdish and Islamist overtones in 1925. However, these two events, followed by an assassination plot hatched in 1926, provided Atatürk the opportunity to hold extraordinary powers. The Maintenance of Order Law (Takriri Sükun Kanunu) in 1925 and the new Criminal Law, adopted from Fascist Italy in 1926, wiped out the opposition. A few well-known rebellions were suppressed instantly. Nevertheless, the people coped daily with dizzying secular reforms, burdensome economic policies and abject poverty intensified by the Great Depression in mostly informal ways, which counterbalanced the high pressure of authoritarian power.

This book probes the everyday politics of ordinary people – specifically, the rural and urban poor and low-income individuals – in a period when formal politics was closed to them. By "everyday and informal politics" I mean the varied dissenting opinions ordinary people expressed about the regime, as well as their daily coping strategies that evoked wider reverberations by affecting politics directly or indirectly. In other words, my main object is to illuminate how the rural and urban masses resisted unfavorable changes and obligations, social injustice, loss of livelihood, monopolies, taxes, low wages and lack of social rights. I then evaluate the impact of their resistance to policy. By underlining the interplay between the top and bottom rungs of society, this book exposes the underpinnings of the official politics – that is, the role of the grass roots in Turkey's social and political change.

I argue that ordinary people, using all means available to them, struggled to weather the crises they confronted and contested their oppressors and exploiters. People's individualistic, daily and spur-of-the-moment but widespread actions to get rid of hardships generated wider, macro consequences. Through informal and indirect mechanisms of negotiation occurring in daily life, those who were excluded from high politics prompted the government to soften its policies, thereby shaping political life and the modernization process. People's covert criticisms and struggles, intentionally or not, generated concessions from the government, notwithstanding the lack of any radical change in the short term.

Undoubtedly, individuals' views and actions could be contradictory and heterogeneous. A person who espoused one policy or reform of the regime might oppose others. There were subordinate individuals who colluded with the authorities. Indeed, a considerable number were true believers in the new rulers. The people's affirmative responses are already well known. Rather, my aim is to elucidate the hitherto unnoticed dissonant views and actions that distorted, rejected or provided an alternative to government discourse and policies.

I mean by ordinary people several segments of subordinate groups in general rather than a single, specific social category. Indeed, opinions and attitudes are not easy to attribute to precisely defined groups. Despite their differences in many respects, segments of the ordinary people like poor peasants and low-income wage earners including workers, artisans and low-paid white-collar workers often spoke a similar language and acted in similar ways to confront the daily challenges of living under an authoritarian regime.

In this book, I approach the most extraordinary years of modern Turkey from the angle of ordinary people and their ordinary life. In the first place, I hope to show that the republic's citizens were not without options for a way out in the face of new challenges. Everyday life was rich with possibilities for action. The bulk of such actions was informal, temporary, pragmatic and spur of the moment – the timeless routines of daily life – while some solutions were devised according to the circumstances. Thus the people's repertory of every-day and informal action has tended to seem irrelevant or trivial to scholars, who have been generally interested in large-scale or well-known events, organizations and individuals. This rich palette of dissonant opinion and action of ordinary people is also hard to detect with the standard radar of historians. Perhaps the most apparent blind spot of this radar is the narrow conception of politics. The politics in this sense prioritizes and therefore traces only legal or organizational activities performed by bureaucrats, institutions or organized movements, thereby obscuring the people's voice and the wide array of struggles poeticized by Veysel.

The common trait of the historical literature on Turkish moderniza-tion is its scant attention to ordinary people and their everyday experi-ences. The people have been considered ignorant and hapless victims, cynical opponents or brainwashed masses due to the lack of their own political organizations and movements. This book draws a different and more complicated picture by revealing the people's critical voices and coping strategies. In this picture, the political actors are not only the state, the elite and the organized opposition but also individuals, families, communities, peasants, laborers, white-collar workers, retirees, widows and orphans – women and men, old and young. It offers an extraordinary history of ordinary people in which the con-flicts and interplays are not simply those between continuity and change, rich and poor, or state and society but also encompass a variety of social, economic, cultural, geographical, psychological and gender-related factors. Understanding the rich experiences of people in those times can also shed light on their resourcefulness under authoritarian regimes in the past and even today, whether in

Turkey or elsewhere in the Middle East, in dealing with challenges by devising solutions on their own terms.

Writing the history of ordinary people entails the use of novel sources and source-reading methods. It is possible to draw new evidence from untapped sources such as police and gendarmerie records, politicians' reports on election districts or inspection regions, petitions and letters, the "wish lists" of provincial party congresses and contemporary newspapers and memoirs. Though many of the written sources and the memoirs imbibed the republican modernization rhetoric, even these may give hints about the people's experiences. Finding traces of people's lives and voices who are mostly illiterate also requires new methods of analysis. Among these strategies is Carlo Ginzburg's advice to "read between the lines" and "cross check the sources" as he did in *The Cheese and the Worms*, which illustrates social conflict in sixteenth-century Italy by recounting the life and thought of a miller, Menocchio, via his trial records. Likewise, Subaltern Studies' method "to read official documents against the grain" for biases and omissions facilitates unearthing the people's experiences and views buried within the texts.[3]

Existing History: Focusing on State and High Politics, Overlooking Ordinary People and Everyday Life

Since the Turkish single-party regime occupied a place on the continuum of authoritarian regimes of the interwar period, studies on early republican history have shared similarities with the classical histories of these regimes. Until the advent of new social history, scholars were more or less united in their appraisal of the authoritarian regimes of the interwar period. Historians of colonial and postcolonial India, Nazi Germany, Fascist Italy, Stalin's Soviet Union and Reza Shah's Iran overemphasized the coercive and transformative features of the state. The concept of totalitarianism was amply used to define these regimes. Society was regarded as being atomized under the absolute suppression of the state.[4] Despite recent studies, for the most part historiography on early republican Turkey has taken place within this genre.

Fortunately, recent works on other countries have revealed social resistance under such regimes. Inspired by the history from below of the British Marxist historians, the Subaltern Studies school has challenged the elitist narratives of Indian history, be they colonialist, Marxist or nationalist by demonstrating how mostly downtrodden rural masses of colonial and postcolonial India displayed everyday and informal actions and thus played a crucial role in shaping modern India. *Alltagsgeschichte* (everyday life history) scholars of the Third Reich have criticized the concept of totalitarianism, underlining the fragmentations inherent to the Nazis and the role of the people's dissent and nonconformity, which resulted in the Nazis' failure to establish the *Volksgemeinscahft*.[5] Social history studies on the Soviet Union have disparaged the totalitarianism model by showing the contestation of communist projects by peasants and workers. Likewise, new accounts of Iran have revealed the masses' resistance to Reza Shah's authoritarian modernizing programs.[6]

Despite the great progress in the history of the ordinary people in other geographies, unfortunately the state and elite prevail as main focal points with a few recent exceptions.[7] Both modernist-nationalist narratives and critical Marxian or Islamist accounts are mesmerized by the republican Kemalist reforms. Their focus exclusively revolves around the state, elites and ideologies. The modernists eulogize the republic as a decisive revolution against religious backlash (*irtica*), whereas the latter questions it by overemphasizing its coercive and transformative features.[8]

Turkish politics of the early republican era is equated with high politics, in which any overt or organized political contests were absent. Bereft of organizations and rights, the crowds receive scant attention and are portrayed as silent masses or cynical opponents. The micro negotiation processes between state and society or between rich and poor that occur in everyday life and that bear little resemblance to the usual political action go unnoticed. Social resistance to the state is reduced to collective protests and rebellions, which are seen as flashes in the pan the state never condoned.

Admittedly, this literature has contributed to our understanding of domination and injustice. Indeed, the early republican state encroached upon people's daily lives by impinging on liberties and rights while economic inequalities deepened. Yet this was only one side of the coin. On the other side were rampant social discontent and struggle. The objective of this book is to flip the coin, illuminating this other side hitherto left in the dark.

Missing Peasantry

Orada bir köy var uzakta	There is a village, far away
O köy bizim köyümüzdür	That village is our village
Gitmesek de, görmesek de	Even if we don't go, even if we don't see
O köy bizim köyümüzdür	That village is our village

These verses of Ahmet Kutsi Tecer, a famous republican bureaucrat and poet, became a popular motto during the 1930s. These words, I think, are applicable to the scholarship. Though peasants comprised more than 80 percent of the population in these years, scholars' interest has barely extended beyond economic policies and agricultural structures. Almost no deep research has been carried out regarding the peasants' everyday life, their struggles for the barest survival and rights and the interaction between the peasants and the government except for a few contemporary village monographs and short papers.[9]

Due to the lack of peasant movements akin to the Bulgarian agrarian movement or to rebellions like those in Russia, Eastern Europe and northern China, even critical accounts portray the Anatolian peasantry as a submissive mass.[10] The fixation on high politics and economic structures has obscured the social conflicts that occurred in everyday life. Scholars generally overrate the abolition of the tithe and the republic's populist-peasantist discourse, believed to have eased the peasants' conditions. Considering smallholding as a static land tenure system is another tendency that has led to underestimation of intra-village conflicts over land and scarce resources.[11]

Except for Kurdish uprisings, the rampant crime and violence plaguing the countryside – including assault, theft, robbery, arson and banditry – is dismissed as *vakayı adiye*, common events of no importance and undeserving of scholarly attention. Banditry has been seen as peculiar to tribalism or to Kurdish provinces. Both Turkish and Kurdish nationalist narratives, covertly but not deliberately, supported each other by focusing on the role of Kurdish tribes and political organizations, portrayed as uncivilized criminals or separatists in Turkish nationalist accounts and as the national forces in Kurdish awakening narratives. Turkish scholars attribute banditry to tribalism, Kurdish separatism or foreign agitation. Critical accounts similarly neglect banditry and rural crimes in Kurdish villages unless connected to the Kurdish cause.[12]

These narratives also tend to overemphasize the power of vertical ties linking poor peasants to tribal leadership through patronage and other hierarchies.[13] Although such ties were indeed important, treating the tribal and village communities as homogenous and free from inner differentiation omits the class conflicts within them. Despite shared culture linking the different classes as emphasized by Clifford Geertz, the peasantry was not a homogenous entity, nor did peasants act as a class in the way Marxian accounts such as Theodor Shanin's defined class for the peasantry.[14] In this regard, the resulting conflicts within the rural communities constitute the main components of peasant politics and warrant the closer examination this book seeks to undertake.

Conventional Labor History: Prioritizing Industrial Labor and Organized Movements

Turkey's social and economic transformation from an agricultural society to a more capitalistic and industrial one accelerated under the republic. State-led industrialization undeniably brought working people certain benefits in the long term, yet in the short term it created enormous burdens. The labor history of the era focuses primarily on these burdens, examining working conditions and the state's economic and social policies. The weakness of organized action is treated as a deviation from idealized labor movements. The first (conditions) and final (organized struggles) stages of working-class formation were overemphasized at the expense of the intermediate stages, such as workers' perception of their conditions and their everyday struggles, which are prerequisites for the formation of class consciousness and organizational movements.[15]

Perceiving organized movements as a unique form of labor politics, the conventional accounts have seen the early and mid-1920s as an active period. This period has been assumed to have come to a halt in the 1930s with the elimination of the left and the organized labor movement with the shutting down of unions and prolabor newspapers.[16] This assumption has led scholars to interpret the social policy measures taken in these years and the labor legislation of 1936 as a product of corporatist ideology, the requirements of International Labor Organization membership or the desire to create a stable and productive labor force rather than working people's struggles. The peasant origin of the vast number of working people and the peasant workers' resistance to being forced into permanent wage labor have been viewed as a deviation from the linear model of development of industrial labor and working-class politics. Therefore these laborers have been seen as a passive industrial reserve army.[17]

Another common argument is that the government pacified laborers by creating a labor aristocracy consisting of well-paid, privileged groups and better-off state officials furnished with social security. Also widely emphasized is the government's attempt to control laboring groups by organizing them on an occupational basis according to the corporatist model. All of these arguments hinder analysis of these people's experiences, perceptions and class conflict within professional associations as well as struggles between rival associations of employees and employers.[18]

Scholars have also tended to feature industrial and organized workers, often those with a leftist consciousness, at the expense of others. Labor history studies on the interwar period have neglected small-scale artisans, who were the backbone of the working class in Turkey at that time. Their response to industrialization has yet to be investigated because they are seen as the declining remnants of the preindustrial society or lumpen proletariat.[19]

Secular Reforms: Partnership of the Modernist and Conservative Accounts

The republic's secular reform, as one of the most comprehensive in world history, is the most intriguing aspect of Turkish history and politics. The new state abandoned the organized institutions of Islam such as the sultanate, the caliphate, *medreses*, sharia courts, *tariqa*s, shrines, the fez, the face veil, sexual segregation, the Islamic calendar and the Arabic alphabet while adopting a new Civil Code, Latin script, the Western calendar, Western dress styles and women's political rights. Almost all studies on Turkish secularism concentrate on Atatürk's intentions, legal regulations or political opposition to secular reforms.[20] Although their points of departure and evaluations differ, nationalist-modernization narratives and critical accounts both view the secular reforms in light of elite motivation. The former regards secularism as a progressive step against religiosity whereas the latter mostly emphasizes the authoritarian agenda of the elite. In this last group, particularly Islamists see the secular reforms as the alienation of the irreligious elite from Muslim society and as a blind imitation of the West.[21]

All of these rival narratives consider the people as passive or without options, overlooking their everyday and more complex interactions with the reforms. And when they consider opposition to the secular reforms, the focus is always upon religious dissidents and riots. Modernists label such contending with secularism as backward reactions of hidebound traditionalists whereas Islamists attribute such reactions to the Muslims' attachment to their values.[22] Both groups ignore the diversity of responses in daily life ranging from selective adaptation to subtle resistance. Moreover, both modernist and Islamist accounts share a preoccupation with the old vs. new dichotomy, failing to notice hybridity – that is, the persistence of more traditional and religious ways of life alongside and intermingled with modern forms.[23] Finally, they have overly relied on cultural explanations and ignored more complex social, psychological and gender-related factors and economic dislocation exacerbated by the economic policies of the government, which shaped people's perception of the secular reforms.

Toward an Infrahistory of Modern Turkey

Fortunately, the new sources and approaches enable us to see this extraordinary era from the ordinary people's viewpoint. Writing a people's history entails not only recalling the awful and dark scenes of their lives but also their active, hopeful and resistant moments. Going beyond the monotone depictions of traditional narratives requires unfolding the divergent opinions and avenues of action available to them. As E. P. Thompson suggested long ago, avoiding the portrayal of ordinary people as passive victims, this book rehabilitates their agency, particularly their struggles for survival and for the recognition of their rights in the context of early republican Turkey, as an infrapolitics of Turkey's politics.[24] I offer an *infrahistory* of what is known as history, or perhaps we can call it a superhistory in the sense of a history of the state and its elites. Instead of concentrating on the superstructure of history in the sense of the well-known history of high politics, this book introduces the ordinary, everyday politics of Atatürk's citizens in extraordinary times; the constellation of opinions, beliefs, practices and stratagems that poor and low-income people in cities and the countryside adopted to resist and survive in these challenging years.

Drawing on Joel S. Migdal's suggestion to grasp the state and society in interaction in everyday life, I present an alternative history of Turkey's modernization, not as a unidirectional process imposed from top to bottom, but as an interactive process shaped by daily negotiations between the state and the society and between distinct social groups.[25] Furthermore, this book reveals the bridges by which the people reached the state informally and indirectly under circumstances that did not allow them to do so otherwise. Briefly, this study explores the *infrapolitics* that interacted with high politics beneath the surface, as Scott puts it.[26]

Such an endeavor requires the use of new sources and lenses to detect the experiences of individuals who were largely illiterate. Indeed, any attempt to shed light on the experience of ordinary people is inevitably beset by conceptual, methodological and theoretical difficulties. The main problem is to overcome the narrow meaning of interlocking concepts key to this work such as politics, public sphere, public opinion, class struggle and resistance.

In the first place, expanding the classical conception of politics, which confines it to high politics, was indispensable for a deeper exploration of popular politics. This work considers everyday life as political. Politics in this broader sense, defined by Harold D. Lasswell, is related primarily to the struggle over the allocation of scarce resources.[27] High politics, on the other hand, has to do with legal and institutional competition. This is only one part of politics. Another constituent part is everyday politics, which is the *infrapolitics* underpinning and shaping high politics. As conceptualized by Scott, *infrapolitics* refers to the strategies ordinary people employ to cope with oppression and exploitation. Excluded from formal politics and with little space for organized and legal action, they substitute them with covert and indirect forms of individualized protest and struggle drawn from the fabric of everyday life and acquired from past generations. These range from rumor, folk songs, satire, petitions, foot-dragging, poaching, squatting, tax evasion and smuggling to pilferage, theft, robbery and even violence. Scott calls these acts *everyday forms of resistance*, a concept that enables researchers to identify and comprehend noninstitutional, hard-to-notice forms of dissent. Motivations for and consequences of these acts may vary from mere survival, to defending acquired rights and interests and forcing state and propertied classes into retreat, to advancing new demands and winning new concessions. Which one will be adopted or stand out is contingent upon the circumstances in which people live. It is these everyday acts that constitute everyday politics, which indirectly impinge on high politics. Everyday politics based on small and individual acts can cause macro problems for the power holders, ranging from the restructuring of control over property to fiscal crises or the failure of state schemes. It can create social turmoil and insecurity, result in policy changes, thwart state schemes or trigger intra-elite conflicts that erode the state's legitimacy and strength.[28] This concept offers deep insight to how the grass roots can play a role in shaping state policy and political life.

Habermas's depiction of the public sphere as a space of critical thinking and public opinion of the middle classes, mediating between state and society, diversified the activities regarded as politics.[29] Later political theorists suggested that underprivileged groups could also constitute counter or subaltern forms of public spheres, thus expanding the concept of politics to include these groups and their different forms of political participation.[30] Hence, social and cultural historians have used the concepts of public and public sphere to define the informal communities, networks and ordinary places, like coffeehouses, pubs, public gardens and homes, where crowds come together and produce and circulate counter discourses. Scholars have also gone beyond the spatialization of the public sphere and suggested enlarging it to include popular forms of political communication and the circulation of ideas and news in informal nonspatial spheres. Oral communications challenging established media have been envisaged as initial, ordinary and informal forms of public opinion and political expression.[31]

Furthermore, mostly thanks to feminist theory, scholars accept the interrelatedness between the private and public spheres, recognizing that private life, seemingly apolitical, is in fact political. Foucault's nuanced conceptions of power, *biopolitics* and *social control* as micro mechanisms diffusing into the capillaries of society contributed to the criticism of private-public dichotomies. Foucault, revealing that modern states seek to control human activities conventionally understood as private, shifted the focus of political analysis from institutional politics to daily life.[32]

With respect to labor history, E. P. Thompson demonstrated the importance of daily actions, means and spaces in class formation and class conflict. By shifting the focus from factory workers and their recognized means of action to other laboring groups (especially peasant workers and artisans) and their everyday experiences, behaviors and opinions previously regarded as apolitical, he offers a new form of class analysis that incorporates nonindustrial laborers and their actions short of strike into the social and historical analysis.[33]

In a similar vein, Subaltern Studies by postcolonial historians of India such as Ranajit Guha and Partha Chatterjee, give ear to what Gramsci calls the *subaltern* – those who were excluded and underprivileged – and point out that especially in rural societies, marked by illiteracy, paucity of political articulation through ideologies and regional, ethnic and religious fragmentation, and the risk of state oppression, the peasants adopt informal and daily resistance forms.[34] The *Alltagsgeschichte* introduced by German social historians also have enabled scholars to bring to light vividly how underprivileged groups resist change imposed from the top through accommodation tactics, forms of getting by and going barefoot.[35]

Historians have long recognized popular culture's role in both expressing and shaping public opinion.[36] Rumor and gossip in an unlettered culture become a means for disseminating news, articulating aspirations and grievances and maintaining group identity, especially when news outlets are censored. They may function as *informal media* that can contribute to the erosion of the regime's legitimacy by recasting and disseminating oppositional views.[37] Popular culture as a set of daily practices through which expressive genres such as popular beliefs and customs are shared also mirrors the extent of continuity and change of daily life, and thus gives clues about how far state projects permeate the population.

Language itself is also an important source for gleaning evidence of popular politics. Conversations, letters, petitions and placards are all discursive means with which the people can contest the power holders. Indeed, as Mikhail Bakhtin showed, words are multivocal and can take diverse meanings according to the context in which they are used. Individuals can ascribe different meanings to dominant discourses for their own goals by selectively appropriating specific components.[38] In parallel, for instance, Thompson evidenced that English laborers appropriated the liberal and constitutional concepts of the upper classes and used them as a weapon against their rulers and employers. In this sense, a deeper inquiry into class struggle requires an analysis of what and how ordinary people spoke.[39]

Finally, Asef Bayat's concept of social non-movement and Albert O. Hirschman's *exit* and *voice* models further the understanding of the different modes of popular politics. *Social non-movements* refers to cumulative and shared practices of large numbers of people. Their fragmented, disparate but widespread and prolonged actions for not only survival but also for striving to improve their life conditions, and their conscious efforts to win rights and gains, may elicit indirect social and political outcomes. Contrary to social movements characterized by organized, ideological and intended challenges to authorities, *social non-movements* are made up of action-oriented, nonideological and covert activities – that is, common daily practices of millions of people. The government's intolerance of direct organized challenges and the state's low infrastructural capacity to fully control the economy, society and culture facilitate, in Bayat's words, "spontaneously collective actions of non-collective actors." Albert O. Hirschman also argues that the people have other alternatives than well-known challenges when they get angry with their governments or employers. They can withdraw from the systems they are involved in through *exit* strategies or express their dissatisfaction or demands via *voice* strategies.[40]

These approaches allow us to go beyond facile generalizations and epithets such as the "strong state–weak society" by getting to the bottom of what happened in the past, which is what I do here for early republican Turkey. Such a framework requires the use of new sources to access the people's experiences. This book draws on novel sources, including petitions and letters, reports of deputies and governors, police and gendarmerie records, wish lists of provincial party congresses and contemporary newspapers, journals and memoirs.

This rich cluster of sources not only informs about the material and mental lives of ordinary people but also gives insight into the avenues through which the state and society interacted. It is worth mentioning this dimension of the matter. The primary communication channel between the government and its citizens – as well as between us and the ordinary people of this period – was the petitions and letters sent to the parliament, state and party administrations, employers and press. In a political atmosphere that restricted the free expression of opinion, these conveyed public opinion to the government. Both the content and language of the petitions tell us about the conditions the people experienced and how they responded.[41] The brief summaries of tens of thousands of petitions evaluated by the Petition Commission of the Grand National Assembly of Turkey (TBMM Arzuhâl Encümeni) are contained in parliamentary yearbooks. Likewise, the petitions addressed to local party branches were echoed in wish lists adopted by provincial congresses. The administrators of public and private institutions also took the petitions seriously. Moreover, the citizens poured their grief out to the press through letters when their petitions fell on deaf ears. Summaries of selected ones were published, with comment, in columns assigned for readers' letters. This huge body of petitions and letters is of great importance for understanding popular opinion and the way the people coped with hardships.

The petitions and letters also functioned as a "subaltern strategy" for manipulating authorities. This required the receivers of these documents to regard the information they contained with caution.[42] The republican leadership therefore employed the report system to keep tabs on both public opinion and how the local bureaucracy functioned. Party politicians were periodically charged to tour both their election districts and inspection regions other than their election district. The report they submitted to the party general secretariat did not sit unread on the dusty shelves of bureaucracy but were taken into account in the governing of the country. The reports were forwarded to specific bureaus, each of which specialized in specific matters ranging from economy, social groups, press, education, health and social assistance to art and sport. These bureaus, sending the specific information in the reports to the relevant ministries, operated as a conduit for these reports between the party and the government. The ministries either put the matter on the agenda of a parliamentary session or ordered provincial administrators to take measures addressing the issues raised in the reports. Another category of reports, general situational reports drawn up by governors and submitted to the Interior Ministry, were also informative about the intersections of state and society. All these reports served to make rulers aware of the people's expectations and complaints as well as enabling them to check the petitions.[43]

Like the petitions, the politicians' reports must be used with caution. They contain incomplete or distorted information due to career motivations or ideological bias. Moreover, politicians did not witness off-the-record conversations or hidden practices. Additionally, the matters warranting reports may have been dictated by the state's priorities rather than by the people's own concerns. However, the reported information can be verified by comparing it with other sources. In this regard, police and gendarmerie reports, insofar as they reflect the closest points of contact between the state and the people, yield additional and more detailed information about popular discontent. Indeed, the security reports differ from the reports of party and state administrators in that they include a large amount of negative comments and events. In contrast to the civil bureaucrats, both the concerns and success of the security forces depended on the detection of "criminals."[44] Fortunately, I had access to a limited number of police records in the General Directorate of Security Archive (Emniyet Genel Müdürlüğü Arşivi), the Interior Ministry Archive (İçişleri Bakanlığı Arşivi) and the Turkish History Association Archive (Türk Tarih Kurumu Arşivi). Apart from these, public security reports by the gendarmerie and court records give priceless information about the social atmosphere.

Popular culture can also be treated as a source of information and a reflection of ordinary people's views and politics. One important expressive genre in this regard was rumors, which were generally recorded in police reports. Again, the journals of the People's Houses (Halkevleri), founded as the RPP's ideological apparatuses instead of autonomous Turkish Hearts (Türk Ocakları), and *Halk Bilgisi Haberleri (Bulletin of Folklore)*, issued by the Folklore Society (Halk Bilgisi Derneği), contain invaluable monographs on rural life. The information collected by contemporary folklorist Pertev Naili Boratav, preserved in the History Foundation (Tarih Vakfı) also contains much about the popular culture of the time.

This work also tracks popular opinion and action through national and local newspapers, collating them with archival evidence. Undoubtedly, these papers upheld the main tenets of the republic as a mouthpiece of the government and worked under heavy censorship. However, this does not mean that they turned a deaf ear to *vox populi* as long as it did not directly challenge the regime and the top leadership. News about social and economic events and reader's letters provide a rich seam of information about the people's experiences and state affairs in provinces.[45]

As Hobsbawm noted, "once our questions have revealed new sources of material, these themselves raise considerable technical problems."[46] The first problem I coped with was the representative power of cases that sometimes seemed sporadic. Again, the police records and reports may reflect the concerns of their writers more than the realities. Historians of the Stalin era who examine OGPU and NKVD reports argue that these documents overestimate the prevalence of subversive conversations because the agents were locked on to them.[47] On the other hand, some scholars suggest that due to the fear of the police in authoritarian regimes, people generally avoid open expression of their views, preferring underground forms. Therefore, it is plausible that the police records reflect only detected cases; in other words, the tip of the iceberg.[48] Yet analysis of official documents raises the problem of how to extract the voices and experiences of ordinary people. To tackle this problem, I apply the source-reading strategies mentioned earlier in this introduction. Another way to fill the lacunas in these sources and to control possible biased information is to cross-check the different categories of sources.

This study is structured thematically in three parts. Each deals with different but interrelated areas of everyday politics and social conflict. Part I contains chapters on poor and low-income peasants' strategies for coping with the unfavorable economic policies and conditions, burdensome taxes, monopolies, the Great Depression and oppression and exploitation by state officials and local notables, and on the impact of peasants' everyday politics on policy and Turkey's politics. Part II examines how low-paid urban wage earners like workers, artisans and white-collar workers confronted the high cost of living, income inequality, low wages, tough working conditions, lack of social policies and pressures of industrial life. The chapters in Part III analyze the reactions of both rural and urban dwellers to shocking cultural changes such as the clothing reforms, the Civil Code modeled on the Swiss laws and the abolition of age-old religious and traditional practices like the Arabic call to prayer, *tariqa*s, shrines, religious education and sexual segregation. These chapters place the people's discontent, apathy and reticence toward secular reforms in the context of the economic problems addressed in the first two parts. This bottom-up foray into the first decades of the republic goes beyond the focal points of the well-established historical narratives and diagnoses the hitherto undetected dynamics and actors of Turkey's history and politics with a micro-historical investigation. By revealing the

complex interaction between economics and culture, formal and informal politics, law and daily practices, I call into question conventional
narratives that characterize the republican period in terms of oversim-
plifying cultural binaries such as "strong state vs. weak society," "elites
vs. grass roots" and "modernity vs. tradition."

As a final word, I am aware that I privilege the broader segments of
the population and their more prevalent patterns of dissent and resistance in daily life at the expense of some other dissent and resistance
forms specific to national and religious sensibilities of Kurds, Alevis
and non-Muslims minorities. Also I give precedence to one aspect of the
people's offstage politics, that is, non-cooperation and discontent
rather than collaboration. I hope that this book, as well as filling a
gap, also arouses curiosity about the other gaps such as the everyday
politics of minority groups or the collaborative forms of popular politics, waiting to be studied in depth.

PART I

Everyday Politics of Peasants

1 | The Price of the Republic for the Peasants

In the 1920s and 1930s, Turkey was like a big village stretched out across the Anatolian Peninsula that had been razed by long-lasting wars depleting the population and economic resources. During the Independence War, not only the occupying armies but also the nationalist forces exploited the peasants to the last drop of their blood.[1] That is why in the midst of the war, Colonel İsmet (İnönü), the future prime minister of the Atatürk era, warned army officers, "Between us, even the nation is your enemy." The nation was overwhelmingly composed of poor Anatolian peasants, whose suffering and discontent would not end after independence.

The devastating wars had sharply reduced the population from 16 to 13 million. The depletion of the urban population and minorities made Turkey a more rural and Muslim society. During the interwar period, the peasantry formed a huge majority, comprising more than 80 percent of the population. By 1927, 81 percent of the people engaged in agriculture. The share of agriculture in the GDP was 49 percent in 1926 and 47 percent in 1936.[2]

In this new configuration, large landowners were the most important parties of the ruling coalition, along with the bureaucratic elites. Therefore, the republic pursued economic policies that favored landed interests and were more in tune with industrial and commercial interests. Furthermore, modernization projects and state-building were to be financed largely through agricultural taxes and the state monopolies' revenues, which weighed heavily on smallholders. Oppression and coercion accompanied the economic exploitation of peasants. The cost of the republican state and its modernization schemes was billed to the peasants in numerous ways. Above all, fertile lands were in the hands of powerful local groups and were distributed unevenly.

Uneven Landownership

Since the mid-nineteenth century, a decisive trend of commercialization and recognition of private property had emerged in the Ottoman lands. A series of laws and integration with Western economies had provided a stimulus for the commodification of agriculture.[3] The national economy policy of the Committee of Union and Progress (CUP) during World War I gave rise to a new and more powerful class of Muslim Turkish notables in Anatolia. From the first days of the Independence War, Anatolian Muslim merchants and landowners had buttressed the nationalist movement for the sake of the preservation of the lands they had recently acquired after the massacre and deportation of Armenians and Greeks.[4] The potential return of Armenians and Greeks to Anatolia alarmed them so much that it was no coincidence that the national resistance took root in the eastern Anatolia, Thrace and Aegean regions, which were exposed to the threat of Armenian and Greek invasion. The local notables had therefore actively taken part in local nationalist Defense of Law Associations (Müdâfaai Milliye Cemiyetleri), which would constitute the nucleus of the RPP.

As soon as the republic was established in 1923, it reinforced private landownership via a series of regulations. First, the Cadastral Code in 1924 and especially the Civil Code adopted from the Swiss Civil Code in 1926 addressed the chaos in land tenure in favor of private ownership. During the 1920s and 1930s, influential households and large landowners, taking advantage of the Civil Code, fraudulently appropriated derelict lands or those lands that had been distributed to refugees, as the interior minister confirmed in his speech in the National Assembly. Deliberately damaging small dams to expose peasants' lands to flooding was another common way to drive the peasants out. The 1929 economic crisis also gave large landowners further opportunity to buy or confiscate the lands of indebted peasants.[5]

Despite a steady trend toward the growth of large estates, the land tenure system varied regionally. Smallholding and middle-sized farms were largely the common patterns. Yet large estates prevailed in certain regions characterized by export-oriented agriculture and monoculture. Adana and the surrounding region, which specialized in cotton, had the largest farms that employed wage labor or sharecroppers. In western cities such as İzmir, Aydın, Denizli and Manisa and their surroundings, large farms were similarly producing cotton, tobacco, grapes and figs for foreign markets. Kurdish provinces in the southeast were dominated by large landowners who held both economic and sociopolitical powers resembling those once wielded by feudal lords. In the mid-1920s, a Soviet expert calculated that around 65 percent of the land was controlled by only 5 percent of the landowners.[6] Hâmit Sadi, a contemporary geographer, calculated the number of large farms as 33,000 and their total holdings as 35 percent of the land. On the other hand, by the end of the 1930s, one-third of all peasant households were either landless or smallholders. According to the 1950 land statistics, the proportion of landless rural households was 14 percent in the Marmara region, 18 percent in central Anatolia, 21 percent in the Aegean, 25 percent in eastern Anatolia and 40 percent in southeastern Anatolia.[7]

The vast fallow lands and relatively high number of smallholders did not necessarily mean that the poor and smallholders did not suffer land hunger. Meager irrigation, undrained swampy land, barren soil and mountainous and rough terrain made much land unfit to cultivate. Fertile, arable land was scarce and at the disposal of a limited number of rich farmers. The republican leaders shunned programs that would lead to a comprehensive egalitarian redistribution of land. Moreover, individual economies reeled under the impact of the crisis. Heavy taxes and

Illustration 1.1 Peasant boy ploughs the field with a mule

increasing credit debt after the crisis would further squeeze the peasantry, causing them to lose their already small holdings.[8]

Burdensome Agricultural Taxes

Hilmi Uran, a prominent politician who investigated the provinces as a party inspector, wrote that the major factor pitting the rural population against the government was unbearable taxes. The high tax rates, abusive or unqualified tax collectors and exhausting procedures created unbearable frustration.[9] Indeed, the most important factor fueling peasant discontent was the heavy agricultural taxes. In the peasants' view, the severe tax burden amounted to exploitation by the government and city dwellers.

On the other hand, the most popular economic reform the republic advertised most was the abolition of the tithe (*aşar*) and tax farming (*iltizam*) in 1925. This has been presented as a huge grant to the peasantry. Despite their abolition and the populist rhetoric embodied in Atatürk's famous saying, "the peasant is the master of the nation" (*köylü milletin efendisidir*), the costs of building a modern state and economy again weighed heavily on smallholders and poor peasants. As in other developing countries, taxation was a central component of state-making and modernization schemes. Thus, the government attempted to compensate for the losses of tithe revenues by increasing other agricultural taxes.[10] Most agricultural taxes were direct taxes, which entailed face-to-face encounters with tax collectors. The proportion of direct taxes in the overall tax revenue increased from 22.6 percent between 1925 and 1930 to 34.3 percent between 1931 and 1940. The taxes on agriculture made up the greatest part of the direct taxes.[11] The government increased a significant direct tax, the land tax, first. The lack of precise cadastral information caused the finance administration to sometimes overestimate land values or impose erroneous or duplicate taxes. What is worse, the rates of the land tax had to be 10 percent at most, but in 1931, some peasants were asked to pay up to 40 percent due to mistakes or abuses by tax officials. Only large landowners and mid-sized farmers had sufficient input and equipment to produce on large enough scales to afford to pay the land tax. Therefore, given the prevalence of smallholdings, this tax mostly endangered the self-sufficient small peasantry. As for the east, along with these taxes, tribal leaders and influential landowners, called *aǧa*s, continued to demand the tithe from the peasants.[12]

Another financial burden for the peasantry was the livestock tax. The livestock tax was the first source of revenue that the nationalist forces claimed the right to collect so as to fund the Independence War. Therefore, the first article of law discussed and enacted in the new National Assembly in Ankara just one day after its establishment was the new Livestock Tax Law. This law increased the tax fourfold in 1920. In 1923, the government increased it once again. Right after abolishing the tithe, the government, seeking to offset the loss of income, broadened the scope of the livestock tax, extending it from sheep and goats to other animals such as cows, buffalo, oxen, donkeys, pigs, horses and camels. The tax rates were raised during the next few years. When the peasants abandoned cultivation for animal husbandry after the 1927 drought, the government raised the tax rates one more time. In the dismal year 1929, the tax rates on sheep, goats and donkeys were doubled once more whereas the rates on other animals were increased by a half percent.[13]

The road tax, which was inherited from the Ottomans, constituted an additional burden that vexed both urban and rural poor. The National Assembly first enacted the Road Obligation Law in 1921 during the Independence War. The tax, levied on each male between the ages of eighteen and sixty except for the disabled, required payment of four days' worth of wages or earnings or working compulsorily for three days on road construction. Just before the tithe was abolished, the government passed a new Road Obligation Law. In 1929, the government increased the tax with the Law of High Roads and Bridges. Taxpayers were obliged to work up to twelve days a year at road construction sites at twelve hours' distance from their domiciles, unless they paid the tax, which amounted to 8 or 10 liras.[14] This tax allowed the government to benefit from an unpaid labor force, most of whom were poor peasants. The road construction companies and local administrators often abused the authority entrusted to them by putting the peasants to work in miserable conditions in more distant places and for longer times than the law prescribed. In the east, the road tax could reach 15 liras, and compulsory work on the roads could last longer than the law ordained. What is worse, even peasants who paid the tax were sometimes forced into doing road work on the grounds that they had not paid the tax.[15]

Illustration 1.2 Road tax obligators doing road construction

On top of all this, the government, in search of additional funds for its wheat purchases, imposed a new tax on the flour mills in 1934 titled the Wheat Protection Tax. The rate of this tax was the cash value of 12 percent of the wheat brought to the flour mills for grinding. In theory, only the mills in towns and city centers were under obligation.[16] However, most towns in those years were no more than large villages, and most of their inhabitants were peasants. Therefore, the peasants living in small towns were affected adversely by this tax. Furthermore, most of those who brought their wheat to flour mills in town centers were peasants from neighboring villages.[17]

The peasants living in the Kurdish provinces also bore the brunt of the taxation. Actually, the state's ability to access the resources in these faraway uplands was quite limited. Together with tribal mobilization, this enabled many peasants to evade the taxes. However, as compared to the Ottoman state, the republican state was more determined to hold sway over the region financially. This partly accounts for the gendarme coercion in the region, which aggrieved the peasants. Moreover, even after the abolition of the tithe, tribal chiefs and *ağa*s did not give up collecting the tithe as well as other traditional taxes and dues. The tax collectors' dependence on the *ağa*s and tribal chiefs as an intermediary group for taxation also allowed them to manipulate the tax collectors and to squeeze the peasants. Hence, the agricultural taxes fell most heavily on the poor peasants. Moreover, the economic crisis caused the depreciation of gold and silver coins called *mecidiye*, which were still in use in far-off Kurdish provinces. This also made the taxes more unbearable for peasants.[18]

The Monopolies

Monopolies were used by states and ruling classes in shaping economy and politics since the emergence of the first states. Even in the cradle of classical liberalism like Great Britain, monopolies constituted the primary source of state revenue.[19] Before the Republic, the Ottoman rulers had benefited from monopolies extensively to fund the sultans' treasuries, military expeditions, state projects and finally payment of foreign debts. The new Turkish state also enjoyed huge revenues from monopolies. Just after the establishment of the republic, the government monopolized the production and trade of items such as salt, tobacco products, cigarette paper, alcoholic beverages, sugar, matches, lighters and forest products. The state monopolies as a sort of indirect taxation smashed the large number of peasant producers, traders and consumers of the items subjected to the monopoly. Leasing the production and trade of many goods to a number of cronies as private monopolies also served the commercialization of the rural economy.

The government first monopolized the match and lighter trade and production in 1924 and transferred the monopoly right to the American-Turkish Investment Corporation in 1930. In 1925, after abolishing the French monopoly over the tobacco market, the Régie Company, the government established the Tobacco Monopoly General Directorate. In 1926, the Spirits and Alcoholic Beverages General Directorate was authorized to produce spirits, *rakı* (an anise-flavored strong spirit) and wine, and to sell licenses for the production and trade of alcoholic beverages. The next year, the government monopolized salt production. Finally, in 1932, the export and import of sugar, tea and coffee were monopolized. All of these autonomous monopoly directorates were merged in the Monopoly Administration General Directorate in 1932 under the Customs and Monopolies Ministry.[20] Although the Monopoly Administration did not include forests, the Forests General Directorate, under the Economy Ministry, monopolized the forests in the early 1920s.

Leasing some forests to timber companies and directly running others, the government deprived peasants of an important economic source.[21]

The state revenues yielded by the monopolies were conducive to industrialization and infrastructure projects such as highway and railway construction. The tobacco monopoly alone generated around 10 percent of the total state income on average during this period. A considerable portion of this was assigned to railway construction as the backbone of the state.[22] Therefore, besides the monopoly laws, the government promulgated the Law about Prohibition and Prosecution of Smuggling in 1927 to crack down on widespread smuggling. This law was amended several times in 1929, 1932 and 1938, when it turned out to be ineffective in the face of rampant smuggling.[23]

As the most lucrative and largest monopoly, tobacco monopoly's revenues comprised most of the monopoly's share within the state budget. Therefore, the Law about Interim Tobacco Administration and Cigarette Paper Monopoly, promulgated in 1925 even before smuggling laws, increased monetary fines on smuggling fivefold. The production and trade of cigarette papers and white carbon papers were banned. In 1930, the government enacted a new and more encompassing Tobacco Monopoly Law to cope with smuggling more effectively. This law remained in force until the promulgation of a new tobacco monopoly law in 1938.[24]

Although the nationalist literature presents the abolition of Régie as a favor to the peasants, the Monopoly Administration also exerted great effort to control the tobacco sector and harshly punished those peasants who disobeyed it. The ban on cultivation, production and trade of tobacco and cigarettes meant the removal of a common livelihood for many tobacco growers and peasant-origin itinerant merchants. From the mid-1920s on, the government sought to wipe out the informal tobacco economy even in the most distant markets by installing new tobacco factories in Bitlis, Diyarbakır, Malatya and Urfa.[25] Besides, the Monopoly Administration determined price levels and the amounts that would be produced. Consequently, conflicts between the state and peasants who resisted the monopoly system continued, though they were not as bloody as in the Ottoman Empire.

Since tobacco was a more profitable cash crop, the number of peasants who preferred tobacco cultivation reached up to 500,000 between 1925 and 1938. Another 30,000 were employed in tobacco processing, despite a slight decrease during the first years of the Great Depression.[26]

However, tobacco growing was a life-consuming job. Cultivators had to obtain a license for tobacco cultivation and expend a considerable sum of money fulfilling bureaucratic requirements. The Monopoly Administration had the authority to limit both the lands the peasants could cultivate and the amount of tobacco they could produce. Cultivators were obliged to sell their produce to the Monopoly Administration or to licensed companies at prices set by the government. Several difficulties arose during dealings with these buyers.

The prices buyers offered were one of the most significant problems facing cultivators. During the Great Depression, both the Monopoly Administration and the private companies offered ruinous prices. Compared with a price of no less than 100 piasters per kilo before the crisis, the Monopoly Administration offered only 10 piasters, while marketing a small package of cut rags at 120 piasters during the early 1930s. Even after prices recuperated in the mid-1930s, the monopolies gave only 25–30 piasters, thereby making a killing by marketing a kilo of processed tobacco at around 300–400 piasters.[27]

Moreover, monopoly officials frequently attempted to deceive cultivators by deeming a large portion – up to 40 percent – of their crop as low quality. Another problem was the long, bureaucratic sale process that lasted weeks. A series of fees required at each stage of delivery burdened cultivators. All of these factors contributed to smuggling and to shrinkage of the total cultivated area until the second half of the 1930s.[28]

As for alcoholic beverages, peasants throughout Anatolia had long produced spirits, *rakı* and wine in their homes. However, the republic established the Spirits and Alcoholic Beverages Monopoly in 1926 and awarded the concession of running it to the Business Bank of Turkey (Türkiye İş Bankası). The Bank transferred this concession to the Turkish Joint-Stock Company of Spirits and Alcoholic Beverages Monopoly, set up by the Bank and a Polish company, Naçelna Organizaçya. Upon the bankruptcy of this company due to the rising costs of license transfers and low demand for its expensive *rakı* and wine, the government directly undertook this monopoly. It continued to sell a small number of licenses to producers. Again, the Monopoly Administration purchased wine produced by peasants at only 17 piasters per liter. It paid no more than 16 piasters per liter of *soma* (the main raw material of alcoholic beverages distilled from grapes or sugar beets), and sold the *rakı* produced from it at a large markup.[29]

Salt was another important item, which had been under state control since the beginning of the Ottoman Empire. The financial crisis of the Ottoman state in the mid-nineteenth century had forced the Ottoman rulers to promulgate the Salt Regulation in 1862, which put salt commerce under a state monopoly. After the Ottomans' bankruptcy, salt revenues were assigned to the Public Debts Administration run by the foreign creditors of the empire.[30] In 1920, the nationalist government in Ankara claimed control over salt revenues to fund the Independence War and raised salt prices several times between 1920 and 1924. In 1925, the government increased the price once again from 4 to 6 piasters per *okka.*[*] Finally, the government took possession of salt production and trade by establishing the Salt Monopoly General Directorate in 1927. Extracting salt from salt lakes and mines was forbidden. Because salt was of vital importance to livestock farming, soaring salt prices increased the costs of keeping animals and hit livestock owners as well as other peasants.[31]

Sugar had been one of the leading imported foodstuffs since the time of the Ottomans. To end this dependence on imports, the republic established sugar factories and gave them monopoly-like rights with the Law on Concessions and Exemptions Granted to Sugar Factories in 1926. The first enterprise the government supported was the Alpullu Sugar Factory in Tekirdağ, set up by a cooperation of sugar merchants, the Business Bank and the Agricultural Bank in 1926. That same year, the Uşak Sugar Factory, owned by sugar beet merchant Molla Ömeroğlu Nuri, was opened. The Eskişehir Sugar Factory and the Turhal Sugar Factory were established in 1933 and 1934, respectively. In order to create a monopoly market, these enterprises were brought under the roof of the Joint-Stock Company of Sugar Factories of Turkey (Türkiye Şeker Fabrikaları Anonim Şirketi) in 1935.[32]

The government benefited from the high consumption taxes on sugar, which increased sugar prices. In the first years, another factor behind soaring sugar prices was the high prices offered for sugar beets in order to promote sugar beet production. Consequently, whereas the price of sugar was 5 to 10 piasters per kilo on the world market, it fluctuated between 40 and 50 piasters in western Turkey and between 80 and 90 piasters in the east. Hence, the number of producers increased threefold, from 22,700 farmers to 65,000, and the cultivated area increased twofold, from 16,700 hectares to 32,500, between 1932 and 1934.[33]

---

[*] *Okka* is an Ottoman unit of weight equal to 1,283 grams.

Although sugar beet cultivators enjoyed high prices from the mid-1920s to the mid-1930s, the sugar plants exploited farmers by making late payments or declaring some portion of the crop rotten or of poor quality in order to justify a price cut of up to 10 percent. The real problems for cultivators came with the government's attempts to lower the soaring price of sugar in 1935 due to increasing demand for contraband sugar. Thus, from 1935 on, prices were reduced from 40–50 piasters to 25–30 piasters. This policy pushed the factories to keep down costs by almost halving the price paid to sugar beet farmers – that is, from 50 paras per kilo to 30 paras per kilo.[34] This caused widespread displeasure among the farmers, while consumers continued to find sugar expensive.

The rulers' interest in forests as a natural resource grew during integration with global capitalism in the nineteenth century. After the establishment of the Forest Directorate under the Trade Ministry in 1839, the first systematic attempts came with the promulgation of the Forestry Regulation and the restoration of the Forest Directorate under the Finance Ministry in 1869. Until the end of the empire, wood cutting remained free in return for a small tax.[35]

The republic sought more systematic control over forests as an income source. The 1923 Law of Peasants' Right to Benefit from the State Forests and the 1924 Ordinance about Forests gave peasants a limited right to benefit from forests with official permission and introduced fines and penalties for illegal wood cutting. These two regulations remained in force until the Forest Law in 1937. The government also banned the grazing of livestock in forests and woodworking without a license.[36]

The republic's burning urgency to generate sources of income turned Turkey into a timber-exporting country. Turkey's exportation of timber rose sharply from 18,000 tons in 1927 to approximately 39,000 tons in 1932. Moreover, state-initiated industrial projects like a paper and cellulose factory in İzmit, mines and railway construction needed timber. Thus the bureaucrats and the press often emphasized the importance of the forests to national wealth.[37]

The state exploited the forests in two ways: directly running them via the General Directorate of Forests under the Economy Ministry, and leasing them to private timber companies. Some of these companies were owned or managed by provincial RPP politicians. For example, the owner of the Bozuyük Timber Factory, İbrahim Çolak, was the RPP deputy of Bilecik province. The Finike Forest Company in Antalya was co-owned by local RPP politicians and merchants.[38]

Although limited rights to benefit from the forest were affirmed in the law, peasants encountered several bureaucratic barriers. Evaluation of applications generally took a long time due to the paucity of qualified forest engineers and officials. Moreover, the absence of a clear legal definition of forest until the 1937 Forest Law caused disputes over pastures, scrublands and bushy, marshy and reedy fields.[39] In addition, the forest policy resulted in mass unemployment in forest villages. For instance, the Ayancık Timber Company and the Zingal Timber Company, which controlled the Kastamonu forests from 1926, took away the livelihood of 200,000 peasants. The Finike Forest Company prevented peasants from accessing even isolated trees. Consequently peasants found themselves in endless conflict with local bureaucrats. These restrictions also resulted in wood scarcity and an increase in wood prices.[40]

All of these efforts to wipe out rural informal economies pressured the peasantry as consumers and producers. The heavily taxed and expensive commodities produced by the monopolies and higher tariffs, especially after 1929, forced peasants to pay more than they had before for industrial goods. Peasants as producers lost control over production and trade. Most of all, the unprecedented economic disaster from 1929 on worsened the situation.

The Great Depression, Declining Agricultural Prices and Running into Debt

After the devastating wars, agricultural production recovered somewhat until 1928. Undoubtedly, the major beneficiaries of the burgeoning production and higher prices were large landowners, who produced surplus to bring to market. The end of the long wars draining the Anatolian people and their feeble economies and recuperating agricultural prices slightly improved living conditions. This positive trend was reversed by the economic slump that shocked all of the world economies during the 1930s. The crisis was a death blow to peasants, who were already shaken by droughts in 1927 and 1928. International trade, further hampered by mounting governmental restrictions, pushed agricultural prices down, whereas the price of manufactured goods increased. Ahmet Hamdi Başar, who accompanied the president on a provincial tour of Anatolia in 1930, described how Atatürk felt depressed as he observed the people's suffering.[41]

Agricultural prices hit bottom during the early 1930s. The prices of wheat, corn and barley – major crops that occupied around 89.5 percent of cultivated land – declined by 60–70 percent. Industrial and exported crops such as tobacco, cotton, raisins, grapes, figs and nuts fell almost by half between 1928 and 1933.[42] Unfavorable prices and a shrink in international demand caused short-term decreases and fluctuations in output.

Especially with rising import duties for industrial goods and the monopolization of basic consumption goods, the domestic terms of trade turned against agriculture by an average of 20 percent between 1928 and 1939. These terms declined around 65 percent by 1933, and from that year on began to recover slowly. During the 1930s, the government took advantage of low agricultural prices to spur industrial development. That is, the peasants needed to produce much more to purchase necessities from the town market. Whereas a cereal-cultivating peasant had to produce 2.71 kg of wheat, 2.71 kg of barley or 4.71 kg of corn in order to buy a meter of cotton flannel in 1927, these amounts reached 7.33 kg, 11.00 kg and 11.38 kg, respectively, in 1934. The price of livestock also dropped dramatically. Sheep prices, which had fluctuated between 8 and 12 liras before the crisis, fell to around 2 liras. The cost of a cow, which had been 40–60 liras, dropped to 15–30 liras.[43]

Running into dire financial straits, peasants resorted to several survival strategies. Diversification of crops was one method they employed

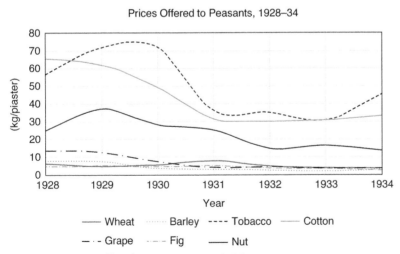

Graph 1.1 Prices offered to peasants, 1928–34

to weather the crisis. Another way to cope with the economic problems included utilizing the labor of all family members and cutting costs by minimizing contact with the market. Child labor was the primary recourse to preserve minimum subsistence.[44]

Taking on debt was another option, but a pretty unsafe one because it entailed risk of further pauperization and even dispossession. There were three lending sources: the Agricultural Bank (Ziraat Bankası) (AB), provincial banks and usurers. First of all, these debts were quite onerous for smallholders. From 1924 to 1935, only 15 percent of AB loans were allocated to peasants. These loans were not enough to meet the pecuniary needs of small producers in dire straits. Most remained below 100 liras, whereas large landowners took on loans of much larger amounts, exceeding 2,000 liras. Moreover, with fifty-four branches mostly located in city centers, the AB was inaccessible to the majority of peasants. Private local banks and usurers filled the gap.[45] Small banks owned by local merchants and politicians offered credit to peasants at higher interest rates of up to 35 percent. In 1931, official interest rates were about 10 percent on the surface, but combined with other fees and commissions, the real interest rate was doubling.[46] The dropping prices further complicated debt repayment. Time-consuming bureaucratic procedures required to apply for bank credit also daunted the peasants, and many therefore fell into the usury trap. The usurers charged ruinous interest of up to 120 percent. However, interest sometimes soared to 600 percent in practice.[47]

Usurers deceived peasants through devious tactics known as "doubling" (*katlama*), "prevaricating" (*kıvırma*) and "getting blood out of stone" (*hendek atlatma*). The first involved charging higher interest than previously agreed. The second comprised refusal to receive payments on time in order to increase the debt burden. The last meant to sue a borrower who had already discharged a debt by falsely claiming the borrower had not yet made payment.[48]

A limited number of agricultural cooperatives, pioneered by the AB in 1929 to fund producers, reached just 3 percent of the peasantry. The administrative boards of the cooperatives were composed of rich farmers. In many cases, peasants who took out cooperative loans paid their old debt with this money to the cooperative administrators, who were their moneylenders at the same time.[49]

The peasants' consequent inability to discharge their debts caused dispossession. As early as 1929, justice minister Mahmut Esat (Bozkurt) addressed the mounting foreclosures, which amounted to more than

1 million in 1928 and 1929. According to the gendarmerie records, in 1935 alone, approximately 350,000 arrest warrants were issued for failure to pay debts, largely agricultural debts.[50] A contemporary observer, İsmail Hüsrev Tökin, pointed out that huge numbers of peasants had lost their lands, vineyards and orchards to moneylenders and large landowners in Konya, Bursa, Ordu, Giresun and Balıkesir-Edremit. The pages of the local newspapers abounded with court announcements of public auctions for expropriated land and livestock. Peasants' debt load led many to accept sharecropping tenancy or to work as part-time laborers on large farms.[51]

These economic policies and the Great Depression resulted in impoverishment in the countryside. In some regions, poor peasants suffered hunger, albeit not on a massive scale. The 1927–8 droughts were a precursor of the difficult times to come. In the areas worst hit by the drought, peasants resorted to eating seeds and adding grass to their bread. In May 1930, sporadic reports of starvation and urgent demands for food aid came from the provinces. The severity of the problem pushed the Interior Ministry to deal with it, especially its repercussions for security. The ministry ordered governors to report on the food question and its effects on security. The reports coming from the provinces indicate that the economic upheaval disrupted security in the countryside by inducing crimes like theft, murder and banditry.[52] Peasants' anguish was doubled with oppression and abuses by local state officials and notables.

Rural Oppressors

Peasants were caught in the crossfire between state agents like gendarmes, tax collectors, debt enforcement officials and forest rangers, and powerful members of their communities such as large landowners, usurers and village headmen. Although the village community was based on several forms of solidarity such as kinship and patronage ties, it also included groups divided along lines of power and property. The economic policies and the Great Depression sharpened these divisions and the tension not only between the state and the peasants but also between these groups.

Despotic Ağas and Households

"The Party here is Ömer Ağa," said the peasants in Konya, a major cereal production center, with whom a party inspector spoke. The inspector noted that rich landowners dominated the Konya party administration. The peasants saw them as equivalent to the state and the party.[53] Most Anatolian villages and towns had their own wealthy and influential farmers who owned larger estates and generally wielded considerable power. Regions that specialized in cash crops and commercial agriculture in particular were dominated by rich and ambitious farmers. They not only controlled the means of production, but they also directly or indirectly intervened in all aspects of village life. They enjoyed the advantages of close relations with local party and state bureaucrats, with whom they cemented good relations. In some regions, they directly assumed or represented state power. In Burdur, a leading wheat center, for example, twenty large landowners occupied the key offices of the provincial government.[54] Likewise, Emin Sazak, the deputy of Eskişehir, was at the same time one of the biggest landowners of the region. In Giresun, a group of large landowners and merchants such as Tir Alizadeler, Hacı Ahmetzadeler, Katipzadeler and Hacı Emin Beyzadeler dominated the local party and state administrations. Indeed, the state and party apparatuses in almost every province were enmeshed with local landowning and mercantile interests. In stark contrast to the widely accepted center-periphery theory, which portrays the republican state and the RPP as the center isolated from provincial society, neither the republican state nor the party was autonomous from its local social partners.[55]

Rich landowners dominated peasants through the patronage system. Mediating between the bureaucracy and the peasants, arbitrating intra-village disputes, and intervening even in family affairs provided them an opportunity to regulate village life according to their own interests. Besides their loyalty, the peasants were expected to submit a portion of their produce, whether crops, fruit, eggs, chicken or livestock, in exchange for aid. Patronage also meant economic exploitation and oppression. Poor peasants' lands, vineyards and even their livestock were under constant threat of takeover by rich farmers on whom the peasants depended financially. Rapacious landowners sometimes sabotaged irrigation systems and dams in order to drive smallholders off their lands. The economic crisis fueled this process by causing dispossession of many peasant households, who incurred enormous debts to local moneylenders, most of whom were wealthy farmers. Apart from this economic mechanism, it was not rare for landowners to physically brutalize peasants. The *kâhya*s, as butlers representing landlords, also exploited peasants and therefore became one of the most disliked group among peasants.[56]

Large landowners had utmost authority in the eastern part of Anatolia. The tyranny of influential landowners called *ağa*s here was not only a discursive strategy the state had devised for the liquidation of disobedient notables – it was a social reality. As the Erzincan governor, Ali Kemalî (Aksüt), reported, in many eastern provinces, peasants owned neither the lands they cultivated nor the houses in which they lived. All of them belonged to *ağa*s. In Urfa, for instance, most villages – including all property, livestock and even the peasants themselves – were in the possession of *ağa*s. One of these *ağa*s had almost 300 villages. Less well-off *ağa*s held 30 or 40 villages. They also continued to collect the tithe and other traditional taxes abrogated by the state.[57]

Two major groups dominated in the eastern regions, which sometimes overlapped. The first consisted of religious figures such as *seyyid*s and *şeyh*s. They represented the religious authority and had their own lands and livestock. The peasants had to pay them religious taxes (*niyaz* and *çıraklı*) and fees for religious services, as well as harvest their crops. These men also had judicial authority. The second group included rich landowners and livestock owners, the *ağa*s. Some of them possessed more than one village, which included peasants, livestock, houses, coffeehouses, barns, mills, forests, pastures and salt mines. Also they continued to illegally collect the traditional poll tax known as *cizye* and commanded great authority over their peasants. Peasants owed them certain obligations, one of which was corvée. The *ağa* could demand a number of days' unpaid labor from his tenants. In the case of disobedience, not only the disobedient peasant but also his family faced the consequences. Poor sharecroppers were generally called *maraba*, which meant the possessor of one-fourth (*rubu*) of the crops they produced on the lands of their *ağa*. *Maraba*s owned their own small plots of land in return for submitting a portion of the yield to the *ağa*. The poorest group was comprised of landless peasants called farmhands (*ırgat*, *rençber* or *azap* – meaning anguish). Lacking even a small plot of land, they worked on large farms for a tiny portion of the crop, a pair of shoes and clothes. In these distant Kurdish lands, the authority of the *ağa* was at the highest level. The peasants could not even marry off their sons or daughters without his consent.[58]

Cemal Bardakçı, the eccentric governor of Diyarbakır from 1925 and 1926 and of Elazığ from 1926 to 1929, depicted how *ağa*s actually governed the region by manipulating state officials and increased their wealth by seizing the animals and lands of poor peasants. In 1926, more than 3,500 peasants were sentenced to prison by default in Diyarbakır and its surrounding area. Most of these prisoners were in fact noncompliant peasants who had resisted their *ağa*s' efforts to seize their lands or livestock. The *ağa*s generally received privileged treatment in the courts and state offices through clientelism in return for providing local bureaucrats food and even gold. Kemal Bilbaşar, a novelist who had witnessed Kurdish peasant life up close when he was a soldier in the east, depicted the conflicts between oppressive *ağa*s and peasants who had to engage in banditry in his famous novels *Cemo* and *Memo*.[59]

Village Headmen

The domination over peasants was generally exerted through the village headman, who led the council of elders, the administrative body of the village. The council and the headman held responsibility for implementing governmental orders and laws in the village. The council of elders, however, usually existed only on paper; the headman actually administered the village.[60]

The main requirement for obtaining the post of village headman, as Mahmut Makal, Turkey's first realist village novelist noted, was to be a property owner. As many contemporary village surveys and memoirs pointed out, most village headmen came from rich and influential households. When rivalries arose within the village, they generally sided with the powerful. Influential families reinforced their authority and economic interests by controlling the office of village headman.[61] Only in villages located in the vicinity of city centers did headmen tend to represent state authority. In isolated and faraway villages, they generally seemed the shadows of tribal leaders or *ağa*s. Headmen had to gain the approval of the local bureaucracy, landowners or both. This made them the most disliked group among the peasants.[62]

The Village Law authorized headmen to carry out state jobs in the villages such as implementing government directives and laws, maintaining security, informing security forces of suspicious persons, criminals, deserters and foreigners, and even settling disputes between peasants. He assisted state officials, tax collectors and gendarmes who came to the village and kept a population register that recorded all births, deaths, marriages, divorces, taxes and livestock in his village. The village headman had an absolute right to impose a vast array of public works and duties on peasants, such as constructing roads, schools, mills or village rooms, and to implement hygiene measures. To pay for such works, they were authorized to levy a tax called *salma* or to force peasants to work in village jobs.[63] Many headmen had a tendency to use *salma*s for private gain or to favor their relatives. The Village Law limited the total amount of levies headmen could demand to 20 liras per year, but in practice, it was not uncommon for them to demand double this sum. The law also authorized them to assess taxes on peasants and to execute debt enforcement proceedings. The Village Law authorized headmen to impose fines of up to 100 piasters on those peasants who refused their directives. Faced with disobedience or opposition, they were permitted to threaten, beat or, if necessary, refer the offender to the gendarmerie.[64] The headmen had the right to hire armed guards called *korucu*. Any disobedience toward these militias was considered a crime against the state.

Tax Collectors

The most hated figure in villages as peasants' nightmares was the tax collector. They referred to tax collectors as *şahna* (hostile, malicious). As a matter of fact, the correct term was *şahne*, meaning tax collector, but peasants pronounced it as *şahna*. The tax collectors were low-income state officials pressed by central and provincial administrators to collect as much revenue as they could.[65] Both the low salary and pressure from their superiors led many to become abusive in order to extract as much money as possible. For the peasants, tax collectors were as perilous as predatory animals. As is obvious from their daily vocabulary and encoded messages, the peasants perceived the tax officials as dangerous as wolves. As a foreign journalist noted, the peasants saw tax collectors as "agents of the devil." Another observer wrote that they represented "the angel of death" in the eyes of the peasants, swooping down as soon as the harvest was collected. A peasant child at the time, future novelist Fakir Baykurt, recalls that peasants in his village called tax collectors "goddam specky four-eyes!" because some of them wore glasses.[66]

Tax collectors toured villages on foot or by horse or mule. Their appearance in a village was a sign of trouble for the villagers, who were obligated to accommodate and feed them. Generally, when a tax collector arrived at a village, he first met with the headman, who helped him to identify the taxpayers and their obligations. On a predetermined date, the peasants gathered in front of the village room or coffeehouse to submit their taxes to the tax collector when the headman called their names. If a peasant did not appear or did not pay his tax, the tax collector, accompanied by gendarmes or guards, raided his house and confiscated whatever he found that was salable.[67] Many peasants had no choice but to sell their livestock and household goods or give them up in place of the tax. Some tax officials or debt enforcement officials derived illicit personal benefit from such sales, which caused further loss for the peasants. As Aydın deputy Nuri Göktepe admitted in 1935, many tax collectors deceived peasants. The party inspectors of Zonguldak, Giresun and Ordu provinces all reported that peasants suffered under corrupt tax collectors.[68] Turkish literature also depicts unfair treatment, abuse and pressure from tax collectors during the early republic. Reşat Enis's novel *Toprak Kokusu* illustrates abuses by tax collectors. Orhan Hançerlioğlu's *Karanlık Dünya-Ekilmemiş Topraklar* also notes how tax collectors, with the help of gendarmes, terrorized peasants who resisted them.[69]

Gendarmes

The gendarmes were perhaps the most frightening state agents in rural areas. They were notorious for beating peasants. Indeed, a folk song titled "Ekinci Destanı" ("Epic of the Cultivator") that Yaşar Kemal heard in villages of the Çukurova region that he wandered in order to collect folk songs between 1939 and 1951, demonstrates the peasants' view of the gendarme as well as their view of the tax collector and the bailiff:[70]

Yazmakla tükenmez hazin macera	This sorrowful adventure does not end by writing
Bir yandan tahsildar bir yandan icra	On the one hand tax collector, on the other bailiff
Çekersin çaresiz kazaya rıza	Haplessly bow to whatever God wishes
Candarma çavuşu Çar gelir sana	The gendarmerie sergeant seems Tsar to you

The upper echelons of the gendarmerie in the provinces usually acted in collaboration with propertied individuals and prominent households. In regard to the rank and file, they were mostly composed of peasant-origin poor and uneducated young men. Along with abusing peasants for their own petty interests, they harmed them by frequently confusing their duties. Beatings and long detention of peasants for days was common.[71]

Gendarmes accompanied tax collectors and debt enforcement officials to extract taxes or impound the property of the peasants. Furthermore, their economic deprivation put them at the disposal of rich landowners. In Turkish towns, high- and mid-ranked security forces generally were assimilated into local interest group who cultivated good relations with the local bureaucrats to get privileged treatment. Sevim Belli, whose father was the Artvin police director in 1936, recalls her father was included in a ruling circle comprising the governor, gendarmerie commander, judge and rich individuals, who socialized at dinners and tea parties.[72] Undoubtedly, their relationships continued outside of social events.

This characteristic of the provincial ruling bloc was not peculiar to Artvin. The party inspectors of Giresun in 1934 wrote that the richest merchant, Hasan Tahsin Bey, had amassed his fortune of about 250,000 liras by means of usury at astronomical interest. He always enjoyed the active support of the local bureaucrats and village headmen in his conflicts with the peasants. In return for their support, he distributed some shares of his earnings to the gendarmerie commander, Major Zeki Bey, the magistrate, Cemil Molla Bey, and village headmen. The gendarmerie commander and the magistrate helped Tahsin Bey by facilitating confiscations and by prearranging back-room sales of confiscated properties to Tahsin Bey at incredibly low prices. Such mechanisms could not be maintained without notorious gendarmerie violence. In a similar vein, the gendarmerie commander in the Alaşehir district of Manisa also cemented close relations with a prominent family in the region. The Manisa deputy warned the government about the risks of such overfamiliarity between the security forces and wealthier families.[73]

As the RPP general secretary reported to the interior minister, the close cooperation between merchants, large landowners and gendarmes was striking in the districts of İzmir. According to politicians' reports and to peasants' petitions between 1931 and 1933, the rich landowners and merchants of the Ödemiş, Kiraz and Kemalpaşa districts, backed by the gendarmerie commander, Lieutenant Fuat, had long oppressed the peasants. Nihat Bey, a prominent farmer in Kemalpaşa, had recently seized vineyards that peasants had cultivated for thirty-five years by falsifying the land registers with the help of land registration official Malik Bey. Upon the persistent objections of the peasants, Lieutenant Fuat set the gendarmes against them and arrested some resistant peasants. In 1933, Fuat Bey, after retiring from his job, was elected to the party administration of the Kemalpaşa district by dint of his partnership with local interest groups.[74]

The story of peasants in the Torbalı district of İzmir, who got into trouble with the gendarmerie commander, Şuayip, demonstrates how the gendarmerie abused the peasants with impunity. In a letter dated 1934, a group of defenseless peasants accused him of suppressing them. According to another letter, the offices of the village headmen had been sold to rich peasants in return for money paid to Şuayip. Gendarmes and tax collectors, hand in hand, collected money from peasants arbitrarily in villages in Selçuk and Torbalı. The government, alarmed by the constant complaints, investigated the case and found the gendarmerie commander guilty.[75]

Peasants who resisted taxes encountered the gendarme. It was the gendarme who arrested and forcibly took peasants who did not pay the road tax to road construction sites. Tax collectors and gendarmes reportedly began to imitate bandits by lying in wait to entrap those who had not paid the road tax. Those peasants who lived off the forests or engaged in smuggling also had to cope with gendarmes and forest rangers patrolling the villages.[76]

Gendarmerie violence reached awful levels in the distant Kurdish provinces. Tribes and *ağa*s had their own armed forces against theft and banditry. These militias integrated the *ağa*s semiofficially with security forces, which exacerbated tyranny over peasants. They had no qualms in mounting a brutal persecution of their opponents. The *ağa*s' intermediary role in tax collection and conscription also made them indispensable to the provincial administrations. The local bureaucracy and gendarmes were embedded in local networks as confirmed by official reports from the region and a report by the general inspector of the First Inspectorate Region comprising several Kurdish provinces. Due to insufficient allowances and ignorance, most of them could be lured by rich households. As Cemal Madanoğlu, a gendarmerie lieutenant who participated in the military operations in the region, noted in his memoirs, gendarmes looked to the local notables for a living.[77] What made things worse was that a significant number of gendarmes in these areas were native young men recruited and fed by *ağa*s on behalf of the government. They generally observed the interests of their *ağa*s when the peasants tangled with the *ağa*s. Mutual hunting between the unyielding peasants and gendarmes was part and parcel of the Kurdish countryside, and it was reflected even in literature like Bilbaşar's novels and popular songs.[78] Bilbaşar's Cemo and Memo were not just fantastic novel heroes. Anatolia was full of such peasants who fought injustice. However, the first choice they preferred was to raise their voice moderately.

2 | *Raising Voice and Rural Discontent*

The government's populist policies, embodied particularly in the abolition of the tithe and in populist and peasantist discourse, did not deceive the peasantry. The peasants were not misled by slogans such as "the peasants are the master of the nation." They, well aware of what was going on in their own lives, formed their opinions independently. Although the literature often portrays these peasants as primarily passive with occasional and brief explosions, they did not remain silent in the face of formidable conditions. Often their first action was to publicly criticize what they found unjust and seek remedies for their problems – that is, they used what Hirschman calls *voice strategies*. The wish lists of local party congresses, deputies' reports on their election and inspection districts, parliamentary discussions, petitions and newspaper reports reveal that the peasants frequently raised their voices and solicited the government to address their economic problems and to live up to its commitments.

Demands for Land

Landless peasants or smallholders, who made a living the hard way with limited resources, often complained of the lack of sufficient land to support their families. Even though most of them produced enough for only their own needs, price drops made it more difficult to earn money from the sale of a marginal portion of their crops when cash was needed. Runaway debt caused many smallholders to lose their plots. Consequently, landlessness and demands for land were among the concerns the peasantry raised most frequently. Their concern was conveyed to the government through various avenues such as letters to newspapers, petitions, politicians' reports and the wish lists of the RPP's provincial congresses. In view of the discontent arising from land shortage, republican politicians, particularly Atatürk and Prime Minister İsmet İnönü, frequently mentioned the necessity of distributing

44

state lands to landless peasants. Such promises further catalyzed the peasants' demands for land.

Balkan refugees, most of whom were peasants who had abandoned their property, constituted a particularly large, vocal group. Land allocations to refugees, fluctuating between 3 and 10 *dönüms*,[*] fell short of their needs.[1] A peasant's remark in a coffeehouse in the Lüleburgaz district of Kırklareli about the land distributions, overheard by a teacher, epitomizes the view of the peasants on the matter: "The government gave me a piece of land of 10 *dönüm*s. The crop that this land yields does not afford a piece of dry bread, let alone clothes, salt and kerosene." In some places, land given to peasants was confiscated immediately due to accrued taxes or loan debts. From their perspective, "the government was expropriating with one hand what it had given with the other."[2]

Landlessness posed a greater problem for the Turkish nomadic tribes known as Yörük or Türkmen inhabiting the Anatolian mountains. Increasing consolidation of private property meant Anatolian land was fenced off and its use restricted for nomadic tribes. Therefore, nomads also sought landownership. Evoking the politicians' promise that every Turkish peasant would have his own land, one Türkmen peasant protested, "We are Turks, but we do not have a piece of land."[3]

The Great Depression and legal reforms consolidating property rights, which led peasants to dispossession, further fueled peasant discontent. Petitions sent to the National Assembly from almost everywhere were replete with demands for arable land or vineyards. In the mid- and late 1930s, individual or collective demands for land distribution increased further because of both the pressure of land deprivation and republican leaders' speeches promising land reform. For instance, in 1935, a group of peasants from the village of Keller in Zonguldak demanded land distribution to the landless peasants in their village. In 1939, a group of landless peasants from Ceyhan wrote to the party and government simultaneously, pleading for the provision of unused tillable treasury land from Çukurova for cultivation. Similarly, a peasant named Ferhad Yaş wrote a petition on behalf of eighty peasant households in need of land in the Mondolos village of Refahiye (Erzincan).[4]

---

[*] One *dönüm* is equal to 1,000 square meters.

Frustrated by the discrepancy between their land famine and the government's promises of land reform, peasants also wrote to newspapers, especially when their petitions received no response. In June 1935, after hearing the promises of the prime minister, a group of poor peasants from Kütahya petitioned the governor in person in the hope of acquiring small parcels of land, but returned to their village empty-handed. Then they wrote to *Son Posta* to call the government's attention to their demands the local bureaucrats had ignored. In a similar vein, a small-scale tobacco cultivator from the Akçaabat district of Trabzon recounted how the local government had rejected his request for a parcel of unused land evacuated by Armenians. He expressed his disappointment, arising from the contradiction between the pledges of the prime minister and the practices of the governorship. In 1936, a group of peasants from İnebolu wrote a letter to *Köroğlu* about their desperate situation arising from landlessness. More than 300 peasants from 54 households had long sought distribution of some portion of the treasury lands. Complaining the government had yet to consider their request, they claimed they had a right to own land.[5]

The complaints about landlessness resonated in the local congresses of the RPP. The wish lists of the congresses in 1936 included land distribution to landless or smallholder peasants. For instance, the distribution of vacant lands and vineyards to landless peasants in the Bergama, Foça, Torbalı, Tire and Urla districts of İzmir was among the requests submitted to the RPP General Congress.[6]

Deputies who regularly toured their election districts also frequently heard peasants' complaints about landlessness. Based on their talks with peasants, many reported that landless peasants or smallholders had expected the government to allocate some fallow state lands to them. The Gaziantep deputy, for instance, underscoring the fact that more than 12,000 households were without land in the villages of Kilis (Gaziantep) alone, suggested that the government apportion some state land to them. Likewise, the Kırklareli deputy reported that the peasants in Thrace desperately needed a sufficient amount of arable land and wished the government would provide it.[7]

Leaders of the RPP also personally witnessed the people's severe need for cultivable land when they set off on country tours. During their 1930 tour, President Atatürk and his entourage witnessed land privation among the peasants almost everywhere they visited. During İnönü's tour of the eastern provinces, the most repeated request of the peasants was for immediate land distribution. The peasants complained of landlessness and deadly fights over scarce arable land and pastures.[8]

Despite a huge number of landless and poor peasants in the eastern provinces, Kurdish peasants nonetheless avoided writing to newspapers and government bureaucrats. Most of these peasants knew only Kurdish and had a distrust of state officials, who were usually manipulated by local notables. In addition, the RPP did not have local organizations in some of these provinces, which lessened the party's contact with the population. Peasant discontent therefore manifested in the form of widespread crimes ranging from theft to banditry, as I discuss in the following chapters. A report by health and social aid minister Hulusi Alataş suggested that Arab, Kurdish and Assyrian peasants generally lacked even a small piece of land of their own and thus engaged in crime in order to survive. According to the report, the main prerequisite for maintaining public order was to supply landless peasants with unused state lands. Similarly, Cemal Bardakçı, the governor of Diyarbakır in the mid-1920s, saw the soaring crime rates in the east as an expression of landlessness and abject poverty. He also highly recommended government provision of land to poor peasants in order to stem the rising tide of crime.[9]

Discontent with Taxes

Ahmet Hamdi Başar, who accompanied Atatürk's tour of the country in 1930, wrote, "Everywhere we go, the people complain concertedly about the weight of taxes." In the village of Kırklareli, peasants who stopped the president's car bemoaned the calamitous agricultural prices, extortion and corruption. In one village, the "sequestering had become a pillage." "One touch, a thousand ouches! What wails are rising," Başar stated. The members of the president's entourage also heard numerous complaints about the livestock tax. In Thrace, people were spiriting away their livestock to Bulgaria in order to evade the tax. In İzmir, Aydın and Denizli, the same complaints about the agricultural taxes reached their ears. In Trabzon, an important center of northern Anatolia, as elsewhere, the peasants were complaining about the livestock and land taxes. Başar noted that many peasants, whose possessions were sequestered, were also jailed. In Sivas, he also saw the peasants protesting the seizure of their livestock by tax collectors.[10]

Indeed, perhaps the most important factor fueling peasant discontent was the heavy agricultural taxes. In their view, the severe tax burden amounted to exploitation by the government and city dwellers. Hilmi Uran, a prominent politician and party inspector, wrote that the major factor pitting the peasants against the government was the unbearable taxes. The high rates, abusive or unqualified tax collectors and exhausting procedures created unbearable frustration.[11]

The land tax, though seemingly targeted at the landowning class, primarily threatened subsistence farmers. Given the prevalence of smallholding in Anatolia, the rise of the land tax resulted in massive public criticism, especially during the Great Depression when agricultural prices plummeted. According to a report by an erstwhile RPP deputy who investigated central, western and northern Anatolian towns in 1930, peasants grumbled about the pretty high estimation of the value of their lands as the tax base.[12]

The peasant letters that flooded into newspaper, party and government offices reveal the common grievance about the land tax. Such letters inundated the editors of *Cumhuriyet*, which conducted a survey about the tax. The first problem was the ignorant officials who erroneously assessed land values at fifteen times higher than their actual worth. The peasants, by means of both petitioning the state and writing to newspapers, called on the government to correct such mistakes.[13]

Peasants frequently compared the abrogated tithe to the land tax, arguing that the latter was more extortionate and arbitrary than the former. As one noted, "The tithe pales in comparison with the land tax." A peasant named Mehmet Emin from Adapazarı found the land tax "more harmful than the tithe." The tax was so high that low-income peasants who needed a portion of the harvest for their own subsistence were required to sell off their entire yield in order to pay it. Some peasants wrote to newspapers to demand a reduction. *Köroğlu* editors, for instance, wrote that the peasants had often been sending letters to the newspaper insisting on a reduction in the land tax rate.[14] Peasants from all corners of Anatolia, collectively and individually petitioning the National Assembly, sought a decrease in the land tax rates. The RPP deputies recorded similar requests when they toured their election or inspection districts. Peasants also demanded settlement of land tax debts by petitioning the government. Likewise, members of local party congresses heard demands for tax relief, as evidenced by the wish lists these congresses adopted.[15]

Peasants' concerns about the livestock tax were also expressed via the RPP's provincial congresses, deputies' reports, petitions and letters to newspapers. The wish lists submitted by thirty-nine provincial party congresses to the Third General Congress of the RPP held in 1931 included the grievances of the peasantry that stemmed from this tax. Their primary demand was the reduction of its rates. Peasants' demands for lower livestock taxes continued to be mentioned in local congresses and included in their wish lists in the following years. Almost all provincial congresses added requests for reduction in the rates and scope of the tax to their wish lists. Deputies' reports also noted that the high rates, unintelligible assessment and collection methods of the livestock tax were major sources of grievance throughout the country.[16]

Petitioning both local and central administrators, many demanded a tax relief program including either an installment payment plan or cancellation of accrued livestock tax debts. Peasants also used the newspapers to criticize the livestock tax. *Son Posta*, for instance, noted that the peasants in Safranbolu had sent a letter describing how animal husbandry had come to a halt in their region due to the high taxes. The peasants, on the edge of bankruptcy, wished for a reduction in the tax rates. Although the government reduced the rates of the livestock tax in 1931 and again in 1932, requests for a further decrease or tax amnesty continued to inundate the government through petitions and politicians' reports. Unsurprisingly, in eastern villages like Dersim where the main livelihood was animal breeding, peasant disgruntlement was highest. In one instance, a group of Dersim peasants wearing a mournful face poured out their grief to an army commander who visited the villages, openly criticizing the taxation of their animals and the wrongdoings of tax collectors.[17]

Perhaps nothing dashed the rural and urban poor so much as being forced to break rocks for the roads because they were unable to pay the road tax. The poor implementation of the tax along with the compulsory work obligation under wretched conditions in road construction in distant places proved traumatic for poor peasants. Children as young as twelve worked on road construction. Fakir Baykurt, who would be a famous social realist novelist of village life in the 1950s, was one of them. Fakir depicted in his memoirs how road tax victims were recruited from among poor peasants by headmen, tax collectors and gendarmes. Once he was forced to do work building in the place of a rich landowner. The taxpayers could be asked to do road work for more than twelve days, longer than the laws permitted. They generally complained by saying, "This is government. It knows taking, but not giving."[18]

Peasants' discontent with this tax frequently appeared in official documents as well as the letters sent to the government and the press. An eager politician wrote in his private 1930 report that he had listened to peasants' criticism of the road tax everywhere he went in central Anatolia, the Black Sea and Marmara regions. According to election district reports from the 1930s, grievances related to the road tax were rampant throughout the provinces.[19] Almost everywhere, wrongdoing in the implementation of the road tax generated complaints. The deputy reports on Konya and Aksaray from 1931 pointed out that the mistakes and abuses of the tax collectors and the detention of peasants who could not pay the tax in cash doubled the grievance of the peasants, who were also hit hard by falling prices. In a Konya village, peasants who had been sent to a distant site by mistake were sent back without having worked. Just after they returned home, the governorship once again sent them to another distant site for days. These long trips on foot exhausted them before they had even started working and provoked harsh criticism of the government. Denizli deputy Mustafa Kazım also stated in his report that "compulsory works that were arbitrarily placed on the shoulder of the peasants under the pretext of the Village Law, and the forced labor obligation of the road tax that lasted about one and a half months under gendarmerie oppression and torture, resulted in general discontent."[20]

Peasants' objections to the tax itself and to the forced labor lasting longer than the laws stipulated were pouring in to the central government and the press. Peasants deemed both the tax and its bad implementation a grave injustice. First of all, collecting the same amount from all people, regardless of their income, did not comport with the state's avowed populist principles. One peasant, in a letter to a newspaper, argued that because building roads was the task of the government, a special tax for this was preposterous. Displeased with the single rate of the tax, low-income peasants demanded taxes be graduated according to income in order to make taxation more equitable. They also pointed out that because roads primarily benefited merchants and the wealthy, who could afford cars, trucks and buses, requiring poor citizens to build the roads was an astounding injustice.[21]

Governors and other officials who exploited the unpaid labor of the peasants under the guise of the road tax also spurred the peasants' objections. The peasants of the İsabeyli village in Denizli, writing collectively to *Köroğlu* in 1929, complained that although they had already fulfilled their work obligation, they were not permitted to return to their villages for eighteen days. More tragically, in some places, the taxpayers had worked about twenty days, sometimes in the construction of bureaucrats' own houses or barns. In the following years, similar complaints continued to be heard. Karaburun peasants in İzmir who faced such a situation collectively wrote to *Köroğlu* to ask the government for help.[22] In a similar vein, in August 1934, the same newspaper, in an article titled "We Received a Letter Signed and Stamped by Several Peasants in Safranbolu," gave space to a poignant criticism of the peasants. The peasants, unable to pay the road tax in cash, had been put at the disposal of a road construction company. They wrote, "We are held captive for twenty-three days, working fourteen hours a day." The peasants queried whether this was a violation of the laws, which had limited the duration of the work obligation to eight days, working nine hours per day.[23] Such letters also indicate that peasants were aware of their rights, at least when they came into conflict with the state.

The wheat protection tax also caused public outcry in rural areas, as evidenced by letters to local newspapers. In one, a peasant from Haymana (Ankara) described the deleterious effects of the tax on all peasants living in the town. In another, a group of poor peasants in Ilgaz (Çankırı) complained that although Ilgaz was a small town inhabited mostly by peasants and smallholders, its inhabitants were not exempt from the tax. They implored the Agriculture Ministry to exempt peasants in the town from this tax.[24]

The local party congresses from several provinces also recorded that peasants requested that the government lower the rate of this tax and exempt the small flour mills in small towns tantamount to villages. A more striking gauge of the tax's impact on poor rural dwellers who lived on wheat was a series of protests by women that occurred in central Anatolian towns during June 1934. In July, the village millers gathered in front of the Finance Ministry to make their voice heard.[25] I elaborate on these events and more in the next chapter on taxes.

Discontent with Monopolies

Peasants, as cultivators, traders and consumers, never liked the monopolies. Tobacco cultivators and smokers were the primary groups that distrusted the monopoly system. The first thing that displeased tobacco-growing peasants was the ruinous prices offered for their crops. For instance, a tobacco farmer named Abdullah in Adana admitted how the prices given by the monopoly doomed the farmers to suffer hunger or align with smugglers. Even in İzmir, whose tobacco was purchased at higher prices, the local newspapers were replete with complaints from tobacco farmers about exploitation and red tape by the Monopoly Administration and licensed private enterprises. Tobacco farmers' discontent was also discussed at the İzmir party congress in 1936.[26]

Peasants' criticisms made their way not only to provincial bureaucracies but also to Ankara. The deputy of Tekirdağ, Mahmut Rasim, underlined in the National Assembly that peasants were complaining about monopoly officials who had cut prices up to 60 percent. According to the investigations a parliamentary commission carried out in January 1931, the tobacco monopoly was the nightmare of the peasants in tobacco-producing districts. The peasants accused the monopoly of purchasing high-quality tobacco at low prices and selling it to private companies at high prices. The commission members admitted that the peasants were right in their objections.[27]

Resentment of the monopoly was treated in Turkish literature. *Tütün Zamanı*, *Zeliş* and *Acı Tütün* by Necati Cumalı depict the blatant exploitation of the tobacco farmers around İzmir from the 1930s to the late 1950s. The author notes that he had always seen his father, a tobacco grower in those years, anxious and unhappy due to the difficulties of tobacco farming. Another novelist, Talip Apaydın, tells the story of a poor tobacco farmer in *Tütün Yorgunu*. Throughout the novel, the farmer complains about cheating by the state monopoly and private companies and calls the monopoly officials traitors and bastards.[28]

The Monopoly Administration, by restricting tobacco cultivation and trade, stirred resentment among peasants. Eskişehir deputies reported in 1935 that the peasants of the Seyitgazi and Mihalıççık districts had become extremely impoverished due to the ban on tobacco farming. The peasants frequently asked the deputies who visited their villages for reinstatement of their right to grow tobacco. Discontent with the ban was common, especially in specific districts of Mardin, Yozgat, Kütahya, Kayseri, Denizli, Erzurum, Bartın, Maraş, Isparta, Niğde and Trabzon provinces, which had long relied on tobacco agriculture. The peasants in these places frequently sought permission to cultivate tobacco as before.[29]

Peasants, who comprised the largest group of tobacco consumers, also resented the poor quality of the Monopoly Administration's tobaccos and cigarettes. The Monopoly Administration produced a cheap brand of cigarette, Köylü, for smokers in rural areas. Moreover, the cut rags marketed by the monopoly did not include adequate cigarette papers, which forced the peasants to buy extra if they could afford it or use newspapers to roll cigarettes. The resulting outburst of anger reached Atatürk himself. As Kılıç Ali, one of Atatürk's best friends, noted in his diary, once Atatürk had been informed of a peasant who had cursed at him. The peasant's anger had been sparked by the lack of cigarette paper, which forced him to roll his tobacco with old newsprint. Atatürk had sympathized with the peasant, recalling how unpleasant it was when he had had to do the same on the battlefield. Anatolia was full of such angry peasants who frequently criticized the poor quality of Köylü cigarettes and cut rags and who demanded price reduction as well as quality improvement.[30]

The salt monopoly also caused public discontent by creating a salt shortage and increasing salt prices. In particular, high prices, beyond the purchasing power of peasants who needed to use salt in great quantities in agriculture and animal husbandry, caused widespread criticism. Writing to the government, the party and the newspapers, the peasants told how they had been deprived of this important staple because of its high cost or a ban on the use of salt resources. Many demanded a decrease in salt prices during the 1930s. The local party congresses also recorded such requests in the wish lists.[31]

After rejuvenating sugar beet production with high prices until the mid-1930s, the government's new move to cut the cost of sugar by decreasing the price of sugar beets from 50 paras per kilogram to 30 paras, as well as doubling the price of the heavy plows used by sugar beet farmers from 20 to 40 liras provoked strong hostility toward the government and the sugar factories.[†] In 1935, deputies from Eskişehir,

---

[†] One lira was equal to 100 piasters; 1 piaster was equal to 40 paras.

an important sugar beet center, recommended that the government increase the price of sugar beets in order to boost the productivity of the Eskişehir Sugar Factory; otherwise farmers might abandon sugar beet cultivation. In 1936, cultivators further pressured the government about pricing. Peasants from Kırklareli, another important sugar beet center, pleaded with the Alpullu Sugar Factory and the government to increase the sugar beet price. In Tokat, cultivators insisted on 40 paras per kilo from the Turhal Sugar Factory. Cultivators in other sugar beet-producing areas such as Edirne, Kocaeli, Bilecik, Afyon, Kütahya and Amasya also demanded higher prices. The amount of scrapped crop was also a matter of debate between the factories and the peasants. The peasants wanted the factories to determine this amount honestly.[32] Perhaps the best gauge of the discontent among the cultivators was the rapid flight from sugar beet agriculture from the mid-1930s on. Indeed, the number of farmers supplying the Alpullu factory decreased from 20,000 to 12,800 in 1938. Likewise, the number of sugar beet farmers producing for the Uşak factory also decreased dramatically, from 18,600 to 5,300 in 1936.[33]

In spite of the sugar factory experts' efforts to convince peasants to cultivate sugar beet, the peasants decisively refused. According to the memoir of a contemporary sugar beet expert working in Turhal (Tokat), the factory officials encountered violent protests. In one instance, Turhal's Dereköyü village peasants confronted the sugar beet experts with hoes in their hands, shouting, "God damn you! Why the hell did you come to our town?" The sugar factory engineers' visit to the village of Perili in Kütahya likewise yielded no results. The peasants did not even haggle, saying, "Efendi, your efforts are in vain. Even if they behead us, we will not plant sugar beets for 30 paras."[34]

The public and private timber companies that took forest villages' livelihoods away were also unwelcome to the peasants. During İnönü's tour of Kastamonu, a province of dense forests, a peasant accused the forest administration of refusing to grant the 10 meters of timber legally allocated to each household, while granting a huge forest to only one entrepreneur. Depriving them of an age-old maintenance of their families was for peasants an injustice. This left them no choice but to cut timber clandestinely. Many languished in prison as a result.[35]

The peasants around the Finike and Elmalı districts of Antalya, which included vast forests in the Taurus Mountains, suffered similarly. The Finike Forest Company, renting all forests from the government, had closed them to the peasants, sparking anger. Likewise, as reported by the İçel deputy, a large timber enterprise, monopolizing the forests, had driven the peasants living in these areas out of their villages. This situation, which increased wood and timber prices in urban areas, frustrated the townspeople also.[36]

Bureaucratic red tape and the rulers' perception of the peasantry as an "ignorant killer of forests" often hindered peasants from exercising their rights to the forests. This situation aroused widespread resentment toward the forest administration. Peasants frequently pleaded with the government to make things easier. Petitioning was the primary way through which the rural population bemoaned the harmful effects of the forest administrations and demanded "free use of the forests for the building or repair of their houses and barns," and "free wood-cutting for firewood."[37] When petitions proved ineffective, they wrote to newspapers. One newspaper reported that peasants everywhere were complaining about the forest officials. The case of Paşalar, a village in Bursa that subsisted on forestry, is illustrative. Unable to obtain licenses to cut wood for six months in 1930, peasants first appealed to the forest director. But he was also reluctant to issue licenses. Then they wrote to the economy minister and a newspaper, claiming that they were going hungry and were unable to pay taxes because their businesses had come to a halt. Finally, their constant complaints and demands forced the ministry to order the forest administration to make things easier for the peasants.[38]

The peasants' complaints found an echo in provincial party congresses. According to the wish lists of the party's provincial congresses in 1931 and 1935, the peasants from many provinces complained that the forest administration had deprived them of timber and wood. The wishes of the peasants included "making the license acquisition easier for peasants," a "decrease in license fees" and "no difficulties for peasants in need of timber and firewood."[39]

Deputy reports also recorded the peasants' displeasure with the forest policy. The deputies of forested provinces like Çanakkale, Bursa, Muğla, Zonguldak, Samsun, Bolu and İçel noted that forest officials and bureaucratic impediments to cutting timber in every village and town they visited angered the peasants and woodworkers. Finally, animal owners and village artisans also grumbled about the forest policy due to the denial of access to pastures, marshlands and reedy fields that were deemed extensions of forests.[40]

Discontent with the Agricultural Bank and Agricultural Cooperatives

A peasant who sent a gloomy letter to *Cumhuriyet* complained about the agricultural loans of the Agricultural Bank (AB) by saying, "The farmers of the Republic are complaining of the Ottomans' red tape"; another letter writer accused the AB of being "an institution of the usurers." Peasants often voiced complaints about the inaccessibility or low amount of credit, daunting red tape, high interest rates and short maturity periods.[41] The first thing that displeased the peasants about the AB was the inadequate number of branches. Thus, the government received many complaints about the lack of access to AB branches. Those peasants who had access to the bank were also frustrated by inadequate loans or blunt rejection of their credit applications. According to a peasant named Osman from the Yomra district of Trabzon, all of the peasants in his village were in debt to moneylenders. The capital of the AB in his district was so low that even if the bank delivered all of it as a loan, it would not save the peasants. Many peasants in Eskişehir, unable to obtain loans from the bank, had fallen victim to usurers. The situation was similar in many other provinces.[42]

Another grievance regarding the bank was the allocation of the lion's share of the funds to merchants and large landowners. Peasants requested that AB loans be devoted to agricultural producers instead of well-off merchants. A 1931 report by a Sivas deputy noted that the peasants accused the bank of funding merchants and large property owners, thereby enabling them to sustain their usury.[43]

The terms of agricultural loans were criticized as too short for low-income peasants. The unfavorable terms of the bank loans further obliged debtors to borrow money from usurers at extortionate interest rates in order to pay back the interest on the bank loans. Therefore, extension of loan terms to five or ten years was a primary demand. Critical letters to the newspapers condemned the bank for charging unaffordable interest rates. Peasants called the bank "a fair usurer."[44]

Peasants also criticized the agricultural cooperatives for profit-seeking, frequently referring to them as "village banks" or "village branches of usury." A peasant from Manisa wrote to *Cumhuriyet* that the debt of a peasant who had borrowed 183 liras from the cooperative in the village of Demirci had grown to 1,170 liras after only a year and a half. The peasant had lost his land, house and household goods to the cooperative.[45]

Beginning in the late 1920s, many cultivators who were indebted to the AB or agricultural cooperatives petitioned the government individually or collectively for debt relief. Especially the bad harvest due to the droughts of 1927 and 1928 and the economic crisis that followed invigorated the peasants' demands for "suspension of debt payments," "debt cancellation" and "a deferred payment plan for agricultural loans."[46]

Wheat purchases at fixed prices higher than market prices carried out by the AB were another target of peasant anger. These purchases had done nothing to alleviate rural impoverishment. Initially, the AB proposed to buy wheat in exchange for erasing wheat producers' loan debt, but the peasants rejected these terms. The government therefore passed the Wheat Protection Law in 1932 and offered higher prices than market levels until 1935. However, the purchases did not reach the majority of producers. Cultivators requested larger-scale purchases until 1935, when market prices moved ahead of the decreasing official prices the bank offered. This time, wheat farmers criticized the bank for offering them low prices for their wheat.[47]

Objecting to Oppression

The ruthlessness and tyranny of village headmen, *ağa*s and gendarmes in the villages were major sources of peasant grievance. Asking for help from the central state authorities was the first method used to cope with the oppression. Peasants sent disgruntled petitions complaining about despotic individuals to the party and the National Assembly individually or collectively. In 1930, for instance, a group of peasants in Giresun province denounced several rapacious and despotic persons in their villages for oppressing the peasants. Over the years, the Giresun peasants continued to complain about the oppressiveness of the *ağa*s.[48] In petitions to the National Assembly, the peasants in a village of Palu (Elazığ) complained of the tyranny of İbrahim Ağa. Likewise, a peasant woman named Münevver in Elbistan (Kahramanmaraş) complained of abuses by Hacı Mehmet Bey. From Siverek (Sivas), a peasant named Hasan complained of a powerful household named Küçükosmanoğulları in his village. In 1931, a retired civil servant named Ahmet Nuri, living in the Kan village of Saimbeyli (Adana), denounced the oppressive attitudes of the *ağas*. A peasant named Enver in Erzurum bemoaned the cruelty of the *ağas*. A group of peasants from the Yalakdere village of Kocaeli also wrote to the National Assembly concerning the oppression of Yusuf Ziya Ağa. In 1934, Mustafaoğlu Veli and his friends in the Karlık village of Adana pleaded with the government to save them from the atrocities of Kadir Ağa. In 1935, a peasant named Abdülkerim from Midyat (Mardin) and a group of peasants from Pertek (Dersim) informed against the despotic *ağas* in their villages. Some of them continued to write to the National Assembly until they received a positive result. The aforementioned Ahmet Nuri once again implored the government to take legal precautions against Halil Efendi, who bullied the village. Likewise, Enver, who had written to the National Assembly in 1931, again petitioned the government to ask for help against the *ağas* in 1934.[49]

Peasant grievances against rapacious landowners were reflected in police reports. Police chief Tahsin from Tosya, for example, reported to the Interior Ministry about the tyranny of an influential landowner, Şükrü Ağa. Peasants in his village were so anxious about the *ağa*'s cruelty that they appealed to security forces in the city center. Party reports also include the discontent of the peasants with oppressive groups. Locals in Sürmene (Trabzon), as one party inspector wrote, spoke of a "class of *ağas*" (*ağalar zümresi*) "buttressed by the party" and "holding the people captive."[50]

Peasants also criticized village headmen who treated them unfairly. The Edirne deputy reported that he had heard peasants in a village coffeehouse complain about the levies and compulsory work imposed by the headman. Likewise, a Denizli deputy reported that the levies and compulsory labor obligations the headman forced on poor peasants had sparked resentment. The peasants in Ankara villages accused the headmen of collecting too much money for village works. Via letters to newspapers and the relevant bureaucrats, peasants raised objections to the headmen. Peasants from a village in Bilecik province, for example, criticized the headman for collecting money frequently. Others, from the Araplar village of Ayvalık (Balıkesir), accused the headman of forcing them to work on his personal projects without payment under the pretext of the Village Law.[51]

Tax collectors and gendarmes took place on the top of the pet hate list of the peasants. The gendarme in particular was the most hated agent of the government. In the eyes of the peasants, "the gendarmerie sided with the *ağa*s." A 1931 report by Denizli deputy Mustafa Kazım indicated that among the most frequent complaints that reached him were "the atrocities and tortures of the gendarmerie."[52] "Gendarmerie oppression," "the torture of the gendarmerie," "beating by gendarmes" and "abuses of gendarmerie commanders" constituted a considerable portion of peasant' complaints in petitions. In an illustrative case, a group of peasants from Ödemiş (İzmir) petitioned the government in 1931 alleging that the gendarmerie commander, Fuat, was involved in corruption in collusion with Nihat Bey, a rich landowner who had his eye on smallholders' lands. Similar complaints regarding the gendarmerie did not disappear in the mid-1930s. In 1934, a group of peasants from Torbalı complained of the gendarmerie commander, Şuayip, accusing him of collecting money from peasants arbitrarily for his personal use. In 1935, a peasant from the Karacabey district of Bursa complained of "the pounding by the gendarmerie." Peasants from the Çakıllar and Rakıllar villages of Gördes (Manisa) also collectively condemned "the corruption of the gendarmerie" by petitioning the National Assembly.[53]

In the east, gendarmerie violence and resulting peasant hostility were more intense. Alongside the gendarmes, militia forces organized by *ağa*s in cooperation with the army also triggered peasant anger. Perhaps the best example of the widespread frustration with the gendarmerie and the militias in the region was a meeting of the chief of the general staff, Fevzi Paşa, and Mardin governor Talat with peasants in Savur district. Their visit to the district drew a curious crowd. As soon as they appeared in the road, peasant women among the crowd wailed, "We are burning! Please, have a heart!" Then, the peasants gave petitions to Fevzi Paşa, complaining about the ruthlessness of security forces and militias. Many demanded the abolition of the militias. Among the Alevi Kurds of Dersim, who incurred the wrath of the state in massacres in 1937 and 1938, the gendarmes were popularly called "djinns with grey dress," owing to the color of their uniform. Rumor had it that these djinns, unleashed by Abdal Musa, an ancient saint, were the enemy of the people.[54]

Peasants often complained of tax collectors' abusive behavior or corruption. Party inspectors also underlined that wrongdoings and mistakes of tax collectors were the main source of the complaints they had listened to in the villages. Peasants did not like the other state officials, either. An RPP deputy, Hacim Muhiddin Çarıklı, for example, wrote in 1931 that he regretfully had to listen to the complaints about the state officials in every place he visited. The memoir of one prominent politician, who served the party inspector, Hilmi Uran, includes observations about rural people's discontent with judges and debt enforcement officials. He wrote that many state officials had sunk into corruption, which resulted in widespread public aversion against the government.[55]

Effects of Peasant Discontent

How far popular opinion in rural areas affected policy deserves analysis. In view of the social need as well as the rural unrest that stemmed from land struggles, the government had already placed land reform on its agenda by the end of the 1920s. Prime Minister İnönü addressed the question of landless peasants in his National Assembly speeches and promised land reform in 1929 and then again in 1936. In 1928, 1935 and 1937, Atatürk touched on the land question and encouraged the government to initiate land reform. The leftist periodical *Kadro*, which attempted to theorize the new regime, championed the idea of land reform. The government took steps, though not comprehensive, to distribute fertile state lands to peasants. The first step was the Law Regarding the Distribution of Land to Needy Farmers in the Eastern Region of June 11, 1929. This law, devised to break the influence of centrifugal Kurdish tribes among Kurdish peasants during the Ağrı Mountain (Ararat) Rebellion, applied to many other regions in western and central Anatolia.[56] The economic program prepared in 1930 included the provision of vacant lands to landless peasants. In 1934, the Settlement Law provided a legal basis for land distribution to peasants. This law also was partially related to the Kurdish uprisings. However, as I discuss in the following chapters, landlessness and social injustice would breed rural unrest and Kurdish rebellions. At the 1935 Congress, the RPP added the land reform policy to its program. The subsequent Settlement Land Law Draft in 1935 intended the distribution of fallow plots to landless peasants, but the National Assembly did not approve it. Two years later, in response to social pressure and Atatürk's insistence, the government prepared a new reform program, the Agricultural Reform Law Draft. This also proved futile. The landed interest within the party scuppered land reform attempts.[57]

Nevertheless, the pressure of the land question forced the government to distribute a considerable portion of fallow land to peasants.
Until 1934, landless peasants, smallholders and refugees received
about 7,113,000 *dönüm*s of arable land and orchards. Between 1934
and 1938, an additional 3 million *dönüm*s were distributed to 88,695
peasant households. Between 1940 and 1944, 875,000 *dönüm*s of
fertile state land – that is, approximately 7.6 percent of the total arable
land – were allocated to 53,000 peasant families. The proportion of this
amount to the total area under cultivation, which was around
43.5 million *dönüm*s by 1927, was about 25 percent. These figures,
although they should be taken with caution due to the state's incapacity
to collect precise data, suggest that the extent of land distributions
cannot be underestimated. Finally, in 1945, the pressure of peasant
discontent, as well as political competition after the transition to
a multiparty regime, induced the RPP to enact the Law of Land
Distribution to the Farmers, the most comprehensive land distribution
program. This law, though not implemented effectively, allocated an
additional 1.5 million *dönüm*s to peasants.[58]

As for the forest matters, the peasants made their voices heard in the
highest state organizations. This is evident from an official notice the
Agriculture Ministry sent in 1933 to the provincial forest directorates,
ordering them to make things easier for peasants and village artisans
who applied for licenses to cut timber.[59] Likewise, in the face of
widespread complaints as well as constant smuggling, the government
was forced to reduce the exorbitant prices of monopoly goods such as
salt, cigarettes, sugar and textiles and to relax limits on production and
trade. The price of salt, the most important input in agriculture, was
notably reduced by 50 percent, from 6 piasters to 3 piasters per kilo.
Notwithstanding some alleviation in public discontent over salt prices,
the salt monopoly continued to elicit reaction from the peasantry
during the 1930s.[60]

The most important components of the populist image of the government were the wheat purchases and agricultural credits implemented through the AB and agricultural cooperatives. Apart from the
populist motivations, the growing discontent of the peasantry during
the Great Depression as well as the fluctuations in wheat outputs led the
government to buy wheat and some other crops at fixed prices.
However, these policies fell short of satisfying the peasantry. The
government tried to alleviate complaints about the agricultural loans

and cooperatives by suspending debt enforcement proceedings and expropriations in 1933. The following year, the AB was ordered to remove commission fees for loans. The 1935 party program also included a promise to reduce interests of agricultural credits, which accordingly was reduced from 10 to 8.5 percent. Payment of existing debt was divided into fifteen equal annual installments in 1935. By 1936, this program covered debts that amounted to 23,703,000 liras, owed by 164,766 farmers. In addition, in 1935, the government ordered the AB not to expropriate peasants' livestock as payment for debt. The government responded to the peasants' demands for debt relief by expanding the scope of the debt relief in 1937. Debts to agricultural cooperatives were also suspended for five years.[61]

All of this tells us that the voice of the peasant found its way in newspaper letters, petitions, politicians' reports and local party congresses' minutes into the state's decision-making. This critical and demanding popular opinion seems to have contributed to the reshaping of policies and practices by extracting concessions from the government and forcing the government to consider protective measures. Undoubtedly, the peasants did not wait for the state to take action. This popular mood in rural areas would cause the peasants to spring into action, as evident in their resistance to taxes and monopolies.

3 | *Resisting Agricultural Taxes*

One day a peasant named Çavuş Emmi (Uncle Sergeant) says to İbik Dayı (Uncle İbik), "If my donkey dies, I will skin it and cover my cow with its skin so that I can escape from the livestock tax." Thereupon, İbik Dayı suggests that Çavuş Emmi should wear this skin in order to avoid the road tax.[1] This was one of the popular jokes that spread across the Anatolian countryside from mouth to mouth in the 1920s and the 1930s. This joke reveals the ways by which the peasants dealt with taxes. To be more specific, it was a reflection of tax evasion in popular culture. Opposition to agricultural taxes by means of deception was so common that such acts became the subject of humor. Both the widespread nature of the tax resistance and its consequences were so far-reaching that, this chapter suggests, a correlation existed between the peasants' resistance to agricultural taxes and the slow waning of the peasantry. The peasants' tax resistance also was among the factors that caused the early republican state's low transformative capacity, which slackened Turkey's modernization.

Dimensions of Tax Resistance

During the interwar years, the increase in tax rates and the extension of some taxes to hitherto exempt areas provoked peasant reaction. Most of the taxes imposed on the peasants were direct taxes, the kind most likely to provoke resistance since they require out-of-pocket payment. Moreover, direct taxation entailed face-to-face encounters with state officials, which could degenerate into quarrels and even fights. Peasants avoided direct confrontation and protest as much as possible. As elsewhere all over the world, the peasants' repertoire of resistance largely comprised subtle ways of tax avoidance.[2] They constantly deployed all of their ingenuity to get around the regulations by cheating, lying or pretending to be ignorant or mistaken. Yet when avoidance was impossible, they did not hesitate occasionally to raise open and violent objections.

One important indicator of tax resistance was the considerable decrease in the state's tax revenues during the 1930s, which dropped from 75 percent of total state revenues in 1930 to 58 percent in 1935 and 50 percent in 1939. The proportion of the collected direct taxes to the levied amount also points out the colossal evasion (see Graph 3.1). Undoubtedly, this downward trend was owed in part to tax relief programs, the gradual decrease in tax rates in the mid-1930s, agricultural price declines and the low extractive capacity of the state. But tax avoidance in rural areas was ubiquitous. Indeed, a discussion in a parliamentary session in 1934 revealed massive evasion of direct taxes, reaching up to 120,500,000 liras.[3] Given that the bulk of direct taxes were levied on agriculture as the main sector of the economy, peasant tax resistance was clearly significant.

A contemporary expert in the Finance Ministry noted that the state failed to collect the greater portion of taxes. Tax evasion, he wrote, was out of control and direct tax revenues never reached target levels. The paucity of educated finance officials, as well as the low wages of tax collectors, also hampered the tax estimation and collection process.[4] Corruption through bribery also fostered evasion.

Tax collection was more challenging in the distant uplands. The figures regarding the land tax suggest that the state encountered great obstacles in collecting it in the eastern regions. According to a 1932

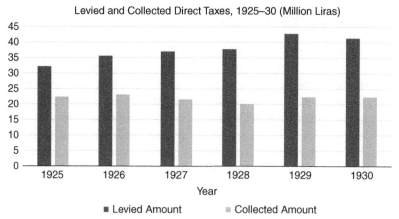

Graph 3.1 Levied and collected direct taxes, 1925–30

report by General Inspector İbrahim Tali Öngören on the Kurdish provinces, including Diyarbakır, Van, Siirt, Hakkari, Muş, Mardin, Bitlis and Urfa, the outstanding land taxes had been gradually increasing. By 1931, 87 percent of the estimated land tax in Urfa was in arrears. The next year, the government collected barely half of the estimated land tax. Resentment of the land tax was so common that İnönü, on his tour to the eastern provinces, had admitted, "We are waiting for the payment of the taxes in vain. They would not pay this high tax. We should not fool ourselves." According to the General Situation Report of the Erzurum governor, whereas the assessed land tax was 192,522 liras in 1932, the collected amount barely reached 47,303 liras. The following year, the estimated tax was 195,900 liras, but the collected amount only 60,838 liras. In 1934, these figures were 159,165 liras and 55,448 liras, respectively. Not only in the eastern provinces but also in developed western provinces like İzmir, peasants refused to pay a considerable portion of the land tax. Thus the provincial party congress in İzmir demanded an amnesty for land tax debt in 1936.[5]

As for the livestock tax, tax revenues in Erzurum, an important center of livestock breeding, remained below anticipated levels. Although the tax amounts levied were 263,036 liras for 1932, 202,495 liras for 1933 and 178,501 liras for 1934, the peasants paid only 163,042, 147,185 and 138,962 liras, respectively. That is to say, taxpayers managed to curtail their tax burden by about one-third in total. The livestock tax revenues in other eastern provinces remained far behind targeted levels.[6] Peasants usually concealed their livestock from the state. The actual number of animals exceeded those registered and taxed. In 1931–2, the number of taxed animals in Dersim, for instance, was 24,000 heads of sheep, goat and cattle, and 7,500 camels. Their tax value was about 59,000 liras. However, 41,428 liras of this amount was not paid in 1932 – that is, livestock owners evaded 70 percent of the tax.[7]

Peasants also avoided the road tax as much as possible. A newspaper reported in April 1932 that the İstanbul governorship had begun to put 8,000 peasants from the villages of the Çatalca district, who had not paid the road tax of 1927, 1928 and 1929, to work in road construction. An additional 3,000 peasants in these villages did not pay the road tax in 1932. They also would be employed at road construction sites. It was also reported in 1934 that many peasants in Kandıra (Kocaeli) had not paid the road tax for years. The demands heard at provincial party congresses for reducing the road tax or cancelling road tax debts also indicate the extent of tax avoidance.[8]

Republican bureaucrats also complained about peasants' avoidance of the road tax. Refet Aksoy, for instance, in his 1936 book *Köylülerimizle Başbaşa* (*Head to Head with Our Peasants*), wrote that the majority of peasants neither paid the road tax nor fulfilled their labor obligations. Local statistics give insight into peasant resistance to the road tax. In Erzincan, for example, the amount of the tax actually collected remained below the assessed levels. Peasants avoided working on road construction at the same time. The proportion of the collected taxes to the levied amount fell from 64 percent to 46 percent between 1927 and 1930.[9]

Repertoire of Tax Resistance

Concealment of Property

When their demands expressed through petitions and letters were not met, peasants resorted to tax evasion. The first way to escape taxes was to hide valuable and taxable properties. Anatolian peasants undertook several subtle avoidance strategies such as either not declaring their property or undervaluing it, or hiding their income and taxable assets. Contemporary observers related the common incommunicative and skeptical attitude of peasants in the presence of a stranger to tax evasion. In her village surveys from the early 1940s, sociologist Mediha Berkes (Esenel) noted how difficult it was to gather information about the peasants' properties due to concern about possible taxes on them. Peasants so suspected Berkes of being a tax collector that she had to record secretly what she saw and heard. Another contemporary sociologist, Yıldız Sertel, also wrote that because their most frightening nightmare was the tax collector, peasants hid the actual amounts of their land, crops and livestock.[10]

In the case of the land tax, tax resistance took two main forms. The first was to avoid registering land and the second was to underreport its size. As Barkan documented, the peasants either did not report or underreported their landholdings. Many did not register their lands under their own names in order to escape the land tax.[11]

Mechanisms of livestock tax avoidance were roughly comparable, though, unlike the fields, animals were movable and easily hidden. Peasants evaded the livestock tax by underreporting or not declaring their animals. In one peasant's words, "the heavy taxes made the peasants thieves of their own property." A contemporary wrote that nobody in his village in Burdur declared all of their livestock. His family, owning two oxen, one cow, one donkey and five sheep, declared only a few of them, thereby saving 305 piasters. Peasant resistance to the livestock tax also can be read from the accusatory statements of the bureaucrats. In an advisory pamphlet addressing the peasantry, a republican bureaucrat accused peasants who hid their animals from the state of being thieves and traitors. Indeed, the number of animals recorded and taxed by the state decreased sharply throughout the country after the tax increase.[12]

Peasants devised several shrewd ways to conceal their animals. Many hid their animals in bedrooms, forests, hills or caves when tax officials came to their village. Press accounts reveal such behavior. In the Titrik village of Giresun, for instance, a peasant named Ayadaşoğlu hid his cow in the forest by tethering it to a tree. In the same village, the preacher concealed his sheep inside a cave in order to evade the livestock tax. Peasant women reportedly hid their goats in their houses, in the bed. Many peasants managed to mislead tax officials by alleging that their sheep and goats were missing, dead or below the taxable age. Such devious tactics were so common that novels like Kemal Tahir's *Sağırdere* included such scenes.[13]

Livestock tax evasion was rampant, especially in the distant eastern uplands, where animal husbandry was the main source of livelihood. Therefore, great gaps emerged between the real numbers of livestock and the numbers taxed. For instance, whereas according to the official records there were 5,000 sheep in the center of Bitlis, the real number was up to 40,000 during the 1930s. Likewise, in Siirt the peasants declared only 12,000 sheep, but the true number was 25,000. In Dersim, the number of declared and officially recorded farm animals was 68,875, but the peasants actually had around 170,000. That is to say, the Dersim peasants managed to shelter about 100,000 animals from the livestock tax within the 1930s alone.[14]

Though not as extensive as in the east, livestock tax evasion was widespread even in western and central Anatolia. In Konya, the number of sheep declined from 2.5 million to 500,000 within four years when the livestock tax doubled between 1926 and 1930. In Aydın, whereas the number of sheep and goats was 404,874 in 1929, this number decreased sharply to 272,318 in 1933. In the same time span, the number of sheep and goats in İçel decreased from 480,927 to 321,484, and in Manisa from 824,043 to 621,214. These drastic decreases stemmed partly from peasants' shift away from animal husbandry due to runaway taxes. However, they also reflect tax evasion. The heavier the taxes, the more animals were shifted to the informal economy. This was reversed in the following years with the gradual decrease in taxes, which rendered concealment unnecessary. Thus the number of officially registered animals would climb rapidly from the mid-1930s on.[15]

The road tax was another front on which the peasants waged a war to escape monetary and labor obligations. One way was to run from tax collectors and gendarmes. There was also a legal way to avoid the tax. Having five or more children exempted a family from the road tax. Some peasants tried to have a few more babies solely for this purpose. Families had reportedly begun to grow crowded in recent years for this reason.[16]

Peasants also exploited popular belief in evil spirits to scare the tax collectors. On tax collection day, they would often hide their livestock in the mountains, a practice tax collectors called *sirkat* (stealing). Folk tales concerning *sirkat* were common, including one that told of a demon in the guise of a naked old woman who had attacked a tax collector on his way to a village. Indeed, such stories and old peasant women pretending to be witches could intimidate tax collectors patrolling in forests to hunt after animals hidden in out-of-sight locations.[17]

Hiding Out and Bribing

The most popular tax avoidance method was to vanish whenever the tax officials came to the village. A peasant in Ardahan told Lilo Linke, a foreign journalist who toured Anatolia extensively in 1935: "The peasants have nothing for themselves. They are so poor that they disappear into the mountains when the tax collector comes near them." Coffeehouses and village rooms were the first destinations the tax collectors dropped by. Therefore, whenever they appeared near the village, these places were suddenly abandoned. For some peasants, the safest way was avoiding coffeehouses and village rooms on certain days so as to escape the tax officials.[18]

In some villages, the peasants set up alarm systems to detect approaching tax collectors. In Diyarbakır, for instance, when Kurdish shepherds caught sight of a tax collector, they spread the encoded news among the peasants by saying, "the wolf is coming!" (*vêr gamê vêr* in Zazaki Kurdish). Those who heard this warning would conceal their animals, beds, blankets, quilts and kitchen utensils and then vanish.[19]

Peasants placed lookouts (*erkete* or *gözcü*) at certain points to alert the village to a probable raid by gendarmerie and tax officials. In June 1936, peasants in the villages of Balıkesir began to stand watch on the roads after hearing the security forces had started to detain those who did not fulfill road tax obligations. Fakir Baykurt's memoirs also include such scenes. Under declaring their livestock by half, peasants in his village were always on the alert for tax collectors during tax season. If an alarm were raised, they hid their livestock in caves or closets for bedding (*yüklük*) inside homes.[20]

Although tax collectors' corruption was a significant problem that bred social injustice, it did sometimes create an opportunity for the peasants to evade taxes. Tax collectors' salaries were low, and many were willing to accept bribes. For peasants, bribing tax collectors was seen as the lesser of two evils. By offering tax officials a certain sum of money or a quarter of the tax in kind or in cash, peasants managed to avoid paying higher sums.[21]

Objections, Protests and Violence

When the peasants could find no other way out, they did not hesitate to confront tax collectors and accompanying gendarmes. In the eyes of peasants, tax collectors posed a threat to their economic well-being; they were agents of the urban elite who transferred the peasants' daily bread to the well-off city dwellers. Whenever a tax collector dropped in, the villagers would say, "The masters in the cities cannot eat stone!"[22] As stated earlier, peasants perceived the tax officials as dangerous as a wolf, "an agent of the devil" or "the angel of death." This negative perceptions of tax collectors often provoked aggression toward them. Individual actions were widespread, but collective resistance and protests also happened at times.

Peasants occasionally took their disputes with tax collectors to court. In 1937, in a village of Osmaniye province, a peasant named Ömer refused the invitation of the headman and the tax collector to come to the village square to pay his tax debts. Their quarrel ended up in the court, which ruled against Ömer. He appealed the decision, but the Supreme Court (*Yargıtay*) upheld it.[23] Ömer lost his legal struggle, but his action suggests that peasants did not hesitate to use legal strategies when they felt they had been wronged.

Only a few collective tax protests occurred due to the high risk they could run under an authoritarian regime. A wave of protest by peasant women that swept central Anatolia in 1934 stands out as a striking example. On June 10, 1934, fifteen women in Kayseri came together in front of the government office and chanted slogans against the wheat protection tax. They then headed toward the governorship, shouting, "What kind of law is that?" and "What kind of government is that?" The same day, another group of women gathered in front of the government office of the Develi district of Kayseri. They also chanted slogans against the tax. Alarmed by the growing protests, the security forces prosecuted the protesting women. One month later, poor elderly peasant women in the İskilip district of Çorum and in the Mudurnu district of Bolu rallied in front of government offices. According to the official who recorded the events, "women made a great fuss in the streets and created an uproar," complaining of poverty and the wheat protection tax. In July 1934, a group of small flour mill owners from several villages around Ankara gathered in front of the Finance Ministry and expressed their objections to the tax burden the district governors (*kaymakam*) had imposed on them.[24]

As a last resort, tax resistance took the form of violence against tax collectors. Attacks when tax collectors were on the road or even in a village, especially during or just after tax collection, were the most frequent pattern of this violence. Newspapers of the time abound with stories about unfortunate tax collectors who were beaten, stabbed, shot or robbed by peasants. Sometimes the peasants confronted the tax collectors and security forces openly and collectively. In May 1929, the peasants in Urfa opposed a livestock census. Their quarrel with the tax collectors, who were escorted by gendarmes, resulted in a serious fight, at the end of which some livestock owners managed to escape with their animals. In April 1930, in the village of Girlavik near the Birecik district, a peasant with a tax debt attempted to escape upon seeing the tax official and gendarmes approaching his house. When the gendarmes surrounded his house, he shot the tax collector dead and escaped.[25]

Such armed clashes were not peculiar to eastern Anatolia. In June 1934, some peasants from the Botsa village in Konya attacked the tax collectors and gendarmes who had expropriated their untaxed livestock and retook their animals. A gendarme battalion then raided the village and beat the peasants. However, the peasants stood up against such unjust treatment by suing the tax officials and gendarmes for overtaxing and torturing them. Another incident of armed tax resistance occurred in Manavgat (Antalya). On the morning of June 3, 1937, a gendarmerie battalion raided the village of Bolasan and sequestered the untaxed livestock. That night, the peasants, under the pitch dark of midnight, sought revenge by preparing an ambush for the gendarmes. One officer was killed in the conflict.[26]

The Anatolian countryside was rife with such attacks on tax collectors and accompanying gendarmes. The attackers were most probably peasants inflamed with anger toward these state agents. For instance, in January 1931, unknown persons murdered tax collector Tahsin Efendi after he collected a sum of money in one Anatolian village. Tax collector Ali Fikri Efendi was also murdered after he collected taxes in the villages of Düzce province in June 1931. Such events continued apace in the years to come. In 1936, a peasant shot a tax collector through the head in Muğla. Another tax collector, Raşid Efendi, was murdered on duty in 1936 after collecting taxes in the villages. When tax collectors traveled to distant villages, their homes were sometimes attacked or robbed.[27] Undoubtedly these are just a few examples among many.

In eastern Anatolia, tax-related armed attacks on tax collectors and gendarmes sometimes grew into local uprisings. Since peasants made use of tribal ties to mobilize other peasants' support, these uprisings have mostly been explained with reference to Kurdish nationalism or tribalism. Undoubtedly, Kurdish nationalists or tribal chiefs engineered several rebellions. Kinship ties also facilitated the uprisings.[28] However, a closer look reveals that the peasants' subjective economic experiences and motivations played a more important role than did nationalist or tribal causes.

The peasant rebellion, named the Buban Tribe Rebellion is an example of how economic struggle underpinned the conflicts between state and society in the Kurdish provinces. In 1934, villages in the Mutki district of Siirt (in Bitlis today) rebelled against the government. This incident is usually considered to have been engineered by Kurdish nationalists. However, as in many other instances of peasant resistance in the region, this insurrection was not motivated by ideological hostility to the Turkish state, but rather by resistance to state control over the local society.[29] The peasants first objected and then rose up against the government when tax collectors forced those who could not pay the road tax to work on road construction sites. The state's policy of disarming the peasants also left them defenseless against attacks by outsiders in the dangerous uplands. This also helped stoke the insurgence, which lasted about a year before the gendarmes put it down.[30]

Less than a year later, in April 1935, Kurdish peasants in the Sason district of Siirt rose up. Again, neither Kurdish organizations nor foreign powers were behind this insurgency. The conflicts broke out due to the growing tension between tax collectors and poor peasants who subsisted on animal husbandry and illegal tobacco farming. The annual census of taxable animals in the spring always caused quarrels between the peasants and the tax collectors. The peasants frequently hid their animals or prevented tax officials from counting their livestock by driving them out of the villages. The intervention of monopoly officials in the peasants' tobacco cultivation also sparked local anxiety. Gendarmerie lieutenant Madanoğlu also poignantly notes in his memoirs that the Sason inhabitants were tired of corruption and oppression by government officials. Their own self-sufficient economy, in which they produced and consumed their own tobacco, salt, food and clothing, was apparently dashing the hopes of state agents to link the region to the national market.[31]

As a result of pervasive noncooperation, tax evasion and smuggling in the mountain villages of Sason, the district governor, accompanied by the *mufti* (official Muslim scholar and community leader), toured these villages in an attempt to persuade them to cooperate with the government. During this tour, a furious fight broke out between the officials and the peasants in the village of Harabak over tax matters. The fight escalated into an armed clash in which the district governor was killed and the *mufti* severely injured. The peasants who were charged with the murder hid in the mountains in order to defend themselves against the security forces. The events, labeled a rebellion by Ankara, spread to other villages in Sason as pressure from the government mounted. Hence, peasant resistance against tax collectors and monopoly officials was transformed into a local uprising, which attracted many other peasants in the region facing similar problems.[32]

Regardless of individual or collective resistance, in confrontation with the tax officials, one important strategy was to mobilize collaboration among peasants. Releasing specific rumors accusing tax collectors of immorality and corruption served this goal. The peasants made use of this informal medium to produce and spread manipulative information in order to encourage disobedience by others, legitimize their own actions or provoke a government reaction against the tax collectors. In January 1939, a few months after Atatürk's death, a rumor alleging that a tax official named Aziz had fired his gun into the air to celebrate the president's death and chanted anti-regime slogans swept through the villages in Kars province. However, an investigation disclosed that this rumor had been put into circulation so as to set the local government against the tax collector because he had pressured peasants who had avoided paying tax.[33]

Certain kinds of rumors prompted public resistance to the tax collectors. Rumors about a government crisis that had allegedly engulfed Ankara were intended to foment the people's disobedience to the government, particularly in regard to taxes. In January 1939, a peasant in Trabzon took advantage of the uncertain political atmosphere. He refused to pay his taxes and sought to mobilize other peasants to join his disobedience by spreading a rumor of a military plot in Ankara. Another sort of rumor concerned the response of state leaders to the brutality of tax collectors. These rumors were intended to encourage opposition to tax collectors by convincing the masses that even the rulers hated them. One such rumor circulated during İnönü's tour of Kastamonu in December 1938. Rumor alleged that the new president, İnönü, had killed three tax collectors. Rumor had it that hearing a denunciation about a tax collector, İnönü wanted to investigate the situation; when the accused tax collector and two of his colleagues attacked the president, he shot them in self-defense.[34] It is not possible to ascertain the source of the rumor; however, it is reasonable to think that peasants sought to justify their hatred of and resistance to tax collectors by fabricating such unfounded news.

Repercussions of Tax Resistance: Depriving the State of Agricultural Resources

Peasants' prolific repertoire of everyday and mostly informal strata-gems, though mostly not intended to change the policies, were not inconclusive. The widespread reluctance in paying taxes, in conjunction with the impoverishment in rural areas caused by the economic crisis, prompted the government to reduce agricultural taxes several times and to forgive a certain portion of tax debt. Tax resistance and the people's rapidly growing sympathy with the short-lived liberal Free Republican Party (FRP) opposition designed by President Atatürk to gauge social discontent in 1930 led even the president himself to contemplate reducing the peasants' tax load. Hence, the government lowered the rates of agricultural taxes during the 1930s. Discontent with the livestock tax resulted in successive reductions in 1931, 1932, 1936 and 1938 that nearly halved it and removed horses and donkeys from the list of taxable livestock. The total amount of tax reductions in 1931 and 1932 alone reached 32.5 percent.[35] These discounts did not cease complaints. Nor did tax avoidance dwindle. Finally, toward the end of 1935, Atatürk, aware of people's discontent with the livestock tax, suggested the government reduce it further. With the new adjust-ments in the tax rates in the beginning of 1936, the total tax discount since 1931 reached 51.75 percent on average. Yet the tax abatement did not put a bridle on tax avoidance. Accordingly, the livestock tax was lowered once again, albeit slightly, narrowed in scope and given clarity in the assessment and collection methods in March 1938. Thus, the government redressed the peasants' paramount grievance more thoroughly.[36]

Similarly, in 1931, people's deep grievance with the forced labor obligation and widespread resistance to the road tax in both rural and urban areas forced the government to lower the rates by around 50 percent and to adjust the labor equivalent accordingly. The tax underwent a considerable reduction from 8–10 liras to 4–6 liras in 1931. The labor obligation also was reduced from 10–12 days to 6–8 days.[37] With regard to the land tax, facing widespread evasion, the government left land tax revenues to the local governments and cut the rate by about 35 percent according to local conditions. In addition, the government forgave some part of outstanding tax debt in 1934, including a huge amount of peasants' tax debts in July that year. In the face of daunting land tax debts, the government remitted the half of this tax in 1935 and 1939.[38] Moreover, alarmed by the women's protests in central Anatolia, Ankara amended the wheat protection tax law one year after its promulgation. The second clause of the law was revised in May 1935 to limit further the scope of the tax by exempting all village flour mills, including those near urban centers.[39]

Undoubtedly, none of these measures signaled a wholesale retreat by the government. Nonetheless, these were serious concessions for a state in need of vast resources, which decelerated the modernization process by depriving the state of funds vital to modernization schemes. In addition to the infrastructural weakness of the early republican state, this social dynamic also reduced its transformative capacity. The last but equally important consequence that would arouse from peasants' struggles to keep their resources by minimizing the tax load was the longevity of the peasantry, which survived until the 2000s, albeit in numbers that have gradually declined.

4 | *Social Smuggling*

Resisting Monopolies

In 1928, the general director of the Tobacco Monopoly Administration stated that tobacco smuggling posed a serious threat to railroad construction, to which the state devoted itself. He emphasized that the government allocated the enormous amount of money generated by the tobacco monopoly for the railroad projects. He requested that the press publish articles portraying smuggling as "a crime committed against the nation." Given the fact that the monopolies yielded a huge portion of the total state income of between 10 and 14 percent during this period, it is not surprising that the rulers stigmatized smuggling as a subversive crime, even as treason.[1] As a sort of indirect taxation, the monopolies were the backbone of the government's economic policies, devised to provide the revenues vital to state projects. The monopoly system also facilitated the commercialization and commoditization of the economy. Smuggling therefore represented another facet of people's resistance to the state's efforts to regulate the economy according to the requirements of state-led industrialization. However, the restrictions in production, high fees and taxes, maze of regulations and high prices of monopoly goods led agricultural producers, traders and consumers to get involved in smuggling.

The Characteristics of Smuggling

Smuggling is the illegal production and movement of goods within a country or across national borders to circumvent restrictions and taxes on them. The production and trade of contraband items was peculiar to neither Turkey nor the republican era. Smuggling was as old as monopolies. It was a long-standing phenomenon that had emerged in other places and previous centuries as a response to strict tax regimens. Leaving aside smuggling before the modern era, even in cradles of capitalism like Great Britain, where monopolies such as the

East India Company played a crucial role in the economy, smuggling challenged the monopolies.[2]

Smuggling had also been an extensive activity in the Ottoman Empire, where the main supplier of the sultan's treasury was extensive taxation through monopolies. Yet it gained new momentum with the advent of modern finance administration by the foreign creditors of the Ottoman state under the Public Debts Administration (Düyûn-u Umûmiye) in the last decades of the empire. Such creditors had established Régie Company as an efficient monopoly corporation in 1883. The tobacco producers and traders driven out of business by Régie had challenged both it and the Ottoman government through smuggling. According to estimates, armed conflicts between smugglers and Régie's own guards resulted in the deaths of between 20,000 and 60,000 people before the Constitutional Revolution of 1908.[3] The republic replaced Régie in 1925 by directly assuming monopoly rights. The foundation of new monopolies and increasing state intervention in the economy stimulated smuggling once again from the mid-1920s on.

Smuggling served largely as a survival method for peasants. It was not under the monopoly of organized bands that made fortunes. Rather, it was an informal web of daily transactions involving untaxed goods to which the great majority of the rural population shifted as producers, traders or consumers in order to avoid the restrictions, obligations and taxes of the monopoly system. Carried out by small operators working individually or in collaboration with relatives or neighbors, smuggling thrived as the "makeshift economy of the poor."[4]

Akin to Hobsbawm's notion of social banditry, the smuggling in this sense deserves to be called social smuggling. It contested to some degree the capitalist restructuring of property rights. That is why, for the government and monopoly firms, smuggling fell into the category of crime against property. In a rural country, most of this crime was committed by the low-income population, particularly poor peasants. Even the press admitted that many people lived on moderate earnings from various activities deemed smuggling.[5] Court cases demonstrate that most smugglers were small dealers living from hand to mouth. In a smuggling trial in April 1935, for example, two defendants from villages near İstanbul alleged that they had become involved in smuggling because of poverty. Both the judge and the press reporter who observed the trial showed sympathy to the defendants. Indeed, poverty fed smuggling, and in return, smuggling fed the poor. The lieutenant governor of Trabzon reported to the Interior Ministry that the poor, including children as young as eleven, were involved in smuggling in order to be able to buy food or pay taxes.[6] In this regard, it fits what Hirschman called an *exit strategy*, which enables people to withdraw from a market that is highly taxed and priced by the state and monopoly enterprises.[7]

Social smuggling was a life-improving activity for the low-income masses. Diverting economic resources to society rather than state and companies, it enabled the people to avoid indirect taxes and high profit margins reflected in the prices. Thus it boosted consumers' bargaining power by providing cheaper alternatives. Undermining the status of the monopoly, smuggling created an informal duopoly that allowed both cultivators and consumers to choose the better alternative. It also prevented provisioning crises in distant markets where the formal economy failed to meet local demands.

Therefore, the people did not give up illegal economic transactions throughout the period. The scale of smuggling can be seen from historical records, most of which are reports on smugglers captured by security forces. Successful smugglers left little or no trace of their activities; therefore the evidence available is only the tip of the iceberg. It is evident from the press and the reports of the Interior Ministry from 1927, 1928 and 1929 that smuggling was rampant during the 1920s under the relatively liberal economic and customs regimes imposed by the Lausanne Treaty since 1923.[8] The more the state intervened in the economy, the faster the smuggling spread in the 1930s. News about smugglers captured together with contraband goods could be found in the newspapers every few days. Gendarmes in Muğla, for instance, arrested 400 smugglers in June 1932 alone. It was reported that 235 smugglers, 17,000 kilos of contraband items, 54,000 rolls of cigarette paper and 800 animals had been seized within the single month of August 1933. During just the first half of October 1934, 67 smugglers carrying numerous contraband items were entrapped. One editorial commented with astonishment, "If these are the smuggled goods caught within fifteen days, imagine those caught in a year!" Such news continued to be reported in the years to come.[9] Smuggling was so widespread that one of the first Turkish movies directed by the most famous director of the time, Muhsin Ertuğrul, was *Kaçakçılar* (*Smugglers*) (1929), telling a tragic story of poor people involved in smuggling.

It is difficult to ascertain from these figures precisely how many of these cases were small or big deals. However, they tell us how heavily smuggling diffused throughout society. The records of the smuggling cases that overwhelmed the courts suggest the extent of the activity. On April 1, 1932, a newspaper article indicated that the specialized court for smuggling in İstanbul alone was hearing eleven cases per day, some of which had been committed in the villages of İstanbul and neighboring provinces. The specialized smuggling court in Gaziantep, a southeastern frontier province, was choked with thousands of cases. The court reportedly heard 4,250 cases in 1934 alone, imposing fines that amounted to 2 million liras. Despite such high numbers, it was reported that many more smugglers had managed to evade the law. According to *Polis Dergisi*, the civil courts were also full of smuggling cases, reaching more than 1,000 cases a year.[10]

A range of reasons led rural people to get involved in the informal transactions the authorities called smuggling. The main impetus for smuggling was, of course, the monopolies. The monopolies meant overtaxation and limitations on production and trade of certain cash crops and consumer goods. This hit producers and traders of monopolized goods as well as consumers. As the state widened its interventionist economic policies, those who continued their informal economic activities automatically fell into the smuggler category. High fees and other costs, bad treatment by monopolies and restriction in production levels led suppliers to produce and sell their items illegally. Concordantly, high prices, low quality and inaccessibility of goods marketed by state factories and monopolies drove consumers to demand smuggled goods. Particularly the price differentiation in two different but interrelated levels encouraged smuggling. First, the heavily taxed and priced licensed domestic products were too expensive compared to their informally produced and marketed untaxed counterparts. Second, price differences between the domestic market and neighboring markets resulted in cross-border smuggling. Consequently, expensive and mostly poor-quality domestic goods did not entice rural customers.[11]

Moreover, many of the transactions the government labeled smuggling were the continuation of practices with a very long pedigree. However, with the restrictions of the monopoly system, these transactions turned into illegal economic survival methods by which low-income people coped with restrictions. For instance, commercial relations between the eastern provinces and Syrian markets, which had long been carried out without restriction, now fell into the category of smuggling due to the new borders. İskenderun under the French mandate operated as an entrance port to Anatolia for contraband until the annexation of Hatay into Turkey in 1939.[12] This is probably why Turkey expended assiduous effort to take control of Hatay, including İskenderun.

Local needs and tastes were another factor that boosted smuggling. Interestingly, domestic goods generally did not appeal to local consumers. The tobacco and cigarettes the monopoly factories produced were not attractive to peasant smokers. Again, peasants, both in the east and in the west, did not like the shape, style and color of Sümerbank fabrics and clothing. Sümerbank's clothes were too close-fitting and delicate for the peasant lifestyle; peasants generally favored thick and durable textiles.[13] As for the forests, the state's strict control resulted in secret timber and wood cutting and trade. Several legal measures in 1924 and 1925 and finally the Forest Law in 1937 restricted the peasants' access to forests. Nevertheless, peasants continued to cut and trade timber and wood clandestinely.

Despite whatever measures the government took, the peasants did not give up the advantages of the informal economy. The government fought smuggling with a series of strict laws, coercive security measures and constant propaganda stigmatizing it as high treason. A contemporary observer admitted, "The smuggling triumphs in spite of the struggle against it that costs millions of liras." In stark contrast to the anti-smuggling propaganda calling smugglers traitors and degenerates, for many people, smuggling was an honorable job due to the risks it entailed and the benefits it provided.[14]

The first body of these measures contained several anti-smuggling laws. Since the smugglers managed to exploit gaps in the law, lawmakers had to upgrade the anti-smuggling laws every few years. The government initially promulgated the Law about Prohibition and Prosecution of Smuggling in 1927. Only two years later, because this law fell short, the government enacted a new anti-smuggling law in 1929. Cross-border smuggling increased after the Turkish government raised tariffs after 1929. Therefore, as of 1931, a semi-military force against smugglers was deployed in the frontier zones under the Customs Enforcement General Command.[15]

These measures prevented neither internal nor cross-border smuggling. In 1931, politicians began to suggest reopening the Independence Tribunals, established to prosecute deserters and rebels during the Independence War. Meanwhile, the government enacted a harsher anti-smuggling law in 1932 on the grounds that smuggling had reached a new dimension that threatened the country. The new law severely punished both cross-border transactions and smuggling of untaxed domestic goods. The Justice Ministry set up specialized civil courts to address smuggling in provinces where it ran rampant. To deal with cross-border operators, specialized military courts were founded in Gaziantep, Urfa and Mardin.[16]

In 1934, a new provision was added to the anti-smuggling law that provided social assistance to the families of those killed in conflicts with smugglers. Its aim was to encourage officials to crack down harder on smuggling. Ordinary citizens were also called upon to inform on smugglers. A smuggling tip-off system was set up and informants were rewarded with money from 1935 on. The tip-off system proved fruitless in part because people feared retaliation. Therefore, the government declared in January 1937 that informants' identities would be kept confidential.[17]

The government reinforced the anti-smuggling measures by launching a propaganda campaign through education in 1927. The Education Ministry issued a circular about the anti-smuggling campaign in schools that stated, "The use and trade of contraband items still astonishingly continue in many places . . . It is nothing but theft [and] a great moral corruption against which the next generations should be protected through education." Courses like *Yurt Bilgisi* (civics) in primary and secondary schools taught the harmful effects of smuggling on society.[18] The National Economy and Domestic Good Weeks programs were established in 1934 so as to promote the consumption of taxed legal goods. What is more, using untaxed goods was considered treason. The media published aphorisms or admonitions praising legal taxed goods and damning untaxed smuggled commodities. One of them went as follows:

Our government loses millions of liras because of the smuggling carried out by bastard persons . . . Dear Countryman! Do not buy even a matchstick from smugglers who come to your village, and report this bastard to the village headman or gendarmerie station.[19]

The railways were expected to reach security goals and to shackle Anatolia's informal economy to the formal economy. The railways were described as "the swords drawn against smuggling."[20] When these measures proved ineffective in curbing smuggling, the government espoused economic recipes, decreasing prices and taxes. This was smuggling's bargaining impact, which forced the state and monopolies to mitigate the profit margins, taxes and prices. That is why contraband production and trade of many widely consumed items such as tobacco, cigarettes, *rakı*, wine, salt, sugar, wood, timber and fabrics was rampant during the period. Of these, tobacco kept its primary place among smuggled items.

Tobacco Smuggling

Pakize Türkoğlu as a contemporary young girl in a village of Antalya province, writes in her memoirs that punishment for tobacco smuggling, called *tabaka cezası*, referring to tobacco cases, was a popular topic of daily conversation in villages. She states that though these acts were illegal, the peasants trying to eke out a living were obliged to commit them.[21] Undoubtedly this was not limited to Antalya. As the most smuggled item, tobacco had a huge market across the country.

The Tobacco Monopoly Law regarded the following acts as tobacco smuggling: cultivating and harvesting tobacco without official permission or in amounts greater than what was reported to the government, trade and consumption of tobacco products without the legal stamp of the monopoly, selling tobacco products outside the places and prices determined by the monopoly, and importing tobacco products illegally. These acts were widespread throughout the country. According to estimates, 70 percent of Kütahya peasants were consuming smuggled tobacco by 1931. Tobacco smuggling was so out of control in Adana, Antep and Urfa that the monopoly's sales had decreased threefold by the same year. The smuggling of tobacco persisted throughout the 1930s. In 1935, Ali Rana Tarhan, the customs and monopolies minister, admitted that the tobacco and cigarette sales of the Monopoly Administration were 400,000 tons less than the previous year's. Consumers preferred to buy cheaper smuggled tobacco products.[22]

The main factor encouraging these acts was the overpricing of monopoly tobacco. Moreover, obtaining official permits for the tobacco trade cost between 5 and 20 liras. Doing business without official permission was therefore more advantageous for low-income traders. In distant regions, tobacco demand outstripped the supply of monopoly tobacco. A consumer market flourished for cheaper, readily available and sometimes higher-quality contraband tobacco and cigarettes.[23] For tobacco cultivators, the unattractive prices offered by the monopoly, long and costly bureaucratic procedures, transportation costs and malfeasance by monopoly officials were incentives to sell their crops to smugglers instead. Evading taxes enabled smugglers to offer higher prices to cultivators. Sometimes cultivators sold their produce directly to smokers clandestinely. The ban on tobacco farming in certain places where it had been the main livelihood also pushed farmers into the illegal cultivation and trade of tobacco.

Smuggled tobacco products were less processed and untaxed. This gave them a tremendous price advantage. Smugglers made a profit even at prices quite below those of monopoly products. The high price of processed tobacco and cigarettes despite the decline in raw tobacco prices encouraged cultivators to enjoy the high profit margins instead of underselling their crops to the monopoly. That is why politicians frequently suggested reducing cigarette prices in 1933 and the following years.[24]

The price discrepancy between the highly taxed expensive cigarettes sold in urban areas and the less-taxed cheaper brands marketed in rural areas also paved the way for smuggling. In 1932, Köylü cigarettes were put in sale about 6 or 7 piasters whereas the other brands marketed in urban areas cost between 50 and 60 piasters. Because the sale of Köylü was forbidden in cities and towns, bringing it to the urban areas for sale underhandedly was a common practice.[25]

Tobacco cultivators were deeply discontented with the monopoly that exploited them. Therefore, many growers cultivated much more tobacco than they reported to the government or set some amount of the harvest aside for their own use and for secret sale. On February 1, 1932, a farmer in İzmir, upon the monopoly's offer of a ruinous price for his crop, set his thirty-eight bales of tobacco on fire in protest. Many others in the same situation entered smuggling instead of destroying their crops. The first social-realist novel of the republic, *Çulluk*, penned by Mahmut Yesari in 1927, described how tobacco growers engaged in tobacco smuggling, popularly called *ayıngacılık*, a term of coded language used to confuse the security forces. Shredded tobacco was referred to as *ayınga* and tobacco smugglers were called *ayıngacı*.

Many cultivators appropriated also so-called waste tobacco leaves (*saman*, or chaff) to sell secretly as cut rags. One such peasant was Rahmi, from the Gönen district (Balıkesir), who, instead of underselling his tobacco to a monopoly company, sold it illegally to consumers. Nonetheless, still unable to pay his taxes, he set his small house on fire in order to escape his debts, whereupon he was taken to court.[26]

Likewise, in the tobacco-producing villages of the Atabey district (Isparta) in 1934, the peasants admitted they sold tobacco illegally because the monopoly was paying chicken feed for their crops and this was the only way to get cash to buy wheat. Many were captured by gendarmes and jailed. The story of a tobacco farmer named Ruşid also illustrates this practice. According to a 1937 court record, Ruşid, who was supposed to harvest 356 kilos of tobacco, turned in only 254 kilos to the Monopoly Administration. He had probably sold the remaining one-third of his crops at higher prices than the monopoly offered.[27]

Famous painter İbrahim Balaban, who depicted the sordid milieu of his village in his art, wrote in his memoirs how his family had become involved in illegal tobacco sale directly to smokers instead of the Monopoly Administration. Consequently he was put in prison, where he met poet Nazım Hikmet, who encouraged him to paint.[28]

In the eastern villages, tobacco smuggling was rampant. Along with cross-border tobacco smuggling, the tribes and peasants, especially in Dersim, Muş, Siirt and Bitlis, produced tobacco without official permission. After the harvest, they immediately sold their tobacco to neighboring villages, together with smuggled cigarette papers. In March and April 1932 alone, the gendarmerie seized tens of thousands of contraband cigarette papers and hundreds of kilos of tobacco in the villages of Bitlis and Muş.[29]

Peasants carried out tobacco smuggling in many ways. Many peasants hid contraband tobacco, cigarettes and cigarette papers in their houses or barns, or in streams, lakes, water wells, caves or forests. In May 1932, the gendarmerie prosecuted the peasants of three villages in the Alaiye (Alanya) district who had stockpiled kilos of tobacco, rolls of cigarette paper and tobacco presses in their houses. In June 1935, gendarmes and monopoly officials found hundreds of kilos of contraband tobacco in villages of Tokat province, some hidden in a stream or in homes.[30]

The peasants also took advantage of legal loopholes. According to the anti-smuggling law, if the value of the contraband items was less than 25 liras or they were apparently for personal use, judges were required to release the defendant. Peasants therefore carried tobacco in small amounts. This trick became so common among small operators that years later, in 1946, the Monopoly Administration alerted security forces against it.[31]

Using or trading cigarette paper that was yellow or cream-colored instead of the white paper banned by the law was another way to circumvent the law. In response, in 1938, the phrase "white paper" in the law was replaced by the phrase "white and whitish paper." Furthermore, smugglers made cigarette paper look like a notebook or placed contraband goods in old monopoly packages in order to mislead security forces. A final category of what the law considered smuggling was *izmaritçilik*, which refers to collecting cigarette butts from streets and coffeehouses in order to obtain the remaining tobacco for personal use or resale.[32]

Fending government officials and even security forces off with violence was a last resort during transactions. Such violent smugglers were not peculiar to the Kurdish-populated southern border zones. As the Trabzon governorship reported, tobacco smugglers did not hesitate to fire back on security forces. In one instance among many, in December 1931, in the village of Tepeköy near Kütahya, seven armed smugglers were busted with 250 *okka*s of tobacco. The newspapers often ran stories on smugglers who fought with or were caught by the gendarmerie in western and central Anatolia during the 1930s.[33]

The violence was more flagrant in far-off Kurdish provinces. The state's pressure on Kurdish rural communities who produced unlicensed tobacco often provoked them into taking up arms against monopoly officials and security forces. Throughout the eastern and southeastern provinces, particularly Dersim, Muş, Siirt, Bitlis, Urfa and Diyarbakır, peasants continued to produce tobacco without a license on their few *dönüm*s of land and sell it clandestinely to neighboring tribes, towns or traders. This caused never-ending confrontation between the security forces and the villagers. These clashes, usually attributed to ethnic conflicts, were in fact related to the locals' resistance to state control over local economic relations. Indeed, the Monopoly Administration exerted a zealous effort to conquer the Kurdish markets. Economic life in these distant and mountainous provinces had remained more autonomous, with strong ties to cross-border markets, since

Ottoman times. However, the republican state aimed to create a unified market within the national borders. The Monopoly Administration, managed by the bureaucratic elite working hand in hand with business circles, desired the profits expected to flow from these places. This was an important reason behind the state's brutality in the Kurdish provinces.

The memoirs of gendarmerie lieutenant Cemal Madanoğlu, who carried out military operations against Kurdish smugglers and bandits in Sason during the 1930s, depict conflicts between gendarmes and peasants deemed smugglers. Madanoğlu emphasizes the Monopoly Administration's diligent efforts to conquer the markets in Kurdish provinces by setting up monopoly factories and stores. His uncle, retired commander and general director of the Monopoly Administration Behçet Günay, had spoken to the economy minister, Celal Bayar, of his desire to establish factories in the region in order to wipe out the informal economy. Hence, in addition to a tobacco workshop in Urfa, the government established two big tobacco factories in Malatya and Bitlis in 1939 and 1940, respectively. The state's concurrent effort to do away with the informal economy brought state violence, which in turn bred peasant violence and a further shift to the informal economy. This vicious cycle exacerbated state violence, which perpetuated bloody clashes. In one incident in 1933, monopoly officials accompanied by gendarmes raided Halikan and Harabak, villages in Sason, in an effort to extirpate the illegal tobacco farms on which these villages made their living. The peasants confronted the officials and security forces. The tension did not escalate until the government took a harsher action against illegal tobacco cultivation in 1935. Along with the conflicts caused by the livestock tax avoidance, the officials' attempt to dismantle the tobacco farms spurred a widespread peasant uprising referred to as the Second Sason Insurgency. The clashes in Sason have been widely considered an extension of Kurdish or tribal resistance, but they were essentially related to peasants' efforts to limit the spread of state-imposed market regulations that undermined their livelihood.[34]

Smuggling in Alcoholic Beverages

Rakı was the most favored alcoholic beverage in Turkey. The smuggling of alcoholic drinks, especially *rakı*, was so persistent that the private monopoly company, Naçelna Organizaçya, folded within a year. Even some legal dealers praised and sold contraband *rakı* and wine. Therefore, smuggling, along with other factors, played a key role in bankrupting the monopoly, whereupon the government undertook the production of alcoholic beverages in 1927 and sold a limited number of licenses to private enterprises. Nonetheless, the state monopoly could not alter the situation. One newspaper reported that not a day went by without news about alcohol smuggling. The number of police and gendarmerie cases related to illegal production and trade of *rakı* and wine reached approximately 1,000 between 1926 and 1928.[35]

There were two main reasons for this: first, high taxes and duties made clandestine production and trade of *rakı* and wine a profitable venture for impoverished local producers. Second, the sharp decline in the price of grapes during the crisis as compared to the high price of *rakı* and wine led grape growers to compensate for their losses via smuggling. By 1933, the monopoly offered 18 piasters for wine that had been purchased for 30 piasters in previous years. Moreover, much of the wine the peasants produced remained unsold in 1933 due to the incapacity of the monopoly.[36] This indicates that the producers most likely shifted into what was called the "black economy."

The huge yawning gap between the price of *rakı* and that of its main ingredient, *soma*, made from grapes, was another factor. The monopoly paid 16 piasters per liter of *soma* to the peasants. On the other hand, it sold *rakı* at great profit, with prices varying between 120 and 300 piasters per liter by 1933. Consequently, the smuggling of *rakı* persisted during the period. In the 1930s, production of contraband *rakı* at homes was widespread in regions like İzmir where viticulture was dominant. Particularly the poor towns of Buca and Bornova and the poor villages of Narlıdere or Değirmendere, where grindingly poor refugees and native peasants suffered hunger to such a degree that they ate grass in 1930, were famous for *rakı* smuggling. In one village, monopoly officials found 2,000 kilos of contraband *rakı* and production equipment. However, the peasants refused to surrender their equipment and protested by spilling all of the *rakı* the officials attempted to confiscate.[37]

The illegal production and trade of *rakı* and wine continued as long as the government offered low prices for grape and *soma*. From western and central Anatolia to the Black Sea countryside, the illegal production of *rakı* and wine for sale or private use was so widespread that 376 cases of contraband *rakı* were recorded in the last two months of 1931 alone. News about peasants caught engaging in contraband *rakı* production in other regions of Anatolia in the following years indicate the prevalence of the issue.[38]

Salt, Sugar and Textile Smuggling

Salt was another vital resource for peasants, used as a key ingredient in animal husbandry, leather and meat processing and daily food. Upon nationalizing the salt mines and lakes, the government levied high monopoly taxes on salt production and trade. This resulted in a concomitant increase in salt prices, which aggrieved both livestock owners and consumers. The soaring price of salt, fluctuating between 6 and 10 piasters per kilogram, led some peasants and traders to extract it from nearby mines and lakes clandestinely. One indicator of salt smuggling is the sharp decline of salt monopoly revenues from about 9 million liras to 6 million between 1926 and 1934, although there was no considerable price reduction. Indeed, in 1935, it was reported from Trabzon that the sale of salt had decreased considerably because the peasants were obtaining it illegally. Salt smuggling was widespread in the southern and eastern provinces too. The share of salt in all smuggled goods was estimated to be 15 percent by the mid-1930s.[39]

One form of peasant resistance to the salt monopoly was to steal salt from salt mines and lakes enclosed by the state. The peasants near Lake Seyfe, an important salt lake in Kırşehir, would shovel the salt from the lake and load it on their donkeys secretly in the pitch dark of night. They sometimes encountered and even clashed with monopoly officials. Contraband salt was so prevalent in Anatolian villages that peasants kept the salt they owned a secret so they were not suspected of having contraband salt. Salt was so valuable that peasants presented it to each other as gifts, like soap. In Antalya's villages close to the sea, peasants produced their own salt by boiling seawater, which the provincial bureaucrats also viewed as smuggling. When raided by monopoly officials, peasants knocked down the boilers containing the seawater. Extracting salt from saline soil was another way to obtain salt, which also was eventually deemed smuggling. Struck by the difficulties the peasants faced to obtain cheap salt, İzmir deputy Halil Menteşe poignantly recounted in a parliamentary speech his encounter with twenty peasants with donkeys laden with saline soil the peasants had dug in faraway mountains so as to extract three kilos of salt secretly.[40]

The conflict over access to salt, concurrent with other conflicts between the government and the locals, occasionally escalated into revolt. For instance, in the Baykan district of Siirt, the dispute that flared up between monopoly officials and peasants over the latter's use of salt mines and lakes without official permission grew into a local uprising with Kurdish and Islamic overtones. The Şeyh Abdürrahman Rebellion (named thus by the state) that broke out in 1926 is one such incident. Although the government claimed the right to all salt mines in the region, the peasants persisted in using them illegally. The theft of a huge amount of salt from the salt depots of the Monopoly Administration in the Melekhan subdistrict triggered the revolt. When gendarmes attempted to arrest Abdürrahman, a local livestock owner, and his friends as the suspected thieves, he and his tribe rebelled. The uprising spread to nearby subdistricts like Mollaşeref, Merijan and Navalan, and the government had to seal the area off to quell the rebellion.[41]

Sugar was also smuggled frequently. Despite the emergence of a nascent sugar industry in the first years of the republic, total production did not come near to meeting demand. Because of low supply, heavy taxation and high tariffs, sugar continued to be a luxurious foodstuff and accordingly was often subject to black marketing and smuggling. Until the early 1930s, sugar in urban centers cost between 40 and 50 piasters per kilo. It was scarcer in rural areas and therefore cost peasants around 60 piasters. In distant places, the prices could reach up to 90 piasters. On the other hand, sugar was far cheaper in international markets. Imported sugar actually came to Turkey at about 20 piasters in 1927, but was put on sale in the domestic market starting at 50 piasters because of enormous profit margins, along with duties and consumption taxes reaching up to 12 piasters. With the economic crisis the government monopolized its importation. Sugar's real price further increased as compared to other agricultural items due to the high consumption tax and customs duties. Whereas a wheat cultivator needed to give 3.23 kilos of wheat for 1 kilo of sugar in 1929, this rate doubled to 6.60 kilos of wheat in 1933. All of this paved the way for sugar smuggling. Cross-border smuggling of sugar became especially common in the southern borderlands. By October 1934, sugar was among the most frequently caught contraband items.[42]

Fabric and clothing were also informally produced, imported and traded by peasants, especially for consumers in Anatolian villages. Two main factors bred textile smuggling. First, despite the drastic price decline of textiles in foreign markets during the crisis, prices in Turkey did not drop evenly. Second, the shape, style and color of the fabrics and clothing produced by the state factories did not appeal to rural consumers. Peasants usually preferred thick cotton flannel, canvas and wool, which were economical and durable. Anatolian women preferred fabrics and clothing printed with oriental features and colors. Peasants found the ready-made clothes produced by the factories of Sümerbank unsuitable or comfortable for rural life. Most peasants sewed their own clothes or bought them from local tailors or itinerant merchants. During İnönü's visit to Kastamonu, a tailor explained that peasants disliked factory-made clothes because they were so tight-fitting around the waist and arm that when the farmer raised his pickax, the cloth suddenly ripped.[43]

In fact, the price of such fabrics dropped slightly during the 1930s. However, the decline in peasants' purchasing power was far sharper. For wheat cultivators, the price of cotton flannel shot up more than two and a half times. For barley and corn producers, the real price increase was about four times and two and a half times, respectively. As for wool, whereas a peasant had to give 44.8 kilos of wheat for one meter of it in 1928, this amount rose more than threefold to 155.5 kilos in 1934.[44] This is why peasants resorted to cheaper, untaxed fabric and clothing, which the state regarded as contraband.

A contemporary writer, Ali Enver Toksoy, wrote that textile smuggling was the lifeblood of the peasant economy for both smugglers and buyers in eastern Anatolia. Smugglers provided the bulk of the most favored cotton and silk fabrics and clothing for eastern Anatolia. Especially after the rise of custom tariffs, smuggled cotton and silk fabrics became more economical for low-income consumers. In the eastern provinces, cotton textiles constituted 60 percent of the cross-border smuggling and silk textiles constituted 10 percent. In 1934, the government permitted the importation of 3,000 bolts of fabric from Syria. However, Mardin province alone consumed about 260,000 bolts of fabric a year. The gap was filled by smuggling. In Diyarbakır, contraband clothing and fabric from Syria was sold by woman peddlers (*bohçacı kadınlar*). On the other hand, the people generally produced their own fabric and clothing. Contraband textiles were also produced locally and sold free of tax. Peasants bought cotton yarn from the town market and made homespun clothing,

Illustration 4.1 Women peddlers in Ankara in the 1930s

which was much cheaper. Many handloom weavers sold these homemade fabrics and clothes tax free.[45]

Resistance to Control over Forests

"People in Anatolia are the enemy of the trees. Anatolian villages are rife with people with axes and hatchets who cut down trees." Thus wrote Ali Naci Karacan, a republican journalist, in 1935. These words can be read as evidence of peasant resistance to the state and private companies' control over the forests. Indeed, the state archives are replete with stories about peasants prosecuted for illegal wood and timber cutting. In 1937 alone, 3,600 cases came before the courts related to conflict between the government and peasants who had violated forest laws. Peasants who had lost their lands to usurers or the government were among those who opened land by clearing forests.[46]

Peasants living in forested areas like Kastamonu, for instance, lacked enough arable land for agriculture. In the words of a republican bureaucrat, they "wrecked the forests" in their efforts to create cultivable land by cutting or burning trees. These practices were popularly known as *hopurculuk* and *göynük*, respectively. The destruction of the forests was in that sense the peasants' solution to land hunger and pauperization.[47]

The decline in agricultural prices also compelled peasants to exploit the forests. Poor peasants who could not live on the cultivation of wheat or barley, whose prices had hit bottom, began to cut timber to sell in town markets. In 1935, a republican bureaucrat came across more than fifty oxcarts loaded with oak lumber and timber on the road in Sivas. When he reminded the peasants of the illegality of what they had done, a woman replied, "How else could we pay our taxes had we not cut and sold these oaks while our wheat was so worthless?" Despite his anger, he acknowledged that she was right, and admitted that many poor peasants destroyed trees for similar reasons. On February 1, 1936, the *Köroğlu* newspaper also reported the prosecution of desperate peasants who had cut firewood for sale by adding a comment that indigent peasants perceived the forests as a resource vital to their survival.[48]

Declining weavers also illegally cut and sold timber for extra income. As a child, Fakir Baykurt had assisted his uncle in weaving and then in timber smuggling in Burhaniye (Balıkesir) in order to offset the slow-down in handloom weaving due to the competition of factory-made fabrics. Timber was cut in the dead of night and then piled in a secure nook far away from the village and camouflaged with brushes, to be moved home later.[49]

A great number of peasants in Ermenek (Konya) had long subsisted on walnut trade. Upon a threefold decline in walnut prices between 1930 and 1935, the peasants began to fell walnut trees secretly for sale to carpenters. A contemporary bureaucrat of the forest administration, Kerim Yund, depicted the situation as "a covert war between the walnut trees and woodcutters." Another contemporary forest engineer, Pertev Erkal, witnessed the same situation in Adana. The peasants involved in timber smuggling were, in his words, "constantly destroy-ing" the forests in the Taurus Mountains.[50]

State control over the forests as well as the increasing export of timber during the 1930s drove up the prices of timber and wood. In many places, finding firewood, wood and timber for furniture, home building or repair work began to pose a great problem. Smugglers offered a solution to this problem. In Adana, for instance, the price of timber was about 4.5 liras in the market. However, the peasants illegally cut and sold timber for only 2.5 liras. There was great demand for cheaper contraband timber in Adana. In 1935, bureaucrats dubbed wood and timber smuggling in Adana "a popular art among the peasants." This "art" thrived due to the scant number of forest rangers as compared to the immensity of the forests. Peasants living along the Seyhan River and in the jungle of Karaisalı were illegal cutters and traders of timber or wood. Some only cut trees, some carried trees on rafts, and some made wooden items. Others stood lookout for gendarmes and rangers. The rafts usually moved on the rivers at night. Once the rafts had been unloaded, peasants either took the contraband items home or hid them to be retrieved and dispatched later. The illegal timber trade was so widespread that there was a huge discrepancy between the official and actual amount of timber consumed in Adana. According to the statistics, total consumption was between 8,000 and 10,000 meters, whereas the actual amount was 30,000 to 40,000 meters. That is, contraband wood and timber met a far greater part of the demand.[51]

The situation was more or less similar in other provinces. Faced with economic instability and bureaucratic red tape in exercising their forest rights, peasants, individually or collectively, cut trees for their own use. Woodcutters who became unemployed after the government leased the forests to the timber companies were particularly apt to become involved in smuggling. Tens of thousands of peasants in Kastamonu who lost their jobs for this reason continued to cut and trade timber illegally, except for a small number of peasants who accepted work as laborers for the timber company.[52]

Another group involved in timber smuggling was the traditional village craftsmen who produced wooden items such as shingles, spoons, plates and mortars. Lacking official licenses to carry out their business, they cut trees and produced wooden items illegally. A group of shingle makers (*hartamacılar*) from the Yağlı Kökçe village of Görele, for instance, was caught cutting trees by the gendarmerie, but managed to escape by opening fire. Spoon making in particular necessitated smuggled cheap timber. In those years, not only peasants in villages but also townsfolk in Anatolia used wooden spoons. Therefore, making wooden spoons was a popular job in towns and villages. However, the forest policy restricted spoon makers from accessing the required timber, so they were forced to cut trees under cover of night and sell their products clandestinely. The woodworkers of Kastamonu, for instance, carried their contraband wooden spoons in oxcarts to neighboring provinces, including Ankara, and sold them in great secrecy.[53]

Nomads called *tahtacılar* (woodworkers), who lived in central, western and southern Anatolia, were also notorious woodworkers and timber smugglers, as is evident from their name. Republican bureaucrats called them "forest monsters" or "forest killers." They hauled the timber with convoys of packhorses to Kayseri, Niğde, Bor and similar forestless places. They carried out a considerable portion of the timber smuggling in Osmaniye, Mersin and Adana provinces. They covered their tracks by using different nicknames in each place they went.[54]

The situation in eastern Anatolia was similar. In his tour of the region in 1935, İnönü noted that the peasants in Ağrı and Ardahan were continuing to "plunder" and "loot" the forests. One year later, economy minister Bayar also described in his *East Report (Şark Raporu)* widespread frustration with the forest policy he encountered during his tour of Kurdish provinces in 1936. He noted that people had no choice but to cut wood illegally or buy smuggled wood.[55]

Effects of Social Smuggling: Mitigating Monopoly Prices

Unrestrained smuggling obliged the government to take economic measures to eliminate the conditions that fostered it. In the face of uncontrolled tobacco smuggling, along with the recovery of tobacco prices easing the worries of further price decline, the government had to permit tobacco farmers to cultivate in the regions raged by smuggling with the 1938 Tobacco Monopoly Law. Undoubtedly, one factor compelling the government to open the lands where tobacco cultivation was once forbidden was recovery of prices. Peasant resentment of abuses by tobacco experts, which was thought to push cultivators into smuggling, compelled the government to decide in April 1934 that tobacco experts could not reject or demand price reductions arbitrarily. The maximum waste portion was officially determined at 15 percent.[56]

Furthermore, smuggling served consumers by prompting the government to take action against the soaring prices of cigarettes. In 1929, Köylü was reduced from 7 to 4 piasters, Hanımeli from 10 to 8 piasters and Gazi from 30 to 20 piasters. The government continued to cut prices during the mid-1930s in order to compete with smuggled tobacco. In February 1936, the price of many cigarette brands was lowered once again between 20 and 40 percent.[57] For similar aims, the government also discounted the price of *rakı* in the mid-1930s. According to a 1935 report by an Urfa deputy, the recent price cuts in cigarettes and *rakı* had reduced smuggling. Indeed, as noted in a popular magazine of the time, *Resimli Ay*, the price reductions partially destabilized the smuggling of these items by 1938.[58]

Escalating demand for contraband sugar also brought a reduction in sugar prices in 1935. The government lowered the cost of sugar by giving less money for sugar beets. In addition, the consumption tax and tariff rate for sugar were lowered in 1937. The former was decreased by about 60 percent, from 12 piasters to 4 piasters per kilo. The import duty on sugar decreased by 23 percent, from 15 piasters to 11.5 piasters per kilo in 1937. Sugar importation increased from 1937 on. Thus, sugar, which was 40–60 piasters per kilo in 1932, dropped to 25–30 piasters in 1935. In the east, prices were marked down from about 80–90 piasters to 50 piasters.[59]

In 1935, the constant complaints about salt prices and salt smuggling also made a price reduction imperative. The government cheapened salt noticeably from 6 to 3 piasters per kilo. The price reductions revitalized the decreasing sales of the salt monopoly around 23 percent by 1936 and 29 percent by 1937.[60] Similarly, extensive textile smuggling contested high textile prices. In 1935, Mardin and Urfa deputies proposed price discounts in textiles in order to prevent smuggling in silk, cotton and canvas fabric. Just one year previously, İnönü also had directed his ministers to drive textile prices down to prevent smuggling. These moves were supported by the press, which blamed smuggling on the high price of domestic textiles. As a result, the government reduced the tariff on textiles slightly in 1937.[61]

No direct evidence exists to connect smuggling to annual declines in customs revenues changing between 20 and 50 percent during the 1930s. Yet it, along with the slowdown of the international trade and the fall of prices, seems to have played a role. Given the high prices of monopoly products despite the disastrous decline in the prices of raw materials, the monopoly revenues, which increased remarkably with the establishment of new state monopolies, also dropped about 40 percent, from 53.9 million liras in 1929 to 32.4 million liras in 1935, and slightly increased in the rest of the decade. Along with the decreasing prices and foreign trade, smuggling also may have contributed to this. That meant the income the government obtained for its industrialization and centralization projects through monopolies fell below expected levels.[62]

In the face of public outcry and the people's challenges to state control of the forests, in 1933, the Agriculture Ministry ordered the provincial forest directories to make things easier for the peasants who needed timber and wood. That same year, the Forest General Directorate issued an order to its provincial bureaucrats to more generously grant permission for timber cutting. Undoubtedly, smuggling did not always generate favorable consequences. Peasant resistance drove the government to turn up the pressure, which was embodied by the 1937 Forest Law. On the other hand, even this law did not deter the peasant resistance, manifested in tens of thousands of violations of the Forest Law between 1938 and 1940 alone. Although the government planned to enclose about 543,200 hectares of forest through nationalization from 1937 on, resistance from peasants, along with the state's capacity problems, meant the total area of enclosed forest was only 28,839 hectares.[63] That is, the peasants managed to intercept the state's efforts to acquire this most important rural resource.

Consequently, the people's struggle against the monopolies constrained the state's capacity to extract rural sources, enabling many peasants to survive. All official or spontaneous outcomes that smuggling generated, ranging from the decrease in demands for monopoly goods, reductions in prices and restrictions and consequent drops in monopoly revenues, epitomize the people's informal and illegal economic activities' impact on the efficiency of the monopoly system. Oppressed peasants, who had no other way out, challenged not only the state's economic monopoly but also its monopoly over the use of violence.

5 | *Theft, Violence and Banditry*

In April 1934, Ömer Ağa, owner of the large Katranya farm in the village of Şember near the Bakırköy district of İstanbul, attempted to expand his farm by driving out the neighboring peasants in the villages of Ayayorgi and Şember from public land they had long cultivated. Upon the peasants' disobedience, the *ağa* called on the police and gendarmerie to evict them. By the end of the fight between the security forces and the peasants, who were armed with stones and sticks, a few women and an infant had been severely wounded and fifty peasants arrested. The peasants continued to claim their property rights. Ultimately the Interior Ministry recognized their ownership rights.[1] Undoubtedly, everybody was not so agile in resorting to the higher bureaucracies; thus, many continued to rely on stones, sticks, knives or firearms when push came to shove. Open confrontation and violence were not the first preference of the peasantry. However, when injustice reached an unbearable level, they had no choice but to resort to so-called rural crimes such as stealing, robbery, arson and fighting individually or collectively. These acts constituted a critical crossroads on which some took a further step by taking up arms.

Increase in Rural Crime and Use of Violence

The severe living conditions of the peasants were the main instigator of rural conflict in the form of "crimes." Perhaps the key gauge of rural conflict was the increasing crime rate. The rural criminals, including thieves, robbers, murderers, smugglers or bandits, came to their offenses from a variety of backgrounds and for many different reasons. But common denominators among the majority seem to have been either agonizing destitution or intolerable oppression.

Indeed, official reports confirm that agricultural security (*zirai asayiş*, as the government termed it) was fragile throughout Anatolia. According to a report of the Interior Ministry dated July 26, 1930, poverty and food shortages were so pervasive in towns surrounding Ankara such as Polatlı, Bala, Ayaş, Haymana, Yukarı Abat, Kalecik, Nallıhan and Keskin that crime had soared in the previous months. Besides deployment of additional gendarmerie forces, an army battalion was charged with keeping security. In Cebelibereket (Osmaniye), food shortages worsened public security. In Kırşehir, provisioning problems deteriorated security in rural areas so badly that there was a severe need of additional armored cavalry troops. In Urfa, food scarcity disrupted the public order and pushed poor peasants into smuggling or theft.[2]

Especially with the economic crisis, food scarcity and rural impoverishment augmented conflicts over limited resources in villages, which ended in quarrels, fights and murders. Ömer Lütfi Barkan, a prominent economic historian who briefly examined the court files of 1,279 murders committed in Kocaeli, Bursa, Denizli, Konya, İçel, Rize, Malatya and Sivas, wrote that more than one-third of the murders were related to disputes over land, pastures, water sources and livestock.[3]

According to the justice statistics published in *Polis Dergisi*, the number of individual offenses and criminals gradually increased from the early 1930s. The proportion of offenders to the total population was 2 per 1,000 in the 1920s. This ratio more than doubled to 4.6 per 1,000 in 1932 and remained around this level during the decade. The majority of the incidents that pushed up the statistics took place in rural areas. Among the criminals, peasants numbered 27,206 in 1935. This number increased by 73 percent to 47,118 in 1937. This shows the intensification of social and economic tensions in the rural areas.[4]

Most data on rural crime, specifically banditry, derive from documents of the Interior Ministry and the gendarmerie. According to these figures, the offenses that fell into the category of brigandage declined markedly after 1924. On the other hand, highway robbery, armed extortion, armed robbery, livestock theft, burglary and murder maintained their importance despite a slight decrease. Some of these acts waned after 1924, but increased again in 1931. After an inexplicable sharp decline in 1932 and 1933, the next year witnessed an increase in apolitical brigandage, highway robbery and murder (see Tables 5.1 and 5.2).[5] These figures indicate that the intensity of social conflict escalated in 1924 and 1925, and then from 1928 to 1931 and again in 1934. In most of these cases, peasants fought for a piece of land, a vineyard or a few heads of livestock, or they had to defend themselves against oppressive and rich landlords or state officials.

Table 5.1 *Banditry in numbers, 1923–32*

Years	Political Brigandage	Brigandage	Highway Robbery	Kidnapping	Armed Extortion	Aggravated Larceny (Armed)	Livestock Theft (*Abigeatus*)	Burglary and Raid on House	Murder
1923	-	25	42	-	149	94	263	10	218
1924	332	331	563	78	2,243	884	2,993	200	3,688
1925	169	231	131	368	2,465	900	2,710	150	2,316
1926	5	130	204	16	778	200	500	677	1,347
1927	4	85	904	104	483	87	400	373	778
1928	10	47	119	24	718	389	1,389	380	2,420
1929	5	55	145	6	641	379	587	387	2,907
1930	10	40	233	5	570	327	384	489	2,975
1931	2	30	330	19	645	500	1,988	1,988	962
1932	2	31	128	2	279	89	269	86	274

Source: BCA-CHP [490.1/227.898.3], February 15, 1938

Table 5.2 *Number of crimes that damaged the public order, 1931–4*

Year	Brigandage	Highway Robbery	Armed Extortion	Murder
1931	30	330	645	962
1932	31	28	279	274
1933	25	10	20	109
1934	70	225	220	1,594

Source: *Emniyet İşleri Umum Müdürlüğü*, 13

Fights over Land

The first and foremost cause of crime in villages was land disputes. Like Barkan, Fahri Ecevit, another astute contemporaneous observer, examined the causes of the boom in rural crime. He argued that in contrast to the ruling elite's oversimplifications ascribing the problem to alcoholism and love affairs, the main reason was economic conflict. Agricultural expert Yusuf Saim Atasagun also drew attention to bloody fights between peasants stemming from competition for land and water.[6] Confirming this, the press frequently published news about furious fights and murders in villages and related these dramatic incidents to land issues. In November 1933, *Ülkü*, the most popular official periodical released by the Ankara People's House, recognized that fights and crime due to land disputes plagued the countryside as the biggest problem of Turkish villages.[7]

Peasants who fought over land generally confronted their oppressors individually. In the Yomra district of Trabzon, a poor peasant, Kamil, killed Mustafa Ağa, who had attempted to take possession of his land. In August 1931, a fight between two peasants in the village of Hacılar in Kayseri over land and irrigation water resulted in one death. According to İnönü's notes on his Kastamonu tour, one of the peasants' common complaints in this northwestern province was murders motivated by disputes over land.[8]

A village survey by contemporary sociologist Behice Boran vividly illustrates one such fight between poor and rich peasants. In a village of İzmir, a young poor peasant, who was aware of the Village Law, occupied a plot of vacant land outside the village under the pretext of transforming it into a village park in accordance with the law. However, the headman and *ağa*, who also had his eye on this plot, agitated the village community against the young man by falsely accusing him of attempted rape. The fight that broke out with the angry young man's knife attack on the headman ended at the courthouse.[9]

Albeit rarely, peasants took collective action against greedy landowners who attempted to seize vacant lands the peasants tilled communally. The provincial governments or landowners who had an eye on these lands often sued the peasants. The lawsuits generally lasted so long that the peasants took possession of these lands. In August 1931, a dispute arose between the peasants of the village of Azatlı and a stud farm owner over a large Karacabey stud farm in Bursa. About 360 landless peasants and smallholders occupied and cultivated a part of the stud farm. Upon the complaints of the stud farm owner, they were taken to court.[10]

From time to time tensions or fights also broke out between the occupant peasants and officials. According to a report in *Son Posta* titled "A Tragedy Because of Land," four peasants were severely wounded in a clash between gendarmes and a group of peasants in the village of Akse in Uşak. The main trigger for the incident was the conflicting interests of the peasants and the Uşak municipality, both of which claimed possession of a pasture of about 100 *dönüms*. Although the local court had given legal ownership of the pasture to the municipality, the peasants had disregarded the court decision and gone to the Council of State (*Danıştay*), the higher administrative court. In the meantime, the mayor, Alaaddin Bey, sold this land to the sugar factory. However, the peasants prevented the factory workers from plowing the land by attacking them with stones and sticks. Then they descended on the factory building to intimidate the factory employees. After this incident, the Uşak mayor accompanied by gendarmes went to the village to enclose the land. The ensuing brawl between the gendarmes and the angry peasants turned into a gunfight, which resulted in the wounding and arrest of several peasants. In another furious fight that occurred in the village of Kullar near İzmit in July 1936, poor peasants came to blow with gendarmes. The reason for this fight was the peasants' resistance to a rich large landowner who wanted to divert the water passing through the village to his rice paddy. At the end of the event, thirty-eight peasants were arrested. However, the peasants' continuing challenge to the landowner and gendarme caused several tumultuous incidents in the village. Similar to this case, continuous clashes were reported between the peasants who occupied public lands and the state officials in the Ceyhan and Kozan districts of Adana province. Sometimes, the peasants killed the state officials who milked them or coerced them to seize the lands they inhabited or plowed, as in the case of a peasant in Aydın who killed a land registry official.[11]

In the east, where *ağa*s were more powerful, the fight for land was much fiercer. According to the observations of the governor of Diyarbakır, the prisons in the eastern provinces were full of peasants who had resisted unlawful land takeovers by greedy landowners.[12] Land disputes would eventually lead some poor peasants to take to the rugged mountains as bandits. The property that was the most visible and therefore the most vulnerable to poor peasants' attacks was livestock. Livestock theft thus became the main economic strategy for impoverished peasants and portended trouble for the propertied classes.

Livestock Theft

Unlike land, crops and especially livestock were movable properties that could be easily lifted. Therefore, the struggle over crops and livestock did not necessarily generate fights. Instead, theft plagued the villages to such a degree that, as contemporary bureaucrat Refet Aksoy noted, farmers had great difficulty in protecting their crops and livestock. The global economic crisis of 1929 aggravated the problem. The Provisional Law for the Elimination of Livestock Theft, in force since 1913, could not alleviate the problem sweeping the countryside. Many farmers began to stand guard with their rifles day and night. Lively accounts from the daily press imply the rampancy of animal theft in the countryside. As *Son Posta* reported in 1932, livestock theft was becoming prevalent in Aydın. Similarly, horse theft in Çukurova exceeded 500 horses per year.[13]

The problem came before the National Assembly in December 1933. The government amended the legal regulations relevant to the issue. The preamble of the amendment diagnosed livestock theft as an epidemic. During the parliamentary discussions of the law, Samsun deputy Mehmet Hacıyunus underscored how livestock theft afflicted his province. "The people of this province, I feel honestly ashamed to say, are thieves. It is not possible to count the number of thieves ... Despite a law to prevent livestock thievery, this law yielded no positive results due to the ignorance of the state officials." The interior minister also stated that poor shepherds and herders often stole the livestock of their *ağa*s and then pretended to have been robbed.[14]

However, legal measures fell short of expectations. In the years to come, the local administrators often reported livestock theft. The Ordu governor reported in summer 1935 that twenty-nine livestock theft cases and forty-five thieves had been brought to the courts recently. Likewise, it was reported from İzmir in 1936 that "agricultural security" was worsening. Many shepherds were stealing crops and animals. Around the same time, the press carried news of theft cases which swept the rural areas. In one news, two poor peasants named Ömer and Mehmet in the village of Kurtcan in Kütahya had stolen forty goats belonging to a rich livestock owner, Kâhya Mustafa. They had been caught while selling the animals' fats and furs. (See Illustration 5.1.) Considering the persistence of the

Illustration 5.1 Livestock thieves in Gediz, 1936

problem by 1938, health and social aid minister Hulusi Alataş blamed it on landlessness and poverty and proposed government distribution of sufficient pieces of land as a remedy.[15]

Attacks on Village Headmen, Tax Collectors and Gendarmes

Although the peasants generally eschewed violence, their frustration often manifested in physical attacks on those who oppressed or exploited them. Times of economic austerity emanating from droughts, bad harvests, economic crises and state impositions exacerbated intra-village class tensions. These attacks were usually related to specific issues rather than a reflection of peasant hooliganism common to all rural societies.[16] For instance, in the Burhaniye village of Adapazarı, the village headman pressured poor peasants to pay a levy for the village fund. The ensuing squabble led one peasant to shoot the headman to death. About the same time, in a village in Balıkesir province, a peasant named Mustafa shot the village headman after a disagreement. In another case, a peasant named Hasan in İzmir shot the village headman, Ali Efendi, who had confiscated the peasant's cow. As a peasant from Ünye (Ordu) recounted, "the republic's headman as an oppressive man serving the state and local dominants" had registered peasants' lands in the name of his relatives and had once smacked a peasant for objecting. After this event, the headman was shot to death, probably by that smacked peasant. The new village headman was also so greedy that his corruption also sparked tension among the peasants. Finally, in the neighboring village of Gölceğiz, a band called Piyan Ali'nin Uşakları (Piyan Ali's Boys) began to attack corrupt headmen, state officials and landowners.[17]

State officials, especially tax collectors, debt enforcement officials and gendarmes, were also vulnerable to peasant attacks. In the village of Akça (Tokat), a debt enforcement official accompanied by gendarmes confiscated the money and property of a poor peasant named Adem Pehlivan, who had not paid the road tax. After that, they went to the neighboring village of Bayat. Adem Pehlivan, accompanied by two angry friends armed with rifles, raided the village and shot the gendarmerie privates to death. After reclaiming all the money the official had taken, the attackers ran away. Likewise, a poor peasant named Hino in the Girlavik village of Birecik shot a tax collector who pressured him to pay his taxes. Thenceforward he lived in the mountains as a famous bandit. Another wrathful peasant, İbrahim, in the village of Yukarı Sal (Bartın) confronted the gendarme who had attempted to arrest him due to his tax debt. Upon İbrahim's opening fire, the gendarme shot him to death.[18]

Perhaps the foremost target of the peasants was the tax collector. The peasants sometimes contented themselves only with assaulting the tax collectors verbally. In Giresun, for instance, a peasant named Yusuf and his wife, Fatma, in the village of Çandırçalış, who refused to pay the tax, walked all over the tax collector and cursed him in the village square. In many cases such assaults turned into deadly fights or direct physical attacks. In one village of Düzce (Bolu), peasants killed a tax collector named Akif Fikri. In another village, a peasant killed a tax collector named Raşid who pressed him to pay his tax debts. In a village of Muğla province, a poor peasant fired a shot at a tax collector and killed him. In İzmir, peasants robbed and killed a tax collector named Tahsin Efendi. Some events were more tumultuous. On May 17, 1929, in the province of Urfa, the quarrel between the tax collectors accompanied by gendarmes and the peasants who opposed a census of their livestock degenerated into armed conflict.[19] The Mutki and Sason peasants' fights with tax collectors and monopoly officials escalated into local riots growing via tribal ties in 1934 and 1935. Contending with the monopolies also engendered violent reactions in the western countryside, though on an individual scale. For instance, in 1931, a poor tobacco cultivator killed the purchasing director of the Geri Tobacco Company, his driver, and a rich farmer who had cooperated with the company. They had pulled a stunt on the cultivator by demanding further price discounts and the "scrapping" of several tobacco bales. Upon the peasant's objection, they infuriated him with severe insults.[20] Some of these unfortunate peasants found themselves in prison, but for some these were only the beginning of new, tough fights.

Taking to the Mountains: Banditry

Clausewitz's idea that "war is an extension of politics by other means" can be propounded not only for relations between states but also for relations between states and their citizens or between social groups.[21] Banditry, though a regular way of life for many criminal-minded robbers and killers, was generally the last resort for peasants resisting injustice. It had been no stranger to Anatolian society since the Ottoman era. As elsewhere in the world, in the Ottoman Empire, banditry and political brigandage emerged in connection with the social effects of wars, economic crises or poor administration. It also sprang up as a response to increasing state intervention or to market forces that destroyed people's livelihoods.[22]

The long war years extending from the Balkan Wars through World War I to the Independence War had turned Anatolia upside down and created a power vacuum that the law of the jungle filled. The new Turkish state exerted great effort to restore the state authority. Only eleven days before the proclamation of the republic, on October 18, 1923, the National Assembly enacted a law against banditry, the Law for Extirpating Brigandage (*İzale-i Şekavet Kanunu*). Two years later, the Sheikh Sait Rebellion in Diyarbakır, Elazığ and Bingöl resulted in harsh security legislation, the Maintenance of Order Law in 1925. This law granted the government utmost authority to eliminate political opposition as well as banditry. However, the republic's attempt to build a modern central state spawned new conflicts that bred banditry. The Great Depression further damaged the social balance. Thus, banditry, albeit in decline compared to the early 1920s, did not disappear during the 1930s. The documents of the Interior Ministry, listing thousands of bandits who were active or caught during the interwar years, show the extent of the matter.[23]

Banditry and struggles between bandits and gendarmes were so common that the *Köroğlu* serialized a short novel titled *Candarma Bekir Eşkiya Peşinde* in 1932. The phenomenon of banditry left its mark in the literary works penned by Turkey's most prominent novelists. Banditry featured in the masterpieces of Yaşar Kemal, Kemal Bilbaşar and Kemal Tahir, all keen observers of rural life during the early republic. The hero of Yaşar Kemal's four-volume magnum opus, *İnce Memed*, is portrayed as a valiant bandit who waged war against greedy *ağa*s on behalf of the poor peasants in the 1930s. Bilbaşar's *Memo* was another figure who rose up against a cruel *ağa* in the same period. On the other hand, Tahir's *Rahmet Yolları Kesti* pointed out to bandits manipulated by *ağa*s or with bad intentions. Admittedly, ruthless and malevolent bandits cooperated with the dominant groups or did not differentiate among their targets. Along with these vicious ones, as a contemporary eyewitness wrote in *Ülkü*, were many good bandits who stood up to social injustice, whom the peasants respected.[24]

Most bandits during the interwar years more or less fit the notion of social banditry, if we define the term more broadly than Hobsbawm did.[25] Most were not ruthless outlaws who wanted to make a fortune by robbing people from all classes indiscriminately. On the contrary, they were oppressed, exploited and abused peasants who strove to survive. Although they struggled only for their own cause and did not champion social reform, they mostly targeted specific people who mistreated them. The well-off propertied individuals whom they saw as responsible for their misery or whom they merely resented became vulnerable to their violence. This distinguished them from malicious outlaws. Consequently, some of these good bandits were admired and aided by peasants or became the subject of popular songs and poems.

On many occasions, the road to banditry was not very long or convoluted and did not require much planning. Any of the aforementioned individual incidents of theft, fighting or murder could open the door to banditry. Some peasants who committed these acts had no choice but to flee to the mountains in order to defend themselves or to take revenge.

Moreover, contrary to the general assumption, banditry was not peculiar to the Kurdish provinces. Nor was it much related to tribalism or Kurdish nationalism. It was the social injustice, domination and resulting peasant discontent that gave rise to banditry as a coping mechanism. Retired judge Hilmi Seçkin, whose father was a civil servant in Garzan (Siirt) in the interwar years, writes in his memoirs how he and his father witnessed that social injustice bred banditry: "Among them [bandits]" he writes, "there were those who had been aggrieved due to the taxes and confiscations, those who had been downtrodden and those who could not make their voice heard because of outrageous domination by *ağa*s and difficulty of access to the courts."[26]

Undoubtedly, collective reactions in the form of insurrection developed wherever tribal and ethnic ties buoyed community mobilization. Furthermore, the sharp inequalities in distribution of land, feeble state and judicial authority, mountainous topography and proximity to frontier zones caused banditry to persevere in a much more noticeable form in faraway eastern provinces.

Other regions were not free from bandits, however. In the Aegean countryside, bandits had long been called *efe*. Famous *efe*s like Çakırcalı Mehmet Efe had given the Ottoman security forces a hard time.[27] Western and central Anatolia as compared to the east were more accessible to the government. These areas were also less mountainous and distant from the long borders. All these factors made banditry risky yet formidable. Nevertheless, even in these regions banditry was among the *weapons of the weak*, in the terms of James C. Scott.

Both in the east and in the west, banditry had to do with peasant aggression wrought by the deterioration of living standards, growing inequality, oppression and increasing state intervention. Peasants could become more aggressive when crop prices dropped sharply, exploitation became more intense and their moral economy, based on mutuality, solidarity, fairness and justice, was broken by market forces.[28] Indeed, by intimidating, attacking and robbing state agents, rich merchants and greedy large landlords, bandits stood for a sort of peasant resistance to pauperization and oppression.

A brief overview of the petitions complaining of bandits gives insight into the nature of banditry. The authors of these petitions were generally rich and powerful peasants, as is clear from the property they lost to the bandits and their nicknames and titles such as *muhtar, hacı, ağa, hacı ağa, efendi, tüccar* and *eşraf*. Merchants and company managers traveling along intercity highways were also targeted frequently. In a petition dated 1928, a timber factory clerk who had been robbed by bandits demanded the government provide security in the region. In 1934, Hacı B. from Ünye complained that a group of bandits had seized 1,500 liras from him. Merchant Hüdaverdi Efendi from Elaziz demanded the government compensate him for a lorry stolen by bandits. Likewise, Ali Efendi, a livestock merchant in Erciş (Van), claimed damages for 700 sheep extorted by bandits. In another petition, a group of notables from Kozan, Dedezade Mehmet Efendi and his friends, claiming that they had taken part in the Independence War as prominent figures of the region, complained of the banditry threatening them. A notable named İbrahim Efendi from Pazarcık (Maraş) complained that the peasants in the villages supported the bandits.[29] These are a few cases among many.

Who were these Anatolian bandits specifically? How and why did they become bandits? What did they do as bandits? Undoubtedly, disputes over land were the primary cause pushing poor peasants into armed resistance. For instance, the rampant banditry in Kadirli (Adana) during the interwar years emanated from disputes over a large uncultivated field called Akçasaz. The story of one of these peasants may shed light upon the events that culminated in banditry in the region. A peasant, Remzi, aggrieved by abusive officials and *ağa*s, opposed them in 1927. In order to silence this angry peasant, the public prosecutor issued an arrest warrant. Remzi fled into the mountains and engaged in banditry. The story of Hacıveli is similar. He also adopted banditry against the *ağa* who had seized his land. Safiye Mehmet, a popular bandit in Kadirli, took shelter in the mountains during his struggle against the *ağa* who had extorted his horse.[30]

Many famous bandits had similar stories. Bandit Cello or Çöllo was a young peasant who herded the cattle of his *ağa* in the İncedere village of Kayseri. Because he had not been paid in return for his service for a long time, he bought a gun by selling one of the *ağa*'s donkeys and began to rob the *ağa*. He hijacked a mail car in order to survive in the mountains until he was killed by the gendarmerie in 1936. Similarly, poor peasants named Feyzo in Kemah (Erzincan) and Deli Omar in Urfa fought their oppressive *ağa*s and other *ağa*s who terrorized the peasants in their region. Alo was another popular bandit of the 1930s. He had been a poor shepherd on the farm of Demiroğlu Molla Hüseyin Ağa in the Keklikoluk village of Maraş. Cheated by his *ağa* several times with unfulfilled promises, he eventually came to hate him. Aware of Alo's resentment, the *ağa* had Alo's mother beaten in the village square so severely that she died soon after. After this, Alo obtained rifles, took to the Taurus Mountains and joined Kara Paşo, another good bandit with a reputation as the nightmare of greedy *ağa*s. Demiroğlu terrorized those peasants who supported Alo and sent his men to the mountains to kill him, but the latter shot them dead and took revenge by raiding Demiroğlu's cottage and killing him.[31]

Bandit Hamo, attacking the subdistrict governor and robbing a retired gendarmerie station commander in Siirt in the summer of 1935, alarmed even Prime Minister İnönü and the gendarmerie general commander, Kâzım Orbay. Orbay admitted that Hamo was not a criminal-minded person, but injustice and poverty had pushed him to become an outlaw. As a poor man, he had run an abandoned grain mill. However, those who had eyed the mill, in cooperation with the subdistrict governor, had thrown Hamo and his family out of the mill on the ground that this mill was a derelict property vacated by deported Armenians, and therefore belonged to the government. Upon this, he had started to take revenge against the corrupt bureaucrats, gendarmes and greedy *ağa*s who had doomed his family to abject poverty.[32]

In another case, a peasant named Reşko in the Çağşak village of Kayseri shot seventeen rich farmers who had murdered his brother due to a conflict over grazing in the late 1920s. The story of a young peasant boy, reputed to be Alim Efe around Afyon in the 1930s, is similar. As a dominant family prevented Alim's family from cultivating their own land in the Dinar district, brawls and fights broke out between them. In one of these incidents, after killing a man of the rival family who attacked him, Alim fled to the mountains to wage war against this family until the 1950s.[33]

Some poor peasants took shelter in the mountains and became bandits after a confrontation with state officials. Girlavikli Hino's fight with the tax officials and gendarmes is a good example. The Kurdish eastern highlands were full of peasants like him. The peasants, afflicted with similar problems, respected, sympathized with and cooperated with such bandits. Peasants even recounted their heroic struggles and composed songs about them.[34] Popular culture likely exaggerated and romanticized these figures. Yet, considering the other evidence, the bandit stories are not entirely unrealistic.

Banditry in the Kurdish Provinces

Many features of the eastern Kurdish provinces further encouraged the banditry there. Among these were the rugged mountains, proximity to borders, a socioeconomic structure characterized by extremely inequitable land distribution, absolute power of *ağa*s and animal husbandry as the main livelihood, which necessitated bearing arms. Local administrators recorded more than eighty bands consisting of about 2,000 men (and a few women) in Urfa, Mardin, Siirt, Van, Hakkari, Bitlis, Ağrı, Elazığ, Dersim and Bingöl alone in the mid-1930s. Most of them were autonomous bands independent of any tribal or ideological affiliation.[35]

The security reports also provide a vivid depiction of the banditry plague in the region. In an earlier date, in May 1929 alone, five armed robbers clashed with the gendarmerie battalion in Hilvan. On the road between Pertek and Hozat, two bandits robbed two passengers. On the highway between Muş and Varto, two armed bandits robbed eight passengers and killed one of them. In Silvan, three armed men killed two peasants. A group carrying weapons robbed a peasant in Ahlat. Bandits seized the money and goods of a peasant in Palu. Another group of bandits waylaid and robbed a passenger in Birecik. Armed men wounded the night watchman in Birecik.[36] According to another monthly gendarme report listing the events, seventy-two robberies and thefts, raids on six villages and raids on three village flour mills occurred in Diyarbakır, Urfa, Elaziz and Muş provinces in October 1932. Apart from these, in the Korukçu village of Bismil, four armed men opened fire on a gendarmerie battalion. Ten armed bandits, possibly the band of Kör Şemo, opened fire on three gendarmes in Silvan. In Beyazıt, the band of Süleyman committed a robbery and the band of Malazgirtli Kamil carried out two armed extortions. In Mardin, ten bandits raided a flour mill, and three robberies and a raid on a village occurred. There were four robberies in Van and three robberies in Siirt. In Gaziantep, four armed robbers stopped and robbed two lorries and one car. The gendarmerie squad patrolling in Nizip came across a band of six armed persons, and the ensuing armed clash cost the life of one gendarme and one bandit. There were twelve robberies and extortions and an incursion into a house in Erzincan, two extortions in Erzurum, six robberies and extortions in Kars and two robberies in Sivas. In addition, the gendarmerie caught the band of Maktul Tevfik and the band of Feyzullah, who had carried out robberies in the region for a long time. Among the bandits caught alive was a female bandit. Another female bandit, named Hayro, was caught in another armed conflict in the region.[37]

A special report on security, prepared for the tenth anniversary of the republic and proudly listing the purged bandits, in fact indicates that the eastern countryside was full of bandits. According to the report, security forces subdued more than ninety bands containing thousands of armed men just in the dismal period 1929–33. Although this report proclaimed that banditry had been reduced to sporadic acts, press and security reports from following years show that the eastern provinces were still crawling with bandits. For example, the famous Reşo's band remained active in the southeast until the mid-1930s and killed eight gendarmes chasing him. Bandits committed numerous robberies and raids within only seven months from September 1936 to March 1937.[38]

In the mid-1930s, banditry continued to be the main form of peasants' open struggle against social injustice in the Kurdish villages. The bandits generally targeted well-to-do farmers, *ağa*s and merchants. İdo and İbo in Diyarbakır epitomize those bandits who waged war against *ağa*s by breaking into the houses of *ağa*s and headmen. Likewise, in December 1935, it was reported from Urfa that two bandit leaders, Kucaklı Hasan and Siverekli Ramazan, had been robbing rich peasants and passengers in the region since 1926.[39]

The bandits frequently attacked and killed state officials. The bands of Keles̨li Halil and Rıza killed a subdistrict director and eleven gendarmes in the first years of the 1930s. A reputed bandit of Kemah, Bandit Zühtü, shot to death the Karacaviran mayor in 1931. He also stole the cars of bureaucrats and robbed mail cars until October 1937, when he was caught by the gendarmerie.[40]

Unsurprisingly, tax collectors were also targeted. In Hakkari, a group of bandits shot to death a tax collector in December 1930. In the Ziravenak village of Erzurum in June 1931, the bandits attacked a tax collector and took the money he had collected from the peasants. The bandit Darih killed a tax collector in the Genç district of Bingöl. Bandits were particularly brutal to gendarmes, many of whom were killed in armed conflicts or ambushes. The press could not report these cases due to heavy censorship. As Oryal Gökdemir's mother related, when her father was an army officer in Siirt in 1932, they felt constantly threatened by bandits who killed the security forces chasing them. Reading between the lines of the security reports about hot pursuits of bandits confirms this observation. According to a report about the gendarme operations against bandits Res̨o, Zaza and Çolak Mehmet Ali, they had killed tens of gendarmes who chased them in the 1930s.[41]

Perhaps the main crime to which almost all bandits inevitably resorted was highway robbery. Cars, buses and lorries generally conveying wealthy men, commodities, crops and foods were among their main targets. Such activity was so common that bandits robbed nine lorries around Pazarcık (Kahramanmaras̨) on July 24, 1929 alone. In

Illustration 5.2 Bandit Zühtü, his friend Abdullah, his wife Feride and the security forces

Illustration 5.3 A bandit with his wife and infant child

later years, bandits continued to operate on the highways. A newspaper article from 1932 on captured bandits noted that more than ten bandits had long carried out highway robberies in Muş, Mardin and Bitlis. In 1935, gendarmes captured the bandit Kato, from Arapkir (Malatya), who had been raiding rich villages and robbing passengers for fifteen years.[42] In 1936, Çoban Mehmet and Hasan, who lived in a cave along with their men, were among the most famous bandits for highway robberies around Malatya.[43]

Some bandits felt remorse and apologized to the people they robbed, as one band did after robbing a bus near Sivas on July 20, 1937. After seizing only money and other basic items but not passengers' rings and clocks, which could be family heirlooms, they apologized to the passengers and asked them for their forgiveness and blessing by saying *"hakkınızı helâl edin."*[44]

An army officer at the time recorded another interesting incident in his diary. When he wanted to go to the second regiment of the gendarmerie in Iğdır (a district of Kars in those times), most drivers refused to take him due to fear of bandits. Bandits were the nightmare even of local administrators. Once a subdistrict governor had been waylaid by four armed men. The governor had offered the bandits all the money he had, but they took only a portion and gave back the rest. Before leaving the scene, they had shared the money among themselves, saying, "Hasso, this is your road tax money. Memmo, this is your building tax, this is my land tax, and this is your road tax."[45]

The roads were so insecure even for soldiers and politicians guarded by the gendarmes that it was impossible to travel at night. Foreign travelers such as German writer Lilo Linke also witnessed the banditry. Her 1937 book illustrates the extent to which banditry held sway in the eastern countryside, taking tolls from army vehicles. Politicians also experienced their share of bandit attacks. For instance, the automobile that conveyed Kars deputy Ömer Kamil and his family was robbed in the road between Sarıkamış and Erzurum by Altındiş Osman's band. Similar incidents recurred in the following years. Despite a gendarmerie escort, Erzurum deputy Asım Vasfi was robbed by bandits on the road linking Erzincan to Sivas in 1934, within walking distance of a gendarmerie outpost. After arriving in Erzincan, Asım Vasfi would write in his report, "The things that happened to me were common here in the villages ... It is striking that even the local bureaucrats took this event in stride as if nothing important happened." In another case, the bandit Şükrü robbed the gendarmerie inspector Kemal toward the end of 1936. In September 1936, bandits robbed the car carrying the Mardin governor and the health director. Robberies of six lorries, one automobile, two gendarmerie officers, the deputy public prosecutor of Diyarbakır and a government physician on March 15, 1937, alone in Diyarbakır indicates the frequency of such events. As late as 1946, bandits stormed the region by robbing state officials like the head of the finance department in Hakkari, as Cahit Kayra, the finance inspector, mentions in his memoirs.[46]

The most valuable property vulnerable to bandit raids was livestock. For bandits, livestock meant both money and food. A security report on livestock theft in the Viranşehir, Harran and Birecik districts in Urfa during the first two months of 1937 gives an idea of the scope of the problem. On January 5, robbers seized 55 sheep in Harran. On the following day, İbrahimoğlu's band stole 100 sheep in Viranşehir. One week later in same district, unidentified robbers extorted 200 sheep from a large farm and clashed with gendarmes the next day. On January 16, seven bandits stole several sheep in Harran. February was more eventful. On the second day of the month, the seizure of many horses was reported from Viranşehir. The next day, three armed bandits killed a person and then another band of ten armed men raided a house in Viranşehir. The months to come were no less eventful.[47] This is only a small snapshot of two months' incidents.

Banditry in the Other Regions of Anatolia

The western, northern and central regions of Anatolia also were crawling with bandits. The bandits in these parts of the country displayed similar targets and methods. However, they differed from their Kurdish counterparts by virtue of their smaller numbers, fewer confrontations with security forces and weaker tribal ties. Like Kurdish bandits, however, they were poor and desperate and mostly targeted rich or oppressive peasants or state officials through raiding the houses of well-to-do peasants, extorting money and livestock and engaging in highway robbery. The main grievances that stirred them up were similar – that is, tax matters, the Monopoly Administration, poverty, landlessness and *ağa* oppression. Banditry was particularly concentrated in provinces where capitalist large-scale agriculture and the resulting social differentiation were sharper, such as İzmir, Aydın, Denizli and Adana. The central and northern Anatolian countryside hard hit by droughts and food shortages also were hotbeds of banditry.

The archives are full of documents reporting plundering peasants who "broke the peace and quiet" (*huzur ve sükuneti bozan*) and their referral to the Independence Tribunals in the 1920s. The band of Muhacir Ali terrorized Niğde and the surrounding provinces until the mid-1920s. Bandits Süleymanoğlu Ali and Hüseyinoğlu İsmail, who had committed many robberies in Bursa province, were captured in December 1926. Kızbekiroğlu İbrahim and his band of fifteen men who had "broken the public security" in the Tavas district of Denizli were caught in May 1926. Bandit Karaağaçlı Ali and his five men carried out robberies around Denizli until caught in 1926. Mustafa Ali and Mehmet Çavuş were popular bandits who panicked Aydın until August 1926. In Eskişehir, Zort Hasan and Bursalı Rıza maintained their banditry until 1927. These are only a few of those who were caught. Many bands survived, whereas new ones sprang up in the following years and gave the security forces and propertied classes a hard time.[48]

Bandits mostly stormed rich peasants' homes and farms. In Adana, for instance, bandits raided a dinner party that included twelve wealthy notables and the Adana gendarmerie commander in May 1929, killing the commander when he fought back. In another raid in January 1931, eight armed men attacked a rich village and two homes in the Kozan district of Adana. In April 1931, twelve bandits entered the Eğridağ village of İçel and broke into the house of Topal Mehmet Ağa, the richest man in the village, to extort him and his wife. In the first years of the 1930s, bandit Çıplak Mustafa (Naked Mustafa) emerged around Adana. His title, Çıplak, probably originated from his poverty and nudity. He became a nightmare to rich farmers such as Molla Durmuş Ağa and Müslim Ağa, who had made him "naked" by exploiting him.[49]

Similar cases occurred in western, northern and central Anatolia. Bandits broke into the house of Ali Ağa in the Bünyanlar village of Akşehir to steal his money. In Uşak (a district of Kütahya in those times), bandits robbed the community praying in the mosque of the village of Kayalı, where wealthy landowners lived. At the moment of prayer, the robbers surrounded the mosque and took the peasants out one by one, collecting about 5,000 liras. In 1934, two poor peasants began to badger rich peasants in Afyon and Isparta like Abidin Ağa, the owner of a large plateau near Lake Eber in Bolvadin. One was a poor peasant named Halil from the village of Korucuova. He was also a draft-dodger. His partner, Osman, was a poor man from the village of Eber. They had worked as shepherds for Abidin Ağa. Upon a bloody fight with the *ağa*, Halil and Osman, taking up rifles, robbed rich peasants, state officials and even gendarmes. In the latest incident, in July 1937, they robbed a gendarmerie commander, two watchmen and four persons in Isparta, and attempted to assassinate Abidin Ağa.[50]

Village headmen, who mostly came from the richest families, were at high risk. In March 1929, for instance, bandit Kel Şükrü, terrorizing the region around Çorum, in his latest raid entered the village of Eymir and stole 300 liras from the headman. Likewise, bandits robbed headman Süleyman Efendi in the Hacılar village of Manisa of all his money in June 1931. The newspaper giving this event noted that similar incidents had become prevalent in the region in recent years.[51]

Some helpful bandits assisted indigent peasants directly. The famous bandit known as Gizzik Duran in the Adana region was one example. Imitating a historical well-reputed bandit, Çakırcalı Mehmet Efe, in addition to robbing rich and oppressive farmers, he assisted poor peasants until he was killed in 1929. The peasants' support for him manifested itself in folk songs expressing grief at his death at the hands of a man they hated.[52] Solving disagreements among the peasants, some bandits served as an expeditious mobile "moral law court" that enabled the peasants to avoid the courts, which were open to manipulation by local notables. The story of a bandit group of sixty-seven armed men in the Kozan district of Adana is interesting. A band, targeting oppressive rich estate owners or local merchants in June 1931, went down to the villages to settle disputes. It was reported in 1933 that peasants admired and supported such bandits in Adana.[53]

Sometimes a whole village was involved directly or indirectly in armed robbery. In the early 1930s, a number of armed robbers hijacking automobiles became famous in İzmir. The supporters of these robbers were poor refugees who lived in the villages of Foça, and perhaps they were involved in or got their share from booty. Besides, they had also been aiding and abetting a famous bandit named İngiliz Memet for years until he was caught in 1933.[54] The remote highways were the main places where wealthy travelers, bureaucrats, merchants, mail cars and lorries laden with whatever could be lifted were ambushed. In Konya, for instance, four bandits robbed many cars and buses on the highways until they were caught in 1929. Two incidents occurred in summer 1931 in Çorum in which motor vehicles were stopped and engineers and other moneyed passengers robbed. Likewise, two bandits named Pelvan Osman and Yozgatlı Battal robbed four lorries on the highway around İzmir in February 1932. In Zonguldak, bandit Gıddık Mustafa conducted highway robberies and home raids during the early 1930s. The newspapers reporting these incidents commented that the roads had become very dangerous in recent times.[55]

In the Menemen district of İzmir, the waters seemed settled after a small rebellion with religious overtones on December 23, 1930. The government had quickly reasserted its power by severely suppressing the rebels.[56] However, the quelling of the rebellion did not bring silence. The unrest continued apace, albeit not ideologically and openly. In 1933, a new kind of outlaw, masked brigands, would emerge in Menemen and rob rich peasants and passengers. Such incidents did not end in the mid-1930s. In the countryside of İzmir, in March 1934, bandits ambushed the car of a doctor. About a month later, again in İzmir, two bandits stopped a car in Akhisar by opening fire on the vehicle and then robbed the passengers. In other western or central Anatolian provinces, bandits were active. For instance, five bandits robbed three buses and a car on the highway between Bursa and Eskişehir in September 1935. Muradoğlu Vahid was a popular highway robber in Düzce. He took to the mountains in 1933 and became famous for his hijackings and home raids on rich individuals until shot by the gendarmerie in May 1935.[57]

The Black Sea region also abounded with bandits and highway robberies. The shortage of wheat and other cereals in the region due to rainy weather and mountainous topography caused serious food scarcities, which intensified the social conflicts that bred banditry. In the late 1920s, several highway robberies were reported from Trabzon and Rize. Two bandits named Şakir and Arif robbed villages and travelers around the Ünye district of Ordu in 1927 and 1928. The Sürmeneli Ahmet, İsmail, Türapoğlu, Mercanoğlu and Nurettin gangs were among those bandit groups who conducted robberies and home raids in the Black Sea region, especially on the Trabzon, Rize and Gümüşhane roads in the late 1920s. By the end of the 1920s, the gendarmerie had eliminated many of these bands. However, American ambassador Joseph Grew, who visited the region in August 1929, noted that although the Rize governor had waged a war against bandits and had caught sixty-seven bandit leaders along with their men, banditry continued to overrun the region. Indeed, the news about the bandits attacking *ağa*s, village headmen and rich passengers kept its place in the press during the following years.[58]

Rural Crimes as Survival and Resistance

Abject poverty and blatant oppression bred rural crime, including theft, extortion, beating, physical attacks, arson, robbery and banditry. Banditry was generally the last resort of peasant resistance. This was not a reflection of peasant savagery. Nor were most bandits connected to tribal groups or the Kurdish movement. It is true that the term *bandit* was largely used by the government to discredit political rebels or to legitimate violence toward those who were recalcitrant. However, this does not mean that banditry was nothing but a discursive strategy of the rulers that served only to legitimate the state's violence.[59] Waging armed struggle against oppression and exploitation, albeit not so preferable for peasants, was part and parcel of rural life. Even many Kurdish uprisings had in fact begun as peasant resistance to taxes, monopolies or social injustice and then escalated via tribal and ethnic ties into local rebellions. The two major forces fueling banditry as well as local uprisings were the state's growing intervention in peasants' lives and concomitant deteriorating economic standing of the peasantry. These were more or less common to all parts of Anatolia. Therefore, not only the Kurdish provinces but all other regions were overrun with poor and furious peasants up in arms against those they deemed responsible for their misery. Violent disputes over taxes, land and animals sometimes led the aggrieved side to launch a sort of guerilla warfare against the perpetrators of the injustice. Undoubtedly, the rural crimes brought further state violence. Nevertheless, it was these rural crimes, together with the critical voices rising from the villages, that alarmed the high-level bureaucrats about the stability of rural areas. Hence, they also unintentionally urged the ruling circles to consider social relief and land distribution programs. Indeed, top politicians and bureaucrats often prescribed land distributions to alleviate the rural unrest. Accordingly, a considerable amount of land was distributed to landless peasants.

Concluding Remarks

The peasantry, which underwent a decline in developing countries, declined so slowly in Turkey that it persisted until the mid-1980s. As is well known, this was partially due to the structural limitations of Turkey's industrialization and modernization. This part has revealed another important but lesser-known reason – that is, the peasants' struggle to survive and the resulting social conflicts that further delayed the dissolution of the peasantry. Well aware of the unpopularity of the government, especially among the rural population, the decision makers tried to contain rural discontent through social and economic schemes as well as coercion. The result was the preservation of the peasantry and agriculture despite steady industrialization.

The founders of the republic chose to lay much of the burden of the extensive state-building and economic development schemes on the peasants. In an economy based on agriculture, the peasants were the main source of surplus. Moreover, the RPP was overwhelmingly dominated by landed and mercantile interests as well as bureaucrats and educated members of the middle classes. Consequently, land became increasingly concentrated in private hands. The craving to increase their lands blinded landowners to anything that might stand in their way. Although smallholding remained prevalent, it was not static but subject to the threat of large landowners, moneylenders and the state. Despite the abolition of the tithe, the sharp increases in other agricultural taxes, monopolies, commercialization of agriculture and the Great Depression put the peasants' livelihood at stake. After a short-lived economic recovery in the early 1920s, all these factors drove down living standards in the villages. Harsh treatment and exploitation by oppressive or abusive landowners, village headmen and state officials exacerbated the problems. Tremendous social and economic upheavals brought misery and anxiety to the rural population.

Undoubtedly, peasant discontent produced no mass rebellions. However, lack of any huge peasant movements did not mean that the peasants remained silent in the face of all these difficulties. Peasants' rich and long-standing repertoire of coping tactics, deeply ingrained in their everyday life for generations, resurfaced. Struggle to ensure subsistence required everyday forms of resistance rather than involvement in high and ideological politics, especially under the authoritarian system. Petitioning the provincial administrators or central government, peasants sought their rights and asked for redress. Appropriating the official discourse, they demanded the government honor its commitments. Conveying complaints to the press was also a way to pressure local and central bureaucrats or to play one against another. Informal communicative strategies like rumor functioned as an informal media through which peasants expressed their aspiration and grief or sought to mobilize others for disobedience. A variety of averting methods and loss-minimizing stratagems that power holders stigmatized as crime were employed in order to weather the economic problems. One important way was to lessen the tax burden with several tax avoidance methods. Aggrieved by monopolies, peasants engaged in illegal production, trade and consumption, which I call social smuggling. This sort of smuggling as a web of daily transactions carried out by mostly poor and low-income peasants contested the monopolies. When they saw no other way, peasants did not hesitate to afford direct confrontations that escalated to the point of violence.

Such efforts, though mostly not intended to change the social or political system, often prompted the ruling circles to revise their policies. Given widespread discontent with taxes, the government had to reduce their rates and contents several times and to forgive a certain portion of tax debt. Rampant smuggling compelled the government to lower the price of monopoly products or loosen the restrictions on the production and trade of monopoly goods. Complaints about agricultural credits and the growing volume of loan debt forced the government to suspend debt enforcement proceedings, limit interest rates and restructure credit debt.

Moreover, the official discourse reflected popular concern over the land question. Both Atatürk and İnönü, vacillating between the landowners' interests and the huge peasant masses' woes, frequently expressed their wishes for land reform. The state bureaucrats advocated land reform by underlining the connection between the land issue and rural security. These land reform proposals generally have been explained with either the RPP's principle of populism or assimilation policies toward the Kurdish population. These explanations sound reasonable to some extent; besides, land-related conflicts embodied in irrepressible rural crimes seem to be one of the major forces that pushed the ruling circles to consider land reform. Consequently, land reform was included in the party program in 1935. From the early 1930s on, the party advocated and propagated peasantism. The republican elite, aware of the rural unrest and of the political costs of a possible dissolution of the peasantry, attached importance to the tranquility of village life. The government did not actually launch land reform and peasantism remained largely confined to official rhetoric.[1] Yet a considerable amount of arable land was distributed to landless and smallholder peasants. All these outcomes of the peasants' efforts to protect themselves facilitated the survival of peasantry and deprived the state of necessary resources for financing its economic and administrative projects. In this regard, the peasants' everyday politics, along with other factors like the state's low infrastructural power, curtailed Turkey's transformation in the direction of the republican rulers' vision.

PART II

Everyday Politics of Urban Labor

6 | *The Price of the Republic for the Working Class*

This part concentrates on low-income working people in urban areas, including industrial and casual workers, artisans, journeymen and low-wage white-collar workers. They composed a huge part of the urban population. Despite the republican rhetoric of a "classless society," the social cleavages based on class continued to deepen. Turkey's economic policy of state-led development and industrialization – embodied in five-year plans, establishment of large state factories, incentives for entrepreneurs and protective high tariffs – brought a doubling of output in a short time. On the other hand, drastic measures to control labor and to keep the cost of the labor force at the lowest possible level resulted in inequitable income distribution and harsh working and living conditions for almost all wage earners. Low-income urban wage earners were asked to pay the price for the republic's economic development programs.

The Main Characteristics of Turkey's Working Class

The Ottoman Empire, especially Anatolia, which formed the heartland of the new Turkey, had remained overwhelmingly an agrarian economy. The Ottomans did not have a mechanized industrial base. The majority of the manufacturing was based on artisanship dispersed in non-mechanized shops mostly supplying the domestic market and striving to survive in the face of European imports. Mechanization, advancing very slowly at the end of the nineteenth century, was limited to a few sectors in big port cities like Salonica, İstanbul, İzmir, Bursa and Beirut. However, nascent industrial workers and artisans working alone or in small shops became important constituents in Ottoman politics from the later nineteenth century. This was not an automatic result of the increasing salience of wage labor. Rather, it was related to the transformation of government strategies over the course of the century. In an age of revolution and socioeconomic upheaval, rulers sought more public support than ever before. This brought the masses into the center of politics. The constitutionalist movements mobilized the masses whose economic standing had deteriorated, and encouraged working people to protest poor labor conditions, low wages and competition from mechanized production and foreign imports. Guilds that safeguarded and monitored professions on behalf of the state declined and increasing numbers of artisan and worker clusters began to come together in unions and professional societies. Strikes became the main part of labor resistance. Only 50 strikes had been recorded during the forty years before 1908. From the July 24, 1908, constitutional revolution to the end of that year, 111 strikes erupted, most of which occurred in İstanbul, İzmir and Selonica.[1]

However, the incipient working-class politics did not take solely the form of a strong and well-organized movement. Working people's ways of struggle and self-protection encompassed many other informal and everyday actions. These constituted the main repertoire of action, especially after the CUP banned labor movements with the Strike Law and the Association Law in 1909. During World War I, the conditions of the working class grew worse with sharp declines in real wages. Under martial law the labor movement was suppressed. However, social upheaval during the war years and the defeat of the Ottomans gave a new impetus to labor activism during the armistice period. Labor organizations and strikes appeared once again along with socialist parties.[2]

Despite this rise in labor activism, the war had depleted the human resources of labor movement in Turkey. Due to wartime calamities, particularly the massacre of Armenians and the deportation of a multitude of Greeks, the working class had lost its most experienced and activist members. This was a significant blow leading to the decay of the organized labor movement. After independence, the new regime, pursuing a state-led economic development program, crushed the organized labor activism. Formation of Turkish capitalism and planned industrialization under the protection of high customs entailed repression of labor. The 1925 Maintenance of Order Law and the 1926 Criminal Law also squashed the labor movement. The civil police were employed to monitor public opinion and left-wing activists along with conservatives. On the other hand, the Encouragement of Industry Law of 1927 was designed to support Turkish industrialists and merchants. Working-class associations and the press were severely repressed. The head of the labor unions, the General Workers' Federation of Turkey (Türkiye Umum Amele Birliği), established in 1923, had been forced to cease its activity in 1924. It was replaced by the less militant Workers' Advancement

Society (Amele Teali Cemiyeti) (WAS) as the chief labor organization. This organization also did not live long and was disbanded in 1928. Repressive laws concerning labor, such as the Assembly Law and the Strike Law, inherited from the CUP, remained in force.[3] Amendments to the Criminal Law in 1936 and the Association Law in 1938 prevented the working class from claiming their rights in an organized manner.

Moreover, industrialization began to alter the social landscape in urban areas. The establishment of state factories created a severe need for an industrial labor force. As a share of the GDP, industry showed steady growth, from 9.7 percent to 18.9 percent between 1925 and 1939. Industry's deleterious impact on artisanal production thus also gathered speed. In contrast to traditional patterns of work, industrial workers now faced strict discipline, unhealthy conditions and a more difficult pace of production. The profile of the labor force began to change. Employment in industry and services was estimated to vary between 600,000 and 800,000 people on the eve of World War II. Total employment in manufacturing, services and mining varied between 10 percent and 12 percent of the labor force. However, the total number was much more than this since most employers evaded the labor censuses conducted by the government. Leaving aside hundreds of thousands of agricultural workers, seasonal tobacco and fig-processing workers and 40,000 railway and transportation workers, urban laborers, including artisans and casual labor, together with their families, amounted to approximately 2 million people, about 85 percent of the urban population. The urban labor force encompassed a wide range of wage earners. A very small number of workers worked in big industries and state enterprises such as iron, steel, mining, cement, sugar, textiles, railways, glass and paper. However, transporters, shippers, dockworkers, porters, construction workers, fishers, postal service employees, artisans, journeymen and self-employed workers such as handloom weavers, tailors, tanners, shoemakers, felt makers, saddlers, carriage drivers, porters and street vendors comprised the largest group. In the Aegean towns alone, 60,000 carpet weavers worked at home. Most were left out of the labor census or avoided the attention of historians because they did not belong to any organization or company.[4]

Despite steady proletarianization, a huge portion of workers maintained ties with their villages. Temporary peasant workers outnumbered permanent and skilled ones. In the absence of a qualified urban labor force, the industry became more dependent on peasantry. In parallel, tough living conditions in rural areas pushed peasants to

seek temporary employment in cities in order to save money to pay
taxes, debts or a bride price, or to weather the economic crisis. With the
impoverishment and employers' tendency to hire cheaper labor, the
number of women and especially child workers also increased.[5]

Wages and Purchasing Power

During the interwar period, real wages recovered but remained below
pre-1914 levels. The wages, though they varied according to sector and
worker qualifications, were too low. Between 1927 and 1938, the daily
wages of workers in some sectors decreased by 10–30 percent. Mine
workers, for instance, received very low wages of between 40 and 140
piasters and lived mostly on bread or corn. A coal miner in Turkey
earned only a tenth of the pay of his American counterpart. The situation
of seasonal workers was not much better. Tobacco workers in İstanbul
received a daily wage fluctuating between 50 and 100 piasters for 10 to
12 hours of hard labor. Unskilled workers in the textile, tobacco and
leather mills were paid 40 to 100 piasters a day, whereas a skilled worker
received an average of 120 to 200 piasters. Women and child workers
received less than even unskilled male workers. In the small towns of
Anatolia, women and children in carpet and silk weaving received only
10 or 15 piasters a day.[6] In the state factories, most workers were paid as
low as workers in the private sector. The daily wage of the average
worker in the Sümerbank Kayseri Textile Factory, one of the largest
public enterprises, was around 50 piasters. Though keeping up by
working much longer was getting harder day by day, working conditions
and incomes in artisanal production were no worse than in industry.
Informal relations with masters and a relatively non-mechanized and
slow pace of work made artisanal production less brutal. Even though
craftspeople comprising masters, journeymen and apprentices spent much
more time in small shops for less money. Journeymen and apprentices
worked up to 14 hours a day and earned 200–300 piasters and 50–80
piasters per week, respectively.[7]

One important factor lowering wages was the heavy taxes imposed
on them. Jules Picharles and Frederic Benham, two American experts
who prepared a special report on the Turkish tax system in 1930, were
shocked by the extremely inequitable tax burden. On average the
government extracted 82 percent of its income tax revenues from the
taxation of wage earners between 1932 and 1938. The bulk of workers'

Graph 6.1 The nominal and real wage index, 1914–39

wages was spent on food and housing. The İstanbul Chamber of Commerce declared in June 1933 that for a family of four in İstanbul the minimum subsistence pay was 122 liras per month. According to one newspaper, if this was taken for granted, low-income people – say, postmen earning 25 liras, teachers earning 30 liras, workers and wage laborers earning 20–30 liras – would not be able to support their families.[8]

As for the elderly, many had no retirement rights or did not receive any gratuity. The minority with retirement benefits contended with small pensions or bureaucratic red tape. In some sectors, payment of wages was delayed for weeks or months, and many factories cut wages arbitrarily. State officials paid by provincial administrations, such as teachers and preachers, were unable to receive their salaries for months, dooming them to poverty.[9]

Working Conditions and Lack of Social Security

In many sectors, except for a few large public enterprises, working conditions were unbearable. The hours were grueling and work sites lacked even basic safety and hygiene measures. Most employers neither followed regular procedures in hiring and layoffs nor provided basic social security provisions such as occupational safety and hygiene measures, retirement funds and compensation for work accidents and diseases.

Working hours generally exceeded ten hours a day. In many workplaces, a normal shift was no less than twelve hours and workers often had to work in unsanitary conditions. In extremely exploitative sectors such as textiles, a workday could reach up to seventeen hours. The shop floors were generally noisy and airless because of outmoded machinery dating back to the previous century even in the largest cotton and textile factories like the Mersin Textile Factory. In tobacco warehouses, the normal workday might be fifteen hours. Large textile factories like the Süreyyapaşa Textile Factory did not allow their workers a day off, even on weekends and bank holidays. In public enterprises, a workday could last in practice up to nine hours. Food factories employed children under the age of ten who worked as long as fourteen hours a day. Low-paid workers and salesclerks in shops and stores too had to work long hours. Bakery workers worked between fourteen and eighteen hours a day without a day off. In the handloom weaving industry, hours were unregulated. Competition from cheaper industrial textiles forced weavers to overwork. All members of a weaver family generally worked nonstop from eight to fourteen hours a day in unhealthy conditions.[10]

Employers pressed their workers to work on weekends, even after the enactment of the 1924 Weekend Vacation Law that determined Friday as a weekend holiday. This law excluded many sectors and allowed employers to cancel weekend holidays up to fifteen times per year. As late as 1935, the government legally fixed the weekend holiday through the enactment of the National Day and General Holidays Law. Sunday replaced Friday as the weekend holiday. This law introduced the paid weekend vacation, but many employers ignored it.[11]

Particularly for peasants and former artisans recruited to the factories, industrial work was unbearable, even unsafe. The separation of home from workplace, formal and strict discipline, the pressure of targeted output levels and deadlines made work more depressing and unfriendly. Large state factories therefore suffered a high rate of labor turnover during this period. Men who worked on public construction projects were among the most destitute. For example, in the most important government railway project undertaken by the Simeryol Company in Sivas, groups of ten to fifteen men shared a single tent and worked more than ten hours under trying conditions. Despite this hard work, their basic diet was rice, bread and a handful of olives.[12]

The mining sector had the poorest working conditions. In Zonguldak Ereğli Coal Mines Enterprise, for instance, a workday sometimes could last fifteen hours under dangerous conditions. The workers of the Fethiye chrome mines suffered similar problems. The high frequency of accidents in the mines was related to poor safety measures and inadequate technical conditions. Increasing demand for coal in railways and new industries pressured workers during the 1930s. Moreover, the piece-rate work system forced workers to reach targeted output levels and caused them to ignore preventive measures. Cave-ins, firedamp, conveyor hits and toxic gases were among the leading causes of accidents. Work accidents resulted in 4,000 casualties between 1927 and 1932. In the Fethiye chrome mines, fatal accidents, for which the company avoided responsibility by bribing officials, occurred almost every day. Printing houses were also unhealthy workplaces due to extreme noise and dirty air polluted by chemicals that caused lung diseases. Tobacco warehouses also had some of the most unsanitary working environments.[13]

The conditions of workers who worked at home were not much better. During the Kayseri stage of his tour, Harold Armstrong observed the poor working conditions of women and children who weaved silk carpets in their homes from sunrise to sunset. Bernard Newman, another traveler in Turkey, also mentioned the destitute female workers weaving carpets in their homes. These workers were left outside the scope of the labor laws. In handloom weaving centers such as Denizli, Aydın, Manisa and Isparta, entire families worked at handlooms day and night by turns with immense industry.[14] In 1936, the RPP inspector of Isparta described the working conditions of the

Illustration 6.1 Child spinners

hundreds of women and children employed at carpet looms from sunrise to sunset every day without a break for between 10 and 30 piasters a day. Another Isparta inspector noted that nearly 10,000 poor women were employed at carpet looms under grim conditions through a sort of putting-out system. These handlooms were purposefully located in humid, dusty, dark places in order to preserve the strength of the rope. In winter, weavers did not heat the rooms in which they worked in order to keep costs down and to maintain humidity. Dying the fabrics and ropes further polluted the air. Diets were so poor that many subsisted solely on bread, cheese and olives. These conditions caused rheumatic, bone and eye diseases. The majority of weavers and almost all of the apprentices in workshops who were employed in return for a few piasters were children. Textile and cotton factories widely exploited child labor. The employment of children around seven or eight years old in return for 10 piasters a day for twelve hours was common in gloomy, unsanitary and noisy cotton and textile factories in Mersin and Adana, although the employment of children under twelve was prohibited with the 1930 Public Hygiene Law (Umumi Hıfzıssıhha Kanunu).[15]

The experts of the American-led Hines-Kemmerer mission, which advised the government on economic matters in the early 1930s, wrote, "Even the best of the social measures taken for the safety and health of the workers in Turkey is at a primitive level ... The measures about the workers' health are horrific ... The social insurance system is rare and covers only a very limited number of people." Except for a few public enterprises, most companies, which were required to employ physicians and establish infirmaries according to the Public Hygiene Law, did not have even a health official. According to an RPP inspector, the employment of doctors in factories was generally eyewash.[16]

No comprehensive social insurance system covered workers in case of disease, injury, pregnancy, death or retirement. The majority were not eligible for occupational retirement funds even in some public enterprises and state institutions. As for the limited number of state officials or qualified workers in a few large public enterprises who depended on these social assistance and retirement funds, many encountered difficulties and bureaucratic delays, often waiting for months or years to receive their pensions or gratuities. In the private sector, recruitment and layoff procedures were extremely arbitrary. Employers, factory managers and foremen were able to fire whomever and whenever they wanted without any redundancy payment. They could dismiss without any compensation a worker who was seriously injured in a work accident. The absolute power of employers and foremen in hiring and firing made female workers vulnerable to exploitation and sexual abuse.[17] Certainly such incidents were not unique to these two sectors.

Several professional associations were designed for mutual social assistance. After the closure of the WAS in 1928, the next year workers and artisans were reorganized by the government in occupational associations. Inspired by corporatism, this move ruled out class conflict by predicating on the idea of occupational solidarity.[18] Indeed, most of these associations were comprised of both employers and employees of the same profession or sector. The main motive of these organizations was to keep the laboring masses under control and fragment them into occupational groups. In addition, by means of these bodies, the government aimed also to collect taxes easily and to relegate social measures to the assistance funds of these bodies that were financed with the premiums cut from wages or membership dues. However, these associations never had sufficient financial and organizational capacity to help their members.

All of these problems and more also haunted agricultural workers. In industrial agricultural regions like Adana, Aydın and İzmir, tens of thousands of agricultural laborers worked in large capitalist farms producing cotton, tobacco and grapes. As economy minister Celal Bayar and party inspector Hilmi Uran noted on the basis of their observations in the Çukurova region and in the eastern provinces, many agricultural laborers toiled in sweltering weather from dawn till dusk in near-famine conditions, sleeping outside on the ground or in graveyards. These workers were harshly exploited by both farmers and their agents, called *elçibaşı*, who hired laborers on farmers' behalf. Their misery led even the most pro-business politicians like Bayar to recommend these people's protection under the Labor Law.[19]

Declining Crafts

Flat-heeled shoe makers (*yemenici*), knife makers and coppersmiths could no longer do a good business. Demand for forged steel knives fell. Colorful, cheaper factory-made knives replaced them. Few people ordered the colorful leather *yemeni*. Shop owners did not have customers; the *yemeni*s could no longer find takers. Instead of these old shops, there were new stores marketing new and ready-made clothes and shoes. Ugly and cheap shoes whose soles were made from automobile tires replaced the beautiful hand-made *yemeni*s. These are cheap and ready to buy. As these new stores prospered, the old shops closed down. People gave up going to tailors for long fitting processes ... Tailors did not receive orders anymore. Only a few tailors resisted by sewing clothes for moneyed customers.[20]

A future leading folklorist, İlhan Başgöz, recorded these observations about traditional artisans in Sivas who lost their jobs during his youth in the 1930s. What he witnessed in his hometown reflected a wider trend of crisis that engulfed artisans. Indeed, notwithstanding their struggle to stay alive, the vanishing of many artisans was not peculiar to Sivas but a general trend throughout Anatolia.

The overwhelming majority of the working class in those years was composed of artisans. They were mostly self-employed masters who worked with their journeymen, apprentices or family members in small workshops or homes. They underwent a deep crisis with the Great Depression and with competition from cheaper domestic or imported industrial products. In fact, their crisis can be traced back to the penetration of the Ottoman markets by European manufactures. However, the absence of industrialization, competition with European manufactures or integration to it if possible somehow allowed some of them to survive.

Of course, it is difficult to generalize about entire artisan groups. Some artisans partly benefited from the recovery of the economy under the republic and even the slowdown in international trade in the 1930s. Yet this did not automatically bring protection for craftsmen. The main crafts comprising hundreds of thousands of handloom weavers, tailors, carriage drivers, shoemakers, saddlers, felt makers and low-income tanners suffered from the Great Depression, industrialization projects and ongoing importation of some manufactured goods. On the other hand, craftspeople like bakers, blacksmiths, masons and carpenters managed to keep pace thanks to the comparative demographic bulge and resulting demand for construction projects.

The first grave blow to the craftspeople was imports. Importation had gained momentum during the 1920s, especially after the Lausanne Treaty under which Turkey reluctantly embraced liberal foreign economic relations. Although Turkey's external trade came to a halt with the global economic crisis of 1929, importation not only in capital goods but also in semifinished and finished products recovered between 1933 and 1938. The Turkish economy still depended on imports. Second, the establishment of new factories, which stimulated the serial production of basic consumption goods, most of which had been supplied by artisans, threatened artisanal production.[21]

Carpet and fabric weaving on handlooms was the primary field to decline during the 1930s. The first shock came with the Great Depression. In fact, the Turkish handloom industry had already fallen into decline because of the cheap carpets and fabrics produced by European industrial conglomerates. The crisis worsened the situation by bringing down prices and decreasing exports. In addition to European textiles invading the markets, Anatolian weavers faced fierce competition from Syrian, Armenian, Greek, American and British textiles. Russian and Japanese draperies also reached Turkey between 1935 and 1939. Fakir Baykurt, who worked at his uncle's loom weaving fabric, points out in his diary how cheaper and abundant factory-made fabric, called American or English fabric, undermined the weavers' jobs.[22]

Uşak, Manisa, Balıkesir, İzmir, Denizli, Burdur and Isparta were among the primary centers for carpet, fabric and spinning manufactures based on handlooms. İzmir was also the export center for Turkish carpets. However, by 1934, the Great Depression had compelled most of them to limit production. Importation of crucial inputs like special sorts of ropes and colorants languished during the global crisis. Incipient mechanized production in newly established large factories also undermined this sector during the 1930s.[23]

According to a 1936 report on carpet weaving in Isparta, both the number of handlooms and total output had sharply dropped within recent years. The high customs tariffs of Western countries had thrown this sector into a grave crisis. While total output in the region had reached 200,000 square meters in 1927, production in 1935 decreased to 60,000 square meters. Stagnation in the sector correspondingly brought about a reduction in wages from 400 piasters to 200 piasters per square meter.[24]

In addition, the Sümerbank Nazilli Textile Factory, installed in 1935, began to supply three times more than the total demand in western Turkey. This induced a further decline in handloom weaving. The Çolakoğulları Carpet and Textile Factory in Kula, founded in 1936 and employing about 300 workers, worsened the situation of the artisans in Manisa. Many people formerly engaged in handloom production lost their jobs and flooded into neighboring counties to look for new jobs. Even in Uşak, the heart of carpet weaving, production dropped to its lowest level during the mid-1930s. In comparison with the 450,000 square meters of production and 2,400,000 liras of profit in 1927, these numbers hit bottom in 1936 at barely 3,000 square meters and 9,000 liras. Of around 1,000 carpet-weaving handlooms in Uşak in previous years, only 100 managed to survive until the end of the 1930s.[25]

In the handloom-weaving centers of eastern Anatolia, the situation was similar. According to a contemporary observer, the mechanized textile factories around Gaziantep undermined home-based handloom production in the 1930s. Likewise, handloom weavers in the Black Sea provinces were also in crisis due to fierce competition from imported goods that came via the Black Sea. By April 1932, hundreds of handloom weavers and traders in Samsun, Ladik and Merzifon were displaced by imported Japanese fabrics, haberdashery goods and clothes.[26]

Another craft hit by importation and industrialization was shoemaking. The Turkish footwear sector, particularly small shoemakers, had already suffered from the competition of imported machine-made shoes before the republic. These imported industrial shoes were cheaper than handmade ones. In the republic, shoemakers faced further competition from the domestic mass production of cheaper manufactured shoes by the Beykoz Leather and Shoe Factory. This factory was actually established by reformist Sultan Mahmut II in order to produce shoes for the Ottoman army. However, with the republic it commenced mass production for civilians alongside the army and then grew after transfer to the newly founded Sümerbank. A few private shoe factories accompanied this factory in the 1930s. As a result of fierce competition from imported and domestic mass production, even as of 1932 the shoe factories drove about 30,000 shoemakers out of business. According to a keen observer of his time, Mehmet Halid Bayrı, whereas Balıkesir had had 150 shoemaking shops until a few years earlier, about one-third of them had closed by 1935. The shoemakers blamed the cheap rubber shoes Sümerbank rolled out. A pair of rubber shoes cost 1.2 liras, but a pair of the cheapest leather shoes cost 2 liras. In the 1930s, peasants throughout Anatolia began to wear the cheaper rubber shoes.[27]

Tanning was another previously profitable and respectable profession that supplied raw materials for shoemakers, saddlers and carriage drivers. Therefore, Debbağ Şeyhi (Sheikh of Tanners) was the most powerful leader of the artisanal organizations of old. However, its members lost out to industrialization. The expansion of railways and tramlines and the increasing number of motor vehicles, automobiles and trucks drove carriage drivers out of business, depriving tanners of a lucrative source of customers. Likewise, tanneries had been the main suppliers of processed leather for shoemakers, who were now in dire straits. Moreover, big leather factories began to conquer the market at the expense of small tanners. In the interwar years, there were 17 big and mechanized tanners, which grew at the expense of 113 small-scale tanners in Kazlıçeşme, the center of tannery in İstanbul.[28]

Among the most prominent traditional crafts in Anatolia was felting (*keçecilik*). Felt makers had been supplying carpets, pads, covers, bags, duffel coats, saddlecloths, clothes and several styles of caps for centuries, but now faced displacement from cheap imported or manufactured products. In Balıkesir, for instance, the number of felters had decreased from twenty-two to fifteen in recent years, fourteen of whom were tenants in their shops. With the 1925 hat reform, the sales of traditional felt caps dropped more than half.[29]

Carriage drivers were also victims of mechanization in transportation. Their decline undermined saddlery by reducing demand for saddles. By 1935, the loss of carriage drivers had created a ripple effect shaking blacksmithing and harness making as well, which had employed up to 50,000 people.[30] However, despite dispossession and unemployment, a considerable number found ways to survive by embracing different jobs or adapting to the changing conditions, as I discuss in the next chapter.

All these factors, with the shrinkage of literate urban workers during the wars and growing state suppression, shaped how working people acted to safeguard themselves. Various groups sought their rights and struggled to survive. Formal means like suing and petitioning, or collective and open actions like walkouts, were undoubtedly more widespread in urban as compared to rural areas. This was largely due to urban laborers' higher literacy, close proximity to state organizations and legacy of organized formal struggle. However, as feeble labor organizations vanished, individual, daily and spontaneous methods in labor's repertoire of action far outweighed formal, organized and well-programmed actions. These struggles remained nearly invisible to historians because they were either despised as atomistic and unconscious or not recorded in conventional sources of labor history. In fact, the working people's daily struggles as a widespread, inescapable part of urban work life put indirect pressure on both rulers and employers.

7 | *Labor Discontent*

"If you are a worker, you do not have as much value as an animal, because there is nobody who is interested in our problems. Nobody looks out for and protects our rights and listens to our grievances."[1] When Zonguldak deputies were taking a short break in a coffeehouse frequented by coal miners, they overheard these words of a worker who had poured out his grief to his friends and even sworn a blue streak. Indeed, low-income wage earners were not deceived by the nationalist and populist discourse of the republic. Aware of the social injustices and the fluctuations in their living standards, they often complained of poor wages, exhausting working conditions, bad treatment by employers and lack of basic social security. They usually expressed their criticisms warily. By invoking the regime's ideological principles such as nationalism and populism (*halkçılık*) against the government, they legitimized their demands. Despite the lack of labor organizations and free press, writing to the state organs and the newspapers constituted the prevailing methods to voice their criticisms. This chapter offers a snapshot of urban laborers' disgruntled views on the matters pertaining to their economic life, which were to shape their actions.

Complaints about Wages, Salaries and High Cost of Living

The main grievance of urban laboring people was low wages or wage cuts. Complaints about these matters filled the pages of newspapers and played a primary role in the emergence of the strikes and walkouts during the 1920s and 1930s. Especially the economic crisis caused frequent cuts or long delays in payment of wages and provoked the laborers' discontent. In 1929, in a letter to *Cumhuriyet*, a female worker from the Sümerbank Defterdar Textile Factory wrote that the workers were very angry because their small wages were paid late and not in full. In 1930, a worker at the Yedikule Railway Depot complained to a newspaper that working overtime despite wage cuts created frustration

138

among the workers. The Navigation Company (Seyrisefain) in İstanbul withheld wages for months as of March 1932, spurring its employees to remonstrate against the company. Likewise, in February 1934, Balya-Karaaydın miners complained about a 25 percent decrease in wages in spite of tough working conditions. The Süreyyapaşa Textile Factory in Balat had not paid wages for two months by March 1936, which caused workers' complaints. That same year, the Paşabahçe Brick Factory delayed payment of wages for two and a half months and created deep resentment among the workers.[2]

Local governments often paid salaries late, causing widespread discontent. Teachers and preachers, as the most literate and at the same time most vulnerable groups, were especially vocal. Teachers were supposed to shape citizens not only by educating them but also by serving as role models. However, in the face of inadequate salaries, they could not help but question the discrepancy between the importance the government attached to their job and their economic deprivations. They asked how they could be role models that reflected the republican modernist vanguardism with a low wage of 40 liras. Teachers from different corners of the country also complained of long delays in distribution of salaries, or of not getting housing benefits, which the government decided to provide from 1932 on. In a petition to Prime Minister İnönü dated August 6, 1932, twenty-two teachers from Niğde province complained about salaries going unpaid for months. They introduced themselves "as starving teachers of the Republic, who were in danger of losing their honor and dignity."[3]

Another low-income group who received their salaries from local government was preachers. Like teachers, they experienced protracted delays in payment and petitioned the Presidency of Religious Affairs (PRA), the central government and the press to criticize this situation. Tax deductions from already very low wages and salaries made things even worse and stirred wage earners' anger.[4]

Above all, the high cost of living and the rise in prices of basic foodstuffs like bread were primary causes of distress among urban populations. Bread prices fluctuated according to wheat prices. When wheat prices shot up in the 1920s and then in the second half of the 1930s, low-income groups whose diet relied heavily on bread became more stressed. When wheat prices hit rock bottom, wages also dropped. All in all, nothing much changed for the urban labor force. During the entire period, difficulties in access to affordable, sufficient, good-quality bread stood as low-income people's basic problem and constant complaint.[5] Even though the government occasionally fixed prices, bakers responded by producing half-baked, poor-quality and lower-weight breads. During the election district inspections by İstanbul deputies in 1929 and 1930, the most frequent complaint they heard was the high price of bread. The unaffordable price of meat, about 60 to 70 piasters per kilo in the mid-1930s, also fueled public discontent in urban areas. Other basic foodstuffs the urban laborers found expensive or scarce were salt and sugar due to the low supply and high taxes on them.[6]

Low-income people did not believe the official discourse promoting domestic products. The high price and low quality of these goods were the primary sources of complaints among wage earners. Questioning the nationalist propaganda that encouraged the consumption of domestic products, consumers satirized the poor but expensive domestic goods as "getting screwed by a friend" (*dost kazığı*). Even the chairman of the İstanbul branch of the National Economy and Saving Association (Milli İktisat ve Tasarruf Cemiyeti) admitted in 1932 that domestic goods were so overpriced that citizens frequently complained to the Association. The high price and low quality of certain goods that cheered ordinary people, like cigarettes and *rakı*, produced by the state monopoly, caused vehement public resentment against the government. Those smokers who found even cheaper cigarette brands very expensive preferred smuggled ones.[7]

Disgruntlement with Working Conditions

Long working hours in unhealthy and unsafe environments stood out as a main source of complaint. The frequency and vehemence of the complaints rose with the economic crisis and the ensuing government policy of industrialization, which galvanized the workers. Many expressed their views via writing to the press. For instance, in a letter to *Köroğlu*, chrome miners in Tavşanlı described poignantly how they were compelled to work more than ten hours a day in abominable conditions. Similarly, spinners in chrysalis factories in Adapazarı wrote about sweating up to fifteen hours a day. They also felt great pain in their fingers from spinning at a stretch. A worker in the Seyhan (Adana) National Textile Factory run by the government in 1929 recounted working up to fourteen hours a day without payment for overtime.

There was nowhere to sit down and have lunch. Tobacco warehouse workers in İstanbul complained about working overtime under threat of firing by the foremen. A tobacco worker wrote that he and his colleagues were locked in a perilously polluted warehouse for thirteen or fourteen hours a day. A group of drapery workers wrote to *Esnaf Meslek Mecmuası* about working long hours in dismal basement workshops. Another 500 women workers from the factories in Adapazarı collectively wrote to *Köroğlu* complaining they were worked a minimum of thirteen hours a day. The utterly awful conditions in the Halkapınar Rope Factory, the Serge Factory and the Acorn Factory in İzmir spurred grievances among their workers. They frequently complained of dirty dust and scorching heat due to the lack of ventilation, and no running water. The lunch break was only about thirty minutes. The factory doctors ignored the workers' health problems.[8]

As seen in the wish lists of the RPP's provincial congresses, among the primary demands of the workers were shorter working hours and improvement of the shop floor environment. The Çankırı party congress, for example, reported that workers frequently demanded that the party give warning to companies that forced them to work longer than the maximum working hours prescribed by the Public Hygiene Law. The 1931 Samsun party congress cited a maximum eight hours of work and betterment of working conditions as frequent demands of the workers in the province. The wish list of the Zonguldak party congress also included shortening the workday and enacting a labor law. Workers also demanded legislation limiting grueling working hours. In 1931, the economy minister, Mustafa Şeref Özkan, promised these needs would be satisfied soon with the forthcoming labor law. Malicious foremen and their abuses were the most common complaint among the workers. Such complaints inundated the press, as evident in a newspaper report writing that every day the newspaper office had received similar letters.[9]

Both the exemptions in the 1924 Weekend Vacation Law that excluded many wage earners from the right to a weekly day off and employers' frequent violation of the weekend right drove workers crazy. Those who could not benefit from the weekend holiday had begun to murmur right after the enactment of the 1924 law. According to a 1924 police report, workers, particularly tramway and railway workers, complained that they were not allowed to take a rest on Fridays and that employers generally fired workers who demanded a day off. They accused the government of favoring employers.[10]

Partly due to this social discontent, the government introduced paid weekend vacation on Saturday afternoon and Sunday applicable to all industrial workers in 1935. Nonetheless, many factories continued to operate on Saturdays and even Sundays in full-time shifts. From İzmit, a tobacco warehouse worker reported that all warehouse workers continued to be worked on Saturdays illegally, though they had informed the Economy Ministry of this several times. In another instance, workers of the Alpullu Sugar Factory asked why they had to work full-time on Saturdays despite the laws granting them an after-noon rest. Workers in textile plants also queried why the textile com-panies could overwork them from morning to night on Saturdays by accusing the government of infringement of their rights. In August 1935, *Son Posta* pointed out that workers in many sectors were unhappy with working full-time on Saturdays and even on Sundays. Workers complained that even merciful employers who allowed their workers a rest from Saturday noon on added half an hour to the working hours of each workday, or paid only half a day's wages to offset the loss stemming from the part-time work on Saturdays. Self-employed artisans, salesclerks and handloom weavers working at home also resented their exclusion from the law.[11]

The newspapers of the time and the lists of the National Assembly's petition commission are replete with petitions and letters complaining of the lack of basic social rights and job security. One common com-plaint was cancellation of labor contracts by employers without any unemployment indemnity. The dismissal of sick or injured workers without any compensation also generated criticisms. Together with coal mines, the cellulose and paper industries in İzmit were known for high rates of job-related accidents and diseases. Workers who were injured or suffered health problems were provided neither protective work accident insurance nor effective medical treatment. Workers felt great anger at this heartless treatment. That is why there is a pretty big quantity of petitions seeking compensation or permanent disability pensions. Many demanded retirement and disability pensions from the government or companies.[12]

The great majority of white- and blue-collar workers, who were not eligible for retirement pension benefits, sought retirement pensions and gratuities by writing to the parliament. On the other hand, occupational retirement and mutual assistance funds or professional associations also failed to meet the needs of their members. For instance, forty workers in a plug factory in Zeytinburnu who were laid off in 1930 complained about their assistance fund to the press. Although they had long paid 4 percent of their wages to the fund, they did not receive any assistance from it when they were laid off.[13]

Social assistance funds established from the late 1920s on for military officers and public factory employees as well as middle-ranking state officials by no means operated perfectly. Many low-ranking government employees, especially officials in local administrations, who were not covered by a retirement fund, viewed this situation as inequality. According to a politician who addressed the matter in the National Assembly in March 1933, even the qualified officials of the Monopoly Administration, who had graduated from the Military Academy (Harbiye) or Civil Service School (Mülkiye), had no social security and this stirred complaints among them.[14]

Apart from this, retirement pensions were generally insufficient. Most retired officials received between 10 and 20 liras per month. Not only low-ranking retirees but also retired government physicians, district governors and mid-ranking military officers were disgruntled by the paltry pensions. Local party officials were also dissatisfied with their retirement pensions. Osman Tan, the party secretary of the Kemalpaşa district of İzmir, for instance, penned a letter to the party general secretary, complaining that his retirement pension fell short of the needs of his family of seven. He pleaded with the party to give him a raise and a small amount of retirement gratuity by emphasizing how he had served in the Young Turk movement and then the Independence War. Likewise, in a letter to the RPP general secretary, a retired district governor, Haşim Yanbolu, drew attention to the unacceptable fact that despite his services in dangerous places like Dersim and Yemen during World War I and the Independence War, his toil was rewarded with a small pension. Poignantly describing the difficulties of living on such little money, he closed his letter by asking for a raise.[15]

Another group demanding assistance from the government was veterans or the widows or orphaned daughters of martyrs. They frequently complained of the government's neglect despite the sacrifices they or their husbands, fathers or sons had made. Appropriating the nationalist rhetoric to justify their petitions, they demanded pension benefits. Their grievances were covered in the national press. In 1932,

Everyday Politics of Urban Labor

for instance, a wife of a Gallipoli martyr complained she had not yet received the pension assigned to widows of war martyrs eight years previously. Another old woman, whose husband had died at the front during the Great War, complained that the government had not yet assigned a pension to her despite her poverty.[16]

As a matter of fact, bureaucratic red tape made all these low-income groups equal, whether covered by social security or not. The paperwork required to disburse a pension generally took too long. The letters sent to newspapers show the people's dissatisfaction with the limited and malfunctioning social security system. In February 1930, based on countless letters sent by indignant citizens, *Cumhuriyet* reported that a great number of old retirees, veterans and orphans and widows of deceased state officials and martyrs were not protected by an efficient social security mechanism. Even if some were covered by a social insurance fund, it took too long to collect pension benefits due to the daunting and confusing procedures. For instance, a former official retired after thirty-six years of service complained that he was living in squalor because his retirement had fallen into abeyance for years. Another retiree wrote that despite his thirty years of service to the government at the cost of becoming permanently disabled, his retirement was still in abeyance after two years due to red tape. His several petitions to the governorship had proven fruitless. Ultimately, he had had to request the newspaper to warn the relevant state officials and even the government. According to the newspaper, this letter was only one of many that flooded their mailbox. The problem turned out to be severely chronic with the Great Depression and generated a flood of petitions to the government criticizing delays in assignments of retirement pensions and gratuities.[17]

Likewise, poor widows and orphans entitled to pensions were unable to collect their allowances. A wife of a deceased state official, unable to receive her widow pension for years due to bureaucratic procedures and living in poverty with five children, complained about red tape in a letter to a newspaper. Another poor widow sarcastically asked whether "the contemporary Republic" (*muasır Cumhuriyet*) was not able to set these simple things right.[18]

Undoubtedly, the main need, which the working class urged and hoped to see, was a labor law. This was a leading demand of industrial workers. Yet, to a lesser extent, craftspeople, apprentices, waiters, clerks and waged taxi drivers also demanded to be included in a labor law. In the first years of the republic, the laboring masses' sympathy with the PRP opposition undoubtedly played a role in fostering the RPP's interest in labor legislation as a way to gain support among the poor. Indeed, the social base of the PRP consisted of mostly poor workers, retired officials, shopkeepers and artisans. According to an intelligence report, in Bozok (Yozgat), for instance, all porters, carriage drivers, laborers and those who had lost their posts with the establishment of the republic had supported the PRP. In Sivas, likewise, the PRP attracted people of lesser means, carriage drivers, coffeehouse owners, unemployed persons and poor refugees.[19] The laborers' support for the opposition compelled the ruling elite to prepare a labor law draft in 1924. However, the RPP, dominated by mercantile and industrial interests, unsurprisingly voted against it. Therefore, the unending labor disputes and social demands continued apace and kept alive politicians' awareness of the urgent need for labor legislation. Ultimately, the government had to prepare two other labor law drafts in 1927 and 1929.

The press also pointed out the necessity of a law regulating work life. In April 1927, the *İkdam* newspaper called for workers to send their opinions about the existing draft of the labor law. Workers who responded mostly criticized the government's draft and demanded more protection. However, even this draft was not brought to the National Assembly. Within a few years, ongoing labor conflicts led the press and politicians to reconsider a labor law. A newspaper wrote about the great strike of tramway workers in 1928 as follows: "The strike of the tramway workers demonstrates once again the need for labor legislation ... The rights and safety of capital are completely ensured by our laws. Let us try to ensure also the rights of labor, particularly of mass labor."[20]

Consequently, the Economy Ministry proposed another labor law draft in 1929, but it was withdrawn within a short time. The labor law was removed from the government's agenda until the FRP opposition was welcomed by laborers with walkouts and street demonstrations in September 1930. In the meantime, the government attempted to partially meet the needs of workers by adopting the Public Hygiene Law in April 1930. It introduced important regulations concerning the health and safety of the labor force and offered free medical services in the large factories.[21]

However, this law could not substitute for comprehensive labor legislation. Working people insisted on labor legislation by writing to the newspapers and the provincial and central administrators. The 1930 provincial party congresses and the politicians' reports also reflect popular demands for a labor law. According to the wish lists of the provincial party congresses, the most expressed demands concerning labor were an eight-hour workday, better working conditions, retirement pensions and gratuities, free medical service and inclusive social security, which could be ensured only with a labor law. Sometimes the party delegates directly demanded labor legislation. The press continued to publish workers' letters and interviews about the necessity of a labor law. In 1932, the newspaper *Yeni Gün* conducted a poll, according to which the great majority of workers longed for a labor law.[22] At this juncture, the government prepared another draft of a labor law in 1932, but once again avoided enacting it.

Neither the workers' demands nor the bureaucrats' recommendation of drawing a labor law faded away. In a meeting on March 20, 1933, Balıkesir deputies met with workers of their province. An urgent telegram sent by the Balıkesir deputy, Hacim Muhittin (Çarıklı), to the RPP general secretary the next day attracted the attention of the party leadership to the workers' stress on the immediate enactment of a labor law. Underscoring the importance of this repeated demand, the deputy closed his telegram by saying, "My lord, I beg for your order to pass this important law in this session of the National Assembly." When the labor law discussions came up again in 1934, even artisans and salesclerks wrote to the RPP, the Economy Ministry and the National Assembly for inclusion of their requests in the would-be labor law. Workers asking why the long-discussed labor law had not been passed yet, were further anxious whether the government would sidestep the issue again.[23]

Finally, in 1936, the new Labor Law was passed. However, both just before and after its enactment, workers greeted it warily. Aside from its failure to include the right to strike and form unions, whether its provisions would be implemented effectively was an issue of concern. In November 1935, a female worker wrote to *Son Posta* that the poor implementation of the Public Hygiene Law over six years had made her suspicious of the proper implementation of the Labor Law. Another worker, from the Yedikule Railway Company, predicted that the law draft in its current form would lead employers to downsize since it covered only big firms.[24]

After the passage of the Labor Law, many workers publicly expressed their happiness, whereas some had reservations. According to a press interview with workers, a chocolate factory worker named Firdevs was happy, but cautious as well. She said, "Before being happy, we must learn which rights this law gives us." A biscuit factory worker, Naime, also expressed her doubt mixed with hope. The eight-hour workday made her happy, but she was afraid her boss would lower wages to make up for the cost of facilities the Labor Law would require.[25] No doubt activist workers disliked the Labor Law's denial of the right of unionization and strike.

These worries would prove well founded. As soon as the National Assembly began deliberations over the Labor Law, some factories began to dismiss senior workers, who were supposed to be bestowed with important rights. Some workplaces cut the number of employees because the law did not cover workplaces hiring fewer than ten workers. Hundreds of companies in İstanbul evaded the Labor Law by dividing their work among several small workshops. Moreover, by dismissing workers on various pretexts, companies discouraged employees from demanding the rights and services introduced by the Labor Law.[26] Nevertheless, the Labor Law provided several opportunities that the workers appropriated for their own causes. Even though it banned strikes and labor unions, it created a legal base and standards to bargain with the employers.

Discontent with the Professional Associations

Workers and artisans generally viewed their professional associations as useless puppets of the government or employers.[27] However, in many cases, they were turned into contestation realms by members who did not remain fully subservient to these organizations. Taxes and premiums deducted from wages prompted criticisms among workers and craftsmen. Bereft of effective social assistance in return for their contributions, they were further frustrated at the corruption in the associations. Moreover, the heterogeneous and cross-class composition of the membership led to internal conflicts of interest between employers and employees. The worker groups among the members demanded class-specific associations sensitive to their needs instead of those of their employers. This was not due to a leftist reflex, but due to their experiences of conflicting interests in everyday life. The wage-earner laborer members sometimes forced their associations to make particular decisions in their favor or to lobby for their rights. A few class-specific professional associations pursued the interests of their members more efficiently.

Most low-income wage earners saw their heterogeneous professional associations as idle apparatuses of the employers and the government. According to a 1931 inspection report, in the eyes of the Zonguldak coal miners, the workers' union was in the palm of the employers' hands, which served commercial interests. Though a certain number of workers' representatives were on its board, they seemed docile workers selected by employers. Workers had to pay dues to their professional association's saving and social aid funds. These dues varied between 5 and 10 percent and were generally deducted from the monthly wages. The coal mine workers usually got nothing or only a miserable pittance in return for these systematic dues. Petitioning the government, they often complained that the union was using this money to pay high salaries to union officials. In view of complaints, the Economy Ministry leveled down the high salaries of all officials of the union in June 1936. Dockworkers in the Zonguldak port also complained that the Dockworkers' Association did not take care of their problems at all. The workers asserted that the money cut from their wages went to the salaries of association officials. They also claimed that despite the unification of the Dockworkers' Association and the Coal Miners' Association under a single association, the dock-workers had been subjected to discrimination by paying higher dues compared to coal miners.[28]

Similarly, the Drivers' Association, with 4,000 members, including low-wage drivers and better-off taxi owners, was a cross-class organization. However, this did not mean the association managed to absorb the conflict of interest between its hard-up and well-off members. Many drivers scraping a living in the İstanbul streets for twelve to eighteen hours a day resented their bosses and contemplated splitting from the association. A driver said, "The taxi owners have been trying to compete with us, rather than looking for a solution to our problems." According to the drivers, some members owned up to thirty cars. Their main goal, the driver alleged, was to monopolize the sector by raising difficulties for low-income drivers. Drivers in İstanbul argued that there was a serious dispute between them and the rich taxi owners over wages and hours and therefore it was unreasonable to place these two groups in the same association. Moreover, despite the large sum of around 20,000 liras that drivers contributed to it each year, the association did not give them help when they needed it.[29]

Workers in other sectors had similar perceptions of their professional associations. A textile worker, for instance, complained that he had been forced to register in a craftsmen's association that also included his master, despite being an underpaid worker rather than a journeymen or an employer. He argued that unskilled workers like him needed a more specific organization comprising only workers to be able to defend their rights. Tannery workers also found odd their membership side by side with their well-to-do bosses in the same association. For a tannery worker, the Turkish Tanners Association seemed bizarre because the bosses, who were called *ağa*s by workers or small tanners, dominated the association. Therefore, the workers and small tanners, who did not expect any benefit from it, opted out of the activities of the association. Likewise, there were no friendly relations between the tobacco workers and the Tobacco Workers' Association. Tobacco workers were of the opinion that the association neither protected their rights nor aided them financially in the case of illness, work accident or unemployment. They also complained that a few administrators of the association had been pocketing the money collected from workers. Indeed, some professional associations were afflicted with chronic corruption, which further alienated their members. According to public perception, rather than safeguarding the interests of their members, these associations were feathering a few officials' nests with the money of working people struggling to eke out a living. That is why many workers frequently objected to the dues and fees their associations demanded or refused to pay them.[30]

Artisans' Discontent

The most significant factor worsening the mood of artisans was competition from cheaper industrial products. Craftspeople often complained about the importation of cheap finished and semifinished goods and the effects of mechanization on their age-old businesses. Carpet and fabric weaving on handlooms was the primary field that underwent a decline during the 1930s. Establishment of textile factories throughout the country together with cheaper imported Japanese and Russian fabrics frustrated handloom weavers. On the other hand, during the 1930s, rising tariff rates on semifinished goods or intermediate materials also increased the cost of some inputs. In a letter to *Son Posta*, handloom weavers in Denizli, for instance, argued industrial enterprises were putting them to the sword. The same newspaper reported hundreds of handloom weavers and other artisans in Samsun were also complaining about the competition of imported fabrics and haberdashery.[31]

Tailors also were displeased with the mass production of ready-made clothes by Sümerbank textile factories, notwithstanding their happiness with the increase in factory-made fabrics as main inputs. Although some of them traded the industrial ready-made clothes and fabrics, their profit was very small, as factories sold them the fabric by charging high prices. Moreover, the textile companies marketed the ready-made clothes at lower prices than the prices of tailors' clothes. In the eyes of tailors, the clothing industry was taking bread out of their mouths.[32]

Both industrialization and imports dealt a staggering blow to shoemaking. Shoemakers complained about stagnation until World War II halted importation. They blamed imported rubber shoes and big factories like the Beykoz Leather and Shoe Factory producing cheap shoes. Small tanners were also anxious and took a dim view of the mechanization of transportation and shoemaking. Mechanical vehicles and manufactured shoes undermined carriage drivers, saddlers, tanners and shoemakers. Even in a remote province like Diyarbakır, rubber shoes so invaded the market that both shoemakers and tanners were on a knife's edge, worried about how to get by. Small tanners were further aggrieved by the leather factories, but they managed to survive by reducing prices or processing cheaper imported leather.[33]

Carriage drivers were among those who were most displeased with industrialization. By 1935, roughly 15,000 people in İstanbul alone subsisted on carriage driving. They held small trucks, automobiles and rail transportation responsible for the deterioration of their lives. This process, they said, would lead them to starvation. By the autumn of 1935, the Carriage Drivers' Association declared that members of the profession were losing their jobs. It was reported that more than 50,000 people in related professions like blacksmithing and harness making had also lost or changed their jobs within the previous fifteen years. Carriage drivers appropriated the government's propaganda for domestic goods by asking why the government in its promotion of domestic products did not protect carriages. They argued that carriages were the best example of a domestic good and should be protected from the fierce competition of imported motor vehicles.[34]

A related occupational group, saddlers, whose business slackened because carriage drivers as their main customers were in decline, shared the hostility of carriage drivers and other professions toward mechanization of transportation, industrialization and importation. Felting was another job field that experienced a deep crisis during the period. The hat reform, growing industrial production in textiles and importation of new industry-made rugs, bags and other goods that replaced felt goods reduced consumption of handmade felt products. Therefore, felt makers sometimes had to sell their products at a 5 percent profit or even at a fraction of the cost, which made them malcontent with the new era.[35] These critical views laid the ground for more active and vigorous forms of urban labor's everyday politics.

8 | Survival Struggles and Everyday Resistance

"My uncle said to treat the townsman according to his appetite. If he says white, do not say black ... My uncle said to handle the townsman with tact." In *Bereketli Topraklar Üzerinde*, the masterpiece of Orhan Kemal, Turkey's most prominent social-realist novelist, the uncle of a poor peasant boy, İflahsızın Yusuf, advises his nephew thus before he leaves the village with his two friends to work in the city. Indeed, the city and industrial life grind up his friends' lives, but Yusuf, keeping his uncle's advice in mind, survives through cunning and returns to his village with some money. Yusuf's story is the best illustration of what the working people's politics meant largely during the interwar years. Unlike the last decades of the empire, during the early republic the labor movement was not so vigorous and salient. The wars, massacres, emigrations and establishment of the authoritarian regime depleted the organized and skilled labor force. Labor activism via unions was impossible. However, working people did not resign to their fate. They drew on every possible informal means that yielded small advantages or minimized losses in their daily lives. Formal mechanisms like petitioning and, to a lesser extent, suing were among the repertoire of actions to influence the state and employers or to seek rights. They also tried to use the professional associations established by the government to their own benefit. As a last resort, violence and protests sometimes proved effective in intimidating employers into retreat. All of these strategies compelled employers and the government to compromise so as to create a more productive and stable labor force.

Self-Help Strategies and Small Acts of Noncompliance

Indiscipline and Pilferage

Under circumstances in which open strikes or protests carried the risk of harsh punishment, most wage earners opted for employing subtle ways to defend themselves. First of all, being forced to work so hard and long with very low wages in return led the workers to seek ways to redress this. One common method was to covertly slow down the work pace by prolonging breaks or pretending to be ill or sleepy. Complaints by employers about the lack of discipline among workers give us clues about such efforts. Undoubtedly, these complaints were sometimes merely tactics to keep pressure on the workers. On the other hand, workers were actually prone to ignore discipline. Workers' indiscipline and apathy to their work manifested itself in defective products. Many workers whose wages did not meet their basic needs plodded away at work and went through the motions carelessly. For that reason, some monopoly factories set up a control mechanism. Each worker was to put a numbered piece of paper inside packs of products identifying who had prepared the packs. Nevertheless, the fact that defective goods constantly spurred public criticism during the 1930s demonstrates that such measures were not a deterrent.[1]

The unsanitary and harsh working conditions in cotton factories in Adana led the workers to display passive resistance. An astute observer of his time, Orhan Kemal, described vividly in his memoirs how workers in cotton factories often worked perfunctorily or slowed down the pace of work by prolonging their toilet breaks. Smoking and having a chat in the toilets, they were able to harness the heavy work tempo. These informal breaks were so widespread that factory guards regularly patrolled the toilets in some factories. Yet the workers continued to spend time wherever they could avoid work. Indeed, workers in Sümerbank's textile factories did their work by halves and procrastinated. Even when they worked swiftly, most of them went through the motions. Therefore, the company's fabrics and clothes contained many defects, which caused complaints among consumers.[2]

The public infrastructure projects accelerating in the republic required extensive construction. This stimulated unprecedented demand for cement and thereby made working conditions in the cement plants even harder. The workers in this sector responded with avoidance tactics. According to the service records filed by the Aslan Cement Factory in Gebze, the first and largest cement factory in Turkey, workers were most commonly faulted for napping on the job. Since some workers held additional jobs outside the factory due to the low wages, they were saving their energy by doing so. Another issue was indifference to the work. Workers lying down on the job were caught chatting during work hours. These behaviors were so common that the factory management imposed fines. Nonetheless, because the factory was located in Gebze, a sparsely populated district of Kocaeli where it was difficult to find workers, the managers generally turned a blind eye to disobedience.[3]

Pilferage and petty larceny were the hidden solutions, albeit palliative and much riskier, to the problem of material misery. Taking advantage of their proximity to money held in safes and to products that could be monetized, many laborers stole from their workplaces. As workers became poorer, their tendency for theft increased. The laws classified pilfering, stealing and thieving as crimes against property. These illegal acts implied the existence of conflict over economic sources. Such daily "anti-property" crimes became so prevalent that the prisons overflowed with those who committed these crimes during the interwar years. Reflecting the impact of the economic crisis, the number of prisoners across Turkey doubled in 1932. The number of those in İstanbul rose about threefold between 1929 and 1935, from 1,350 to 4,000. In August 1932, a newspaper article titled "2,500 Thefts in One Year" pointed out the sharp increase in theft. Theft was on the rise in Adana, another industrial base, in 1932. The situation was similar in İzmir, the second-largest industrial and trade center. Due to the crime boom, the capacity of the İzmir prison fell short of accommodating all offenders, most of whom were thieves. More striking was the class composition of the prisoners. The urban dwellers among them were mostly poor individuals with occupational backgrounds such as industrial workers, porters, drivers, carpenters, butchers, shoemakers, grocers, tinsmiths, coffeehouse owners, tailors, fishers, low-ranking civil servants and prostitutes. As for the cause of imprisonment, theft, larceny, embezzlement and pilferage overwhelmingly outnumbered other crimes.[4]

A crime map of İzmir during the Great Depression confirms the close association between the deterioration of the economic standing of the working class and escalating crime rates. This upward trend continued in the following years. According to the statistics compiled by the Justice Ministry, the number of crimes committed by people of working-class background climbed from 5,550 in 1935 to 9,866 just two years later. The bulk of the crimes were those against property like theft, larceny and pilfering.[5]

This was similar to what was going on in rural areas. Here what is particularly relevant to our discussion is the proliferation of stealing from the workplace. Workplace theft was so widespread that employers needed to take security measures. In the Sümerbank Kayseri Textile Factory, for example, one of the biggest problems that troubled the factory director was the stealing of factory goods by the workers. A foreign observer who visited the factory wrote, "Every evening the men had to be searched for stolen goods. During the past months they carried away everything that could be moved."[6]

At the Aslan Cement Factory, workers stole materials like ethyl alcohol or bags from the factory for resale. A myriad of similar cases can be traced in the press and in court records. In a silk factory in Mahmutpaşa, women workers had been stealing kilos of silk and selling in the market for a long time. According to court minutes, a female worker in a sugar factory had been caught with a lot of sugar concealed under her clothes. Workers in the stamp factory in İstanbul stole stamps worth about 300 liras. In the factories of the Monopoly Administration in İzmir, workers stole alcohol, spirits and aniseed from barrels and replaced them with water. Shop workers also made use of the opportunity to steal goods. A storekeeper of the Karaağaç Plug Factory stole a grinder, drill, cap screw and screws and then passed them to his brother, also a worker in the factory, to

Illustration 8.1 Workers of Sümerbank Kayseri Textile Factory being searched for stolen goods

sell. Another storehouse clerk, working at a large grocery store in Galata, pilfered coffee, soap and many other items from his workplace.[7]

Apprentices, who seemed obedient to their masters owing to the bonds of loyalty, resorted to similar covert activities. In 1937, newspapers reported that the number of apprentices who stole from their masters was rising. This was the way, a newspaper noted, apprentices obtained pocket money for holidays (*bayram harçlığı*). The quest for barest survival drove female domestic workers such as maids and cleaners, who were recruited from the poorest families, to filch money, food, jewelry or clothes from homes in which they worked.[8]

Low-income civil servants also resorted to illegal self-help methods or, in moral terms, to corruption as a way to ameliorate their destitution. As Joseph Grew noted, the widespread corruption among Turkish civil servants was bred by low salaries. Like Grew, a public prosecutor, Reşat Tesal, recalls in his memoirs how low salaries led officials to such acts. In one case, Tesal had tried to save a poor state official who had committed embezzlement by finding mitigating causes. Embezzlement and pilferage cases involving low-salaried state officials reached epidemic proportions from the late 1920s with the economic crisis.[9]

The most common type of misappropriation was to secretly steal money belonging to the state. Many tax officials, bookkeepers, treasurers, postal officers, bank officials, municipality officials, debt enforcement officials and personnel of the Red Crescent and the Turkish Aviation Society were involved in embezzlement. In October 1936, a civil servant in İstanbul was arrested for stealing 17 liras from the municipality. In his defense, he stated that the poverty of his family with six children had led him to yield to temptation, and therefore he pleaded for mercy. In December 1938, a postal officer who had pilfered cash asserted at trial that he was unable to support his family on his salary.[10]

Changing Jobs, Absenteeism and High Labor Turnover

"In our country, the workers do not feel attachment to their jobs firmly. This may cause a great danger for the industry. A worker comes to the factory; we train him as an apprentice by paying him in our factories; he starts to work in the factory; he works for two or three months perfectly; but one morning we see nobody at the machine on the shop floor; in this way many leave the factories and return to their villages in groups."[11] The new prime minister, Celal Bayar, said these words in a parliamentary speech in 1937, addressing the shortage of permanent qualified workers due to absenteeism and temporary work, and the dangers this situation created for Turkish industry. His speech shows how much the labor turnover startled the government. Indeed, the labor turnover soared, curtailing productivity and alarming both the ruling circles and industrialists during the period.

Changing jobs when wages or working conditions became intolerable was an alternative to the aforementioned risky behaviors. Surely workers did not have the luxury to quit a job whenever they disliked it. Nevertheless, they often left as soon as opportunities arose for higher wages and easier job opportunities. Workers of peasant origin who maintained ties to agriculture especially had more room for maneuver. The strange working life in industry, characterized by strict discipline, dangerous and convoluted machines, serious accidents and impersonal relations stood in stark contrast to what even urban society was accustomed to. On top of these issues, low wages, lack of social security and epidemics that spread in crowded towns precipitated the high circulation of labor in industry.

Scholars have appraised the high rate of turnover as an unconscious floundering of workers, a result of their rural background and the prerequisites of seasonal industries. These explanations have some merit. In particular, workers in seasonal sectors left their jobs against their will. Hundreds of thousands of peasants worked in urban areas only until they saved a certain amount of money. Both factors contributed to the high turnover rates. On the other hand, a considerable portion of the turnover emanated from the sheer efforts of workers to find better working conditions. The peasant workers' tie to the land was not the sole reason for their reluctance to work permanently in industry. The most important reason was the repulsive labor conditions. Their ties to the land only enforced their bargaining power with the highly inhumane industrial production by allowing them to leave the factory whenever they could not endure. Absenteeism and high labor turnover rates, which increased during the 1930s, thus skyrocketed in the first half of the 1940s due to the social impact of World War II, which further aggravated working conditions and wages. Temporarily working in factories, for peasants or those urban workers who kept their connection with agriculture, meant a resistance to utter proletarianization. Short-term work in industry protected them from dispossession by enabling them to save money for debts, taxes and other urgent needs, as experienced in other industrializing countries.[12]

The peasants especially engaged in casual jobs as doorkeepers, cleaners, domestic servants, wage laborers, porters or street vendors in urban areas. A considerable number of these workers were peasants in acute need of cash who had left their agricultural work for a short period in search of temporary jobs owing to the pressure of high taxes or debts to moneylenders. Newspapers of the time and a report on the Turkish economy by foreign experts in 1933 and 1934 also confirm this. Throughout the late 1920s and especially the 1930s, government railway and highway projects provided temporary jobs for peasants. The foreign engineer of the Simeryol Company in Sivas complained that the workers, most of whom were peasants, stayed until they had saved some money and then fled back to their villages. Simeryol's manager said to a foreign journalist, "They save every piaster they can, and when they have enough to pay their taxes and buy a new suit and sugar and a few knick-knacks for their family, they say goodbye to us to go home again to their villages."[13]

Another job field peasants incessantly moved in and out of was the textile industry. Most workers in the Seyhan National Textile Factory and the Kayseri Textile Factory were peasants who often left the factory to resume harvesting or sowing. Almost half of the workers at the Seyhan National Textile Factory were smallholders. As a Turkish industrial expert complained, "a peasant comes to work in a factory, but too often, after a few years, the call of the land gets too strong and he goes home to his village." This was an important reason for the high labor turnover.[14]

Undoubtedly, working conditions were not attractive for either peasants or urban laborers. This was also an important factor that induced high labor circulation. At a later date, in 1949, the International Labor Organization argued that the primary cause of the high labor turnover in Turkish industry was not only the seasonal labor movement between agriculture and industry but also the poor working conditions, low wages and the absence of social security and of basic social services. Well aware of this situation, RPP deputies warned the government about the problems that led workers to quit frequently. The worse the working conditions were, the higher the absenteeism and turnover rates, as evidenced in coal mines. "Supplying enough workers for higher productivity," the deputies' report stated, "requires bearable working conditions based on the Labor Law." Sümerbank's own reports also admit that in existing working conditions, any enterprise could not expect workers to not leave the factory as soon as they found slightly higher pay or more favorable working conditions.[15]

Adana and Kayseri textile factories also suffered the instability of the labor force since most of the workers went back to their vineyards to harvest grapes in the summer. This was a way to supplement their low wages. It also served as a form of unemployment insurance, if they wanted to break with the highly disciplined and exhausting industrial work. In a large cotton factory in Tarsus, there was a high instability of labor due to dark and depressing workshops full of unsafe machines making a deafening noise. Bad treatment by foremen made matters worse. Therefore, whenever they saved some money or a better job opportunity arose, the workers left the factory. This drove employers crazy. Epidemics also distressed the workers. For instance, a malaria epidemic that plagued Kayseri and Denizli throughout the 1930s pushed workers to leave the textile factories and return to their villages.[16]

The aforementioned high labor turnover in Simeryol Sivas railroad construction was not only due to the peasants' strong desire to return to their villages after a few months working. The turnover was mostly due to the working conditions. Simeryol workers had complained several times about the company's indifference to their problems. A 1936 inspection report recorded that the workers lived in destitution. The low wages, unsanitary conditions, long working hours and short breaks caused constant complaints. Because the company delegated the housing and provisioning of workers to another company in return for a 6 percent share of the profit, the workers had to pay far more money for accommodations and foodstuffs. Distributing the monthly wages late, the railroad company kept the workers in debt to the provisioning company. The workers felt so exploited that they fled whenever they could. In the Aslan Cement Factory, the major problem factory management faced was absenteeism and high labor turnover. The workers' service record files tell us that this was related to their response to industrial discipline and tempo.[17]

Despite the scarcity of accurate figures, it is possible to draw a general conclusion from some data belonging to the public enterprises, which offered better conditions and higher wages. The total number of starting workers at the Sümerbank Kayseri Textile Factory was 19,761 from 1935 to 1950. This was seven times the total number of workers. Again, from 1937 to 1941, 11,272 workers had entered the Sümerbank Nazilli Textile Factory, about three and a half times more than the total staff of the factory. The turnover rate in the sugar factories reached 300 percent in 1940. In the Etibank Ergani Copper Enterprise, labor turnover was about 247 percent. This rate was 64.8 percent in the Bursa Woolen Cloth Factory. The workers of the Sümerbank's Defterdar Textile Factory and Beykoz Leather and Shoe Factory also frequently quit their jobs without permission.[18]

High labor circulation was the nightmare of manufacturers. It forced companies to rely on temporary novice workers instead of a qualified and permanent labor force, jeopardizing productivity. Indeed, total output remained far below the levels the government had targeted in the First Five-Year Industrial Plan between 1934 and 1939. Labor instability reached such acute levels that in 1935, the state railways decided to sell tickets at the reduced rate of 1.25 liras instead of 5 and 3 liras for passengers traveling to the industrial zones for work. Similarly, alarmed by high labor turnover, the textile factories in Kayseri and Adana sought to attract workers by providing them additional services like accommodations that included heating, electricity, laundry, running water and hot meals. Furthermore, toward the end of 1936, the Kayseri Textile Factory decided to distribute a pair of shoes and clothing once a year to all workers. Such measures continued in the following years. The Aslan Cement Factory took measures to control high labor turnover, including turning a blind eye to minor misdeeds – even pilferage. The management also avoided depriving disobedient and undisciplined workers of benefits such as wage increases and social services.[19]

In 1937, the prime minister's speech in the National Assembly underlined social measures such as providing housing, vocational education and sanitary conditions as prerequisites for the creation of a permanent labor force. That is, the high turnover would give a covert bargaining power to the workers by compelling the politicians and employers to appreciate the importance of basic social measures. Especially during World War II, soaring labor turnover would compel the government and employers to adopt new social policy measures or at least the idea of social policy, which ultimately culminated in comprehensive postwar social policy legislation that included the establishment of the Labor Ministry.[20]

Diversifying occupations was among the people's methods to curb deterioration in their economic conditions. The additional jobs they held were generally simple ones requiring no qualifications or capital. Even though these jobs marginally boosted their incomes, the importance of such incomes for people living on the edge of survival cannot be overestimated. Artisans hit by industrialization especially adjusted to changing conditions by shifting their business to more feasible fields. Upon losing their customers, saddlers and shoemakers, for instance, engaged primarily in repairing used and damaged leather goods. In 1934, *Esnaf Meslek Mecmuası* reported that changing jobs was common among low-income and self-employed workers. Due to the high cost of living, many people moved every day from one job to another. One of the most preferable jobs during the Great Depression was to open a small diner serving cheap and simple meals to impoverished customers. From 1927 to 1932, the number of such diners in İstanbul increased from 400 to 2,200. The main cause for this increase was the poor people's struggle for survival. Those who were recently unemployed or impoverished could open such places with just a small amount of capital, a gas range and a few dishes.[21]

Late payment of salaries and lack of social security pushed elementary school teachers to seek supplemental sources of income. Village teachers, for instance, shirked their duties and took up agricultural work together with the peasants. Sarkis Çerkezyan's mother, a teacher, had to work also as a house cleaner in order to supplement her family's income. Some impoverished teachers sold schoolbooks and stationery supplies. This practice was so widespread that booksellers in the towns complained that teachers were undermining their jobs. Preachers, whose economic status eroded under the republic, also picked up additional money by performing other spiritual rites. Some of them, just as teachers did, ran bookstores, sign-lettering businesses or groceries. Teaching the Quran or Arabic script clandestinely was among the main sources of income. Finally, the decrease in their economic standing led some to engage in sorcery, writing amulets or faith healing.[22]

Another way to earn extra money was street vending. On the streets of İstanbul alone, roughly 50,000 people reportedly made a living by peddling. The more the purchasing power of wages eroded, the more the number of street vendors expanded. In seasonal sectors like tobacco, workers lived by working as peddlers, shoe shiners or porters during the off seasons. Workers who were fired also held alternative jobs such as running coffeehouses or diners, working as wage laborers or trading sundries.[23]

Pursuing Rights

Writing to the Newspapers

When a tobacco warehouse owner named Mehmet Kavala laid off his workers in İzmit without any unemployment pay, a worker objected. Kavala's men attempted to beat the worker, but other workers intervened and threatened to write to the newspapers. Intimidated by this threat, Kavala agreed to pay workers enough additional money to last through the winter.[24] This instance best exemplifies the effect of submitting a diatribe against an entrepreneur to the press. Indeed, voicing demands and problems through writing to the press or the government was a widely used, efficient way for urban laborers to struggle for their rights and survival. Those who encountered a wrongdoing in daily life intimidated their adversaries by saying, "Do not make me write to the newspaper!" Indeed, since the press had become a primary channel through which public opinion reached the government, many turned to newspapers to express their opinions or to make their grievances visible to government authorities. Letter writers also expected newspapers' help and advice to overcome their problems.

Despite press censorship, which silenced direct political criticism, newspapers with large circulations gave space to citizens' letters. For the press, in the absence of a fully fledged network of reporters, such letters virtually constituted a channel of news. Therefore, selected letters touching on public grievances were published under the titles "Okuyucu Mektupları" ("Letters of the Readers"), "Halkın Sesi" ("The People's Voice"), "Halkın Köşesi" ("The People's Column"), "Karilerimizden Mektuplar" ("Letters from Our Readers") and "Kari Gözüyle" ("From the View of Readers"). These small columns served as platforms for people to express their frustrations or to publicize a malfeasance or wrongdoing so as to pressure employers and local administrators to concede their demands.

One of the main themes in these letters was delayed or unpaid wages. Many state officials and workers who had not been paid their salaries or wages for months demanded payment in this way. In their letters to *Cumhuriyet* in September 1929, teachers in Kemaliye and Urfa, for instance, demanded that their salaries, which had not been paid for five months, be paid as soon as possible. In May 1932, teachers in Konya also sent a letter complaining of long delays in payment. One month later, a group of teachers from Gaziantep wrote that they had not received their salaries for six months. Mosque employees who experienced the same hardship bombarded the newspapers to publicize their predicament of not receiving pay or receiving very low salaries for months.[25]

Factory workers raised their voices individually or collectively by writing to the press. In a letter to *Cumhuriyet* in January 1930, a worker in Karaağaç, whose wages had not been paid for months, complained of this situation. Similarly, writing to *Son Posta* in May 1932, Seyrisefain workers in Kasımpaşa asked why the company had not paid them for two months. In February 1934, workers of the Balya Karaaydın Mine Company reported to *Köroğlu* that the company had cut their wages sharply. A few years later, the same workers wrote to *Köroğlu* that they had been shortchanged by more than 100 percent. Although the company had promised to pay them 140 piasters a day, they had received only 60. The workers requested the newspaper call for the government's intervention in this violation of their rights.[26]

Submitting letters by visiting the newspaper offices personally was another method to augment their effect. In 1932, fourteen workers of the Bakırköy Textile Factory went to the office of *Son Posta* and submitted their complaint about the unpaid perks. They probably poured out their troubles to the editors and asked them to stress their problem in the newspaper. Many old retirees who had not received their pension or grant for months or years, aged workers or civil servants in deprivation of retirement rights, relatives of deceased civil servants and workers without any protection requesting pensions bombarded the newspapers with their emotional letters, complaining about how they had been ignored and cast aside by the state institutions and companies they had served for years.[27]

Another topic about which the letter writers complained the most was working conditions. Textile workers in Adana who worked hard for a minimum of twelve hours a day wrote to *Köroğlu* requesting it to call the attention of the state to their inhumane working conditions. In August 1932, workers at the tobacco warehouse of the Monopoly Administration in Samsun collectively wrote a diatribe to *Köroğlu* deploring the exhausting working hours in stuffy workrooms polluted with nicotine and poor treatment by merciless foremen. A group of chrysalis factory workers in Adapazarı also penned a letter to *Köroğlu* to express their criticisms of the eleven-hour workday that injured their bodies. Workers in Tavşanlı (Kütahya) chrome mines, by writing to the same newspaper, also declared concertedly their objection to the more than ten hours of very hard and dangerous daily work. Alpullu Sugar Factory workers, who believed their employer had violated their right to a weekend holiday, together penned a letter to a newspaper inviting the factory to observe the law.[28]

Last, just one of numerous examples, was the collective objection of Mersin dockworkers to the wage payment system of the dock company. The company was not paying wages in cash but giving only gift vouchers. This system was to the disadvantage of workers because the contracted groceries accepted these vouchers with a 10 percent deduction. The workers, complaining of the situation via a letter to the press, wanted to be paid in cash.[29]

Workers who had been fired without reason also wrote to the newspapers to criticize their arbitrary dismissals. A group of waiters employed in the Taksim Municipality Garden were fired after objecting to being pressed into additional jobs by their foremen. Upon their dismissal, they got into *Tan* in no time flat with a letter criticizing the garden administration. The newspaper published the letter with a comment supporting the waiters.[30]

Petitioning the Employers and the Government

Petitioning employers, relevant state administrators or politicians was the most common way to prompt them to take action. Concerns about wages and working conditions are paramount in these petitions. In March 1932, workers of the Seyrisefain Company, who had not received wages since January, wrote a petition to declare that they would not work until their accrued wages had been properly distributed. In the autumn of 1935, the Haliç Company, another navigation company in İstanbul, first froze the annual social aid it delivered to workers in kind such as clothing and shoes due to a financial bottleneck and then suspended its activities, laying off its employees without any compensation. The company personnel, petitioning the company directorate, objected to the cancellation of the social aid and demanded half its cash value. Then, the senior employees, who had worked in the company about twenty years, laid claim to unemployment compensation.[31]

Another example of pursuing a right via petitioning employers came from the security guards of İstanbul museums, who were seeking a wage hike. They collectively penned a petition addressed to the Directorate of

Illustration 8.2 Street petition writers (*arzuhâlci*)

İstanbul Museums arguing that they were paid only 25 liras per month, which did not meet the needs of their families, and asked for a raise.[32]

The service record files of workers kept by factory managers confirm that workers frequently submitted petitions to their companies. Burhaneddin Tezcan, a worker at a cement factory in İstanbul, stated in a petition that he and his father had loyally served the factory for years, but now he was in acute need of assistance from the factory in the form of a small wage hike of 2 piasters per hour. Many similar examples are found of petitions to factory managers.[33]

A dispute between the İzmir Port Company and dockworkers in July 1935 is a good example of workers' active use of petitioning as a negotiation strategy. The dispute arose from wage reductions and the piecework wage system disfavoring the workers. Hundreds of workers collectively petitioned the company's management to object to both. The next day, the management declared that they would find a middle way. Indeed, the company found a compromise with the workers by satisfying some demands.[34]

A great number of working people contacted the government directly by petitioning the National Assembly, party leadership, ministers, governors and party administrators. The number of petitions filed with the National Assembly's petition commission each year far exceeded the number sent to any other institution. The petitioners invited the lawmakers and the government to defend or boost their rights, implement the laws, keep their promises, take social policy measures and redress their grievances. Petitions to the top leadership were sometimes so effective that the leaders personally investigated the cases set forth by the petitioners. In a petition addressed to Atatürk himself, teachers in Kırşehir complained about delays in payment of their salaries. After hearing this, Atatürk first consulted the education minister and then, due to the minister's vague reply, went to Kırşehir right away, where he personally talked with the teachers about the problem.[35]

The RPP central administration was the most important beacon of hope for workers who had trouble with their employers. For instance, in 1935, a porter in Gemlik Customhouse was fired upon complaints from the Gemlik district governor and an RPP bureaucrat, without his statement being taken. The porter sued the administration, but the local court dismissed the case, declaring that the complainant had ignored his duty by leaving Gemlik frequently for İstanbul. Thereupon, in November 1935, the porter petitioned Recep Peker, the RPP general secretary. His petition described how he had fought in the Independence War with heart and soul. Then, he stated that the unjust treatment he had undergone had injured his family's honor. He had incurred the wrath of certain individuals in the Gemlik Aviation Society by reporting them to the government for corruption. The porter requested to be appointed to a position in İstanbul. Peker then sent an inspector to Gemlik to take the district governor and party administrator's statements. Upon his investigation, Peker decided that the porter should not have fallen victim to slander and ordered his immediate reemployment.[36]

In another case, porters in Büyükada who had accused the chief porter and administrators of the Porters' Association of corruption, appealed to the party general secretary via a petition in September 1936. They alleged that the chief porter, Hüsameddin, had unlawfully seized a certain portion of their incomes. His assistants Eyüp and Hızır, also salaried officials in the Porters' Association, had not professed to be porters in any way. Eyüp ran a coffeehouse and Hızır owned a restaurant. They treated porters who did not frequent their shops unfairly. The petitioners requested the party to prevent these injustices. The same year, the Sivas railway workers employed by Simeryol petitioned the party, complaining about unsanitary conditions, bad housing, exhausting overtime work and other abuses by the company. All of this dashed their hopes about the RPP's populist promises.[37]

In two related cases in İstanbul and İzmir, workers once again took collective action by petitioning the party. In 1936, right after the government took over the port monopolies in these cities, controversy arose over the vested rights of the employees. The government had ignored these rights, especially those of the dockworkers, by refusing to extend them to the new enterprise. However, in response to growing demands from the İstanbul port's employees, the government had to recognize their previous rights. But the İzmir port administration firmly resisted the port employees' demands for approval of rights acquired previously. Therefore, the employees of the İzmir port collectively petitioned the RPP administration, asking the party to include approval of their vested rights in the wish list of the party congress. Ultimately, they compelled the government to recognize their vested rights.[38]

Not only workers but also self-employed weavers in Anatolian towns sought the party's help by petitioning. In petitions to the party general secretary, handloom weavers in the Babadağ district of Isparta described how large industries and imported goods were hurting them. Unable to compete, they begged for assistance from the party and the government.[39] Artisans and their professional associations also sought aid from the party and the government through petitions.

Another official institution within close reach of the people was the provincial government. When faced with a problem, many turned to the governor or the Industrial Directorate (Sanayi Müdürlüğü). In June 1932, a newspaper reported that complaint petitions from workers to the Industrial Directorate had significantly increased in recent times. The dominant theme was delay in wage payments and adverse working conditions. Inundated by the petitions, the Directorate reportedly was carefully investigating these cases.[40]

A petition signed by 500 employees of a tobacco warehouse of the Monopoly Administration in İstanbul was submitted to the İstanbul governorship in person. It called for fewer working hours, better hygiene, safety, clean water, nutritious food and a ventilator to remove polluted air. At the end of negotiations, which the governorship mediated, the workers merely received a promise their requests would be taken seriously. In another instance, 900 workers in textile factories in İzmir who had been furloughed in January 1935 dispatched a collective petition to the İzmir governorship seeking reemployment or unemployment compensation. The government found the reasons of the employers invalid and the companies accepted that these workers would be rehired in the spring.[41]

Workers also did not hesitate to send petitions higher up the government hierarchy. They often wrote to the ministries with oversight of their occupational fields. Workers employed in tobacco factories, for example, complained of ill treatment by ruthless factory administrators to the Customs and Monopolies Ministry. In one instance, workers at the tobacco factory in İstanbul directed by the Monopoly Administration sent a petition to the minister, accusing certain foremen and administrators of sexual harassment. They called authorities to protect their honor against foremen who led females to prostitution by forcing them into having sex with their bosses.[42]

Railway workers petitioned the Public Works Ministry when they got into trouble with their employers. Indeed, construction companies exploited their workers to the last drop of their blood. One of these companies forced workers to sign a labor contract full of unfavorable terms. According to its terms, the company could employ the workers without payment for months and fire them without payment of accrued wages or any compensation. In a collective petition describing how unfair the contract was, the workers asked the Public Works Ministry to disentail the terms and conditions imposed by the company. However, their efforts did not succeed.[43]

In another case, the Public Works Ministry declared that all money accumulated in the mutual assistance fund of the nationalized Eastern Railways Company would be distributed to company workers. However, the ministry later abandoned this idea. Workers criticized this decision and called on the minister, Ali Çetinkaya, to fulfill his promise. They also injected some humor, as shown by the following satirical poem.[44]

Çok sevindik hayal kurduk bekledik aydan aya
Ümitlerimiz boşa çıktı kaldık bakın hep yaya
İkramiye vaadi ile cebimizdekini harcadık
Halimizi arzedelim bari Çetinkaya'ya

We got very happy, dreamt and waited for months
Our hopes came to nothing, look, how we all are stranded
With the promise of bonus, we spent what we had in our pockets
Let us submit our situation to Çetinkaya at least

The letter writers mostly made use of a rhetorical language to convince bureaucrats of the validity of their arguments. Invoking the nationalist and populist discourse and adorning their petitions with the principles of the regime, they skillfully legitimated and enhanced their claims. This did not mean they were fully adherent to the government. On the contrary, they challenged it subtly from within by inviting the authorities to keep their promises and act in accordance with the principles they parroted. The language of the petitions was in itself a dynamic of working-class struggle. They took advantage of the multifarious implications of concepts in language by appropriating the official discourse for their particular causes.

Some petitioners recounted how they had sacrificed their family members to the national cause. One old woman introduced herself as a woman of the motherland whose father and two sons had been martyred in World War I and the Independence War. Arguing that she therefore deserved to live comfortably in her remaining years, she pleaded with the government to help her financially.[45] Nuri Aksel, a night watchman in a gunpowder depot, requested social aid from the government to supplement his paltry wages. He stated poignantly that although he had made sacrifices for the sake of his country in the Independence War, he was not able to support the six children he was raising for the growth of the nation. In another letter, an ex-official of a timber factory in Ayancık complained that although he was an ethnic Turk who had served in the National Forces (Kuvâyı Milliye) during the Independence War and been tortured by the enemy, his employer had replaced him with a man of Armenian origin. He asked the "nationalist and Turkish" government to correct this wrong by reappointing him to his previous post. In a petition addressed to Atatürk, a chef from Nazilli wanted to be awarded the Independence Medal owing to his service in the Independence War. He also pleaded with Atatürk to find his son employment as a bank clerk. In so doing, he did not forget to eulogize Atatürk, expressing his respect and love with reverential words such as "worshipful" (*mübeccel*) and "honorable." Workers routinely pretended to adopt the hegemonic discourse that exalted the president and the government. İstanbul tramway workers, whose 1928 strike was put down, placed their hopes in "the people's government" (*halk hükümeti*). They requested help from Atatürk via a letter stating how they trusted his "great sublimity."[46]

Appropriating the Laws

Although they resorted to the legal system less frequently, working people, especially industrial workers, also individually or collectively sued employers who violated their rights. Zonguldak dockworkers were among them, filing suit several times against their employers as well as against the coal miners' union. On December 15, 1932, a dockworker named Hüseyinoğlu Hasan sued the Ereğli Coal Mines Enterprise for unlawfully deducting a premium from his wages. Upon dismissal of the case by the local court in Zonguldak, the worker filed an appeal. Ultimately, the Supreme Court reversed the judgment of the local court, finding the appellant right.[47]

Based on this case, in April 1935, the dockworkers of the Zonguldak port brought an action against the coal miners' union. The workers had long disliked the union because it represented the interests of the mining companies rather than those of the workers. The union's director was the director of the Enterprise. Therefore, the union remained fully indifferent to the problems of the workers. By the spring of 1936, a big dispute had erupted between the union and the dock-workers over an 8 percent premium the union took from the workers' wages. In the past, there had been two workers' organizations, the Zonguldak Dockworkers' Association and the Zonguldak Ereğli Coal Miners' Union. The former had all along been collecting 8 percent premiums from its workers while the latter had only been collecting 2 percent. When the two organizations merged, the union continued to cut 8 percent of the dockworkers' wages, but only 2 percent of those of coal miners. The dockworkers, claiming this was unfair, demanded the union pay back the excess premiums to the dockworkers. The second issue was the union's support for the government's economic plan to keep down the costs of the transportation of coal through the reduction of the wages. This was the last straw for the dockworkers, and finally they filed a lawsuit against the union, demanding it pay back some part of money collected unfairly. The local Zonguldak court dropped the case. Nevertheless, the dockworkers went for an appeal. After deeper investigation, the Supreme Court overturned the decision of the Zonguldak court and ordered the defendant to pay 1,000,000 liras to the dockworkers. However, the union passively resisted this order by delaying payment. The dockworkers subsequently petitioned the general secretary of the RPP, persuading him to charge two inspectors to investigate the matter.[48] I could not find any information about what happened thereafter. Yet it is obvious that whether they won or lost, the workers defended their legal rights fervently.

Zonguldak coalminers and dockworkers also fought for overtime payments. The Enterprise often ignored the payment of overtime wages, which led coalminers and dockworkers to sue. Workers injured due to work accidents also sought compensation by bringing suit against the Enterprise. Even though the local court usually dismissed the lawsuits, the workers did not hesitate to appeal, and some managed to win reversals. A ship worker who was severely injured due to a defect in the crane of the ship filed a claim for damages of 10,000 liras against the Haliç Company. Similarly, a worker discharged for no reason by the İstanbul Tramway Company appealed to the court.[49]

Handloom weavers also sought their rights through legal means. In one case, a group of weavers working at handlooms in their own homes for a textile factory sued the factory, which had refused the weavers' demands for one day off per week by disregarding the Weekend Vacation Law. The local court ruled that the law did not include those who worked at handlooms in their homes. Thereupon, the weavers appealed, but the Supreme Court affirmed the local court's decision.[50]

After the Labor Law went into force on June 15, 1937, workers attempted to benefit from its provisions. According to the law, individual or collective labor disputes were to be settled through a reconciliation process led by governmental organs. The first stage required workers to discuss the problem with their employers through a committee of worker representatives. If no agreement was reached, the next stages were the provincial and then the national arbitral boards of appeal. For the control and inspection of the implementation of the law, the government established labor bureaus directly linked to the Economy Ministry.[51]

The Labor Law accelerated workers' attempts to demand that employers regulate working conditions in accordance with the law. The employers complained that their employees, who had been submissive before the enactment of the law, began to call them to account over many issues. The labor bureaus were soon overwhelmed by applications. Thousands of labor disputes flooded into the labor bureaus within a year and a half after the law went into effect. Some employers were taken to court or forced to implement the provisions of the Labor Law.[52]

In the face of this pressure the Economy Ministry issued the Regulation about the Reconciliation of Labor Disputes and Arbitration in March 1939. It introduced a more bureaucratic reconciliation mechanism for collective disputes. Following the promulgation of the regulation, the first big labor dispute erupted at the İzmir Tramway and Electricity Turkish Joint-Stock Company. The company had cancelled some social benefit provisions three years previously. In response, the workers had resorted to the reconciliation procedures. In the end a resolution was reached that satisfied the workers with recognition of paid leave of absence, a paid day of rest and a shorter workday.[53]

The following case also demonstrates how the workers appropriated the Labor Law in order to legitimate their protests. In a leather factory in Adana, workers, upon the rejection of their demands for an eight-hour workday and betterment of workplace conditions in accordance with the Labor Law, stopped work. The factory owner declared the workers were striking illegally and called the police. However, this time, in accordance with the Labor Law, labor bureau inspectors accompanied the police. After a quick investigation, the inspectors concluded there had been no strike and the Labor Bureau issued an official warning to the factory.[54]

Another example of appropriation of the Labor Law was a collective action by the Flemenk Tobacco Warehouse workers in 1938. This was one of the biggest tobacco companies in İstanbul, employing roughly 800 workers. The workers lacked basic social rights and facilities and wages were too low. After passage of the Labor Law, the workers, whose awareness of social rights had risen, submitted their requests for wage hikes, free lunches and paid weekend vacations to the company. After the negotiations, the management accepted most of the workers' demands.[55]

Struggles against or through Professional Associations

Despite the decline in handicraft production since the nineteenth century, artisans had not resigned themselves to their fate. Many had survived by resisting or adapting to European capitalism. They had also forced the government to take action in their favor via petitioning or other means of self-defense. In the 1930s, the rise of domestic industry and the ongoing integration, even though slowing down, with the world economy hit craftspeople once again. The artisans were not swept aside, but they obviously faced important problems to which they actively responded. During the interwar period, not only Turkey but also other parts of the preindustrial world invaded by imported goods from Europe and Japan witnessed rising discontent among artisans. Tens of thousands of them in Aleppo in the early 1930s, for example, rallied in mass demonstrations against imported textiles. In the footwear industry, workers and artisans protested the importation of ready-made items from the Czechoslovak firm Bata.[56]

In Turkey, artisans resorted to several methods of survival. Like other labor groups, they widely used petitions. Artisans' associations also played a key role in this regard. Despite their inherent flaws, these organizations were not merely passive administrative tools to collect taxes and dues, supervise labor and maintain professional standards. Sometimes they formed the basis of resistance to the adverse effects of industrial production and penetration of imported manufactures.

The experiences of shoemakers give us an idea of the big picture. Turkish shoemakers shared the fate of neighboring Syrian shoemakers, who rallied at street demonstrations against imported shoes driving them into extinction. However, the newly emerging Turkish footwear factories, owned by the government, were under state protection. Massive protests by Turkish shoemakers was very risky, and therefore absent. Yet the shoemakers, making use of available means, resisted that Sümerbank items and imported shoes gradually pushed them out of business. Lobbying through their professional organization was one important way. According to the chair of the Shoemakers' Association, the factories producing cheap rubber items were damaging not only the small shoemakers but also tanners and saddlers as suppliers and users of processed leather. According to the shoemakers, at this rate, shoemaking and other related crafts would die out completely.[57] Subsequently, the Shoemakers' Association petitioned the government to protect shoemakers against cheaper industrial and imported shoes. In June 1932, together with the Saddlers' Association, it demanded that the government stop the importation of products made from rubber. As a result, in part of their active lobbying and petitioning, in 1934 the Economy Ministry levied a consumption tax of 150 piasters per kilo on rubber shoes and 250 piasters per kilo of rubber. On the other hand, the government withdrew the tax on rubber to 150 piasters the next year. The Shoemakers' Association's objection to this came to no fruition this time.[58]

On the other hand, although big industry had put thousands of shoemakers out of business, about 20,000 shoemakers in İstanbul alone endeavored to compete by producing much cheaper shoes. This competition required them to keep costs down through intensive labor. If the need arose, they did not hesitate to put their wives and children to work from dawn till dusk. Indeed, four shoe factories in İstanbul went out of business in the face of this zealous competition from craft production in 1934.[59]

Industrialization's other victim was some 15,000 carriage drivers hard hit by mechanization of transportation. They too pushed their professional organization to save their jobs from extinction, and it submitted a petition asking the government to prevent the imminent termination of the carriage profession. The carriage drivers demanded a regulation banning lorries from carrying less than a minimum authorized weight. They argued that, as domestic products, carriages deserved to be protected against lorries and cabs, which were made outside the country.[60]

Another group of low-income people in transportation service was taxi drivers, most of whom were poor wage earners. Their occupational organization was the Drivers' Association. In 1920s, before the Workers' Advancement Society was shuttered, the association was not under the hegemony of rich car owners. When İstanbul drivers went on strike in the mid-1920s, the WAS supported the strike actively. However, after the RPP began to penetrate professional associations by liquidating the WAS, the Drivers' Association, like many others, began to be controlled by well-to-do RPP-affiliated members of the profession. This dominant group consisted of taxi owners. They continued to make their drivers work up to eighteen hours a day. Waged drivers therefore frequently came into conflict with taxi owners over wages, working hours and the weekly rest day, and became convinced that the association did not represent their interests. Many believed that they needed a more class-specific organization to fight for their rights. Accordingly, drivers challenged taxi owners' control of the association from within. In 1935, by means of effective petitioning, drivers compelled the Drivers' Association to recognize a few basic rights such as a shorter workday and one paid day of rest per week. Their resistance was so efficient that the taxi owners considered establishing a different association.[61]

The Tanners' Association, ostensibly representing all tanners, was also not free from internal conflicts of interest. The association included two antagonistic groups: a limited number of big capitalist tanners who had managerial control, and more than 100 small-scale traditional tanners known as Black Tanners (Kara Tabaklar). The latter outnumbered the former, but they were not strong in the administration. The fierce competition of small tanners who took advantage of processing cheaper imported inputs caused a significant decrease in the price of leather by 1932. Thereupon the capitalist tanners who headed the association called on the government to raise the tariff rates not only on leather products but also on all cheap inputs widely used by small tanners. Undoubtedly, the protection from the cheaper leather and rubber commodities of Europe was to the benefit of the small tanners too, but the association's demand for an increase in customs duties on cheap inputs ran counter to their interests. Therefore, the proposal of the association sparked a debate among tanners, which led the small tanners to object to this proposal.[62]

Some class-specific professional associations protected their members against employers. The Cooks' and Waiters' Association was a more homogenous organization. It vigorously supported particularly waiters in their struggle against restaurant owners. In June 1935, restaurant owners and waiters were embroiled in a sharp dispute over wages and tips. The chair of the association officially petitioned the government and the press, declaring the restaurant owners had unjustly appropriated tips amounting to 59,000 liras per year. The Restaurant Owners' Association objected that the employers had cut only 20 percent of the tips in order to provide the waiters with hot meals. Upon this debate, waiters presented their case to the press and the government. According to one waiter, the employers did not permit waiters to keep the 10 percent tips they earned from customers. The employers seized the tips on the pretext that they would compensate for losses such as broken glasses, dishes and free lunch for waiters.[63]

Bakery workers' associations in İzmir and İstanbul were also more class-specific and defended the rights of their members against bakery owners. Dough kneaders and bread bakers were generally forced to work up to sixteen hours a day for wages that were disproportionally low, around 5 liras per week. Apprentices were perhaps the most helpless, working hard in return for a few loaves of bread or a few piasters. None of them had social guarantees in case of layoffs or work accidents. The İstanbul Bread Makers' Association, petitioning the press and the government, publicly declared that bakery workers urgently needed a raise in wages and better working conditions. The İzmir Bread Makers' Association had gone beyond petitioning by bringing the strike option up for discussion on May 11, 1933, in a meeting at which an RPP inspector was present. Workers planned a sit-down strike, which would leave the public short of bread for a day and thereby draw attention to their problems. However, the warnings of the party inspector about the risk of a police attack and legal prosecution dissuaded them from striking. The inspector noted in his report that unless the sufferings of these workers were relieved, they would go on strike sooner or later.

The same inspector also reported widespread grumbling among printers in İzmir. The printers' voice was expressed by the Printing House Workers' Association. In the first months of 1933, several disputes arose between the association and printing house owners over squalid working conditions and poor wages. The association decided that its members would stop working in printing houses that mistreated workers. It also denounced such printing houses to the government. Then the association decided to put the strike option to a vote. After weighing the advantages and disadvantages of a strike, the association committee changed its mind in a meeting on May 14, 1933. However, as the party inspector underlined in his report, printing house workers' struggle for humane working conditions would continue as long as these miserable conditions remained unchanged.[64]

Consequently, the authoritarian polity, decrease of the urban skilled workforce and an increase in the number of peasants in the labor force shaped working-class politics. If possible, workers relied more on nonconfrontational forms of resistance and protest. Undoubtedly, higher literacy, closer proximity to the bureaucracy and the legacy of labor unionism gave workers opportunity to use more formal means like petitioning, suing and organizations, as compared to peasants. However, the peasants filled the ranks of the workforce and imbued the repertoire of urban laborers' action with the peasants' political culture based on much subtler and more covert ways. Many workers' ongoing contact with agriculture allowed them to exit industrial work whenever it was unbearable. Temporary work in industry enabled them to resist dispossession by providing cash for their urgent needs like paying taxes, debts or bride prices. Changing jobs as an exit strategy in the face of tough working conditions or ruinous wages was also common among urban workers. The result was enormous labor turnover, which had far-reaching implications such as falling productivity and rising instability in the industrial labor force. That is, the working people's struggle for survival limited the capacity of the new republic to fashion a stable and productive labor force. This situation was aggravated by more direct threats like physical violence toward employers and sudden walkouts. All these further alarmed the government and employers, compelling them to give concessions, albeit limited, to the workforce and to consider social policies.

9 | Violence, Protests and Walkouts

Under an authoritarian regime that prohibited strikes, working people often resorted to daily, spur-of-the-moment protests. Despite the ban on strikes, workers adroitly took actions resembling strike such as abruptly stopping work, coming to blows with employers and foremen, walking off the job or staging protest marches in the streets and in front of government buildings. Often the evidence offers no indication of direct political intent behind such acts. These acts, which directly brought no positive result in many cases, were not completely ineffective. The tragic incidents and the decrease in productivity that the working people's struggle and resistance engendered were intimidating to employers and could directly or indirectly force them to offer concessions to their workers.

Threatening and Attacking Foremen and Employers

Scholars have generally emphasized how the labor force was exposed to oppression during the first two decades of the republic. How workers used methods, which comprised open protests and even violence against employers, remains a less well-known aspect of their experience. Actual or threatened violence was a widespread tool of workers' resistance. The primary targets were foremen and workplace managers. Workers occasionally targeted company owners who were directly involved in disputes.

Foremen, having the utmost authority over workers' lives, particularly in hiring, firing and fining, were the most hated group on the shop floor. Overseeing productivity was also incumbent on them. They were authorized to regulate working hours and payroll issues, which made them representatives of the bosses in the eyes of the rank and file. Workers generally viewed foremen as "greedy servants," "ass-kisser agents of the bosses" and "pawns of the employers" who wanted the workers to work harder and imposed fines on them at every

178

opportunity. Many foremen, who were paid better, did not see themselves as in the same boat with workers.[1]

Disputes over working hours, wages and treatment of workers
ignited fierce fights, which could end in the police station. Workplace
brawls were so common that workers taught each other boxing tactics
and how to defend themselves in a fight. Showing their aggressiveness
through gestures such as clenching fists, knitting brows and dirty looks
were also tactics workers used to frighten foremen and employers and
thereby compel them to compromise. Memoirs by workers offer
insights into the evolution of such fights and brawls. For instance,
upon the firing of twenty workers from a tobacco factory, a fistfight
broke out in which workers beat up the foremen and their helpers.
Workers were especially responsive to bad treatment of female workers. In such cases, male workers did not hesitate to take a stand against
cruel foremen. In Bursa, tobacco workers beat a foreman who had
insulted women workers.[2]

Female workers also did not hesitate to attack merciless foremen. In
one case, the foreman of the tobacco warehouse of Bordalı Ahmet in
İzmir had banned drinking water during shifts and kicked a pregnant
Kurdish woman who drank water secretly. Seeing the woman fall to the
ground in pain, women workers assailed the foreman with blows. Then
they suddenly staged a protest by marching and shouting in the streets.[3]

Workers of peasant origin especially deeply resented the strict industrial discipline and frequently attacked foremen who tried to impose it.
At the Sümerbank Kayseri Textile Factory, where workers of peasant
origin were employed, the workers attacked foremen so often that "not
a single day goes by without a riot," said the factory manager. Unpaid
or underpaid laborers attacked those they deemed responsible for their
economic situation. Adnan Binyazar recorded in his childhood memoirs, for instance, that at a small glass factory where he worked, angry
workers who had not been paid for months assaulted the employer,
directors and foremen before quitting their jobs.[4]

Sometimes, workers who had been fired threatened foremen to hire
them back or face dire consequences. Their threats were quite functional in reemployment. Indeed, many foremen and factory managers
who were scared of a possible attack rehired them even when they did
not need additional workers. A considerable number of workers went
beyond beating and savaged more severely those who had taken their
bread from their mouths. Such cases seem to have increased in

frequency during the economic crisis, which sharpened economic conflict. A worker, Hüseyin, who had been fired by his foremen, Halil and Muhittin, stabbed them to death. Two tobacco workers in İstanbul severely wounded their boss, David Efendi, because of a disagreement. In another case, the chief porter at the Hasır seaport in İstanbul, Pötürgeli Mustafa, stabbed foreman Ahmet Ağa to death for refusing his pleas for reemployment. Like Mustafa, Kürt Memet, who went hungry after being fired and sought repeatedly to be rehired, ultimately shot the foreman dead. In İzmir, a worker fired by his company followed his boss home and stabbed him to death. Another worker, named Abdullah, fired from the Munitions Factory in Ankara, stabbed the factory director to death when his objections fell on deaf ears. In another incident, a worker named Ziya in a tobacco warehouse in Kantarcı, who was dismissed and unable to find work elsewhere, continuously asked for work from his former foreman, Ahmet Efendi. Upon being rejected at every turn, Ziya went mad and murdered Ahmet Efendi. In an intriguing event, three workers, Rahmi, İbrahim and Nebi, at the tobacco factory of the Monopoly Administration in İstanbul, planned to dynamite the factory but were caught. According to the statement they gave at the police station, they wanted revenge on the factory management for imposing unfair fines on them.[5]

As a result of pressure over labor movement and the socioeconomic and cultural characteristics of the labor force, individual protests were ascent. The workers' individual grievances and protests, which came together and gained spontaneous collectivity on shop floors, triggered bigger and more collective tumultuous events.

Workplace Fights and Walkouts

Strikes well prepared by activist workers and unions had decreased as the government had ruled out labor organizations and the left in the second half of the 1920s. Yet workers did not give up collective struggle; instead, they adjusted their actions to the realities of the political landscape. The workers brought the battle to a new front, that of everyday life, by staging unannounced and unorganized walkouts and protests. Conventional accounts of Turkey's labor history have often focused on the strike as an organized action engineered by left-wing parties or unions, and paid little attention to everyday and informal forms of strikes that manifested as sudden walkouts.[6] The collective struggle of the working class in this or that way did not come to a halt either in the 1920s or in the 1930s even after the liquidation of communist intellectuals and the WAS. Actually, most of the strikes that occurred in the mid- and late 1920s had not been prepared by the left. The ruling circles often characterized every worker resistance as communist intrigue in order to delegitimize them. In fact, the Communist Party of Turkey (CPT), as the sole communist organization, was illegal and handicapped by internal rifts and police surveillance. A report by the American intelligence agency noted that strikes by İzmir tobacco workers and Adana railway workers in 1927 were not attributable to communists. Communist activists were even unaware of grassroots conflicts between workers and employers in factories. Regarding the walkout of Defterdar Feshane Textile Factory workers in 1932, *Kızıl İstanbul*, the publication of the CPT, wrote that neither the CPT nor the communist workers were behind it. Likewise, according to police reports, a communist organization did not take part in bargemen's resistance to the İstanbul Port Monopoly Company in January 1927, the bloodiest clash between labor and capital in the interwar period. This firm resistance lasted for weeks and caused casualties among the bargemen and the police. That is, the socialist movement had already lost its vibrancy of the armistice period, but this did not mean workers' struggles stagnated.[7]

From the beginning of the Independence War to the proclamation of the republic in 1923, Turkey witnessed a wave of strikes.[8] This wave continued immediately after the establishment of the republic. Strikes unfolded in mid-1923 in İstanbul, İzmir, Zonguldak and other cities. Coal miners in Ereğli went on strike three times in the summer of 1923. Bomonti brewery workers followed them. At the same time, hundreds of Oriental Textile Factory workers, 4,000 fig-processing workers in İzmir and İzmir-Aydın railway workers stopped work. In September, printing house and textile factory workers mounted a resistance for their basic rights. Then workers of the Eastern Railway Company went on strike in November for higher wages, a shorter workday, improvement of working conditions, paid vacation and free medical care. Strikes forced the Economy Ministry and companies to implement a few social measures. It was partly in reaction to such strikes that the government put labor legislation on its agenda.

Interestingly, the existing labor unions and associations opposed some of these strikes. During the İzmir-Aydın railway workers' strike, the president of the Aydın Railway Workers' Union tried to prevent the workers from striking. Likewise, the İstanbul Labor Union opposed the strike by printing house workers on the grounds that they were paid much better than workers in other sectors. However, the workers' strikes continued in the first years of the republic, no matter that the left and labor organizations were weak or suppressed. In 1924, black-smiths in Adana protested heavy taxes. Cocoon-processing workers went on strike for three days demanding a raise. Both groups achieved their goals. In July 1924, tramway workers in İstanbul protested the dismissal of their worker friends, then postal workers went on strike for higher wages. Around the same time, female tobacco workers in Ortaköy protested unsanitary working conditions. In August, a conflict arose between railway workers and the Eastern Railway Company. In November, workers of the İstanbul municipality demanded a paid day off per week. This strike wave compelled the ruling circles to make concessions to the workers like promulgation of the Weekend Vacation Law in 1924.[9]

The workers' resistance continued the next year, although the social-ists and labor activism were further paralyzed with the Maintenance of Order Law in March 1925 to quell the Kurdish and Islamist Sheikh Said Rebellion. Though the left blamed the rebellion as reactionary and supported its suppression, the security measures taken against this rising also were used to oppress all opponents, including the left and labor activists. At the beginning of 1925, tramway workers, flour mill workers and employees of gas companies in İstanbul came out on several walkouts demanding higher wages, fewer working hours, better working conditions and a paid weekend holiday. Again, in July and August, there were protests and work stoppages by telegraphers in Samsun, Adana and Erzurum. Then slaughterhouse workers in İstanbul stopped work for one day. The same year, workers in the private Şirket-i Hayriye ferry company in İstanbul went on strike. In Zonguldak, coal miners staged about ten strikes in 1925 in which thousands of workers participated. Among the strikes of 1925, a walkout by tobacco warehouse workers in Tokat forced the company to accept the workers' demand for a wage increase of 50 percent.[10]

In 1926, the frequency of workers' open protests decreased once all oppositional activity was banned after the Sheikh Said Rebellion. The major event that year was the Soma-Bandırma railroad workers' strike in the summer. Workers collected 12,000 signatures supporting their cause and submitted them to the government. After ten days, the workers ended the strike with a slight wage increase.[11]

The working class entered the year 1927 with new collective actions. In January, bargemen of İstanbul ports refused to work for the İstanbul Port Company due to a 15 percent cut in wages. Three thousand of them besieged the scows belonging to the company. The director of the company, Ahmet Hamdi Başar, noted in his memoirs how he had felt helpless in the face of the bargemen's resistance. More than 100 police officers clashed with striking bargemen armed with sticks and hooks. The police forces, which faced the strikers' firm resistance, were reinforced by gendarmes and firefighters. The resistance of the bargemen ended when the police fired into the crowd during the third week of the strike. Fifteen bargemen and five policemen died and many were wounded. The police arrested more than 300 strikers.[12]

In another instance, more than 3,000 tobacco warehouse workers in İstanbul came out on strike in May 1927. The fear that the strike would encourage workers in other public enterprises to also go on strike led the government to meet the strikers' demands by increasing daily wages by 20 piasters. Only one month later, the railway workers of Adana submitted several demands to the Eastern Railway Company, including an eight-hour workday, one weekly paid day of rest, a paid annual vacation, the right of collective bargaining, free medical service, control over production and a labor law. Upon the refusal of such demands on August 9, the workers went on strike. The workers used all possible means to win their cause. Lying down on the rails, the frenzied crowd held up the trains and fought with the police, strikebreakers and gendarmerie several times. The wives of demonstrators joined their husbands in their fight. The involvement of wives, other family members and neighbors in the strike made the situation more delicate for the security forces. When the security forces tried to force the women from the rails, the strikers made use of the power of the rumor about the abuse of women, which spread like wildfire and led the neighboring villages to support the workers' resistance. Moreover, they availed themselves of the official nationalist rhetoric by asserting that they were "Turkish workers" struggling to protect the "Turkish people" from exploitation by the foreign-owned company. When the security forces offended them, the women shouted slogans like "Long live the republic!" and "May God be pleased with the republic!" to show their commitment to the government. Finally, the strikers built solidarity with other groups of laborers in Adana such as shoemakers, black-smiths, printing house workers and carpenters. This resistance did not yield the desired results in the short term. The railway workers accepted a small wage increase and other conditions proposed by the company. A few months later, in October, the government initiated a new antic-ommunist campaign to divert public attention from the labor question and to discourage workers from going on strike.[13]

In 1928, automobile body workers in Adapazarı, tramway, textile and tobacco workers in İstanbul, and Eastern Railway Company work-ers all rose up. Some of their actions resulted in full or partial success. The İstanbul tramway workers' strike, supported by the WAS, gained widespread public attention. On August 26, the tramway workers presented to the governorship and the Tramway Company a detailed list of demands, including a 50 percent raise, a bonus payment each year, an eight-hour workday, overtime payment, paid vacations, unemployment compensation, free medical service, toilets and water fountains in terminal stations and special clothes. The company agreed to negotiate. However, upon the breakdown of negotiations, the work-ers marched in the streets on October 7. According to police reports, despite the work stoppage, the tramways continued to operate without interruption, owing to "loyal workers" bought by the company. Consequently, the striking workers, most of whom were fired, gave up the strike on October 15 and asked the government's help. The company rehired some of the fired workers. The remaining discharged workers wrote a collective letter addressed to Atatürk. Employing the nationalist and populist discourse of the regime and venerating Atatürk as the "soul of the people," the workers asked him for help. Yet most of the work stoppages in 1928 engendered higher wages, albeit slightly, and some small concessions. On the other hand, these collective actions paved the way for the closure of the WAS in 1928, which played a role in the organization of some strikes. This, however, did not put a stop to worker resistance. In 1929, workers at a tobacco warehouse in Beşiktaş fought with foremen and employer-allied workers. The protesting workers were taken to the police station, whereupon they demanded labor legislation.[14]

Workers' protests and collective actions persisted during the next decade in spite of the growing authoritarianism. The establishment of the FRP in 1930 aroused great expectations among labor. The arrival of opposition leader Fethi Okyar in İzmir created a great excitement among workers. Fig-processing workers, vineyard laborers and dockworkers staged walkouts in August and September. The dockworkers' demonstrations turned into a tumult with the intervention of the police and gendarmerie. About 2,000 workers marched in the main street and gathered in front of the hotel where the opposition leader was staying. Okyar was welcomed with cheers by workers wherever he went in his western Anatolian tour. In İstanbul, huge crowds including workers who saw the FRP as a harbinger of good days also flocked into the streets. During Okyar's visit to İstanbul, tobacco workers, tramway and railway workers, dockworkers, bargemen and workers from many other sectors walked along Beyoğlu shouting slogans like "Long live Fethi Bey!" but they did not neglect to show their attachment to the regime, shouting, "Long live the republic!"[15] Dismayed by this great show of interest by workers as well as other discontented groups, the RPP forced Okyar to dissolve the FRP within three months. From then on, the RPP turned into an unrivaled single-party government, but nevertheless this did not bring an end to working-class struggle.

After several months of silence, in July 1931, employees of the Ortaköy tobacco factories took a strike action. Galata tobacco warehouse workers followed them in August. In December 1931, Defterdar Textile Factory workers protested wage cuts. Wavering between going on strike and petitioning, workers decided to take their demands to the factory administration collectively. At the beginning of 1932, workers in İzmir's tobacco warehouses and of the Seyrisefain Company staged walkouts. In İstanbul, a protest by Seyrisefain workers, particularly engine department workers, over the withholding of wages lasted from March to May. On April 12, the workers of steamships decided not to work until they received pay. The company broke the resistance by hiring new workers. Upon this, petitioning the newspapers and the government, which pressured the company, the striking workers finally obtained their accrued wages.[16]

As a precaution against labor unrest as well as for other reasons, the government began to consider a labor law and at the same time increased the dose of repressive measures in 1932. However, coercion did not avert labor protests. Nor did populist discourse delude workers. Labor disputes in similar forms continued to erupt even during the rest of the 1930s. In 1933, Balya-Karaaydın miners attempted a work stoppage as a protest for better working conditions and a wage increase. Ginneries in Adana witnessed several tumultuous incidents caused by the rejection of workers' wage demands, which mostly ended with police intervention. The same year, tobacco workers who had heard of an English company's rush order from their warehouse turned this foreign demand into an opportunity to demand a raise by stopping work. The employer, fearing an interruption of production, accepted negotiation, by which the workers got a 10-piaster increase in daily wages.[17]

The most remarkable incident of 1934 occurred in the İzmir Halkapınar Serge Factory of the Orient Carpet Company in September. A change in the wage system had brought wages down by 30 percent and spurred protest among workers. More than 100 workers petitioned the factory management. Upon the refusal of their demands, the workers occupied the factory. After police forces entered the factory, the workers headed for the İzmir RPP branch to ask for help. Protests and incidents inside and outside the factory lasted for a week, during which workers blocked the operations of weaving looms.[18]

The following year's first quarter witnessed two striking events. In March 1935, dockworkers at the coal depot in Kuruçeşme, İstanbul, demanded a wage hike. The rejection of this demand provoked a walk-out. Toward the end of that month, at a tobacco warehouse in Tophane owned by the Adapazarı Turkish Trade Bank, a walkout occurred. That summer, another firm resistance occurred in the Nemlizade's Tobacco Warehouse Company in Üsküdar, owned by Mithat Nemli, the chair of the İstanbul Chamber of Commerce. The employer's negative response to the workers' demand for a 10-piaster raise in daily wages prompted a work stoppage. Just after the protest began, the police surrounded the warehouse. Fights with stones and sticks between striking workers and foremen, guards and workers siding with the boss inside the warehouse grew into a mass demonstration in Sultanahmet Square, where clashes continued. Simultaneously, the strikers took their concerns in person to Yunus Nadi, the chief editor and owner of the *Cumhuriyet*. Finally, in the face of the unyielding challenge by workers, the employer compromised with some of their demands.[19]

Perhaps the most active year with respect to labor protest was 1936. The year began with resistance mounted by workers of the Samsun Tobacco Factory in January and hosiery factory workers in Taksim and continued with walkouts and demonstrations by Süreyyapaşa Textile Factory workers in March; walkouts by tobacco workers of the

Nemlizade, Herman, Seden Kolar and Flemenk companies between March and November; protests by Yedikule Gas Company workers and the resistance of porters to the İstanbul governorship in April; and Paşabahçe Bottle and Glass Factory workers' strike in July. The walkout by workers of the Samsun Tobacco Factory owned by the Monopoly Administration was one example of significant collective action. The workers used various tactics to resist poor working conditions, low wages and the cruelty of the chief foreman, whom workers had already taken to court for insulting them. On January 22, upon the workers' demands for a higher wage, the chief foreman scolded them angrily once again. In the wake of the ensuing quarrels between workers and the foreman, twenty-two workers were fired. The following day, simultaneous rejection of the wage demands by the administration prompted hundreds of workers to stop work. The administration declared that the affected department would be closed down and its workers would be dismissed. The workers, continuing their sit-down protest, were mugged first by the factory guards and then by the police. Women and child workers thrust themselves to the forefront in order to prevent a harsher attack. After the police emptied the factory, hundreds of workers spontaneously marched to the main street and gathered in front of the Samsun party building. For the strikers, this was an illegal lockout. After submitting a petition listing their complaints and demands to the RPP chair of Samsun, the workers ended the demonstration. However, police arrested fourteen of them. Next day, upon hearing about the detention of their friends, hundreds of workers including women and children gathered in front of the Samsun governorship. The number swelled to 2,000 with the participation of other workers and artisans such as blacksmiths, shoemakers, tanners and saddlers who were friends or relatives of the workers as well as fellow victims of industrialization and government policies. In the face of vigorous protests, first, the governor accepted the release of the arrested workers and transmitted the workers' petition to the Customs and Monopolies Ministry. The ministry immediately rejected the workers' demands. Then the factory dismissed about 300 of the striking workers. The workers did not give up pursuing their right by petitioning the government. By November 1936, the workers' incessant demands along with the lack of qualified workers had forced the factory to begin rehiring the dismissed workers group by group.[20]

In February, workers of the Taksim Hosiery Factory also stood against the wage decrease from 10 piasters to 7.5 piasters for knitting a pair of stocks. However, workers' firm resistance and lobbying via the hosiery association compelled the factory to withdraw the wage reduction. On top of that, this time workers decided to exert pressure for a wage raise of 2.5 piasters and forced the factory to accept their demand.[21] Another big work stoppage took place about two months later in İstanbul. On March 16, 1936, the Balat quarter witnessed a tumultuous incident by employees of the Süreyyapaşa Textile Factory, who had not been paid for two months. Workers had complained about the factory management to the governorship, but to no avail. Moreover, the factory management fined each worker, cutting 37.5 piasters from the wages for the broken shuttles. This was the last straw. Six hundred fifty workers on the night shift stopped all machines and shuttles and occupied the factory. As usual the police raided the site and emptied the factory and in the ensuing brawls arrested three workers. Soon after, hundreds of angry workers raided the Fener Police Station to rescue their friends but did not find them. Then the furious workers met in Sultanahmet Square and held a mass demonstration in front of the İstanbul governorship, shouting, "We want our wages! We are hungry! We want our bread!" The workers' representatives met with the governor, who assured them the detained workers would be released soon and he would speak with the employer directly to resolve the problem. Believing the governor, the workers ended the walkout. However, the factory management delayed paying the back wages and then fired fifty of the striking workers.[22]

Toward the end of March and in April 1936, several conflicts arose between workers and employers in the Herman, Seden Kolar and Flemenk tobacco companies in İstanbul. In July, Paşabahçe Brick Factory workers, who had received no wages for two and a half months, gathered in front of the factory and declared that they would not leave until they were paid. This protest also ended with brawls between the police and the workers. The brick factory then halted production and announced that it no longer needed the workers. However, the workers did not give up pursuing their rights by petitioning the relevant state departments.[23]

At the beginning of November, workers at the Nemlizade Tobacco Company staged a strike again. This time they were against the company's new pay schedule, according to which workers were paid every ten days instead of on a weekly basis. The workers also demanded a wage increase, healthy working conditions, clean drinking water and a ventilation system. Rejected in all their demands, the workers occupied the warehouse. The company reluctantly accepted the workers' demands, but subsequently fired some workers in revenge. Frustrated by layoffs, hundreds of workers gathered in front of the warehouse. They argued what the boss had done was a kind of lockout, which was forbidden by law. Upon the company's calling the police, a furious fight broke out between the resistant workers and the police. The clash resulted in many workers being hospitalized, but that did not deter the protestors. The fights between the workers and the police continued the next day. Seeking to avoid intensification of the dispute, the company reinstated the weekly payment system and rehired most of the fired strikers.[24]

Another noteworthy worker resistance occurred at the Zonguldak Ereğli coal mines. As mentioned before, the dockworkers had objected to an 8 percent deduction from their wages by the Coal Miners' Union and demanded reimbursement of the sum of money they had paid extra so far. Meanwhile, in the first week of April, the dockworkers had come together in the Zonguldak port holding a public demonstration against the Ereğli Coal Mines Enterprise and the union. The police had taken many workers to the police station, but had been shortly forced to release them in the face of the workers' resolute protests. Eventually, the strikers sued the enterprise and the union, and won their legal struggle with the verdict of the Supreme Court.[25]

After the Labor Law went into effect in June 1937, labor disputes, workplace fights and walkouts continued as before. In fact, the Labor Law prohibited strikes, lockouts and labor unions. However, its protective articles gave the workers the opportunity to pursue their rights or legitimate their causes. In 1937, for instance, tobacco warehouse workers in Beşiktaş protested the quality of the lunch they were provided. During the protest, the workers and foremen fought each other in the streets of Beşiktaş. A subsequent labor dispute occurred at another tobacco warehouse in Beşiktaş when the employer decided to lock out workers demanding a raise. Well aware that the lockout was forbidden by the Labor Law, the workers declared that the company was in violation of the law and then beat a foreman, whom the workers called "ass-kisser Yaşar."[26]

One case in which the workers managed to exploit the Labor Law was a work stoppage at a leather factory in Adana. The workers refused to work until the employer met their demands compatible with the Labor Law. The employer attempted to disperse the workers via police. However, this time, officials, tasked with investigation of the labor disputes, accompanied the police and decided that the employer had violated the Labor Law in many respects. The officials issued an official warning to the factory. Another work stoppage in 1938, by workers at the Flemenk Tobacco Warehouse in Tophane who wanted a wage hike and social rights stipulated by the Labor Law such as free lunch, medical service, paid vacation and a weekly day of rest, resulted in the granting of most of their demands.[27]

Concluding Remarks

The first decades of the republic were very arduous times for low-income wage earners. In Turkey, working people were more heterogeneous than the labor forces of industrial countries were. It encompassed different groups such as skilled and unskilled industrial workers, workers of peasant origin, casual laborers, artisans and their workers and low-wage white collar employees. Although their experiences could differ, they all suffered from a high cost of living, a decrease in purchasing power and wage cuts, freezes or delays. Their common affliction was disastrous working conditions and long working hours. Work environments were mostly unhealthy and unsafe. Except for a limited number of large public enterprise employees and state officials, no effective social security protected workers against accidents and sickness. These conditions and the state's control over labor have become recurrent themes in the conventional accounts. Working people are portrayed as victims of their employers and the authoritarian state. Due to its exclusive focus on organized movements, the literature depicts the early and mid-1920s as a period marked by labor organizations and social activism. The late 1920s and especially the 1930s are seen as an interim period when labor was silenced. Peasant workers and self-employed artisans are regarded as backward remnants of the preindustrial world, which ought to be swept aside by industrial capitalism. The role of other labor groups and the daily, widespread struggles of working people are overshadowed by the stories of left-wing intellectuals and labor unions.

In view of such gaps in the literature, the chapters in this part have focused on these previously unnoticed aspects of the working-class experience. The first finding is that working people were not an unconscious mass silenced by the authoritarian state or rising capitalism. Elimination of the left and labor organizations under authoritarianism did not necessarily mean that working people lapsed into inactivity. They thought autonomously according to a subjective sense of self and were not deceived by the official populist and developmentalist rhetoric. Aware of the social injustice they experienced, they did not see themselves benefiting from the republic's progress to "the level of contemporary civilizations." Despite the official representation of the "people's republic" without antagonistic classes, working people viewed their world as polarized between those with power and money and those without.

Going beyond voicing their opinion, working people actively struggled for their survival and rights. The labor struggle increasingly tended to comprise informal, individual and mostly unorganized actions, adapting to the authoritarian single-party politics. Workers resorted to a large reservoir of everyday and subtle coping mechanisms that provided small advantages and benefits, ranging from writing to the press, petitioning the government, work slowdowns and pilfering to changing jobs. Suing employers was among their options, although that occurred less often. The official nationalist and populist discourses were widely used to legitimate arguments or urge the government to keep its promises.

Professional associations were more than mere puppets of employers and the RPP. They were not homogenous entities free from internal conflict. The wage-earning members of heterogeneous professional associations challenged the employer members. They pressed their associations to be more effective in helping them. On the other hand, wage earners did successfully fight through a few class-specific professional associations and obtained concessions from their employers.

When push came to shove, workers individually or collectively made a stand in several ways short of formal strikes. Threatening, beating, wounding or even killing employers or foremen were part and parcel of working life. Clashes in factories that spilled into the streets and even into city squares also occurred frequently. These events caused employers to feel that the productivity and stability of their businesses were imperilled. The everyday politics of the working class accordingly yielded some considerable successes. Apart from large and small improvements in daily life, the mostly individualistic, occasionally collective, but cumulatively massive actions compelled the government and employers to consider or adopt basic social and economic measures. The ruling circles needed to consider several labor law drafts in 1924, 1927, 1929 and 1932, which finally culminated in the Labor Law of 1936. Despite prohibiting unions and strikes, the law provided a framework which workers could partially appropriate. Before this law, the government had attempted to meet the partial needs of working people by enacting the Weekend Vacation Law in 1924 and the

Public Hygiene Law in 1930, which brought protective provisions for child and female laborers, medical services in large enterprises and rules for workplace sanitation.[1] Faced with workers' support for the FRP in 1930, the RPP brought a few workers to the National Assembly as deputies in the 1931 elections so as to create a labor-friendly image. Atatürk delivered a speech honoring these worker deputies and promised that the state would always work for their welfare. Moreover, in 1931, the RPP included populism among the "six arrows" (*altı ok*), delineating its main principles like nationalism, etatism, republicanism, reformism and secularism.[2] The National Days and General Holidays Law regulated the paid weekend holiday in 1935. From the early 1930s onward, the government accelerated the establishment of occupational social assistance and retirement funds in many sectors. The retirement rights of officials on the payroll of provincial governments were regulated in 1933. Many retirement funds were established for employees in a number of public enterprises. Large private enterprises also granted certain social rights to their workers. Apart from these, the government lowered the income tax deducted from salaries and wages by 16.6 percent in May 1936.[3] Another symbolic but important step that indicates how far the government took account of the mood of the labor force was the adoption of May 1 as a holiday in 1935, albeit under the title of "Spring and Flower Holiday." By this regulation, the government undoubtedly intended to create an image of itself as a benevolent father to the workers.

The critical question here is why the rulers needed to create such an image. Until today, all of these symbolic or social policy measures have been explained as the state's efforts to control workers, increase productivity and ensure the stability of the labor force. But it is equally legitimate to ask why the state and the companies needed a stable and productive labor force and why the government explicitly embraced populist discourse. The answer lies partially in urban wage earners' struggle for survival and rights in everyday life, which played a considerable role in the laborers' instability and low productivity. Along with other factors like scarcity of skilled labor and adequate equipment at work, the high turnover rates pushed productivity down and costs up. This was a heavy blow to the industrial drive of the young republic and nascent Turkish manufacturing. Of course, it would be an exaggeration to call the limited concessions to labor a success for working people. Yet it is possible to see them as the partly intended and partly unintended positive results of the people's efforts to improve their lives. Moreover, in a society with limited resources in which even a loaf of bread could make a big difference, these social policy measures and the small advantages everyday politics yielded should not be underestimated. Finally, the growing labor movement of the 1950s and 1960s did not materialize out of thin air, but took inspiration and derived lessons from the experiences of the interwar years. The survival of artisans, the high number of casual laborers and the workers' ongoing ties with the villages would also leave their marks on the labor movement in the following decades.

PART III

The Power of Popular Culture

10 | Hotbeds of Opposition to Secularism

Mosques, Coffeehouses and Homes

"Our departure from İzmir was not so grandiose. Rather than the people, the official administrators sent us off. The situation was similar in many places we went to. In Bursa and Balıkesir, most of those who sat in front of the coffeehouses in the main streets watched the convoy of Gazi (Atatürk) passing by them without standing up ... This is also because of the secular reforms."[1] The author of these lines is Ahmet Hamdi Başar, who accompanied Atatürk on his provincial tour to gauge the mood of the citizens in November 1930. They were not always greeted with applause as often depicted in images supplied by the Anatolian Agency. People did not always stand in respect, but instead projected a cool aloofness to them by remaining seated while the president's cortege was passing through the main streets right before them. This was not only because of the economic difficulties but also because of the profound secular reforms, which had vexed the people further.

The republic's spurt of secularization provoked a series of uprisings and harsh criticism, especially in its first years. A small number of collective uprisings or intellectual oppositions are well-known aspects of Turkey's experience with secularism. Less well known is the widespread nonconfrontational criticism, protest and resistance by ordinary people in daily life that prevailed during the entire period. Popular discontent and resistance to the secular reforms appeared mostly in the form of apathy and unwillingness in embracing them or preserving customary beliefs and practices. Feigning ignorance was a common way of foot dragging in accepting the state directives. Many criticized the regime, reforms or politicians in daily conversations without challenging them openly. Individuals who lost their authority and economic resources in the new order especially championed the production and dissemination of anti-secular opinions. In the absence of free channels of political expression, the oppositional views came out in various everyday ways such as daily conversations, sermons, rumors, jokes and placards. Likewise, due to the strict control over spaces in which public opinion was formed, non-elite venues such as mosques, coffeehouses, houses and town and village squares served as hotbeds of dissenting views and alternative social spaces. Neither the People's Houses or People's Rooms – devised for political and cultural indoctrination – nor the official secularist discourse and worldview were unrivalled.

The Losers of the Secular Reforms and the Social Base of Opposition

Undoubtedly the most important and indelible imprint the republic left in Turkey's history is the secularizing reforms. The first wave of the reforms consisted of constitutional and political changes such as the banishment of the sultan, moving the capital from İstanbul to Ankara, the proclamation of the republic and finally the abolition of the caliphate. Political reforms were followed by other cultural and social reforms. The *medrese*s were closed in 1924 and religious education was eventually removed from the curricula of high schools and then primary schools. The government tried to gather Quran courses under its official control by introducing a license system.

The Education Ministry introduced compulsory secular education for all school-aged children in a coeducational system in 1927. The Kurdish-Islamic Sheikh Said Rebellion in 1925, accusing the government of godlessness, gave an opportunity to the RPP to assume a repressive attitude toward political opponents through the Maintenance of Order Law from 1925 on. Alongside the conservative opposition PRP, all religious spheres of socialization such as the dervish tombs (*türbe*), Islamic *tariqas* (*tarikat*) and their lodges (*tekke*) were shut down in 1925. Another law closed down religious foundations (*vakıf*) and banned religious titles such as *sheikh* and *dervish*. Spiritual activities such as writing charms and amulets (*muska yazmak*), practicing magic (*büyücülük*), fortune-telling (*falcılık veya gaipten haber vermek*), faith healing (*üfürükçülük*) and giving and receiving oblation or sacrifices to saint' tombs (*adak*) were also banned. For the ruling elite, all these practices were incompatible with the secularism, rationalism and science they admired. The government directly undertook the education and employment of preachers[*] through the

---

[*] In Turkey prayer leaders called *imam*s also carried out the task of giving a sermon, called *vaizlik* or *hatiplik*. I call all of these groups preachers.

Faculty of Theology at İstanbul University and preacher schools (İmam Hatip Okulu), but these were abandoned by 1933.[2]

Atatürk also tried to transform society by changing symbolic codes such as clothing. The Hat Law in 1925 discarded the fez, a fundamental hallmark of Ottoman men, and introduced the Western hat as the new headgear. The government never banned veiling officially, but encouraged unveiling through local campaigns. The state's intervention in clothing was partly related to the state-building process and devised to make people understand the fact that the new rulers would henceforth make the laws. Another aim was to change the status of women by removing the symbols that had supported segregation of the sexes. Finally, the ruling elite expected such symbolic changes to erase the Oriental, backward image of Turkey in the eyes of Western countries.[3]

In 1926, the adoption of the Civil Code from Swiss law heralded new rights for women. The Civil Code banned religious marriage (*imam nikahı*) performed without civil marriage. It also abolished polygamy, prohibited early marriage for girls and granted women the right to choose their spouses, initiate divorce and inherit and acquire property. Women were granted the political rights to vote and to stand for elections gradually between 1930 and 1934. The state's surveillance over religion and religious functionaries was carried out by the Presidency of Religious Affairs (Diyanet İşleri Riyaseti) (PRA). The PRA was established in place of the Sharia Ministry (Şeriye Vekâleti) in 1924. In 1928, another radical step was taken with the casting off of the second article of the constitution, which recognized Islam as the state religion. The RPP went much further by replacing Arabic script with the Latin alphabet the same year. This change was also designed to bind Turkish society more tightly to Western culture and to intellectually disempower the devout old generation. A few years later, in 1932, came the mandate that the call to prayer and sermons in mosques be delivered in Turkish. Finally, the official weekend was shifted from Friday, the traditional Muslim holy day, to Sunday in 1934.

The republic employed a series of ideological or coercive mechanisms to consolidate these radical changes. Not only young pupils in new secular schools but also adults in the Nation's School (Millet Mektepleri) were educated in new Latin script and secular principles. The RPP set up People's Houses in provincial centers and People's Rooms in villages as sites for indoctrination and socialization. Secular rituals, ceremonies and balls attended by both modernly dressed men and women together in contrast to the old segregation of the sexes (*haremlik selamlık*) were also meant to secularize society. The Criminal Law prescribed several penalties for anyone who meddled in politics through their religious capacities and who "imperiled the reforms." The press was taken under close control and even censored. The anti-secular and anti-regime talks were also monitored through secret civil agents.[4] This spurt of cultural renewal provoked a deep resentment among the overwhelming majority, which was expressed only in the privacy of daily life with talks and acts out of fear of the authoritarian state. The aforementioned social and economic discontent further alienated the masses from the secular reforms and their upholders.

***

Both Islamist and modernist narratives tend to explain people's resentment against secular reforms with reference to the conflict between modernism and tradition, overlooking one vital factor: the dramatic deterioration in the social and economic status of the ordinary people, explained earlier. The impoverishment in rural and urban areas coincided with a grave blow by secular reforms to those impoverished people's age-old religious practices and beliefs. The Turkish modernization drive was overshadowed by feeble and slow economic development. The reforms were not able to substitute material welfare for the old values. This led the people to approach the secular reforms warily and even negatively.

On the other hand, the state's infrastructural power was not capable of transforming the huge rural population along the lines of secular reform. Moreover, one major change the republic wrought was the loss of power of religious institutions and of clerics. Those whose livelihoods depended on religious institutions lost their jobs or experienced a sudden fall in status. The new regime gave precedence to new secular schools and culture centers like People's Houses, which virtually resembled temples of the republic, over mosques. Opening new mosques never became a priority of the new state. Ankara was called a "city without minarets," except for the minarets of the Hacı Bayram Mosque, built in the fifteenth century. The PRA's share in the state budget remained insignificant. The PRA dismissed many mosque employees gradually through removing or merging mosque jobs. In İstanbul alone the number of employees in forty-four large mosques was cut from 312 to 188. The government avoided appointing new staff to fill the vacant posts.[5]

The fear of job loss was accompanied by the reduction of salaries and the elimination of customary informal incomes such as Islamic alms and donations like *zekat, sadaka, adak* and *kurban*. First, in 1928, the PRA officially declared that mosque personnel were not state officials, but wage earners bound by a wage contract. This deprived them of employee rights, wage and salary raises and social security benefits. The salaries of village preachers were delegated to village funds collected from peasants. Second, pious foundations that once funded the mosques were closed down. This sharply cut the resources that had previously gone to the mosque employees. The preaching in mosques was subjected to a license issued by the PRA after a police investigation.[6]

Preachers often found their wages delayed for months due to budget constraints.[7] The government called citizens to donate to state-sponsored associations such as the Aviation Society, the Red Crescent or the Children's Protection Society. Some religious scholars who cooperated with the government reinterpreted the meaning of religious donations according to governmental interests. Yusuf Ziya Yörükân, a religious scholar, proposed that Muslims who fulfilled their tax obligations did not have to give Islamic alms (*zekat*). Abdülbaki Gölpınarlı, a *sufi* theologian who collaborated with the government, strongly recommended donating to the new associations instead of mosques. All this undermined the interests of religious functionaries who had long subsisted on these revenues.[8]

The prohibition of faith healing and similar spiritual practices removed another economic source for preachers, sheikhs and dervishes. Likewise, the outlawing of *tariqa*s and sacred tombs caused a crisis of subsistence for those who lived on the funds coming from believers' donations, alms and sacrifices, and on the sales of amulets, charms, sacred soils and waters, votive candles and petitions to God. Indeed, prior to the republic, *tariqa* lodges and tombs were a substantial source of income and ideological power for a large number of clergymen. With the transfer of all properties belonging to the *tariqa*s, dervish lodges, mosques and Islamic pious foundations to the state, as contemporary republican politician Asım Us wrote, many sheikhs and dervishes together with other staff members of these institutions started to beg in the streets.[9]

These institutions were not only for these people. The poor, widows, orphans and patients had relied on the spiritual and material assistance provided by them for centuries. Their closure deprived a great number of low-income or poor recipients of their assistance. İstanbul alone had 365 dervish lodges by 1925, with a total staff and disciples (including their families) of about 90,000 people. These people benefited from these networks materially and spiritually. A conservative woman writer of the time, Sâmiha Ayverdi, described the dervish lodges as "spiritual insurance" in the absence of a modern social security system. Famous leftist humorist Aziz Nesin shared this view, noting how the lodges fed the poor. He also wrote that his uncle, who had been living in Çürüklük Lodge in İstanbul, had become impoverished after the lodges were banned.[10]

Another novelty that undermined the authority of clergymen was the Civil Code. Compulsory civil marriage particularly was a major blow to their monopoly over the approval of marriage. Finally, secular education and the adoption of the Latin alphabet rendered these former scholars and teachers illiterate. They found themselves as students whom the secular young teachers taught the new alphabet in the Nation's School. The elimination of religious education with the closure of *medreses* and the prohibition of Arabic instruction and Quran courses without license also narrowed their employment opportunities.[11]

The decline in the economic and ideological status of clerics was noticeable. Furthermore, low salaries and irregular payment forced many clerics to work in additional jobs. The extent to which being a preacher had lost its charm and economic advantage under the republic became the subject of a poem by a contemporary folk poet,

Illustration 10.1 Preachers learn the Latin alphabet in the Nation's School

Zuhuri, composed in 1930 in Merzifon (Amasya). The poem includes these verses:[12]

Biz işe başladık geçtik mihraba	We started to work we stood in the *mihrab*
Bazı çuha giydik bazı şal aba	We at times wore broadcloth, at times shawl cloak
Bir selam kazandık felekten caba	We won [only] a gratis greeting from fate
Eğildik hüdaya eyledik niyaz	We revered God, we supplicated
...	
Bizle merasimi değişti felek	Fate has changed its protocol with us
Çıktı elimizden varidat tek tek	Revenues escaped our hands one by one
Hayırı kalmadı bozuldu meslek	[Our] profession went to pot, deteriorated
Bağı her taraftan kuruttu ayaz	Black frost dehydrated the vineyard all around
Çocuk okutmayı öğretmen aldı	Teacher undertook the education of child instruction
Bayramlık haftalık o yola saldı	Festive [aids] weekly wages departed to that way
Bize bir cenaze yuğması kaldı	Only washing the dead remained to us
İstersen çok su dök istersen az	If you wish, pour a lot of water or pour a little
Fitreyi zekatı verdik havaya	We gave *fitre* and alms to the air [Aviation Society]
Nikahı muhtara vakfı araya	Wedding to the headman, endowment to intermediaries
Nushayı doktora ettik hedaya	We bestowed the amulet to the doctor
Elimizde kaldı parasız namaz	Unpaid prayer remained in our hands.

...

A limited number of high-ranking religious scholars managed to integrate into the new system by working in the İmam Hatip schools and Faculty of Theology. After the closure of these schools between 1930 and 1933, they resumed working in other schools and state departments.[13] Nevertheless, those who had no such opportunities responded to the changes in a somewhat different way. Faced with economic hardship, initially they resorted to the government to demand a job, wage increase or financial aid. Danish writer Carl Vett, who spent two weeks in the Kelami *tariqa* lodge in İstanbul, noted even prominent sheikhs were living in material need and seeking help in Ankara. Many religious scholars and preachers who lost their jobs had no access to retirement benefits. For instance, deprived of his regular pay, Eyüp Sultan Tomb's keeper, Ahmet Ziya Efendi, petitioned the government and recounted how he had become destitute. A *müezzin* (reciter of call to prayer, *ezan*) with seven children who had recently been fired from the Evliyâzade Mehmet Efendi Mosque petitioned the PRA for a job in another mosque. Old *medrese* teachers, most of whom had also lost their jobs, sought employment in government institutions. For instance, Süleyman Efendi, teacher of Islamic history and geography in the *medrese* of Süleymaniye, who went unemployed after the closure of the *medrese*s, petitioned the PRA by poignantly depicting how his family of five was in need and asking to be reappointed.[14] The same fate befell an Arabic and religion teacher named Mahmut Celalettin Ökten after the removal of Arabic and religion courses from the new school curriculums in 1926. Ökten, who would work actively in the reestablishment of İmam Hatip schools from 1949 on, was among many who suffered unemployment in this period.[15]

As for the active preachers and Islamic scholars, those preachers who worked under contract demanded to be put on the payroll of the central government or a wage raise. For instance, toward the end of 1928, many mosque staff demanded a raise as well as the benefits enjoyed by other state officials, but the PRA refused. Despite being often declined, similar demands inundated the PRA during the 1930s.[16]

Mosque employees pursued their economic rights collectively through the Pious Foundations Employees' Association (Hayrat-ı Şerife Hademesi Cemiyeti), established in 1922. Giving voice to the demands of its members, the association issued a petition to the National Assembly. After a rhetorical eulogy for the new regime, the petition described the miserable conditions of mosque employees and listed their needs, particularly higher wages and employment.[17]

All this made them hostile to the secular reforms and the republic. Common economic grievances of people and preachers found expression in the latter's critiques of the elites and their fashionable lifestyles, which they often condemned as extravagance. Given that even communists availed themselves of religious discourse for political agitation, it is not surprising that the preachers used the language of religion to disparage the system that had disenfranchised them. The 1929 trials of communists accused of being both "communists" and "religious reactionaries" (*mürteci*) at the same time indicate how poor workers, allegedly communists, made use of anti-secular discourse in order to delegitimize the government and to mobilize the masses.[18]

Imperial officials who shared the same fate as clergymen under the new regime were also among the firm upholders of the anti-secular views. According to secret police reports, dismissed state employees as well as low-income laborers and artisans spearheaded opposition by talking about the immorality of the reforms at every opportunity.[19] Certain reforms spurred reaction from artisans whose jobs they undermined. Clothing reforms, for example, hurt the interests of the producers of traditional clothes such as the fez, the veil called the *çarşaf* (a large garment covering the body and even the face, similar to the Iranian chador) and baggy trousers called *şalvar*, *potur* or *karadon*. Moreover, state support for big industry and modern lifestyles, at odds with traditional consumer culture, also led artisans to oppose the regime, often in religious terms.

This entire social base along with many other factors fed discontent with the secular reforms. A limited number of dissenters openly criticized and even rebelled against the reforms. We know this side of the story. However, much more was going on at the grassroots level. Ordinary people mostly opted to cope with the secular reforms through more elusive and informal means such as seditious talk, critical sermons, rumors and placards. Many resisted the state's intrusion into their life by maintaining age-old prohibited educational, mystical and religious practices clandestinely in the privacy of everyday life. Mosques, coffeehouses and homes especially turned into main centers of expression of hostility toward the secular reforms and antipathy toward the state.

The Hotbeds of Anti-secularism

The novelties of the republic frequently became the subject of critical conversations in daily life in non-elite social spaces. Mosques, coffeehouses and homes where ordinary people congregated, socialized and exchanged ideas were the major sites of discursive challenge. For the government, it was difficult to fully control these places. Despite police surveillance, subversive and critical views about the secular reforms were often articulated. Surely, those who were discontented with secularism mostly tended to eschew inviting others to join the rebellion or directly criticizing Atatürk or the regime. Instead, nostalgia for the caliphate, the sultanate and old days functioned as a sort of criticism or rejection of the current situation. Yet some people more explicitly criticized and even cursed the reforms and the political leadership. Another discursive weapon was the rumor. Disgruntled citizens fabricated and spread fake news, distorting and challenging the official discourse and propaganda. Disobedience and resistance to the reforms in daily life would be the culmination of widespread challenging opinions burgeoning in ordinary public spaces.

Mosques: Centers of Opposition

One major hotbed of such discourse was the mosque. It was the primary gathering and social space of ordinary men. As Ahmed Emin (Yalman), who examined the development of the press in modern Turkey, wrote in 1914, prior to the printing press, the mosque, along with dervish lodges, coffeehouses and bazaars, was the most important site for intercourse between people. He noted, "The spreading of opinions and the molding of news were the business of preachers."[20]

   Indeed, mosques have always been at the center of towns and villages both spatially and ideologically. In the Ottoman Empire and during the early republic, most provinces had a central square with a mosque. During imperial times, mosques and preachers were the most important ideological and educational apparatuses of the state as well as of opposition groups. The mosque constituted a social place where Muslim men came together for prayer as well as a center for information, education and dispute settlement. The mosque also served as the oldest social policy institution by collecting Islamic *zekat*, *sadaka* and other donations for both the poor and the clerics. That is, mosques were not only temples but also a complex of education, indoctrination, social assistance, public service and socialization with schools, courtyards, soup kitchens, fountains and baths adjacent to them. Even the Grand National Assembly of Turkey was to be located in the Ulus district of Ankara, whose center was the Hacı Bayram Mosque.

Moreover, their ideologically, socially and spatially central position brought them to the heart of politics. *Tariqa*s and religious leaders had controlled politicians, bureaucrats and millions of people through mosques. The mosque had shown its influence during World War I and the Independence War by mobilizing hundreds of thousands of people. Both the Ottoman and Ankara governments had used them against each other.[21]

Cognizant of such potential, the republican rulers did not allow mosques free rein. From the first years, the new regime curbed the influence of mosques and preachers over the masses. The new city plans did not allocate a place in the city center for a mosque. The activities and sermons of the clerics were placed under strict control by the PRA and the secret police.[22] Moreover, alternative public places such as the People's Houses and People's Rooms were devised to disseminate pro-republican views.

Nevertheless, the mosques continued to constitute the primary socialization and communication space for menfolk. Even some women in the big cities continued to visit clerics in mosques in order to receive counsel. In villages, peasants socialized in mosques as well as in coffeehouses and homes. In these places, many clerics spewed their hatred against the government in their sermons or daily talks. They not only expressed their own views but also articulated what the frequenters of their mosques felt and thought. Discussions took place inside the mosque and in the courtyard, where people frequently congregated before and after prayers to talk about local affairs and politics.[23]

Guesthouses or village rooms were also located in mosque courtyards, and peasants often gathered at the mosque when a stranger came to the village or an important issue was raised. It was not a coincidence that most of the uprisings against the Hat Law, which erupted in the last two months of 1925, were triggered by crowds gathered in mosque courtyards just after prayers. In Rize, agitated by a preacher in the mosque, worshippers marched to the governorship to protest the hat reform. In Maraş, a crowd gathered at the mosque courtyard in the city center to protest the hat. Protests against the Turkish call to prayer in Bursa also began in meetings held in mosque courtyards just after prayers.[24] Likewise, the Menemen Incident in 1930 began just after prayers in the mosque.

Subversive talk in the mosques did not always lead to protest. Many who gathered expressed their dislike only in daily conversation.

Preachers frequently delivered counter-sermons by disregarding the official sermons the PRA dictated to the mosques. Such sermons were so widespread that the government admonished religious functionaries several times. Noncompliance continued in the following years. Religious holidays, when people flooded mosques, were especially likely to fuel such critical conversations. Anti-government sermons in mosques gained momentum toward the end of the 1920s and again in the late 1930s, which were marked by overlapping economic and political watersheds. In 1928, the government repealed the constitutional principle establishing Islam as the state religion and accelerated the reduction of clerics on its payroll. The next year, the global economic crisis hit Turkish society. The economic and cultural discontent of the people and the clergy overlapped and manifested as pessimistic and critical talk in mosques. The second watershed came with Atatürk's death in 1938 and the devastating Erzincan earthquake in December 1939. These events caused a new wave of rumors and sermons, spreading hopes for a retreat from the reforms and the collapse of the republic. In 1938, receiving numerous intelligence reports and denunciation letters about the anti-regime sermons, the ministry once again needed to warn provincial governors and *mufti*s.[25]

The state archives are full of documents about challenging sermons. One of them was given by Trabzon Merkez Camii preacher Hacı Hafız İsmail Hakkı Efendi during the Friday prayer in February 1928. Referring to the Quran, he declared that Islam required men to control their wives by beating them and keeping them away from modern civilization. Likewise, the preacher of Yozgat Merkez Camii, Ethem Hoca, expressed his animosity toward the secular reforms, particularly unveiling. He accused "bareheaded women" of prostitution, and said "all Muslim women will become prostitutes at this rate."[26]

Comparing the republican regime with the Reza Shah regime in Iran, a preacher in İstanbul accused both of being infidel. In both countries, he said, the men cut their beards and mustaches like women, women uncovered their heads like infidels and the rulers put hats on their heads like chamber pots. Another preacher in Mersin spoke against the hats and the new image of women in his sermon. In Adana, a preacher criticized the new lifestyle as well as the economic policies, saying, "Smuggled goods are legitimate for religion (*helal*)." He also accused people who played gramophones of being infidels.[27]

The consumption of alcoholic beverages by the new elite and dancing at balls were also criticized in the mosques. Although Islam forbids drinking alcohol and prescribes the veiling of women, Atatürk was a habitual drinker of *rakı* and a supporter of women's entrance into public life without the veil. As the symbol of the new regime, Atatürk received his share of criticism for drinking *rakı* and dancing with women. Many criticized only the balls, dancing, gramophones and *rakı*, without reference to Atatürk. Actually these criticisms implicitly targeted Atatürk and the new regime. For example, Abdülkadir Hoca in the Beyşehir Mosque often sounded off against the reforms and the regime in his sermons. In 1933, he attacked drinking: "In short, all of the wives of those who enjoyed drinking *rakı* are not considered married, but free." Then he moved on to dancing: "Those men who are dancing are pimps in this world and devils in the underworld." Fakir Baykurt notes in his memoirs that the preacher of his village in Burdur frequently condemned the politicians for being infidel (*gavur*) and claimed that the nation would blow like a gun sooner or later.[28]

Some preachers were prosecuted for "giving affront to the personality of Atatürk" (*Atatürk'ün manevi şahsiyatını tahkir*). Sometimes they declared that Atatürk had died, or was about to die, in order to discourage people who modeled themselves after him or to encourage the community to abandon the republic's novelties. Another target was secular teachers, seen as representatives of the regime. The preacher of the Kemah Mosque, Hafız Sabri, declared that the new teachers were godless and that their main thrust was to remove religion. Mosque sermons and conversations also targeted secular associations with an eye on worshippers' religious alms and donations. Numan Efendi, a *mufti* in Kayseri, repeatedly encouraged the community to disregard the Aviation Society's official announcement on mosque doors soliciting donations and then alleging that such illustrated posters were forbidden according to Islam, he tore up the poster. Preachers who wanted to prevent believers from giving their alms and donations to the secular associations argued that they were not holy. Some preachers condemned airplanes, for instance, as unholy vehicles directed by devils.[29]

Allah vs. Tanrı: Resistance to the Turkish Call to Prayer

Perhaps the foremost reflection of the mood in the mosques was the disobedience to the Turkish call to prayer. Since the beginning of the

Islamization of Anatolia, the call to prayer had been recited in Arabic from the minarets of mosques five times a day. As a liturgical language, Arabic had been regarded sacred for ages. However, in parallel to language reform and ardent nationalism, the republican state put Turkification of the liturgical language on its agenda. The first Turkish Quran was read during the first Friday prayer of the holy month of Ramadan in 1926 at the Göztepe Tütüncü Mehmet Halis Efendi Mosque. Shocked worshippers complained about the preacher, Mehmed Cemaleddin Efendi, to the *mufti* of Üsküdar. Upon the protest letters and complaints, the PRA had to appoint Mehmed Cemaleddin Efendi to another mosque. However, the government did not give up reforming the liturgical language. The first Turkish formal homily (*hutbe*) was delivered in 1928. After the preparatory phases, a committee comprised of some of the leading religious scholars and linguists suggested the Quran permitted believers to use their native language in prayer. Then the PRA released a circular on July 18, 1932, prescribing the Turkish call to prayer (*ezan*), the opening prayer (*kamet*) and the formal homily (*hutbe*) to all mosques in Turkey and ordering all religious staff to use Turkish in all stages of prayer. The following year, the PRA declared Turkish would be used for knelling (*salâ*) and saying "*Allahuakbar*" (*tekbir*). *Allah*, the sacred word for God that Muslim people, religious or secular, repeat on all occasions, was replaced with a Turkish equivalent, *Tanrı*. On the other hand, the government did not pass legislation banning the Arabic call to prayer, *salâ* and *kamet*.[30]

This change also spurred widespread reaction in daily life. Negative feelings especially about the change of religious language continued throughout the 1930s. Most people felt guilty or weird, especially when the Turkish call to prayer saying "*Tanrı uludur*" ("God is great") was given. When the Turkish call to prayer sounded from minarets, people grumbled or cursed. Hopes for a return to the Arabic script and call to prayer remained alive at the end of the decade. Some spoke ill of the Latin letters and attempted to discourage use of the Latin alphabet by claiming infidels used it. In Malatya, for instance, after a preacher delivered the call to prayer in Turkish, placards written in Arabic script and criticizing the government and the Turkish call to prayer were hung on the door of the Yenitaş Mosque and on walls in the city center.[31]

From the first years of the change, many preachers did not give up delivering the call to prayer, *salâ*, *tekbir* and *kamet* in Arabic. The press reported the prosecution of preachers and citizens disobeying the new regulations. Official reports in the archives also confirm widespread disobedience to the Turkish call to prayer. In letters to provincial RPP chairs on the eve of the holy month of Ramadan in 1936, the general secretary of the party, Recep Peker, warned governors to be on the alert for "religious reactionaries" attempting to chant the Arabic call to prayer, *salâ* and *tekbir*, noting that such actions had increased compared to previous years.[32]

Traces of disobedience can also be found in the state and police archives. According to correspondence between the Konya governor and the *mufti* in 1938, a preacher sang *tekbir* in Arabic during the morning prayer of the sacrifice feast. Police reports from 1938 indicate that many preachers violated the government order by using Arabic. Some *müezzin*s called the Turkish call to prayer the "Song of *Deccal* (Anti-Christ)" or *ulumak* (howling), associating it with the new pure Turkish word *Ulu* (great) in the first line of the Turkish call to prayer, "*Tanrı uludur.*" Preachers also recited the Arabic call to prayer quietly along with Turkish one.[33]

Much evidence from memoirs of contemporaries suggests that the Turkish call to prayer met with passive disobedience and even blunt rejection in rural areas. According to Ali Nar, a peasant boy in those times, the preacher in his village had not given up the Arabic call to prayer. Another contemporary recalls that the preacher of his village likewise continued to give the Arabic call to prayer. When the gendarme appeared, he pretended to comply with the official rules by turning immediately to Turkish. The memoir of an Armenian peasant records that the call to prayer was sometimes recited in both Arabic and Turkish in the villages of Çorum during the 1930s.[34] Another way to evade prosecution and fines was to pretend to be mentally disabled. Some even received medical reports proving their mental disorder so as to circumvent accusations of being anti-republic. In some districts, because preachers refused to deliver the call to prayer in Turkish, the call was not heard at all. Another solution preachers preferred was to give the morning summons in Arabic in a flash because an attack by the security forces was less likely at the break of dawn, and then skip the four remaining calls to prayer. The choice of language for the call to prayer was in most cases contingent upon the attitude of the security forces or the presence of a state official near the mosque. "God-fearing gendarmes," in locals' words, might turn a blind eye to the Arabic call to prayer. As for those who worshipped in their homes, the Arabic Quranic verses they whispered were unalterable. Women likewise continued to use Arabic in religious ceremonies at home, where the government never meddled.[35]

Individuals who knew no law foreclosed the Arabic call to prayer often sued the security forces and officials who prosecuted or fined them. The courts, especially the Supreme Court, usually rescinded the sentences and fines. Furthermore, by referring to case law, the high court determined there was no legal basis for the penalties imposed on those who recited the Arabic call to prayer. That is why, in 1941, the government felt obliged to amend the Criminal Law to ban the Arabic call to prayer.[36]

Imposing the Turkish call to prayer proved much harder in the Kurdish provinces. Since the native language there was Kurdish or Arabic, the prohibition of Arabic in worship all but prevented Kurdish clerics and local communities from performing prayer. Therefore, the security forces frequently faced open challenge from Kurdish clerics who insisted on using Arabic. In some districts, the Kurdish population simply stopped attending mosques for a while.[37]

Coffeehouses and Homes: Popular Sites of Contrary Opinions and Religious Education

Along with mosques, coffeehouses constituted the most important social institutions in villages and towns. Coffeehouses continued to play their traditional role as main centers for exchanging ideas. Local issues were settled in meetings held in these places. Coffeehouses as non-elite spaces of socialization attracted far more people than did the People's Houses and People's Rooms. Indeed, it is evident from party reports that coffeehouses distracted people from going to the People's Houses. Even members of the People's Houses spent most of their spare time there.[38] They operated as an extension of homes. They were not centers of oppositional views inherently; rather the impossibility of state control over them made them the main area where dissent could be voiced more freely. That is why the losers of the new regime such as sheikhs, disciples of forbidden *tariqa*s, low-income preachers, craftsmen, workers, peasants, civil servants and the unemployed criticized and even swore at the government and politicians in coffeehouses. The government therefore took measures to weaken the influence of these fulcrums of subversive discourse.[39]

Forbidden religious lodges continued to exist under the guise of coffeehouses. Laborers and the poor frequented workers' coffeehouses. These places also harbored critical discussions about secular reforms as well as workers' economic problems.[40] Worshippers usually dropped by coffeehouses prior to and after going to the mosque. Therefore, it was no coincidence to hear anti-government and anti-secular talks in these places.[41] During the rise of both the PRP and the FRP opposition parties, coffeehouses and their owners played a considerable role in generating anti-government propaganda.[42] Aware of this potential for harboring dissenting views and subversive talks, the secret police kept coffeehouses under surveillance. According to police reports, opponents of the new regime and advocates of the opposition carried out their activities in coffeehouses. As noted in intelligence reports dated 1924 and 1925, the "opponents of the regime" frequently spoke of the "deleterious" effects of the "importation of Western civilization into Turkey," the "extravagance of the new rulers," the "elimination of the Quran and religion from schools and mosques" and the "immorality of Muslim women who danced with foreigners," all of which they claimed laid bare the "new rulers' irreligiosity." Therefore, they said, "a great rebellion was underway in Adana and Konya" or "the RPP was repellent and in a desperate situation." An intelligence report indicated proponents of the PRP in Bursa also "propagated" their subversive views in coffeehouses. In İstanbul, in a coffeehouse near Nuruosmaniye Camii, Seyit Tahir and his followers accused the regime of being irreligious and argued that this regime would no longer survive. According to another secret police report, many former Ottoman officials in İstanbul who had been deposed by the new state harshly criticized the reforms in coffeehouses. Informed by the police, the Sivas governor reported that both coffeehouse owners and their clients like retirees, cabbies and refugees were among the RPP's opponents.[43]

Coffeehouses were particularly important to the dissemination of dissent during the short-lived second opposition party experience. Many coffeehouse owners sided with the FRP and spread views challenging the RPP and the regime.[44] During the 1930s, in spite of the consolidation of the RPP's power, coffeehouses continued to provide discontented people with a non-elite space in which conflicting views were expressed and transmitted. Expression of critical opinions gained

momentum toward the end of the decade, after Atatürk's health worsened in 1937. According to the Denizli police, the coffeehouses were
full of "reactionary" and "religious" people belonging to "plebian
groups," who often talked against the regime, politicians and reforms.
Rumors concerning the hat, Atatürk and the RPP mostly originated
from coffeehouses, as did allegations that the Aviation Society, the Red
Crescent, and other state-sponsored associations wasted citizens'
money or were irreligious. Crimes committed against the honor of the
government, the regime or the president mostly occurred in
coffeehouses.[45] Moreover, in an implicit challenge to the ban on
Arabic and Turkish classical music on state radio, which broadcast
only Western music, coffeehouse customers preferred listening to
Oriental music and Arabic Quran broadcasts on Egyptian radio.[46]

Probably owing to coffeehouses' influence in shaping the popular
mood, the National Assembly discussed closing them in 1926. The
government opted instead to closely monitor them through the police.
The government also sought to put them into the service of the state in
disseminating the party's ideology. Faced with the impossibility of
control over coffeehouses, the government once again attempted to
close them in 1933.[47]

Another measure was to create alternative pro-government socialization centers like the People's Houses and the People's Rooms.
However, the people continued to congregate in coffeehouses.
Therefore, a large number of People's Rooms in villages remained
vacant. Official reports abound with descriptions of inactive People's
Houses and People's Rooms, abandoned by their members. Even some
of their own employees and members stopped by coffeehouses at the
end of the workday.[48]

Coffeehouses were not the only meeting places available to ordinary
people. If the government closed the coffeehouses, people could still
come together for candid discussions in their own homes. The people
had always ascribed to houses the highest degree of privacy, as is
evident from the concept of *mahrem* (private). However, the house
was not merely a private space disconnected from public life. The non-
elite culture of ordinary people was reproduced and transmitted there
to the next generations. Generally free from the eyes of the civil servants
and security forces, houses enabled people to conserve their age-old
habits, norms and beliefs. Religious and traditional lifestyles continued
to be practiced in the privacy of homes.

In Ottoman Muslim society, whereas women spent much of their time in a special section of a house called the *harem* or *haremlik*, another room known as the *selamlık* was reserved for men. Despite certain differences such as sexual segregation, the *selamlık* was a counterpart to the Western salon. Long chats between acquaintances and relatives in these rooms were the main component of social life. These chats, accompanied by smoking and drinking coffee, were often called *selamlık sohbeti*. These home meetings and conversations persisted during the republic. What people talked about in houses varied according to their agenda or the course of events in the province, the country and the world. Some comments had an explicitly political edge. Sometimes elders told heroic stories about their military days. By transmitting their experiences, they educated and shaped the younger generations.[49]

As Mitat Enç describes in his memoir, *Selamlık Sohbetleri*, *selamlık* meetings in Gaziantep constituted a sort of home school, not only for young boys but also for all attendees. Close friends of Enç's grandfather and father gathered there to smoke and discuss various matters. The secular reforms were the most debated topics of their conservations in *selamlıks*. Attendees compared the positive and negative aspects of the reforms and did not hesitate to criticize them. Such *selamlık* meetings were not peculiar to Gaziantep, but widespread across Anatolia. Sometimes people shared folk tales or poems or read passages aloud from folk books like *Aşık Garip*, *Kerbela Vakası*, *Köroğlu* and *Sahibi Buhari* or from religious books like the Quran, *Mızraklı İlmihal* and *Mevlid*, thereby reproducing popular and religious culture. Preachers, who felt monitored in mosques, preferred to meet their disciples in houses, where they could freely comment on politics.[50]

Women's home receptions were among the well-known communication channels. Women gathered in homes discussed not only fashion and recipes but also religion, the economy and politics.[51] A keen observer of provincial society, novelist Reşat Nuri Güntekin in his *Anadolu Notları* (*Anatolian Notes*), published in 1936, defined homes "a kind of club" (*bir nevi kulüp*), in which people including women came together, discussed various matters and worshipped. These home meetings were also rumor mills. For instance, according to the police reports, one of the women at a house reception in Eskişehir said, "Atatürk is dead, therefore the hat will be removed, we will wear the *çarşaf* again, the dervish lodges will reopen, and our old costumes will return." The content of women's conversations at these meetings was so rich that prominent figures in the provinces encouraged their wives, daughters or mothers to keep in touch with the female relatives of provincial bureaucrats so as to obtain information about economic and political developments.[52]

Mostly among the women, *mevlid* ceremonies, popularly called *mevlids*, were an important part of home gatherings that has survived until today. A *mevlid*, a long poem praising the birth and life of the Prophet Muhammad, was chanted in homes in association with deaths, births, circumcisions and other life events. *Mevlids* created occasions for attendees to gossip, talk about worldly matters and feature critical views about republican reforms.[53]

Religious education was also carried out in private residences. After religious instruction was removed from school curricula and religious instruction in mosques was banned, preachers secretly taught religion, Quran and the Arabic script at homes. The disciples of banned *tariqas* whose lodges had been closed also used houses to carry on their activities. Police reports confirm that lots of people kept their affiliation with the *tariqas* that operated clandestinely in houses. In Manisa, in June 1932, a group belonging to the Bektashi *tariqa* was caught in a house they used as a lodge. In Ankara, in January 1936, a group of *tariqa* disciples was caught in a *zikir* (an Islamic devotional rite in which attendees try to gain spiritual transcendence as well as to strengthen their community ties). In Gaziantep, the police prosecuted a group of people who had met for a religious rite in the house of a *sheikh*.[54] During this period, a famous religious leader, Saidi Nursi, and his followers operated clandestinely through house meetings. Atatürk's death especially gave rise to the performance of numerous illegal religious rites at homes. Indeed, the police departments in Ankara, İzmir, Kayseri, Van, Konya, Manisa, Bursa, Kırklareli, Muş, Rize, Kırşehir, Çorum, Yozgat, Tokat and Niğde reported an increase in private religious home meetings. These secret religious rites were usually held at times such as bank holidays when a no-knock raid by security forces was less likely.[55]

Secret Quran Courses at Homes and Mosques

Houses and mosques had another function: maintaining religious education. Despite the gradual elimination of religion from the educational system, both the preachers who had lost their official teaching function and the parents who still cared about Islamic training kept religious education alive through secret Quran courses. Coeducation of girls and boys in the same classes and the lack of religious instruction discouraged many families from sending their children, especially daughters, to the schools. Many parents preferred having their children take Quran courses, mostly at homes or mosques.

Along with this, many other factors slowed down the increase in the schooling rates. The first one was infrastructural problems. The new secular schools, especially in the countryside, were not capable of enrolling all school-aged children due to the inadequate number of schools and teachers. The second issue was that locals generally perceived teachers as representatives of the state and the new order. Indeed, teachers were often used for work people hated such as tax collection, conducting population censuses or military conscription. Therefore, people kept away from teachers as much as possible. Besides, children, especially in villages, constituted an important source of unpaid labor. It is not difficult to understand why the peasant majority in particular opposed compulsory education. Children were expected to work alongside their families in the field, grazing livestock, collecting wood, carrying water and running errands. Therefore, a considerable number of townsmen and villagers did not enroll their children in school.[56]

All of these factors, along with secular coeducation, further estranged parents from schools. Indeed, as a monograph by İbrahim Yasa about the Hasanoğlan village of Ankara points out, the abolition of religion courses hurt people. Especially after the language reform, attendance at the village school further decreased, and during some years, the school remained completely empty. According to Yasa, one of the primary reasons behind the low rate of attendance and enrollment in schools, besides opposition to secular education, was the importance of child labor within the family. As for girls, the peasants preferred to marry them off at twelve or thirteen instead of sending them to school. Hence the average enrollment rate even in villages of the capital city dropped from 41 percent to 34 percent during the 1930s. Rates were lower in the distant provinces. In Erzurum, for instance, both attendance and enrollment were far lower. As of 1935, of all school-aged children in Trabzon, only about 20 percent were enrolled in school, of which less than 10 percent were female.[57] To sum up, during the early republic, low schooling rates in the countryside were related to people's avoidance as much as the insufficient number of schools and teachers.

Many parents worried that their children would not receive a proper religious education in the schools. Provincial society often did not take kindly to the modern-looking young teachers and their new education methods. Some asked them pejoratively whether they knew and would teach the religion to their classes. Some went so far as to threaten them because they ignored the Quran or religious education. In some cases, local inhabitants shunned teachers in order to make them feel isolated and power-less. Some men openly requested that teachers teach their children the Islamic religion and the Quran. Village teachers who attempted to inform local people about science or the new curriculum were often criticized as patronizing, talkative, pedantic and even godless. Turkey's most prominent leftist political humorist, Aziz Nesin, wrote in his memoirs that his father did not want to send him to school during the 1920s because he believed schools converted Muslim children into infidels. Aziz's father was not exceptional. According to the secret police reports, many peasants refused to enroll their children in the schools on the grounds that the teachers did not read the Quran. In the Hasanoğlan village of the capital city, an old woman expressed her dislike for the new education by arguing that "in contrast to good old days when pupils learned good things, prepared for the afterlife, and never walked in the streets bareheaded, in the republic these good old things have disappeared. But the demons of hell will sizzle them in [the] otherworld."[58]

Hostility toward secular teachers often found expression in rumors, such as one that circulated in Yozgat that the teacher of Karakışla village had died in a traffic accident because he had urinated on the wall of the village mosque. In the spring of 1935, a striking rumor about vanishing children spread in İstanbul. According to the rumor, schoolchildren were being kidnapped by cannibals, and many families consequently refused to send their children to school.[59] These rumors expressed the people's dislike of the new secular education. This nega-tive perception could unleash violence. In one incident in Kayseri in 1931, a mob of hidebound men leveled to the ground the newly built school adjacent to the mosque and then opened fire on the houses of the teachers.[60]

Coeducation particularly frightened parents in the countryside. As a matter of fact, even some teachers did not feel comfortable with it. Therefore, even when the girls were permitted to go to school, teachers and school administrators in some faraway towns separated girls and boys by seating or dividing the class into two sections. In Gaziantep, for instance, girls and boys were seated in separate areas. The school administrators gave boys and girls breaks at different times, thereby limiting face-to-face contact. All of these measures were taken as a result of pressure from the parents of the female students. Nevertheless, many parents did not send their girls under the pretext of sexual harassment by teachers. There were even attacks on teachers who insisted parents to enroll their girls.[61]

As an alternative to secular education, religious instruction in underground Quran courses was widespread throughout the country, even though the government licensed many Quran courses under official supervision. The memoirs of people who grew up during the interwar years describe how they received illegal religious instruction. Mehmet Kara, alias Kutuz Hoca, recalls attending a Quran course in his neighborhood in Rize during the mid-1920s, where his instructor used to seat him on the broad windowsill and told him to keep watch for a possible gendarmerie raid. Nezih Neyzi recounts in his memoirs how preachers taught the Quran at the homes of well-off pupils by pretending to be guests in İstanbul. On many occasions, female *hafız*s (reciters of the Quran) who taught the Quran at home often escaped police prosecution by pretending to have gathered for *mevlid*.[62]

As noted by a contemporary expert on popular culture, religious education was still alive in Safranbolu in 1939. In this informal educational system, the first stage of instruction included arithmetic as well as reading the Quran and memorizing Quran verses. Tarık Ziya Ekinci, a future Kurdish physician and leftist politician who spent his childhood in the Lice district of Diyarbakır in the 1930s, recalls that only a few children went to school in his neighborhood. Most children were taught in homes or mosques secretly by preachers whose basic needs were met with locals' assistance. Likewise, Pakize Türkoğlu recalls how peasant children in his village in Antalya received religious education in the house of Hasan Hoca Dede during winter nights in the late 1930s. Islamic training was so important to being regarded as a good person that even some Armenian families sent their children to secret Quran courses held at preachers' homes in order to avoid condemnation from their Muslim neighbors. Ferman Toroslar was an Armenian child whose family had been exiled from Sason to Çorum. He was one of those pupils who had to receive Quran instruction in a large cellar of a preacher's house that could accommodate around sixty children. In Kayseri, many people like Külekçizade Ali Efendi, Çorakçızade Hüseyin Aksakal and others taught Quran and Arabic at their homes. These people were to obtain official posts and carry out these activities under an institutional roof with the reestablishment of İmam Hatip schools in 1949.[63]

Teachers utilized interesting methods to carry on religious education secretly. Infringing on the laws, one contemporary preacher, Süleyman Efendi, taught religion and Arabic script clandestinely at his farm in the Çatalca district of İstanbul during the 1930s. His young students pretended to be laborers working on the farm. At times of tightening police control, the courses were held in public gardens or during short rail trips between İstanbul and neighboring provinces in a cabin whose doors were always locked. In the Black Sea region, teaching the Quran was carried out in the dense forests. In the Of district of Trabzon, *medrese* education of students who came from other provinces, as well as local students, continued at specific houses. In the east, learning Quran, Arabic and hadith took place in hidden caves.[64]

Such stories are corroborated by the state archives, which are replete with documents listing illegal Quran courses and the preachers prosecuted for unlicensed religious instruction. According to the police reports, the instruction of the Quran and the Arabic alphabet were so widespread throughout the country, even in the mid-1930s, that it was difficult to eradicate. While the police detected many illegal Quran courses and even the active *medreses* carrying on Islamic instruction adjacent to mosques, governors needed to warn the government about the illegal religious courses. Likewise, public prosecutors in many provinces took to court village headmen and preachers for teaching Arabic and religion illegally.[65]

In later years, the Quran courses did not disappear. For example, one preacher in Rize was prosecuted in 1938 for teaching Arabic to sixteen children. Another preacher in the same province was fined for teaching tens of children. A few preachers in Adana were arrested for secretly training quite a few students in a *medrese*. Police records indicate many women were also teaching Arabic and the Quran by 1938.[66]

Well aware of the prevalence of underground religious instruction, the republican state never prohibited Quran courses. Rather, the government, accepting the existence of such courses, tried to keep them under control, outlining the rules instructors had to obey and framing the courses within legal limits through official PRA regulations. The prosecutions generally targeted courses outside official control. Indeed, during this period, the PRA licensed more than 700 Quran courses. In addition, the Education Ministry opened 164 Quran courses before the end of the 1930s. The number of these courses would reach 883 by the end of the 1940s. However, the memoirs and security records suggest that far many more than these continued to operate secretly.[67]

Popular and traditional socialization places and institutions such as mosques, coffeehouses, homes and Quran courses never faded away with the republic. All of these popular spaces harbored the popular communication systems and a shared language through which the people expressed their resentment and aspirations, as I discuss in the next chapter.

11 | Informal Media vs. Official Discourse

Word of Mouth, Rumors and Placards

During the 1920s and 1930s, the state, the party and the cultured middle classes all dominated the formal public sphere and public opinion through the People's Houses, the People's Rooms and state-sponsored associations propagating official views. The press was under heavy and therefore turned into the mouthpieces of the government. The new regime rested in large measure on coercion, used sometimes harshly against alternative political views. Therefore, the official discourse seemed dominant and free from challenge. However, given the unlettered culture of the ordinary people, heavy censorship and political oppression, word of mouth functioned as a popular media through which dissenting opinions were articulated and disseminated. A sort of underground media aired alternative news challenging the mainstream media. This popular media, or *informal media* in Robert Darnton's term, encompassed daily conversations, rumors, folk songs, folk poems and anonymous handwritten placards, which served as an outlet for voices and views that were otherwise impossible to express.

The main venues where the informal media operated were common places where ordinary people gathered and socialized. As discussed earlier, these places had nothing to do with the public sphere in the sense of Habermas's bourgeois *public sphere* in which educated middle classes produced "rational" opinions through critical discussions. They represented the more inclusive and broader conception of *public sphere* comprising the *plebeian public sphere*, where non-elite subordinate social groups gathered. This contrary, alternative and shielded sphere comprised the social spaces of those ordinary people who lacked equal access to the bourgeois public sphere or who wanted to avoid the restrictions of official and bourgeois spaces. Diffused into capillary of the society, these spaces such as homes, coffeehouses, shops, mosques or Quran courses were harder to be monitored or invaded by the state. The content of the *informal media* corresponding to this *plebeian public sphere* was more dissident and addressed the concerns, hopes and priorities of the people. It was largely these places in which dissonant voices were raised and resistance germinated.

This wider conception of public sphere and public opinion shows us there is no fixed expression of social discontent. Instead, both the form and the content of people's political expression varied according to people's social position, literacy status or the conditions under which they lived. They also fluctuated according to specific events, moments, discourses, rulers or institutions. Indeed, during the early republic, the non-elite and illiterate individuals expressed their views in their own terms through more flexible and easily transmittable oral forms of expressions such as daily talks, jokes and rumors. The anonymous placards as written pieces of paper containing criticisms of the reforms or the government sprouted here and there in public places. However, under an authoritarian polity, popular opinion, especially criticisms and opposing voices were produced and disseminated most often by word of mouth.

Word of Mouth

Most of the contrary views were expressed in daily talks less timidly. Comparatively safer places like homes, coffeehouses, mosques, gardens, pubs and other non-elite social places hosted such conversations. In these daily talks, certain themes and forms featured prominently. First of all, views contrary to those of the secular regime found expression in vilifying the current regime and longing for old times. Many equated the republic with "godlessness" and "irreligiousness." A young Turkish man interviewed by a foreign observer described the cultural reforms as "frightful decadence." Another foreign traveler, visiting Turkey in the mid-1930s, wrote of a preacher in İstanbul who criticized the government as *dinsiz* (irreligious or unbeliever).[1]

In the eyes of many rural people, the republic meant impiety. They argued that the new government had brought bad luck to the country. According to a 1937 police report from Denizli, people in coffeehouses drew a parallel between droughts and the new regime. Some said, "We have not seen abundant rains since the proclamation of the republic." In a similar vein, the big earthquake of 1939 that devastated Erzincan province was seen as a consequence of godlessness. Many frequently connected the natural disasters that befell the country to secular reforms.[2]

Nostalgia constituted one form of expressing discontent with the power holders. Without criticizing the present regime directly, yearning for the old golden Ottoman times was, although not always, a disguised expression of dissatisfaction with the new regime. In making rhetorical and covert comparisons between the sultanate and the new regime, the latter was criticized on the grounds that the old days were more cheerful and blessed. The time of the sultans was remembered as one of abundance, and people wished for it to come again.[3]

Opponents of the reforms compared the reign of the sultan caliphs to the republic, praising the former and denigrating the latter. As reported by the Samsun police, peasants from the village of Şıhlı praised the caliphate, which they contrasted with the "evil deeds of the republic." A civil policeman, entrusted with the task of listening to what people talked about in public, had gone to the Cumhuriyet Hotel, where he found a person blaming the reforms. An excerpt reads: "Mehmed Ali, living in Kadıköy Zühtü Paşa Neighborhood, works at the Mineral Research and Exploration Institution (Maden Tetkik Arama Enstitüsü) in İstanbul, Kızıltoprak. He was staying at the same hotel where I was also staying. Four days ago, I went to the Cumhuriyet Hotel. . . . There I heard him saying, 'The new government is secular! So what? Predecessors worked better than today's rulers.' Then, he talked about the good old days of the sultanate at every opportunity, asserting that 'the revolution should not mean the abolition of Arabic script . . .'; that 'today's rulers [are] complete thieves.'"[4] Such talks, circulating on the grapevine, could turn into rumors.

Rumors: Alternative and Informal Media

As an information channel beyond the control of the government, rumors had the potential to spread like wildfire and prevail over official propaganda. Motivating the people in the direction of certain behaviors and fostering noncompliance, it could operate as a catalyst of popular resistance.[5] During the early republic, Turkey was awash with rumors about the secular reforms and the regime at crucial turning points. These rumors generally expressed distrust of official propaganda about the good intentions of the government and the benefits of the reforms. Rumors made the ideological hegemony of the new government more fragile.

There were two sorts of rumors. Certain rumors fueled pessimism, inciting the people to disobey the government's orders by connecting disastrous events such as earthquakes, droughts or floods to the regime. These rumors suggested the state would go too far in harming religion.

Other rumors were optimistic and predicted a return to the "good" old days. They expressed hope for the retreat of the reforms by discouraging and demoralizing officials and pro-government individuals. Rumors about political chaos, the assassination of leaders, the death or incurable illness of Atatürk or the imminent occupation of Turkey by foreign forces insinuated that the reinstitution of the ancien régime or the abandonment of reforms was imminent.

The rumors' subversive potential obliged the government to closely monitor them. The Interior Ministry considered rumors the propaganda of the opponents that might shatter national unity and solidarity. Governors were ordered to be on alert in the face of dangerous newsmongers. In addition, the ministry wanted the People's Houses and People's Rooms to inform citizens the rumors were all groundless and merely the lies of enemies.[6]

The first significant wave of political rumors arose toward the end of the 1920s, cresting in 1929. The main themes were the forthcoming "evil" reforms and the president's "impiety," incurable illness or death. The second wave appeared with the Great Depression and the subsequent FRP opposition in 1930. These rumors reflected the people's hope for a regime change with the possible replacement of the RPP government with the FRP. The third and largest wave came with Atatürk's death and the Erzincan earthquake toward the end of the decade. From the introduction of the secular reforms between 1925 and 1929 on, word of mouth criticizing the reforms ran rampant throughout the country. The rumors reflected both the religious discontent and the economic grievances of the masses. Given bad harvests due to the droughts of 1927 and 1928, increasing taxes, the burden of the monopolies and the unfolding economic crisis, which all coincided with the radical secular reforms, it is not difficult to understand which social groups fueled them.

In this first wave, just after the dervishes' lodges were closed down and the hat reform and the new Civil Code were introduced in 1925 and 1926, a rumor spread throughout central Anatolian towns and villages that the government would soon collect all young virgin girls and widows and export them to foreign countries. Local administrators warned the government about this unfounded news and its catastrophic results. In some villages, this rumor led to the rape of virgin teenage girls. Undoubtedly this rumor was connected to another one regarding the president's private life. Rumors had it that the gatherings of men and women, including Atatürk's adopted daughters, in

Çankaya Mansion were the "scene of debauches at which drunkenness and immorality were flagrant" or the "scene of his promiscuous relations with women." Similar rumors about Atatürk's private life laid the ground for arguments that his reforms actually aimed at imposing a non-Muslim lifestyle on the people.[7]

Another rumor that circulated throughout Anatolian villages a few years later, in 1928, concerned a ban on circumcision that was believed to be imminent. Due to such rumors, many peasants in Manisa hurriedly had their sons circumcised. Hasan Kudar, who was a child in those years in a village of Balıkesir, recalls hearing villagers saying, "From now onward we will live like infidels, the kids will not be permitted to be circumcised." Therefore, many people circumcised their sons immediately.[8]

Objection to the clothing reforms was expressed via rumors about ancestors being resurrected in their graves due to the increasing number of "bareheaded" and "whorish-looking" women. In April 1928, for instance, the Mersin police reported that the wives of some porters and tinsmiths had circulated a rumor that a corpse had been observed sitting up and wailing in his grave, whereupon a doctor and a public prosecutor went to the grave and heard him say: "I am a living soul and I am burning in fire, since neither mothers nor fathers take care of their children; women in the streets are nude, and cut their hair and wear overcoats." At the end of the investigation, the police prosecuted four women for spreading this rumor. These women were all wives of impoverished artisans.[9] This rumor was an expression of discontent with the clothing reforms as well as poor people's resentment toward the rich political elite. It was also a way to discourage women from unveiling, as I discuss in Chapter 13.

Other rumors that spread both in the east and in the west in February 1929 reflected anxiety over the perceived threat to Islam represented by the republican reforms. On February 14, 1929, in the villages of Elazığ, for instance, peasants began to say that Ankara would soon send church bells to be put up in the mosques. In the same month, people in the Kasımpaşa quarter of İstanbul talked about 3 million Christian crosses that would be imported from Europe. In the years to come, millenarian rumors would allege that Qurans were being thrown onto floors and torn apart and that Deccal (the Antichrist) would soon appear in Anatolian towns.[10]

Some rumors predicted the approaching end of the republic. The main theme of these rumors, which pervaded the country especially in 1929, was the poor health of Atatürk. Rumors about the president's ill condition accompanied rumors about a possible invasion of Turkey. Given the shocking changes and the worsening material conditions that stemmed from the drought just before the global economic slump, the discontented people seemed to have cherished hope for the death of the president, especially after his second heart spasm in May 1927. In January 1929, the Interior Ministry reported a rumor about the president's death was circulating in many places. In April, preacher Hacı Hasan in Gerede disseminated a rumor that "the Ghazi is seriously ill, the government will surrender İstanbul to the Greeks in return for Salonika, then İsmet Pasha will escape to Europe." It was alleged in Balıkesir in June 1929 that "the Ghazi died three months ago and the cabinet fell, therefore Kazım (Karabekir) and Ali İhsan (Sabis) Pashas (two conservative opponents of Atatürk) will take the lead and save Islam." Rumors alleging that the president had died or would die soon from an incurable illness or an assassination ran wild in other provinces. A rumor alleging that Atatürk had been assassinated caused a panic in some provinces in February 1929. During the 1920s, rumors continued to circulate that the president had been paralyzed in one leg and was on the brink of death due to cancer.[11]

In 1930, the establishment of the FRP led many people to speculate what would happen when the party came into power. Discontented people's expectations were reflected in what the RPP generally stigmatized as "poisonous propaganda," rumors that predicted the reinstitution of Arabic script, the amendment of the Civil Code, the reopening of *medrese*s, religious lodges and tombs, the removal of the ban on the fez and the reestablishment of the sultanate and the caliphate. Other rumors added to these the cancellation of certain taxes or tax debts, the abolition of the Monopoly Administration and lower prices for basic goods.[12]

Perhaps the most prolific period with respect to rumors was the year Atatürk died and the following few years, marked by anxiety as to what was going to happen. World War II would give rise to new scenarios. Rumors of these years suggested that the government would revoke the secular reforms and even the republic itself. Hopes for the reinstitution of the previous order were not rare. Nostalgia for the "divine sultanate" was so prevalent that rumors circulated throughout Anatolia in the 1920s and 1930s about the sultan's imminent return. The RPP's general secretary, Saffet Arıkan, warned party inspectors about rumors that the "dynasty which had been unjustly expelled from the country would return, and the sultanate and old order would replace the republic." Such rumors could be dangerous for the rulers, as happened during the Menemen incident. The rebels in Menemen had disseminated rumors that the former caliph Abdülmecid was ready to enter the country and assume power. This rumor stimulated the active and passive consent of the people to the insurrection.[13]

In the weeks following Atatürk's death in November 1938, rumors were afloat about future developments. The police reported people in a coffeehouse in Bandırma had said "Atatürk died and Sultan Vahdettin's son will take his place." This statement reportedly had aroused excitement among the people. In 1939, rumors such as "soon the time of the old sultans will come" were reported from the eastern provinces.[14]

Encouraging rumors heralded a return to old times. The Rumors were afloat that the new president, İnönü, would make concessions to the people or be overthrown via a plot or assassination. The subversive talks in the forms of rumor in mosques and other public places mushroomed again. According to one police report, "There are those who preach in mosques against the regime, who wear illegal clothes against the hat law, who speak against our respectable leaders, and who strive to stimulate *tariqa*s and dervish lodges. ... In Anatolia, rumors and groundless allegations circulate among the people. It is generally said that 'the government is planning to repair the mosques and to educate "new teachers" for the villages'; 'the government has decided to put a religion course in the curriculum of primary schools'; 'female students will not be permitted to go to beyond secondary school, and they will be educated in schools separate from male students'; 'those women who are working in government offices will be dismissed and these women will be housewives, thereby the population will increase.'"[15]

Likewise, peasants and preachers in the villages of Muş speculated about what would happen after Atatürk. Peasants were reported to have said the following: "İsmet Pasha is our father; we believe he will shut down the schools for girls." "We will return to the old sultanate." "The government will grant an amnesty to all the tax debts and prisoners." "İnönü will remove the ban on *kalpak* [fur cap] and cement good relations with Syria." A denunciation letter written by a retired army general toward the end of 1938 shows similar rumors were in circulation in İstanbul schools and coffeehouses. Rumor had it that "girls will not be permitted to go to high school," "girls who went to high school will not be hired in state offices," and "İsmet İnönü will permit women to wear their head covers."[16]

Indeed, as the İstanbul police reported to the Interior Ministry, people in some districts were saying by December 1938 that the fez would replace the hat and that dervish lodges would reopen. Upon this report, the ministry ordered the İstanbul governorship to investigate the sources of such rumors and to prevent their further spread. One month later, in January 1939, word of mouth got about in İzmir that laicism would be abandoned, religious education would be reestablished, and female personnel in state offices would be fired. In Edirne, in February 1939, the police prosecuted a number of people for alleging women would wear the *çarşaf* in the near future and Arabic script would be reinstituted. The same month witnessed the circulation of similar rumors in Kastamonu that the government had assigned 5 million liras for the repair of mosques and that religion courses would be added to school curricula.[17]

Rumors that ran rampant throughout Anatolia alleged a conflict within the government had caused chaos and the assassination of İnönü. According to one such rumor, three of Atatürk's closest men, Ali Çetinkaya, Kılıç Ali and Şükrü Kaya, had assassinated İnönü or plotted to overthrow him. Police departments in Ankara, Bolu, Çoruh, Elazığ, Erzurum, Giresun, Isparta, İstanbul, Kırklareli, Konya, Malatya, Maraş, Mardin, Mersin, Muğla, Ordu, Seyhan, Van and Yozgat reported similar rumors in November 1938. Kept informed about such rumors through intelligence reports by the police and the Turkish intelligence agency, the National Security Service (Milli Emniyet Hizmeti, MAH)), the interior minister issued an encrypted message warning governors about "the prevalence of such propaganda in almost all places of the country." The ministry requested them to use all necessary means to combat the word of mouth.[18]

İnönü's succession to the presidency undoubtedly disappointed antirepublican dissenters. He was Atatürk's closest friend and one of the most enthusiastic advocates of the reforms and the state-led economic policies. Therefore, rumors implying the profanity of the republican regime sprang up once again. As reported from Kars, one rumor alleged "engaged men and women will be forced to put on Christian crosses and subsequently the mosques will be closed down."[19]

Natural disasters like the earthquake that ravaged Erzincan and the surrounding regions in 1939 and flood disasters in 1940 gave an opportunity to those who sought pretexts to condemn the government. Some blamed the devastation on the irreligiosity of the country's rulers, saying, "Since they have been dancing, God has punished them." A similar rumor circulating in Trabzon coffeehouses predicted that because "Turkey has lost its religion ... it will be ravaged within forty days." In İzmir, İstanbul, Kocaeli and Bursa, another rumor making the rounds alleged that İsmet İnönü was a jinx, so the natural disasters had come with his presidency. In Afyon, people heard an apocalyptic tale of a French fortune-teller who had foreseen the Erzincan earthquake and warned new earthquakes would devastate the western regions of the country, after which the greater part of Turkey would sink into the sea.[20]

Seditious Placards

Placards in the forms of handwritten paper sheets were another avenue by which critical views were expressed and publicized. Anonymously written notices that were displayed in public spaces (affixed to walls, doors and even trees) were designed to deliver a message to the masses, to specific institutions or to the local and central administrators. As a technique of opposition, placards had the potential to shape public opinion and galvanize protest. Raw in content and style, placards were a sort of half-written and half-spoken intercourse. They turned the spaces in which they were posted into a kind of public sphere and wall-newspaper where people communicated with each other and challenged the government. Their anonymous character made it hard for the government to get rid of them.[21] The style of such messaging ranged from polite criticism to profanity. Appearing in association with specific developments, the placards generally focused on secular reforms as well as economic hardships and bureaucratic malfeasance. Many mixed a call for a return to the old "golden" times with an attack on the regime and its rulers.

Immediately after the Hat Law was passed, dissenters expressed their opposition by means of anonymous placards plastered on walls or doors. One appeared on the wall of a central building near the marketplace in Sivas in November 1925. One month later, during the anti-hat protests, critical posters were plastered on buildings. Opposition to the alphabet reform was also expressed in anonymous manifestos that criticized the new alphabet and called for a return to the Arabic script.

One was posted on the wall of a shop across from the Çarşı Camii in the Kula district of Manisa, a few months after the alphabet change. The police investigation divulged that a shoemaker named Kamil had penned it. Arguing the new script would harm the people, it called for using sacred Arabic scripts. From the censored part of the manifesto it was understood that it severely insulted the president.[22] In 1932, a number of placards mushroomed across the country criticizing the government's decision that the call to prayer would henceforth be recited in Turkish. In Bursa, for example, placards were affixed to the doors of private houses in November 1936 that read, "We should not forget our religion."[23] Interweaving religious discourse with criticism of high taxes and political corruption, some placards cunningly aimed to provoke anti-government action. Of them, perhaps the most redoubtable and inflammatory was one attached by pins to the back door of the Army House (Ordu Evi) in Bandırma and on the door of the Bandırma Cinema in 1937. Written in Arabic script, it enumerated its points like a manifesto.[24]

Hey Muslim Nation! Hey Soldiers!

1 It is the Ghazi who disregarded Islam.
2 Prostitution disregarding Islam dominated the country.
3 Women became naked, where is Islam?
4 Girls and boys live and work together. Is this appropriate for Islam?
5 Balls are being held and everybody bangs women. Where is Islam?
6 The bugger, fuck-brained Ghazi will be called to account.
7 We will put Ghazi to death soon.
8 You bastard ministers and top politicians who are panderers fucking each other's wives and you pimps who are seeking to curry favor with the bugger Ghazi will also be called to account.
9 You have robbed the Muslims and the Turkish nation, enough is enough you pimps!
10 The laws and taxes are too onerous for the people. You sons of bitches, bastards, especially the Ghazi and ministers, you pimps and corrupted people.
11 Hey Muslim Turkish nation, do you still keep silent? All these have accounts in foreign banks in order to leave the country. Enough is enough! The Muslim Turkish nation whom you have robbed is no longer tolerant of and patient about you.

12 They have discarded the religion. Hey, all Muslims and the Turkish
    nation, raise your heads. Those people you feared are in fact sided
    with you. Your small message will completely solve the problem.
    You will see within a short time. Those who will not participate in
    rebellion will be put to the sword. Anatolia, East, and West, all
    together, the Ghazi will account before the people, so let us see his
    ass, let us see this pimp bugger.

Poor people affiliated with the Communist Party of Turkey also used
the counter-hegemonic language of anti-secularism in their placards.
Expressing their discontent with social injustice by labeling the cultural
reforms "bourgeois extravagance" and "eyewash", they played to the
religious sensibilities offended by the reforms. In İzmir in 1929, for
example, a group of communist artisans and workers were accused of
writing a placard titled "To Hapless and Poor Brothers Who Were
Deceived and Poisoned Everyday by the People's Party's Opium."
Blaming the secular reforms, the placard alleged that young virgin
women were being forced into prostitution and sports and dances
were distracting young men from earning a living.[25]

Some placards comprised melodic and satirical content, resembling folk
poems or short rhyming quatrains called *mâni*. These short sayings of four
to seven lines conveying political messages, in an indirect and satirical
style, allowed the teller a right of expression that was otherwise inhibited.

Memurlar dansta	Officials in dance
Tüccar iflasta	Merchants in bankruptcy
Köylü hasta	Peasants sick
Esnaf yasta	Shopkeepers mourning
Millet hastadır	The nation is sick
Esnaf yastadır	The shopkeepers are in mourning
Mektep muallimleri danstadır	School teachers are in dance
Vali bey baştadır	Mr. Governor is at head
Uyan milletim uyan	Wake up my nation wake up
Halimizi arayan yok	Nobody cares about you
Yazık bu millete acıyın	Shame, show mercy to this nation

Such sayings, whether written down on pieces of papers affixed to
here or there or transmitted through word of mouth, offered

a legitimate travesty of mostly unsayable reality in a rhymed form. Pointing out the people's economic desperation, they targeted the secular lifestyle of the top elite. During the 1930s, sarcastic rhymes similar to the ones just cited, written on pieces of paper and pasted in public places, sprouted across the country.[26] This shows the ingenuity of the Anatolian people in articulating their views shrewdly under the guise of folk culture. Another way to demonstrate their discontent as well as to keep their identity was *symbolic politics*, which came over in people's approach to the new clothing rules.

12 | Neither Fez Nor Hat
Contesting Hat Reform

"The Hat Law forbade him to wear the fez. At first, he had tried to disobey it but the *muhtar*, 'the bastard of a pig,' had fined him. Then he stayed indoors for a week or two. But he could not gaze at the walls forever, so he had ordered his son to buy him a cap in [the] Sivas market. When he got it, he looked at it with contempt and did not touch it for many days. At last, his peasant avarice had gained the upper hand. He had paid for it, so he might just as well wear it. ... One day, *inşallah*, the wicked Government would be swept away, and for the moment he kept his fez carefully hidden."[1] Thus wrote foreign journalist Lilo Linke after interviewing a peasant wearing a flat cap. This observation shows that even among those who obeyed the Hat Law, venomous hatred for the new hat and hope for a retreat from the Hat Law remained alive during the 1930s. The Hat Law was perhaps the most successful sartorial reform. It swept away the fez. However, even this reform encountered widespread resentment. Many refused to wear the Western brimmed hats worn by the elites and the middle classes, and instead adopted different forms of headgear.

The Meaning of the Hat Reform

Clothing as a political symbol was peculiar neither to Turkey nor to Atatürk's republic. Many states during the interwar period pursued a politics of clothing in order to legitimate their rule. Stalin adopted a worker uniform so as to emphasize the triumph of the proletariat in the Soviet Union. Mao wore clothing similar to that of Chinese peasants and laborers. Hitler and Mussolini preferred militaristic uniforms to demonstrate their aggressive nationalism. In India, Gandhi, the leader of the independence movement, turned his cap into his symbol, making it popular among Indian nationalists. Clothing functioned as a symbolic instrument through which these rulers transformed their societies or showed their political motivations.[2]

The founders of republican Turkey made use of the symbolic force of clothing when they replaced the fez with the Western hat in 1925. This new headgear, once known among Muslim subjects of the empire as *şapka* (Russian *shapka*), a term derived from the French *chapeau*, had long been the distinguishing mark of non-Muslims.[3] Scholars tend to explain this reform with respect to republican elites' admiration for the West. There were, in fact, more complex aims. The first was to replace religious bonds with a new national identity binding society's allegiance to central authority. The abolition of the fez was part of a nation-building project that sought to distinguish Turkish citizens from the rest of the Islamic *ummah* and the Ottoman past. The second, related to the state-building process, was to make people understand who was in power. Indeed, only a year before the hat reform, one of the Atatürk's close friends, Ali Çetinkaya, wearing a fur cap in the independence tribunals, had criticized a Turkish journalist wearing a panama hat of being non-Turkish by disparaging his hat. Just after the hat reform, and wearing a Western hat this time, he harshly criticized and condemned to death an Islamic scholar of the Fatih Mosque, Atıf Hoca, a zealous opponent of the Western hat and the republican regime.[4] Çetinkaya's sudden U-turn is not surprising because what was important was not the content of the law or the shape of the hat, but obedience to the new authority.

The new Turkish rulers, well aware of the European imperialist powers' perilous depictions of non-Western societies as backward and uncivilized, took as their third aim to blur the conspicuous distinctions between Turkey and the West. The idea of a homogenous Muslim world conceived and shared by European and Islamist intellectuals as the antithesis of Western civilization actually caused an "othering" of Muslim societies. Erasing the basic symbols identified with the Islamic and Oriental cultures, secularism sought to challenge not only Islam's hegemony but also this misconception so as to save the Turkish state and society from such discriminative Orientalist representation.[5]

The most important aspect of the Hat Law as it related to society was that it created symbolic equality among citizens by erasing old symbols of religious, ethnic and sexual identities. Under the Ottoman Empire, headgear was a major symbol that defined one's religious belief and socioeconomic rank. As ideological agents of the regime, clergy had enjoyed a privileged status indicated by their clothes, turbans (*sarık*) and robes (*cüppe*), which distinguished them as Islamic scholars (*ulema*). Despite initial opposition when it was introduced in 1829, the fez had gradually become an important symbol distinguishing Muslims from non-Muslims. Its brimless shape and red color (the same as the Ottoman flag) was suitable for prayer. The brimmed Western hat was seen as non-Muslim. Communal tensions and class conflict in the Ottoman Empire had sometimes manifested in the form of attacks on such symbols. One popular insult Muslims subjects directed to non-Muslims was "Shit on your hat."[6]

Apart from this, the brimmed hat was not suitable for praying because it prevented the forehead from touching the ground while prostrating oneself. Moreover, Ottoman artisans and merchants producing or trading traditional clothes had vested interests in the conservation of the old clothing codes. The clothing also pinpointed the gender status of the wearer.[7] The segregation of sexes was based on certain clothing codes. The veil and *çarşaf* protected a woman's face and body from the gaze of men.

This is why any attempt to alter clothing codes generally triggered a popular backlash. The introduction of the fez by Sultan Mahmut II, who had initiated an extensive reform in the state administration and army, had caused rebellions. Many individuals who disapproved of the fez referred to the sultan as the "Infidel King" (*Gavur Sultan*).[8] Likewise, the new clothing codes of the republic, proclaimed on November 25, 1925, were also unwelcome and triggered a series of local protests. After the state's harsh response, people's resistance shifted to everyday life. Undoubtedly the fez was immediately discarded. However, the great majority did not accept the Western hat and circumvented the law by adopting different sorts of headgear.

Coping with the New Hat

Historical accounts of social responses to the hat reform have generally focused on a series of uprisings against the Hat Law that erupted in İstanbul, Bursa, Erzurum, Trabzon, Rize, Giresun, Malatya, Kayseri and Kahramanmaraş. These are well-known incidents in which small crowds protested the law. However, much of the defiance took place in everyday life.[9] Many simply refused to wear the hat. In some areas, men withdrew from public life for a while in protest. Those who disapproved of the hat and the new regime discouraged their neighbors, friends and relatives with derisive jokes and rumors. Some wore the hat in public while continuing to wear the fez or turban at home. Some pretended to be preachers or mentally ill so they would be excused for wearing traditional clothes. People who disliked the hat avoided prosecution by wearing various kinds of brimless skullcaps, fur caps and conical hats that were mostly worn before the Hat Law. Even men who obeyed the law adopted the *kasket*, a flat cap with a smaller brim, often turning its brim back to leave the forehead exposed.

The reasons people refused the new hat were not always specifically religious. On many occasions, rather than anti-Christian impulse or strong Islamic bonds binding them to the fez, people found the Western hat weird, strange or unsuitable to their lifestyles. While some people had religious motivations, some had psychosocial, class or political causes for refusing to wear the hat such as social shame or discontent with the regime, reforms or the upper classes. As Hobsbawm noted, in revolutionary France, wearers of the old stocking caps had been class enemies of wearers of the tricorne hats. The dress codes were status and even class markers over and through which social groups conflicted. The 1899 uprising of Bolivian Indians had targeted urban elites wearing trousers and forced them to dress like Indians. Finally, the widespread economic interests vested in the manufacture and trade in traditional costumes and the high cost of the new hat also discouraged its adoption.[10]

Ridiculing the Hat, Anti-hat Rumors and Placards

Wearing a Western hat subjected one to mockery, especially in the countryside. Harold Armstrong wrote of an incident in which a man who had donned a hat was laughed at and accused of being an unbeliever by his companions. He subsequently refused to wear a hat even in front of the security forces. Indeed, poking fun functioned to discourage people from wearing hats. One popular anecdote concerned a Greek merchant who mocked Muslims for wearing European hats. According to the anectode, he had said to his Muslim friends, "It must be difficult to wear this hat. You had always cursed us by saying, 'Shit on your infidel hat'; now, how will you put on these hats stuffed with your shit?" When the Hat Law was passed, people in Erzurum thought up a joke ridiculing those who wore it. According to the joke, the people deliberately mistook the hat for a chamber pot. One day, a person wearing a panama hat had taken his hat off to respectfully greet another person. The person he greeted responded, "Forget it, my friend, forget it. It is suitable only for bears to fill it."[11]

Anti-hat rumors also worked toward the same goal. Word of mouth alleging the reacceptance of the fez and the abolition of the Hat Law was widespread. Anti-hat talk gained momentum toward the end of the decade, especially with the deterioration of Atatürk's health. According to police records, rumors against the hat and modern clothes sprang up in coffeehouses and homes. In some places, dissenters expressed their negative feelings and opposition to the hat by means of anonymous placards affixed to walls or doors. One such placard was hung on the wall of the large covered shopping center called Taşhan in the Sivas city center in November 1925. Another placard written by a group of communist activists in İzmir criticized the secular reforms, including the hat reform.[12]

The pressure of the local social milieu and culture was generally more influential than state coercion in the provinces and even in certain quarters of the big cities. People who disliked the hat advised and warned their friends and relatives not to wear it. According to İrfan Orga's memoirs, for instance, one day, the barber in his quarter kindly requested him to take off the "ill-omened" hat. He had said, "The hat is inappropriate for a Muslim because it is a Christian headgear. Therefore, if a Muslim wears it, Allah will never forgive him." Similar requests and warnings by influential preachers also sharpened negative perceptions of the hat. Even some provincial notables who wanted to join the RPP's local administration had to withdraw from politics because the elders, preachers or sheikhs they followed requested them not to wear the hat under any circumstance.[13]

Families and relatives were an especially important factor in discouraging men from wearing the hat. Sarkis Çerkezyan recalls that in their village, Mustafa Ağa had not left his home for a while after the proclamation of the Hat Law in order to protest the change. In the end, he had to buy a hat in order to go downtown without risking a fine. When he returned home wearing it, his wife and daughters began to cry out, lamenting, "Our father, you also became an infidel." This attitude of his family distressed the *ağa* for a long time.[14]

Therefore, even in urban centers, hat wearers walked in the street timidly during this period. In some quarters, young naughty boys accosted hat wearers by mocking and sometimes throwing stones at them and shouting "Infidel" (*gavur*) or "Tango" from behind. Men traveling in such risky quarters therefore preferred to carry their hat in their hand. Naughty street boys and vagrants scoffed at the hat wearers in the streets. They mocked them by yelling "*mon cher*" ("*monşer*") at them in a derisive manner. Some children concertedly shouted from behind, "Snob!" (*züppe*).[15] Such behaviors were not only childish jokes but also reflected their parents' negative approach to the hat.

Everyday Resistance and Selective Adaptation to the Hat Reform

Anatolian men resisted the Hat Law in daily life in several ways. They did so passively by withdrawing from public spaces. Indeed, some men in Anatolian towns avoided leaving home for weeks or months just after the proclamation of the Hat Law. As Mitat Enç noted, in Gaziantep, so many people began to lock themselves into their houses after the Hat Law that the number of people shopping decreased significantly. Many swore, "If I wear it, let my wife become divorced" (*Giyersem, avradım boş olsun*).[16]

For men who insisted on wearing traditional headgear, there were several ways to escape prosecution. Pretending to be a cleric was one. According to law, preachers were not obliged to wear the hat and were allowed to wear religious costumes during working hours. Therefore, many people tried to get around the official clothing codes by pretending to be preachers. During his trip to Turkey, Armstrong noted that ordinary people dressed eclectically after the republican reforms. He was also surprised by the great number of preachers wearing fezzes with turbans and robes. In fact, some of these men were merely pretending to be preachers in order to avoid prosecution. Consequently, applications for official certificates to wear religious garb, especially the turban, increased in these years. Only a small number of men wore the fez in town centers or in distant villages. These unyielding men took it off and hid it inside their clothes as soon as they noticed a gendarme or policeman. In villages, those who wore the fez or turban often pooled their money to purchase one hat and kept it in one of their homes or, more frequently, in the Village Room, for use by those who had to go downtown. In addition, some peasants who needed to wear the hat in public simply put it on over their fez. When they were out of sight of the officials, they took off the hat. In Sinop, for instance, even peasants who lived in villages close to the city center kept a few knit caps they had sewed in the guest room of the village. Peasants who needed to go to the city center left their customary headgear in the guest room and put on one of these hats. In other words, many people gave up the fez reluctantly and reservedly, but refused to wear the Western hat. Instead, they either did not wear headgear in public places or wore brimless hats. Such headgear, as Linke described, was usually a handmade cap such as a fur cap, skullcap, conical hat or woven wool cap, which were cheaper and more widely available than the Western hat.[17]

Accordingly, two other contemporary foreign observers noted that even though most people seemed to comply with the new regulations, they did so in such a superficial way that they had seen "the old Turk in all his glory." Giving up the fez did not necessarily mean embracing the hat. According to the memoirs of a contemporary, the elders of his village chose to wear a turban, a kind of fur cap called *papak* or a woven skullcap called *takke*. A 1930 election district report of Çanakkale deputy Yusuf Ziya Gevher indicates that even in a western province like Çanakkale, people did not comply with the Hat Law. Gevher was aggrieved to find that the citizens viewed rejecting the new hat as heroism.[18]

İstanbul police records from the late 1920s indicate some people had taken to wearing an odd, brimless form of hat in a sarcastic manner in the city. A 1933 report from the Eskişehir governorship to the Interior Ministry called attention to the growing number of Eskişehir inhabitants who wore skullcaps similar to old-fashioned nightcaps instead of the hat. The governorship recommended that the ministry officially ban these skullcaps. Likewise, the Bolu governorship, in a report to the Interior Ministry, noted widespread noncompliance with the Hat Law in the form of wearing different headgear such as woven wool berets, skullcaps and conical hats.[19]

As late as 1940, the general inspector of Thrace, Kazım Dirik, reported that the citizens even in this western region still wore several kinds of traditional headgear as a middle ground between the fez and the modern hat. During inspection tours, he had seen men wrapping turbans on their heads and wearing skullcaps even in the shopping districts of the provincial centers.[20]

Brimless head coverings as an alternative to the new hat were so common some governors prohibited them. Nevertheless, such prohibitions did not intimidate the people into surrendering to the official headgear. Notwithstanding the punitive measures, as an eyewitness observed, the streets and marketplaces were full of vendors with colorful conical hats made with paper. By 1935, upon a countrywide increase in the number of men wearing skullcaps, which resulted in an increase in lawsuits stemming from conflicts between the security forces and the people, the Justice Ministry alerted the Interior Ministry to this acute problem. In order to prevent a tide of lawsuits, the Justice Ministry requested the Interior Ministry to take the necessary administrative measures. In distant provinces, it was impossible to implement the clothing reforms effectively, and quarrels erupted between gendarmes and locals wearing fezzes and turbans, which escalated into serious fights.[21]

Individuals harassed by security forces for resisting the Hat Law did not hesitate to sue them. This betokens individuals' – including peasants – awareness of their legal rights. In Trabzon, for instance, two peasants sued a police officer for insult and physical violence. In another case, a subdistrict director (*nahiye müdürü*), whom a peasant had complained of using violence to take his traditional headgear to the Interior Ministry, was removed from office. According to the interior minister, Şükrü Kaya, "such a cruel administration itself might pave the way for an insurgency."[22]

Correspondence between local and central administrators indicates local judges usually found accused citizens not guilty. In some cases, public prosecutors launched investigations into members of the security forces who resorted to physical force. That is why the general inspector of the third inspectorate region, Tahsin Uzer, accused judicial authorities in Erzurum, Ağrı, Kars, Artvin, Rize, Trabzon, Gümüşhane and Erzincan provinces of hampering the struggle against "reactionaries" and "illegal headgears." Police officers intervened in the wearing of improper headgear; however, the courts usually regarded such interventions as outrageous and unlawful. Even when the local courts punished the wearers of local headgear, the Supreme Court reversed their decisions. In many cases, the Supreme Court decided that wearing wool berets, *papaks* and even *puşi* according to the local and climate conditions could not be considered as opposition to the Hat Law.[23]

Another selective adaptation method people employed to evade prosecution was to wear a flat cap with a smaller brim. Hence it was possible to use it when fulfilling the religious duty simply by turning the brim around. Some who disliked even the flat cap wore it sideways or turned the peak back at other times.[24]

The death of Atatürk gave further rise to anti-hat hopes and accordingly to acts of noncompliance. İstanbul police began to record

Illustration 12.1 People wearing flat caps sideways

Illustration 12.2 A man taking off his hat and wearing a skullcap while performing ritual ablution before prayer

conversations and rumors claiming that the ban on the fez would be lifted soon. The old fez manufacturers, some of who had had their fez stocks confiscated by the police, also played a role in the emergence of such expectations.[25] However, the strong commitment of the republic's second president, İnönü, to the hat reform dashed such hopes. Still Western hats, except for flat caps, did not meet with widespread approval. After the transition to the multiparty regime, although the Hat Law remained in effect, neither the judicial authorities nor the governments were to enforce it. This was partially due to the unwelcoming response to wearing Western hats on one hand and partially due to the disappearance of the red Ottoman fezzes on the other.

13 | *Negotiating Anti-veiling Campaigns*

Mediha Esenel, who conducted village surveys in the western Anatolian countryside in the early 1940s, writes, "The peasants believe that angels do not visit those homes in which the women do not cover their hair." She had personally witnessed a peasant woman being beaten by her husband because she had forgotten to cover her head even at home.[1] Both men's and women's strong desire and insistence for veiling and the deep meanings attributed to the veil were not unique to the region Esenel surveyed, but prevailed across the country. The republic's anti-veiling efforts, which were carried out with local campaigns without any law banning veiling, could not eradicate the veil.

The next major dress reform of the republic was to target this widespread veiling practice and the deep meanings attributed to it. The clothing reforms, starting with the hat reform, culminated in the anti-veiling campaigns that started with female civil servants of a few provinces in 1925 and gradually extended to other provinces and to all women in the mid-1930s. However, the people's experience of anti-veiling campaigns was complex and quite different from that of the few elite women's stories of liberation from the veil. Like men's headgear, what was experienced in the transformation of women's clothing proved once again that local norms, habits and peer pressure outweighed the state's influence. However, changing women's dress proved much more difficult than transforming men's headgear. Both women and men displayed several forms of resistance and utilized selective adaptation strategies to cope with the anti-veiling campaigns. In contrast to the culturalism that dominates both modernization narratives and Islamist accounts, the main thrust that motivated popular resistance was more than religiosity. Social, economic and psychosocial factors and gender relations played a crucial role in shaping people's attitudes toward anti-veiling campaigns. Aware of all these factors, the government would deal with the people's response in a much more flexible manner.

Unveiling Muslim Turkish Women

During the early republic, the *çarşaf* was the most common form of veil among Muslim women. Though varying in length, style, color and fabric, it generally covered the body from the head to the foot, knees or waist. It was only rarely combined with another kind of thin face veil called the *yaşmak* or the *peçe*. In fact, before the *çarşaf*, the *ferace* and the *yaşmak* were a popular combination among urban women, whereas the *atkı* and the *peştemal*, large cotton towels wrapping the upper part of the body, were widespread in Anatolia. The *çarşaf* replaced them partially during the reign of Abdülhamid II as a new fashion imported from Baghdad. The Ottoman rulers had begun to rely much more on Muslim subjects, principally Arabs, after nationalist movements emerged among Christian communities. This eastward orientation, embodied in pan-Islamism, also had cultural and ideological repercussions, like increasing religious conservatism. Although Abdülhamid II initially banned the *çarşaf* for security reasons, his pan-Islamist strategy, which fostered close relations with Arabs, created a sociocultural ground that made its adoption easier. The constitutional revolution of 1908 brought comparative freedom for women and secular intellectuals. Women's *çarşaf*s became more varied in terms of color and shape. These years saw an unprecedented audibility of women's voices. Educated women, along with men who advocated a change in the strict patriarchy, discussed women's rights and fashion in new periodicals where they criticized extreme forms of veiling.[2]

The republic decisively invigorated the unveiling of women through state-led campaigns. Encouraged by the hat reform and the new Civil Code, a number of municipalities had initiated local unveiling campaigns from the mid-1920s. These were limited to women officials or to local elites' wives and daughters. The anti-veiling policies gained new momentum after the RPP consolidated its power in the 1930s. In 1934, just after women's acquisition of the right to vote, the government directed municipalities and provincial governors to launch official campaigns for change in women's dress. Local administrations conducted special public ceremonies at which a few women, mostly the wives or daughters of local bureaucrats, removed their veils and were celebrated by the provincial administrators so as to embolden other veiled women to discard theirs. Although local administrations occasionally imposed bans on heavy veiling, particularly the *çarşaf* combined with the *peçe*, the government resorted to neither legislation banning the veil nor to a vulgar use of physical force against veiled women, as Reza Shah in Iran and Amanullah Khan in Afghanistan did in the same years.

The people gave various responses to anti-veiling campaigns. Educated and middle-class women, representing a tiny minority of women, generally supported the clothing reforms. The press and official documents, exaggerating this support, declared Turkish women had bravely discarded their veils. Critical accounts, especially those by Islamists, have emphasized the coercive measures against veiled women. However, contrary to conventional accounts that depict women as "liberated proponents" or "intimidated victims," people's experiences were far more complex. The majority resorted to several strategies to deal with the change, ranging from selective adaptation to active confrontation. This was not due to their ignorance or religious fundamentalism, but was a result of multiple, overlapping socioeconomic, gender and psychosocial determinants. Women's dress remained largely under the influence of local norms and customs rather than official principles. More precisely, fear of condemnation by neighbors and relatives outweighed the rules and measures of the government. Although European dress comprising hats, coats, overcoats (*manto*) and skirts was fervently advised by the government, women were given great latitude in choosing alternatives to the *çarşaf* and the *peçe*. Consequently, women's veiling practices, both in old forms and in different styles, persisted almost everywhere, except for a few big city centers that saw limited change.

Tenacity of the Veil

Numerous native or foreign eyewitnesses during the late 1920s and 1930s pointed out that the great majority of women in Anatolia continued to wear "old-fashioned" clothes and cover their heads and bodies. What was called "old-fashioned" clothing was in fact still popular and fashionable among ordinary women. Harold Armstrong, visiting Anatolian towns in the mid-1920s, wrote, "The townswomen were shapeless masses of black clothes with their black *çarşaf* cloaks drawn over their heads and shoulders down to their wrists, and thick veils: peasant women in baggy stripes bloomers, blouses and brocaded coats, and a white towel drawn across their faces, leaving one eye only exposed." He found the women in Kayseri within the *çarşaf*. "In Kayseri, women were not unveiled. I never saw a Turkess unveiled. . . . They wore thick, black veils drawn down." The province where he saw women unveiled for the first time was Ankara. Only 50 percent of women in the capital were covered. However, İstanbul had changed little. In the great part of İstanbul, women continued to cover their heads and even their faces with veils especially when a man looked at them or talked to them.[3]

The first American ambassador to Turkey, Joseph Grew, who also visited the Anatolian provinces, described similar scenes. In his memoirs, he emphasized how little effect the reforms appeared to have on the lives of women in the early 1930s. He wrote, "Almost all the women in Turkey, except for those in bigger cities, are veiled. When men pass by, they hide their face and turn their back to these men." Depictions of Anatolian women by Italian traveler Corrado Alvaro, who visited Turkey in 1931, confirm Grew's observations.[4]

Lilo Linke, touring across Turkey in 1935, told of her first impression of Turkish women in detail in her book *Allah Dethroned*. Her account shows that the religious order was dethroned in legal and political life, but not yet in everyday life, especially for women. She had seen a woman for the first time in a government office when she had arrived in İstanbul. "Most women, more strongly tied to tradition, were wrapped from head to foot in their black cotton *çarşafs* which some of them had even half drawn across their faces." On her voyage from İstanbul to Samsun, she shared a cabin with two wealthy Turkish women who wore black silk *çarşafs*. When she traveled to Sivas, she saw that "most women were veiled by a straight piece of black cloth tied round their heads underneath their *çarşafs*." In the Sivas governorship, she came across "the women in their cotton *çarşafs* checked in red and white." At a textile factory she visited in Tarsus, almost all of the women were wrapped in cotton *çarşafs* that left only one eye exposed, in spite of the blazing heat. She writes in a realistic as well as sarcastic manner, "Apparently, Tarsus had not made its 'big jump forward' yet."[5]

Turkish observers of the time present similar scenes. In Alanya, a southern region, the situation was similar. Arif Balkan, a contemporary entrepreneur, observed that women wore their black *çarşafs* even in the sweltering days of summer in the 1930s. They also strolled through the streets with black umbrellas, which they used to shield their face and hair if uncovered. This was a tactic known since Ottoman times as a fashion. The memoirs of Pakize Türkoğlu, who grew up in the same district in those years, confirms the widespread use of umbrellas by women to cover their faces. Şükûfe Nihal, a woman writer of the time, portrayed the women in a western center, Kütahya, as covered with the *ferace* and the *atkı* combined with the *şalvar*. Women in the villages of Söke, a large district of Aydın, donned large baggy trousers and colored soft veils called *yemeni*. According to a monographic study on the central Anatolian district of Safranbolu by a folklorist of the time, Enver Beşe, even in this town near the capital city, as elsewhere in Anatolia, young girls were expected to don the black *çarşaf* as soon as they turned eleven.[6]

In the east, veiling took more extreme forms. A field study conducted in the villages of Erzurum and Kars between 1936 and 1942 by Mümtaz Turhan found peasant women wearing the face veil and the *çarşaf*. According to the memoirs of Tarık Ziya Ekinci, his mother, as a wife of a state official in Lice, reluctantly left the *çarşaf* and wore an overcoat and headscarf, but never exposed her hair. Other local women continued to wear the *çarşaf*. Another contemporary, the wife of a staff officer, described how all the women in Elazığ in the mid-1930s wore black *çarşaf*s in the city center.[7]

The reports of provincial governors and police departments also indicate that women's clothing did not undergo a significant change. In a report dated 1930, for example, the Gaziantep governor admitted the assiduous effort made to modernize women's clothing had fallen short of its targets. Even after the ban on veils by the Adana municipality in 1934, police reports reveal that women's clothing changed little. It was reported from Sinop in 1935 that the local women had not abandoned their old clothes. Even unveiled women who had come to vote in their modern clothes wore *çarşaf*s in daily life. A general situation report by the Ordu governor in 1935 stated that despite the struggle against the veiling, 80 percent of the women continued to cover their head and body in some way. The number of unveiled women was small. Toward the end of the decade, in 1939, it was reported that women in Anatolian provinces still wore *çarşaf*s and other kinds of veils.[8]

Newspapers of the time also complained about the persistence of veiling in Anatolia. For example, in January 1934, a newspaper reported that women in Kütahya could not leave their houses without a veil and *çarşaf*. Similarly, it was reported from Aydın in April 1934 that the number of women with a veil and a *çarşaf* was quite high. As of June 1934, the women in Amasya had not yet given up the veil and *çarşaf*. One year later, another newspaper reported that many women in western coastal towns like Ayvalık continued to wear them as well.[9]

Dynamics and Forms of Resistance to Anti-veiling

Opposing Secularism and Men's Worries about Their Authority over Women

Understanding of women's response to unveiling entails comprehending the patriarchal constraints that shaped women's attitudes. Indeed, the most fervent resistance to unveiling came not from women but from men. By and large, the overwhelming majority of the male population did not lean toward gender equality and the image of the modern woman the government promoted. Quite to the contrary, they never liked the idea of strong, unveiled women. They therefore championed passive resistance to unveiling and other reforms equalizing gender relations. Women were not passive bystanders either. They had their own causes to challenge or to avoid anti-veiling campaigns. Some concerns were common to both women and men.

First of all, as Leslie Peirce has shown in the Ottoman context, clerics' and other religious men's objections to women's equal status or participation in politics under religious terms was to some extent a tactic aimed at preserving their own authority. "The debate over women," Peirce writes, "was thus not always about women; rather, they were often a metaphor for order."[10] In this sense, under cover of the "morally degenerative effects" and "irreligiousness" of the new appearance of women, in fact, the clergymen targeted the new secular regime that had disempowered them.

Accordingly, the unveiling policy of the government especially annoyed clergymen. For them, the veil symbolized Islam and the chastity and piety of Muslim women. Those who hated the new regime took every opportunity to denounce unveiling in their sermons. From the initial phases of the anti-veiling campaigns in the mid-1920s on, clerics delivered sermons condemning women who uncovered their head and dressed "immodestly." As stated before, Hacı Hafız İsmail Hakkı Efendi in Trabzon during the Friday prayer in February 1928 declared Muslim men could beat their wives in order to control them. A preacher in Yozgat expressed his animosity toward the unveiling of women by accusing all bare-headed women of prostitution. Similar seditious sermons continued in mosques in the following years.[11]

Other men were not passive consumers of such sermons. Nor were they fanatical opponents of all novelties. They had their own subjective reasons behind their attitudes. Above all, the Civil Code, in establishing legal equality between women and men, the compulsory education of girls and the abolition of sexual segregation, vexed many men. After legal reforms equalizing women and men in the private sphere and political life, the state's anti-veiling policy assuming authority over women, so far the prerogative of their male relatives, aroused new anxieties and a sense of weakness among Anatolian men. Therefore, they were the first to defy the unveiling campaigns. As a contemporary female observer stated, "there were many men who objected to seeing their wives or their daughters appearing in public without the traditional clothes." Men feared these developments would reduce their authority within the family. Indeed, women's veiling was closely associated with male control over women's sexuality. A contemporary observer recalled how a male visitor criticized the reforms by saying, "Petticoats (*eksik etek*) cannot be considered equal to men. If there are no men to control their families, the dependent women will go astray. What the hell is that equality?" Some men thought reforms concerning women threatened their masculinity.[12]

Another reason behind men's opposition to the anti-veiling campaign was the possible adverse economic effects of women's liberation for men. Most low-income men perceived the entrance of women into working life as further competition in the labor market. Due to the shortage of labor after long wars depleting the male population, a crucial prerequisite of the newly emerging Turkish economy was to free women from the bonds of traditional gender relations that had barred them from the labor market.[13] Indeed, the number of female workers slightly increased during the 1930s. Therefore, male workers, who saw the female workforce as a threat to their jobs, disliked women's entrance into work life. A newspaper article titled "Male Workers Complain about Women" reported that men, particularly unemployed men, insinuated that employment of women had resulted in unemployment among men and a decrease in wages.[14]

What is worse, female workers were susceptible to sexual harassment and rape, which aggrieved not only them but also their male relatives. For instance, in a tobacco factory directed by the Monopoly Administration, a group of mostly male workers complained of sexual harassment of female workers by the factory managers. A 1933 report about working life in the industrial enterprises of İzmir drew attention to the widespread sexual abuse of female workers. According to the report, most of the female workers in the factories of İzmir had become prostitutes and were morally depraved. This attitude prevailed in other industrialized regions as a universal fact of capitalism. For that reason, most women did not enthusiastically welcome being visible without their head covers in public. Even in Ankara, the people, including women, did not take kindly to women working outside their homes. Likewise, although the Sümerbank Kayseri Textile Factory, one of the largest factories of the time, needed female workers, both women and their male relatives disliked the idea of women working alongside men, and therefore the factory had to employ children about twelve years old.[15]

Economic Costs of Unveiling

One of the reasons the clothing reforms discomfited people was their inability to afford new dress. The new image of women had thrown low-income families into financial distress as they incurred unexpected expenses for new clothes. An article titled "Overcoat or Bread?" quoted a letter from a group of men in the Akseki district of Antalya. The letter writers said, "We are poor people who live on bread. In spite of this, the state has ordered us to buy new outfits for our wives." Indeed, the new, fashionable clothing was expensive, whereas the *çarşaf* was both easily made and cheaper. As low-income men did, women complained about the financial burden of unveiling for their families. Furthermore, veiling was an egalitarian practice. Its modest and uniform style was very functional for low-income and poor women, enabling them to conceal old, cheap or dirty clothes under their *çarşafs*. Even educated women ready to wear it found the new women's hats unsuitable for their bodies, which stressed them terribly.[16] On the other hand, uncovering their hair and wearing new fashions could make it necessary for women to adopt other fashions such as makeup and haircuts. All these meant new costs, which lay a further burden on poor and low-income families.

Manufacturers and merchants of traditional women's clothes were also terrified of the state policies that sought to transform women's

clothing. They generally perceived the anti-veiling campaigns as detri-
mental to business. Ahmet Şevki, a textile manufacturer producing
*çarşaf*s and headscarves in Aydın, was one exemplar of these opponents
of the change in women's clothing. According to intelligence reports,
his main interest was to ensure his income by the continuation of the
old clothing styles. Upon the start of the anti-veiling campaigns, he sent
petitions complaining of these campaigns to Atatürk and to the RPP.
Addressing the individual rights of citizens rhetorically, he wrote, "The
law of individual freedom has been trampled on." In a similar vein, the
RPP organization in Maraş reported in 1936 that handloom weavers,
tailors and sellers who for a long time had produced and marketed
black cotton fabrics and traditional women's clothes opposed the
elimination of the veil. They requested the government to lift the anti-
veiling campaign launched by the city council; otherwise, they would
lose their jobs.[17]

Local Community Pressure

All of these issues created social pressure that obstructed giving up
veiling. One of the most important factors that discouraged women
from accepting modern clothing was peer pressure. Beliefs about veiling as a symbol and requirement of piety and chastity and negative
perceptions of unveiled women outweighed state propaganda. Not
only men, but also women played an important role in this regard. As
a study on Pakistani women points out, "Women are susceptible to
other women's evaluations regarding their responsibilities. ... Mutual
surveillance – subtle or projected – keeps [them] within the proper
boundaries."[18] Likewise, in many Anatolian towns, women who
broke the age-old rules risked public criticism or even physical attack.
Even in the poor quarters of big cities, both men and women fixed their
eyes on modern-looking women in the streets. Monitoring by neighbors and especially mocking by men in public kept women from
adopting modern clothes. In a 1936 report, the Çankırı governor
addressed the adverse effect of the negative attitudes toward bareheaded women on the anti-veiling campaign. For this reason, most
women, except for the women of a few educated families, did not
dress according to the official regulations.[19]

Indeed, Anatolian men and especially old women frowned on
unveiled women. Old women believed and often said that God would

punish women who exposed their heads and legs. As Pakize Türkoğlu wrote in her memoirs, when she wanted to enroll in a school during her childhood in the early 1930s, her female relatives and neighbors told her, "What the hell do girls have to do with school? Female students do not cover their head there; if you go to school, you will burn in hell tomorrow." Community pressure was so intense that women of Armenian families who had been deported from Mutki to Çorum due to the uprisings in the region in the mid-1930s needed to wear the *çarşaf* wherever they were sent because the locals harshly condemned women who did not.[20]

The main reason behind such behavior was a common popular understanding of the ideal woman, which was at odds with the republican perception of the "new woman" free from piety and chastity. Many thought the image of the new woman promoted by the government was so immodest that these women looked like prostitutes. Adnan Binyazar mentions in his memoir that his poor master running a small diner in the Kasımpaşa quarter of İstanbul often blamed unveiled women and their men for being "whores" and "cuckolds."[21]

This was not an exceptional example. A notice sent to the Interior Ministry by the police reported many inflammatory and scornful comments circulating among the people, such as "Nowadays they have made women look like whores." According to police records, "reactionaries" (*mürteci*), accusing the anti-veiling campaigns of going against moral values, were discouraging women from abandoning the veil. Interestingly, among them were the administrators of the provincial RPP branches. In Eskişehir, the party directors of some districts avoided waging an anti-veiling campaign. Likewise, as party inspector Adnan Menderes reported, party administrators and members in Konya and in some districts of Antalya such as Alanya, Korkuteli and Serik were unwilling to carry out anti-veiling campaigns because of narrow-mindedness or fear of public criticism. Some party members had said, "We have no right to hurt people's feelings."[22]

Consequently, as police reports noted, women in some provinces or districts could not leave their homes or walk in the streets comfortably. For women who were unready or unwilling to go out unveiled, exposing their head was a source of shame, because veiling was closely associated with honor. Walking in streets or bazaars created anxiety for women who had newly given up veiling. When shopkeepers and artisans in the shopping district gaped at them, some of these women stumbled due to their increasing anxiety.[23]

Intimidation into Veiling

Like men with Western hats, unveiled women were often subjected to verbal or physical assault. This was another deterrent to going unveiled. Indeed, dressing in the modern way proved more difficult than veiling, except in a few cosmopolitan city centers. Modern-looking women frequently encountered harassment and verbal attacks in the streets. Some of those who disturbed and molested these women were only vagrants; however, there were those who deliberately treated modern-looking women badly owing to their resentment of the anti-veiling campaigns, the regime or the government. It was a way of intimidating women into veiling and expressing discontent with the regime or resentment of the rich. Some poor individuals targeted modern-looking women as symbols of the elite they perceived as a cause of their misery.[24] There were several cases of assaults on these women in the streets. In his memoirs, Kılıç Ali, a close friend of Atatürk's, notes that such events occurred right after the clothing reforms. In Adana, for instance, molestation of women by rough men called külhanbeyi ran so wild that women could not go out.[25]

In another example, according to a telegram sent by three female teachers from Sivas to the government, a rough man named Nergiszade Boyacı Ahmed intimidated female teachers and other unveiled women into wearing the çarşaf. Likewise, it was reported from Afyon in November 1935 that upon the appearance of bareheaded women in public, some men began to shout at them, "What wonderful 'domestic goods' we have!" ("Ne eyi yerli mallarımız varmış!"). According to the bureaucrats of the Interior Ministry, such rude behaviors kept women from unveiling.[26]

A popular slander against a woman in modern dress was to call her gavur in the streets. In addition, some verbally attacked unveiled women by calling them Tango, as the tango was widely perceived as an immoral dance performed by couples who dressed indecently. Women with modern dress were shouted at concertedly in the streets: "Tango, Tango, in his back bow-tie!" ("Tango, tango, arkasında fiyangoo!"). Some children shouted at women with hats, "Madam, Madam, let the dog pee on your neck" ("Madama Madama/ Köpek siysin yakana"). Verbal attacks occasionally turned into physical ones.

In Zile, a group of men who criticized a female teacher for her embrace of modern clothes ultimately raped her. The memoirs of Adnan Binyazar are a good example of how marginalized and desperate individuals vented their anger on well-dressed women. Binyazar, a poor boy who had migrated from Diyarbakır to İstanbul in those years, harassed modern-looking women and fancy girls who seemed to him spoiled members of the elite. Once he threw a rotten tomato at them.[27] The government, aware of the adverse impact of such events on the unveiling campaigns, took stringent measures. The Justice Ministry issued a circular in September 1929 ordering local courts to prosecute those who molested or accosted women. In the following years, numerous men who verbally attacked women in the streets were imprisoned or heavily fined.[28]

Compounded by the popular dislike of unveiling, rumors served to express and to disseminate the views inimical to anti-veiling campaigns. Alarming rumors that the state would soon deport Muslim women to foreign countries and import Christian symbols shook popular trust in the government's intentions. Women both produced and disseminated similar rumors at gatherings of close friends. As mentioned before, rumors circulating among the people alleged that their forebears turned over in their graves and even resurrected due to the "naked women." In another case, false news that "policemen and gendarmes had been killed by the people when they attempted to remove women's veils" circulated in 1935 in Konya.[29] Rumors also frightened women into keeping away from public life and thereby from unveiling. In Gaziantep, rumor had it that police officers had begun to tear off *çarşaf*s and scarves. Upon hearing this rumor, women stopped leaving their homes. Another rumor, circulated in Hınıs in 1939, was more fear-provoking, claiming that the government was preparing to put Turkish girls into the service of Russian men. After the death of Atatürk, rumors claiming that the state would retreat to the old sublime days and accordingly to old clothes and even old sexual segregation circulated in almost all regions of the country.[30] All these rumors encouraged disobedience to anti-veiling measures.

Open Disobedience, Petitions and Threats

Although the government passed no law banning veiling, provincial administrations locally banned or restricted veiling, particularly its

extreme forms such as the black *çarşaf* and face veils. Police and gen-
darmes occasionally issued warnings or fines. On rare occasions, officious
security forces attempted to remove women's veils forcibly. Despite these
local measures, women did not give up veiling. In the Tirebolu district of
Giresun, for example, the municipality decided to eliminate the veil on
October 7, 1926, but obtained no result in the face of women's resistance.
The women in the province continued to cover their heads and faces. In
Trabzon, the city council banned the veil in December 1926, but most
women refused to comply. Although the police prosecuted a few women
for intimidating others, many women stood up to these measures. One of
them was Sakine Arat. Despite warnings and fines, she continued to wear
the *çarşaf* and once loudly protested by saying, "Even if you tear off my
çarşaf ten times, I will not give up veiling. This is my tradition." In the end,
the police stopped warning her.[31]

Resistance to the anti-veiling campaigns took the form of writing complaint letters to local and central politicians, sometimes in a threatening
manner. The government received many complaint letters from Ordu
province against the anti-veiling campaign launched by the municipality.
Police reports generally pointed out that locals had greeted the anti-veiling
campaign organized by the provincial administration with general aversion. Among the documents in the police archive are also warning letters
sent by prominent and influential individuals in the provinces. These
people, who had their fingers on the pulse of public opinion, warned the
government not to force women to expose their heads. One such letter,
sent to the Interior Minister by a prominent farmer in Ödemiş, reported
a night watchman's zealous enforcement was causing furious conflicts
between security forces and women or their husbands. He invited government and civil servants to show understanding of local customs and
lifestyles.[32]

In Nazilli, the strictness of the district governor spurred a group of
women to affix an anonymous complaint letter with implicitly threatening contents to the door of his house. One of the women, named
Pakize, who was suspected of writing the letter, was prosecuted by the
court. In a similarly threatening manner, Gaziantep inhabitants, displeased with the anti-veiling campaigns of the municipality, wrote
anonymous letters warning the governor not to intervene in women's
clothing choices. In the face of these letters, the Gaziantep governorship
put off the campaigns in June 1936 and let the women have their way.[33]

Albeit rarely, women who were aware that veiling was not outlawed defended themselves via petitions or legal ways against members of the security forces who attempted to punish them. Two sisters in Sivas, for example, who had been fined upon entering a government office in çarşafs, refuted the accusations on the grounds that they could not be regarded as guilty because no law banned their attire.[34]

Selective Adaptation: Combining Veiling with Modern Styles

Many women dealt with anti-veiling campaigns by finding a middle course between the official rules and the accustomed clothing styles. Caught between the pressure from the state and the disapproval of their relatives and neighbors, many women sought a compromise in stylistically eclectic clothing. Some wore long overcoats and headscarves covering the head and neck. Others used only a headscarf tied under the chin. These new combinations, more or less suitable under both the anti-veiling campaigns and traditional clothing codes, enabled women to balance the pressures of two opposite forces.[35] Even when they were exercising their official rights, like voting in 1935 and later, they were often photographed veiled in different ways (see Illustrations 13.1, 13.2 and 13.3).

Another alternative was to hide the face with an umbrella. According to a news article entitled "You Cannot See Any Women without Umbrellas in Alâiye," almost all unveiled women had begun to carry umbrellas in order to hide their face and head, even at night. Likewise, in Gaziantep, women who wore a headscarf instead of a çarşaf substituted umbrellas for their çarşafs. The memoirs of Nahid Sırrı Örik, a republican bureaucrat who toured Anatolian towns in the late 1930s, indicate how women circumvented anti-veiling measures by partly incorporating these policies into their usual clothing styles. In Kayseri, according to Örik, many women had withdrawn from public life. After quite a while of waiting in the city center, he had seen a few women wearing black overcoats and black gloves. Some also carried black umbrellas with which they hid their faces. He wrote that he could not see the face of even one of these women.[36]

A contemporary young woman from a middle-class family in İstanbul, Necla Pekolcay, witnessed how her mother began to wear an overcoat, a headscarf called a *sıkmabaş* to cover her head and another scarf to cover her neck. Although this style would be preferred

Illustration 13.1 Women and men in the bazaar of Sivas, wearing traditional clothing in 1935

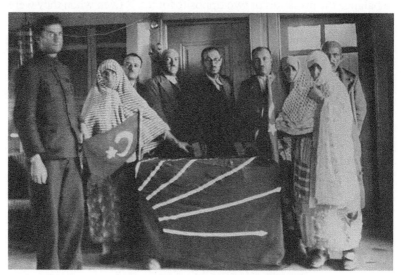

Illustration 13.2 Women in Afyon wearing local style *çarşafs* vote in 1935

by Islamist women somewhat later, it actually first burgeoned in this period as an eclectic and adaptive form of veiling, but not as a symbol of a political movement. Likewise, a lot of women in Black Sea

Illustration 13.3 İstanbul's poor women in Topkapı in 1937

provinces gave up their *çarşaf*s but invented interesting forms of veiling in 1934. Women reportedly replaced the *çarşaf* with large towels wrapping their heads and upper bodies.[37]

Impact of Popular Response

State-sponsored anti-veiling campaigns as a part of secularization projects in the Muslim world were not peculiar to Turkey. Reform attempts in women's clothing swept across other Muslim countries from the Balkans to Central Asia. One of the earlier attempts was made by the Afghan state. King Amanullah Khan, the founder of the Afghan state, ordered Afghani police to tear off women's veils in the streets in 1928. Hearing of this, Atatürk said to his ambassador to Kabul, Yusuf Hikmet (Bayur), "Tell him [the king], a man should not hit his head on the rocks." Indeed, Amanullah Khan would have to flee the country shortly after due to the religious backlash. Atatürk, on the other hand, was sensitive and forward-thinking about the probable consequences of any forceful intervention in women's clothing. Atatürk's words summarize the republic's approach to veiling. The republican rulers were aware of the possible dangers of forcible intervention in gender relations, especially in women's clothing, and therefore adopted a more moderate attitude.[38]

After the political consolidation of the regime in 1934, the government opted to encourage provincial party and state administrations to take locally suitable measures to promote the elimination of veiling. However, despite intense propaganda and campaigns encouraging women to give up the *çarşaf*, the *peçe* and other forms of the veil, the overwhelming majority of women did not abandon veiling. People contested anti-veiling policies in covert and subtle ways in their everyday lives. Many women insisted on their usual outfits, whereas many others creatively adopted new and eclectic styles of veiling. The local society's control outweighed the influence of state propaganda in shaping women's clothing. That is, the state's secularization drive did not overcome the provincial society's local cultures and lifestyles. Consequently, women's usual clothing styles based on veiling persisted throughout the country, except in the centers and certain quarters of big cities. This was not due only to the society's religiosity or opposition to the regime. The reasons were more complex and multifaceted, and the rulers were aware of them. Both men's and women's approach to veiling or anti-veiling were shaped not only by religious conservatism but also by gender relations, economics, age-old traditions and psychosocial factors.

Accordingly, well aware of all of these factors and especially people's sensitivity to women's clothing as the primary extension of gender relations, the republic's response to veiling was somewhat flexible and moderate. No law forbidding the veil was passed. Nor did provincial administrators strictly forbid it. The mayors or governors who locally banned or restricted the veil never strictly observed the implementation of these bans or kept the restrictions limited to state buildings. When fervent governors asked permission from the Interior Ministry to use their security forces against women who defied their directives, the ministry refused and warned them to avoid outrageous measures. The Antalya governor was one of those bureaucrats who were eager to exercise physical force against veiled women. Upon women's indifference to the local ban, he asked the ministry for authorization to employ police force. The ministry refused. One month later, on December 14, 1934, the Interior Ministry sent a circular to all governors and general inspectors ordering them not to resort to force. The next year, the fourth general congress of the party would witness a debate about whether veiling should be legally prohibited. Whereas some politicians like Asım Us argued for legal prohibition, interior minister Şükrü Kaya regarded legal measures as unnecessary. His comparatively pliant approach to the issue exposed him to accusations of gradualism.[39]

In view of widespread discontent, the government had to further soften its stance toward the end of the decade. On November 14, 1938, new interior minister Refik Saydam issued a circular to all governors stipulating security officers should by no means force women and girls to take off the headgear they had been using since old times. The minister recommended provincial authorities take measures appropriate to local conditions so that such customs would disappear in a gradual manner. One year later, the next minister, Faik Öztrak, issued a similar circular ordering governors to show tolerance to women's noncompliance with clothing laws.[40]

The implementation of republican secularism with regard to women's clothing was not determined by top-down decrees. Everyday resistance and selective adaptation compelled the republican elites to be more tolerant and compromising in practice. The government granted the local bureaucrats the leeway to adopt policies appropriate to local conditions. This distinguished the Turkish experience from that of Iran and Afghanistan. The republic's approach to the issue, as Kandiyoti argues, was pedagogic and indirect compared to Reza Shah's drastic ban that intervened even in the headscarf.[41] The Turkish government gave passive consent to the headscarf and even to the black *çarşaf* in daily life. In this regard, republican secularism was flexible and moderate rather than assertive and uncompromising. The continuity of many other religious and traditional beliefs and practices I will show now also proves this.

14 | *Old Habits Die Hard*

Tenacity of Old Lifestyles in New Times

The young republic took further steps in tailoring the new Turkish nation to Western European standards. In the sphere of gender and women's status, the Civil Code, adopted from Swiss law in 1926, was a radical rupture with Sharia law. The republic also envisaged a mental transformation of the masses from mysticism to rationalism. Science, modern medicine and the visual and plastic arts were ardently advocated as a bulwark against supernatural beliefs and superstitions. Popular spiritual practices such as amulets and faith healing were banned. Sacred tombs of Muslim saints entitled to public veneration and believed capable of interceding for people on earth were closed. However, it was easier to make regulations than to enforce them. The Civil Code was not able to put a lid on the age-old practice of gender bias. Popular perceptions of women's role in society and marriage patterns changed little. All forms of spiritual belief and practice survived. The republic could not fully impose its vision of modernity on society.

The Tenacity of Established Gender Relations

"Popular Code" vs. Civil Code

"Official marriage requires a complex preparation process for our villages. Population registers, physician's examination, and similar paperwork ... However, there is a very easy way of getting married that has existed for centuries: religious marriage performed by preachers. Men resort to religious marriage in order to make things easier, to divorce their wives easily without any legal responsibility whenever they want or to marry a second woman. Therefore, there is still a huge number of illegal marriages and illegal children from such marriages. From time to time the National Assembly needs to make laws to deal with these problems. This proves the resistance of the old traditions and practices to the Civil Code. .... Some argue that peasants marry more than one woman because of their need for a labor force to employ in the field."[1]

Tezer Taşkıran, the daughter of a liberal-leaning RPP elite, Ahmet Ağaoğlu, wrote this in the 1970s. Indisputably the republic made great contributions to women's rights and freedoms in the long run. Nevertheless, age-old gender biases, deeply embedded in the social fabric, were to long outweigh the new rules and principles. The majority of people did not keep pace with the republic's ideal of modern family and gender relations. Extremely patriarchal gender relations, unregistered and unofficial religious marriages, female seclusion and, to a lesser extent, polygamy survived.

The chief principles related to marriage adopted by the Civil Code were monogamy and official registration of the family union. Under Islamic law, the consent of both parties given before two witnesses in the presence of an imam pronouncing the marriage was sufficient for the establishment of a family union. The Civil Code changed this by requiring the official registration of the union by a government official. In the case of divorce, it introduced the principle of reciprocity. Scholars interpret this change as revolutionary, as it superseded the religious code and Islamic provisions for marriage and divorce.[2] Unquestionably it was revolutionary in the legal realm, but the revolution in practice would not come as quickly.

As a prerequisite of a modern state, the new Turkish state attached great importance to population censuses and statistics. However, the civil government institutions and bureaucracy were not ready to collate detailed and precise information on people. The government had to overcome several impediments before monitoring the population. According to a 1938 report by the General Directorate of Civil Registry (Nüfus İşleri Umum Müdürlüğü) about the obstacles to obtaining an exact census of the population, the primary ones were unregistered marriages, childbirths and deaths. The report gives insight into how widespread unregistered marriages were. The 1935 population census recorded 2,729,980 unregistered childbirths, 159,718 unregistered deaths and 852,676 unregistered marriages. These figures undoubtedly represent only those cases that could be detected. Unregistered religious marriage was quite easy in terms of both performing and concealing it from the state. Such marriages did not require the red tape, financial cost and lengthy procedures of official marriage. In a country where about 85 percent of the population lived in villages, the Civil Code had charged village headmen with the registration of marriages. However, the great majority of headmen were not capable of carrying out this task. Many were illiterate and negligent. The details of the paperwork often tripped up them. In Kurdish provinces many did not know even Turkish, let alone being literate. Therefore, even in western villages, the report says, the pages of population registers remained blank. The high financial costs of a civil marriage arising from fees for postage, registration, marriage declaration forms and certificates, health reports and photographs for the marriage certificates were another deterrence to official marriage. The last but most important reason for unregistered marriages was the popularity of the religious marriage called *imam nikahı*.[3]

Contemporary sociologist Niyazi Berkes notes that religious marriages, performed secretly by preachers and unlawfully not complemented with compulsory civil marriages, were still widespread throughout Turkey. The *imam nikahı* was essential to the establishment of the family union even in Ankara. Similarly, according to a monograph by Joseph S. Szyliowicz on Erdemli and Koyuncu villages in Mersin, as of the 1940s, religious marriage was prevalent. Almost all marriages were unregistered owing to the expenses and bother of the necessary trip downtown. The peasants did not consider a marriage valid unless a preacher had sanctified and announced it. A survey by the Justice Ministry in 1942 confirms this reality by noting, "Peasants still continue to value a marriage by an imam who read aloud a verse from the Quran above an official marriage performed by an ignorant village headman who does not know what to do."[4]

The prevalence of religious marriages over civil marriages is reflected in the wish lists prepared by provincial party congresses. In these lists, the most striking issues pertinent to the Justice Ministry were about the population's disregard for the Civil Code. In Eskişehir, for instance, the avoidance of civil marriage was among the primary causes of the large number of unregistered school-aged children. The citizens demanded the legal marriage age be reduced to seventeen for men and sixteen for women. The relatively high minimum age for marriage dissuaded parents from civil marriage. From Maraş and Kayseri similar demands were raised. The party branch in Kastamonu requested the government simplify the official procedures for marriage, which were daunting for peasants. The party congress in Bolu demanded the amendment of the

Civil Code and the criminal laws, whose gaps people manipulated in order to escape civil marriage. Article 237 of the Criminal Law prescribed punishment for preachers who performed religious marriage without civil marriage and for couples who married without civil marriage. However, there was no punishment for people who were not imams but performed religious marriages. This allowed people to bypass the Civil Code and the Criminal Law by falsely claiming that their marriages had not been performed by preachers, but by other persons. For the judicial authorities, it was impossible to prove whether a marriage had been solemnized by an imam or someone else. Another common demand of the provincial party congresses was to relieve the financial costs and to ease the daunting procedures of civil marriage. It was also difficult for illiterate people and barely literate village headmen to fill out the marriage forms. All of these factors encouraged people to avoid civil marriage. As of 1933, the *imam nikahı* not complemented by civil marriage was so prevalent across Anatolia some bureaucrats urged the government to prevent more effectively those religious marriages made without the official procedures.[5]

Indeed, of all marriages during the first decades of the republic, civil marriages accounted for less than half. Even three decades after the adoption of the Civil Code, in the mid-1950s, the number of civil marriages did not exceed 70,000 a year, whereas the annual number of marriages in countries that had approximately the same population as Turkey reached 180,000. The widespread avoidance of civil marriage led the ruling elite to think of solutions to the problem during the 1930s and later decades. In 1936, the government had to amend the laws by introducing harsher punishments such as prison sentences of six months to three years for spouses who violated the Civil Code's ban on unregistered religious marriage and polygamy. Village headmen who avoided reporting marriages performed illegally would be fined between 5 and 500 liras.[6]

Many other reasons also caused illegal marriages to be performed in old ways. The minimum legal age for marriage made marriage for younger people impossible. Therefore, the Civil Code, along with other factors, led to an increase in prearranged abductions of young women. In this regard, the abduction of girls, a widespread phenomenon in rural Anatolia, was a popular way to get around the requirements of official marriage. On the other hand, poor young men especially resorted to this method to bypass other obstacles such as the bride price. Thus the abduction of girls in this sense required an urgent marriage to save the couple's honor. Such cases therefore caused the persistence of religious marriages, which could be completed very quickly.[7]

Another reason for the persistence of religious marriage was the fact that men in villages whose wives were infertile or had not given birth to a son were seen as having the right to take a second woman as a substitute wife called *kuma* in order to produce a child, most preferably a son. In such cases, a second wife could be taken only by means of a quick religious marriage. Moreover, the fact that women were seen as a production factor in the village made it reasonable for a man to marry more than one woman, which was permissible only in religious marriage. Finally, widows who wanted to continue receiving a widow's pension after remarriage had to resort to religious marriage in order to retain their legal status as widows.[8]

Although Islam gave men the right to up to have four wives at one time, this situation had never been as widespread as assumed in Ottoman Anatolia. Foreign travelers even in the eighteenth and nineteenth centuries wrote of the infrequency of polygamy in Asia Minor. In late nineteenth-century İstanbul, only 2.5 percent of men had more than one wife. Polygamy, or *taadüd-i zevcât* as the Ottomans called it, even among the Ottoman upper classes had begun to decline because the supply of "women slaves" called *cariye* (concubines) from the Caucasus and the Balkans had diminished with the contraction of the empire.[9]

Finally, the republic legally forbade men to marry more than one woman under the new Civil Code. Yet polygamy, though it remained low as before, survived during the early republic. The main reason for this was the proportionally smaller male population due to war losses in the last years of the empire. In addition, polygamy provided a social insurance mechanism for women without any breadwinner relatives. Consequently, in spite of the Civil Code, polygamy would not disappear, particularly among the people of remote eastern villages.[10]

It is indeed difficult to estimate the rate of polygamous marriage because it was forbidden and thus hidden. Researchers interested in the issue therefore focused on the later decades of the republic on which more information exists. The statistics from the 1960s and 1970s point out the marriage of men with more than one woman. However, limited data regarding the interwar years demonstrate also the persistence of polygamy during that period. According to a survey by the Justice

Ministry in 1942, polygamy in rural Turkey varied between 2 percent and 10 percent on average in these years. Research conducted in the later years showed that about one-third of polygamous families lived in the eastern provinces. Village monographers also confirmed the existence of polygamy in spite of the Civil Code. In Ankara villages, although monogamy was the general pattern, some men married more than one woman. Such marriages did not vanish even in the decades to come, reaching about 20 percent in the villages of Konya, Kayseri, Çankırı and Yozgat by the end of the 1950s.[11]

The main reason for polygamous marriage was not the religiosity of the Anatolian people. In many cases, the infertility of the first wife and the need for additional labor within the family led men to take more than one wife. Especially in the case of infertility or serious illness of the first wife, this practice provided social security for her, who otherwise would be divorced. Sometimes first wives even welcomed a co-wife as additional help with domestic chores and farm work. Polygamy was by no means outmoded in the Anatolian countryside, especially among peasants and nomads. According to the records of an observer, many polygamous men lived in the villages of the Taurus Mountains in 1928. A Turcoman peasant stated, "For us, women are capital. In the cities, the rich build homes; here the rich Turcomans marry." Even in the western countryside, polygamy was alive. In the rural areas of İzmir, a remarkable number of men married more than one woman, even as many as four. In his monograph on the village of Hasanoğlan, İbrahim Yasa notes the number of men who wanted to marry more than one woman was not a few. Other field surveys from the period also prove polygamy still existed in the villages of both the eastern and the western provinces. Samsun deputy Ali Tunalı's report also complained of widespread marriage to more than one and even up to three women, which, he argued, harmed women's rights and honor.[12]

In the towns and villages of Kastamonu, men who married a second woman illegally pretended to be hiring a housemaid or a woman laborer. Likewise, in İçel, a considerable number of men reportedly married a second wife covertly. This was not a matter on which the state was open to compromise. The persistence of polygamy prompted the Interior Ministry to promulgate a circular in March 1937 increasing the penalty for polygamous marriage.[13]

The legal age limits for marriage were also trespassed by the people via *imam nikahı*. The Civil Code determined the legal age for marriage as eighteen for men and seventeen for women. In spite of this, younger boys and girls continued to be betrothed by their parents. The average age of marriage for women in the countryside ranged between twelve and fifteen. By the age of twelve or thirteen, most girls were regarded as ready for marriage. In the villages of even the capital city, the age of marriage was reaching down to twelve or thirteen. Single women older than seventeen were seen as spinsters since many girls married as soon as they turned twelve. Certain early marriages, especially between cousins, were regarded as a protection against division of the family estate. Whatever the reason, any early marriage was impossible under the due process of law. In these cases, *imam nikahı* without official marriage was inevitable. As another solution, which guaranteed the legal rights of couples, some families legally revised the ages of their daughters two or three years upward so as to make them eligible for marriage. Prominent families especially received the help of local bureaucrats to cover up early marriage by forging documents.[14]

In the face of the people's resistance to the Civil Code and in accordance with the government's pronatalist population policy, the government declared an amnesty on the tenth anniversary of the republic. Couples who had married only via a religious ceremony and their unregistered children were officially accepted as legitimate. Yet this did not end the problem. One year later, with the Law for Registration of Hidden Population, all marriages, whether official or religious, and all births, whether legitimate or illegitimate, were accepted as legal and recorded in basic census rosters. Compulsory prepayment for stamps was cancelled on marriage, divorce and birth documents. In February 1937, the fees for official documents such as the "marriage declaration form," "written notice," "medical report" and "marriage certificate" were decreased or abolished. Marriage procedures were simplified. Two years later, the price of official marriage forms was to be further lowered.[15]

Debates on the suitability of the Civil Code for Turkish society with respect to legal age limits for marriage came to the fore in 1938. The Turkish legislature amended the Civil Code in order to accommodate local conditions. Article 88 of the Civil Code, amended on June 16, 1938, lowered the minimum age for marriage to seventeen for men and fifteen for women, and in exceptional circumstances to fifteen for men and fourteen for women.[16] Three years before this amendment, the Supreme Court had already authorized judges to lower the minimum age without restriction for women if the woman had become pregnant or had lost her virginity. This clause would be exploited by those who wanted to marry before being of age through prearranged abductions, another example of the local social landscape's influence over the laws. Finally, another amnesty in 1945 would accept as legitimate all families established through religious marriage and all children of these families on the condition that such religious marriages and illegitimate children were registered in population registries.[17] This was an important concession to society. Protecting the rights of children and women and preventing the growing number of inheritance disputes occupying the law courts made this legal concession imperative.

Little Change in the Status of Women

"Those days I was a young woman. One day I accidentally overcooked the food and burnt it. Then, 'Oh,' I said to my mother, 'You cannot beat me; we are living under the Republic.' My mother replied to me immediately, 'That Republic is not at home, it is outside.'"[18] Such is the recollection of an Anatolian woman who was aware of her rights in the 1930s. It illustrates how far republican modernization reached ordinary women. Modernist historical accounts of the early republic, focusing on educated middle-class women and their legal rights, argue that women were emancipated under the republic. Drawing such a conclusion from educated and middle-class urban women's experiences can be valid. However, it does correspond to a lesser extent with ordinary women's experiences. Indeed, republican leadership strived to end the seclusion of women, sexual segregation and the religious notion of women's "inferiority by nature." The republican regime broke the old conception of women to some degree, especially in the legal domain. However, real life was beyond the reach of the laws and regulations. The secondary status of women and sexual segregation, albeit in lighter forms as compared to imperial times, proved more enduring throughout the country.

For most women in rural areas, the republic and its reforms represented something intangible. The republic could neither penetrate the private sphere nor change women's secondary status in actuality. In interviews with provincial women experiencing these years, most of them underlined the continuity rather than the change in daily life. Just as one peasant woman, Emine Akay, summed up the novelties of the new regime by saying, "Nothing has happened in our village."[19] Many provincial bureaucrats did not give up their usual strictly patriarchal relationships with their wives. According to Cahit Kayra, in Sürmene, where he went as an inspector for the Finance Ministry, there were generally no women in the streets in the early 1940s. Men and women could not walk together. Even the subdistrict governor and his wife walked separately along different paths. "It was," Kayra noted despondently, "really very difficult to change the Anatolian people." Moreover, for the most part, women had no right to choose their husbands and continued to be married off by their fathers.[20]

Perhaps the best way to gauge the continuity of women's secondary status is women's dress as an extension of gender relations. The government's efforts to change women's clothing and sexual segregation did not find ready acceptance, as discussed earlier. Whereas some women wore tall cotton frocks, overcoats and loose robes combined with headscarves, others never discarded the *çarşaf* or its derivatives. Most men disliked seeing their wives, daughters or sisters in public without a *çarşaf* or a headscarf. In even western Anatolian villages, peasants continued to believe that the angels did not come into houses in which the woman was bareheaded. A contemporary female sociologist wrote that she personally witnessed a peasant woman beaten by her husband since she forgot to cover her head inside the house.[21]

Segregation of the sexes continued in everyday life throughout Anatolia except for the large city centers. Especially in the countryside and eastern Anatolia, it remained as strict as it had been before the republic. Provincial society was generally shocked by the very idea of women working side by side with men. This was one of the reasons behind the employment of small girls and boys under twelve in newly established factories. Even in the capital of the republic, Ankara, people took a dim view of women working at jobs outside the home. In the Kurdish provinces, patriarchy and seclusion of women were intense. Sex segregation continued to shape the organization of rooms in the house by reserving *selamlık*s for only men. Like worship, wedding celebrations and even receiving guests continued to be performed separately for men and women throughout the country.[22]

Traces of gender discrimination in public life could also be seen in big western cities. In some seaports of İstanbul, segregation was still evident by 1929. Even in the biggest cosmopolitan city, İstanbul, keeping women passengers in separate areas of the ferries and ports of Şirket-i Hayriye lasted until the 1930s. Similarly, although local governments had abolished separation of the sexes in public transportation, women and men continued to travel in different sections as late as 1936. In public places like cinemas, men and women were still supposed to attend at different hours or on different days. As reported from Manisa, a western province, men and women, most still veiled, could not attend the cinema together. In some districts, women were not allowed to go shopping or the shops women frequented were still separate.[23]

Another indicator of the continuing women's isolation from public life is girls' low schooling and high drop-out rates. This rate steadily increased during the republic. However, even girls belonging to the middle classes were hardly permitted to enroll in primary schools. That is why literacy among women increased slightly to 15 percent by 1950 and to 55 percent by 1980.[24] The story of a high officeholder living in Ankara shows how the patriarchal culture influenced even the republic's educated men. Saliha, one of two daughters of a bank director in Ankara, covered her head with a headscarf like her mother when she was twelve in 1930. Subsequently, she and her sister were taken out of school. Especially in villages, the common view was that girls did not need to learn reading or writing. Accordingly, girls' school attendance was lower by far than the average, and this changed little during the period. Even in the western Anatolian towns, only a small number of girls were permitted to go to school. Girls had to assist their mothers at too many chores, such as washing dishes and clothes, sweeping rooms and taking care of their brothers and sisters. Learning to do these things was thought imperative to become a good wife. In the villages of the Tavas district in Denizli, for instance, girls were not sent to school and women's literacy remained quite low even into the 1970s. In the east, the situation was worse. In some Kurdish districts, there were almost no girls in school. Tarık Ziya Ekinci recalls only one girl student among 100 students in the primary school in Diyarbakır, and she was the daughter of the gendarmerie commander. Hilmi Seçkin, a future judge from Siirt, writes that if the children of state officials had not attended the schools, classrooms would have been empty. As for girls, their number was much less.[25]

Moreover, parents did not like the new schools in which girls and boys were taught in the same class. Aware of the popular distrust of coeducation, some teachers separated male and female students into different classes or areas within the same class and had them take breaks at different times in order to prevent intermingling. In Diyarbakır High School, female students were segregated from male students and interaction between them was forbidden. They had separate playgrounds and entrances. Boys entered the school from the back door while girls used the front door. This informal segregation also existed in Sivas, as İlhan Başgöz notes in his memoirs. Any male student who spoke to a girl even for an instant became the subject of gossip. Some parents, including his own, terminated their daughters' education for this reason. Friendships between male and female children were often not tolerated.[26]

Atatürk and the new regime exerted great effort to overcome the traditional concept of chastity (*iffet*), which was the main obstacle to women appearing in public places alongside men. Atatürk's dancing with women at balls and wedding ceremonies and special receptions usually held at the People's Houses in which men and women were both present were meant to promote social mixing between men and women. However, most upper-class men and bureaucrats, particularly in provinces, often refused to let their wives and daughters accompany them to such events. Sevim Belli, the granddaughter of an affluent ship owner living in a coveted mansion in Beylerbeyi, wrote about how her uncle never allowed his wife to accompany him on such public occasions. Even top politicians preferred to attend balls alone.[27]

On the other hand, many women felt more secure holding on to the old ways and preferred not to attend such balls and receptions. The wife of the Edirne governor, for instance, rejected her husband's invitation to a ball in the 1930s, saying, "Please do not ever offer me such a thing. Even if I go to the ball out of regard for you, I will sit in a corner with my headscarf. I will not dance and do not let children ridicule me." Among the wives of the top elite were some who were reluctant to attend the events since they were expected to be uncovered. A good example is Reşide Bayar, the wife of the economy minister, later the prime minister, Celal Bayar. She refused to go bareheaded to a reception at İsmet Paşa's mansion, Pembe Köşk. When Atatürk asked about her headscarf, she replied admonishingly, "If you will permit it, let us leave some people's heads covered." Like Reşide

Bayar, most wives of high bureaucrats disapproved of such occasions where women whom they called "improperly dressed" or "naked" had fun together with men. Moreover, probably the attendees also felt insecure at balls due to the possibility of a raid by conservative mobs. Such incidents could occasionally happen even in İstanbul, as an army officer of the time, Salahattin Tanç, witnessed.[28]

Women teachers, supposedly the primary agents to disseminate secular ideals, also hesitated or were not allowed by their husbands to participate in special events where both men and women were present. In one instance, for the celebration of the day of Atatürk's first visit to Antalya, the People's House had prepared a program in which a chorus consisting of male and female teachers would sing the national anthem. However, the female teachers left the choir, asking the pardon of the governorship, because their husbands did not consent to their participation.[29]

Despite the image of equality the republic sought to project, women's basic legal rights granted by the Civil Code were barely applied in practice. The lack of a remarkable advancement in women's rights of inheritance in practice is a good example of how far the Civil Code could transform gender relations. The laws prescribed equal distribution of a deceased husband's or father's inheritance to both male and female heirs. Yet the popular practice of distribution of inheritance to only the male members of the family changed little. Women continued to be disinherited or receive only a small amount. Disputes between husbands and wives were settled within the community, usually in favor of the men, since women mostly had very little contact with the state administration. Due to society's negative perception of divorced women, women rarely dared to divorce their husbands. In other words, the Civil Code granting women the right to divorce had only limited impact on the real lives of women, at least in the first decades. Women's literacy rates, working and visibility in public life – even among middle- and high-income families – would remain low in Anatolian provinces into the 1950s.[30]

The Persistence of Spiritual and Customary Beliefs and Practices

Faith Healing, Amulets and Magic

Joseph Grew, the first American ambassador to Turkey between 1927 and 1933, wrote in his memoirs that what struck him during his stay in

Turkey was the great contrast between what he saw in daily life and Atatürk's motto, "The only real guide in life is science" (*"Hayatta en hakiki mürşid ilimdir"*), which embodied his enlightenment vision. Grew wrote, "Amulets against ill will and illness were so widespread in almost all villages of Ankara that for now a catalogue of amulets is more useful than a catalogue of Zeiss microscopes therein."[31]

Atatürk had made his famous speech praising science in his meeting with teachers of Samsun in 1924. Indeed, his strong attachment to rationalism and enlightenment ideals became the lynchpin of the republic. Great effort was exerted to eliminate religious fundamentalism, mysticism and superstition during the interwar years. Nevertheless, age-old popular spiritual and mystical beliefs and practices persisted in both rural and urban areas. It was pretty difficult to overcome these unless modern medicine, hospitals, doctors, teachers, schools and social policy measures replaced them in satisfying the people's needs. In the absence of such socioeconomic backing, the poor masses especially had to grapple with economic bottlenecks and sociocultural upheaval by using every accessible popular means, including faith healing, amulets, sorcery, melting lead and pouring it into cold water over the head of a sick person in order to break an evil spell (*kurşun döktürme*), oblation and sacrifice to God.

One widespread superstitious behavior that derived from Islamic disapproval of representations of humans was bias against photos and figurative art. Undoubtedly, modern figurative arts and artists, which had sprouted in the last decades of the Ottoman Empire, flourished under the aegis of the government. Atatürk statues were erected in the squares of big cities. However, given the society's bias, even secular intellectuals and the middle classes did not readily embrace them for a long time. Even educated young individuals were suspicious of the camera. When Lilo Linke asked a few educated, middle-class Turkish women if she could take their photos, they vigorously refused because of their religious bias. A folklorist of the time, Musa Kâzım, in an article about superstitions in Anatolia of the mid-1930s, pointed out how deep the hostility toward photography was among the people. Many did not like to have their photos taken because they believed it to be a sin.[32]

Similarly, the belief in the evil eye (*nazar*) was the most popular superstition in Anatolia. A contemporary account of Turkey penned by Millingen and Shah in 1932 mentions how much the Turkish population feared the destructive effects of an envious eye. Having no access to medical facilities, much of the Turkish population, like other rural societies, pinned their hopes on divine intervention in the treatment of diseases. Most inhabitants of İstanbul believed that both good health and fortune were given and taken only by God. Therefore, the most used method to get out illness and bad fortune was mystical practices and folk remedies called "old wives' medicine" (*koca karı ilacı*). In İstanbul alone, there were more than 200 such recipes, which mostly poor old women concocted. Perhaps the most popular and reliable one was the amulet, a piece of paper on which a preacher or anyone believed to have divine authority wrote a prayer in Arabic for a price. Verses of the Quran believed to remedy certain health problems or bad luck were copied onto a piece of paper and placed in a small leather pouch. Almost all children were given an amulet, which some cherished throughout their lives. Fakir Baykurt wrote that, as a village child in Burdur during the 1930s, he had become ill and was taken by his mother to a preacher who hung several amulets and a shoulder belt called a *hamaylı*, which included healing prayers.[33]

In the legal sphere, amulet writing, faith healing, sorcery and similar activities were outlawed under the 1925 law banning dervish lodges and saints' tombs. However, all these activities were extensively carried out here and there. For many, amulets and faith healers were more accessible than doctors and modern medicine. Such practices yielded a good income for a great number of unemployed people. Particularly preachers who lost their previous economic and ideological power relied on faith healing by writing amulets for 1 to 6 liras. There were even expensive amulets that cost up to 15 liras. Faith healing and the beliefs that bred it did not vanish, as is obvious from the news about faith healers caught in the act.[34]

The scarcity of free medical services left poor and diseased people no choice other than to resort to these practices. However, such beliefs and the vested interest in them were so deeply rooted that even when free medical care was available, people did not abandon them. In cases of disease, resorting to sheikhs, preachers or specific faith healers for their divine touch or prayer even after or simultaneously with medical examination was a widespread practice. Both eastern and western villages were rife with faith healers. The Hasanoğlan village of Ankara alone had twelve faith healers and four special people who prescribed amulets. In the Erdemli and Koyuncu villages of Mersin, the treatment of disease was spiritualistic and ritualistic, having been handed down from generation to generation. Although the Village Law obliged headmen to report sorcerers and faith healers to the security forces, many headmen disregarded this obligation. As contemporary sociologist Mediha Berkes stated in a detailed survey in 1941, neither such mystical beliefs nor the faith healers lost their significance with the republican era.[35]

In the Anatolian countryside, people suffering from pain, tuberculosis, malaria and jaundice generally appealed to wise and religious old women faith healers and preachers instead of seeing the government physician. Malaria patients wore special bracelets made of cotton yarn knotted nine times and blessed by preachers. They might also be taken to bodies of cold spring water known as the eye of malaria (*sıtma gözü*). To cure malaria-stricken children, women healers would pretend to cut the child's bloated abdomen with an axe while reciting magical words or prayers. Children with whooping cough were treated by passing through a tunnel inside a huge mound of droppings. Carl Vett, bearing witness to the period, describes ill children being brought by their mothers before a dervish. In order to cure them, the dervish stood on the backs of these small children and touched them with his bare feet. Tomb keepers' prayers and breath were recognized as the best remedies for headache, pain and many diseases.[36]

Folk medicine was popular even among the upper classes. In her memoirs, Sevim Belli tells how her mother and relatives often applied popular nostrums and remedies resembling magic. When her older sister was infected with meningitis, they invited a faith healer. They also resorted to a ritual called *kurşun döktürme* against the possible adverse effects of the evil eye. It was the most popular mystical ceremony, performed by a preacher or elderly women who prayed and blew continuously into the patient's face in order to render the evil spirit deaf and dumb. Meanwhile lead was melted and poured into cold water over the head of a sick or unfortunate person so as to break an evil spell by saying "lead into the Devil's ear." To treat infertility, many people relied on the prayers of faith healers, preachers and sheikhs famous for curing this problem. The clients in need of their help hosted these mystical healers lavishly in their homes. Certain foods such as water and sugar blessed by preachers, sheikhs and faith healers were used to cure specific illnesses and many other earthly troubles.[37]

Convicted by the local courts, some faith healers appealed to the Supreme Court. The high court often reversed the decision of the local courts. In many cases, it acquitted the convicted party by deciding the acts of the defendants did not violate the law shutting down the dervish tombs and religious lodges and forbidding the mystical jobs carried out by those who claimed to be on the staff of these institutions.[38] Finally, the republic, tolerating the practices that were popular among the masses, unless not systematic and politically challenging, did not come down too hard on such popular beliefs and practices.

Visiting the Tombs of Dervishes

Another indicator of the persistence of religious culture was the continuing visitation of tombs and other sites considered sacred. Although the government closed the shrines, they were still active centers of attraction. The Muslim saints' tombs continued to be highly revered places. People troubled by health questions, economic difficulties or family affairs did not give up praying at or near the tombs for the saints' intercession. Women particularly prayed to conceive a child and get married. Many simply visited the tombs as a relaxing practice and to obtain the blessings of the saints. It was popularly believed that danger could be averted or wishes granted by hanging a piece of cloth on the railing of the tomb of a dervish, lighting a candle or kindling in the tomb, sacrificing a sheep, goat or chicken, or donating money or food.[39] Even the land around the tomb was believed to be so holy and blessed that merely touching a tree or stone or eating a pinch of its soil or water was reckoned that could relieve one's grief or troubles.

Despite the official closure of tombs in 1925, within less than a decade many had secretly reopened. Locals and visitors, hand in hand with the so-called tomb staff functioning as tomb keepers and faith healers, mounted a passive resistance to keep them open. In some places, they claimed that the doors of the tombs, locked by security forces, had been opened at night by invisible beings, *djinn*s, or the ghosts of entombed saints.

The Kemal Ümmi Tomb in the Tekke village of Bolu was one of them. It remained open and active even after the ban on tombs. This famous tomb also was the main source of income for the peasants who ran it. The sacrificed sheep, goats and chickens and other offerings went to them. Therefore, although the security forces shut down the tomb, the peasants reopened and ran it, claiming that the door of the tomb opened by itself on visiting days.[40]

In a similar case, residents of an Aegean village believed that a trivet near a particular tomb had healing powers. If an ill person could pass through it, they would recover. If not, they could offer a sacrifice instead. The district governor moved it to a distant place in order to cut people's ties with it. However, it soon appeared back in its original spot. Although the villagers did it, in order to escape the law, they invented a rumor that the trivet had magically reappeared on its own.[41]

Indeed, in order to preserve their popular holy places, people fabricated mystical stories to dissuade the officials from closing them. The Yuf Baba Tomb in Gaziantep was one of the tombs the people managed to rescue from the government. Rumor had it that a holy person named Yuf Baba had once lived there. When he was angry with someone, he would shout "*yuf!*" at them, inevitably causing some misfortune to befall them. One day in the first years of the republic, a district governor attempted to demolish the tomb and move the grave elsewhere. But after losing his children and his house to various disasters, he abandoned the plan. This unfounded story had likely been manufactured with the intent to dishearten the local bureaucrats, and apparently it achieved this goal. People somehow contrived to get past the guards unnoticed. Asking for help from the souls of saints was popular even among the families of educated bureaucrats. The family of Hilmi Seçkin, whose father was an official in Siirt in the 1930s, visited the tombs of Veysel Karani and Sheikh Abdülkadir Geylani.[42]

Throughout the country, vast numbers of people habitually visited the tombs of holy persons or miraculous places believed sacred, which existed in almost every town and village. In Afyon, for instance, natural spring water dripping from a source near the tomb of Sarı Çoban Dede was recognized as a cure for eye disease. In that area, people resorted to faith healers or preachers near the tomb to improve eye health and cure blains. In the Adana region, a desolate tree known as Cennet Ana was considered sacred. This place was a veritable children's hospital in the region. Many women brought their ill children there, prayed, sacrificed a chicken, cooked it and after leaving the food under the tree, had their small children kiss the tree. In another holy place known as Karataş in Adana, women with sick children passed between two boulders with the hope of recovery. In Konya, people often visited a tomb named Çileder, where they bathed with the water from a nearby well and prayed in the tomb by giving 15 piasters and lighting a votive candle. Patients were made to lick a pinch of soil bought from the tomb keeper, which was believed to be healing.[43]

Likewise, in Gaziantep, the locals continued to frequent several tombs and holy places. Touching one's head to a black stone column in Şeyh Mosque was a recognized way to relieve headache. The tombs of Bozgeyikli Mancubun, Hacı Hamza, Memik Dede and Hallacı Mansur were among the most popular places in Gaziantep. In addition, a popular fountain was believed to be a strong cure against malaria, a major affliction at the time. As another popular remedy, children with a cough were taken to a cemetery and made to pass between two gravestones.[44]

When petitions to the government proved futile for ensuring aid, people dispatched petitions to God via the souls of the dervishes buried in the tombs. Ready-made and short petitions written in Arabic by tomb keepers were bought by people and then left on the surface of a river or grindle near the tombs or a special place reserved for petitions. In Bursa, at the Molla Fenari Tomb, for instance, these petitions were left on a grindle named Alişar Suyu. These papers usually were collected by tomb keepers and resold over and over.[45]

Urfa province and its surrounding districts were famous for healing places and tombs regarded sacred and frequented not only by locals but also by those living in other provinces. The Hacı Taş Bekir Ocağı attracted those afflicted with chronic diseases, as did the Bedri Zaman Tomb and the Şeyh Tüfh Tomb. The Abdurrahman Dede Tomb was usually frequented by women suffering from infertility. After they tied a cotton rope sold by the tomb keeper to their waistband, they prayed and promised an offering to the soul of Dede. The Hakim Dede Tomb was another sacred place believed to be curative, and the Latif Efendi Tomb was particularly sought out by the paralyzed. In the Şeyh Ocağı, supplicants were washed with the water boiled in a sacred fireplace and then blessed by the preachers. When they recovered, they had to give free alms to the preachers.[46]

As the capital of the Ottomans, İstanbul for centuries housed the prominent memorials of piety like mosques, lodges and tombs together with holy relics. The devout dwellers of İstanbul, attached to age-old traditional and religious practices, also kept their tomb visits alive. Even after tombs were deactivated, tombs like Kahbar Baba in Halıcıoğlu, Yavuz Er Sinan and Nalıncı Dede in Unkapanı continued attracting visitors, although secretly. Baba Cafer in Zindankapı had, for example, well water believed to have healing effects. The Çifte Sultanlar Tomb in the Kocamustafapaşa district continued to attract visitors who offered sacrifices if their wishes came true. The Gül Baba Tomb was in the backyard of the Gül Camii in Fatih, where visitors gave alms to the Gül Camii staff for their services in the tomb. The Yuşa Çelebi Tomb in Beykoz and the Ya Velût Sultan Tomb in Ayvansaray were two other sites to which people flocked.[47]

Illustration 14.1 People visiting the Eyüp Sultan Tomb in 1929

The Eyüp Sultan Tomb in the courtyard of the Eyüp Sultan Mosque was the holiest place in İstanbul. It was believed that Eyüp el Ensari, one of the Prophet Muhammad's companions, was buried there. Therefore, since the time of Fatih the Conqueror, Ottoman sultans girded their sword before the Eyüp el Ensari Tomb just after their ascent to the throne in order to legitimize their rule on religious terms. This tomb was in the courtyard of the mosque and therefore never went without visitors. Aziz Nesin wrote how he accompanied his father on visits to sacred tombs during the 1920s and 1930s. The Sümbülefendi Tomb, which continued to hold a place in the hearts of İstanbul dwellers, was one of them. Once, he had seen many people lying in the tomb's suffering house (*çilehane*), where they underwent a period of suffering in order to take the edge off their worldly desires (*nefs*).[48]

Such practices also persisted in the villages of the capital of the republic. Infertile women lay flat on their backs and touched their faces to the stones of the tombs. The Sultan Baba Tomb in the village of Teberik especially was the first and last resort for persons in ill health in Ankara. The village of Hasanoğlan alone hosted five such tombs: Hasandede, Çaldede, Sarıdede, Asiyeabla and Hüseyin Gazi.[49] This situation was similar in other villages.

Surely the main reason behind the persistence of such popular spiritual culture was the weakness of the state's infrastructural power. Neither the social security provided by the government nor economic welfare had been developed enough to replace these traditional sources of hope. Needy individuals, chiefly those who lived on revenues from the tombs and those who relied on the mediation of souls to reach God, contested the closure of tombs. The tombs also constituted a business field, employing many people informally as tomb keepers and faith healers. They subsisted on believers' alms and sacrifices and on the sales of petitions, amulets, sacred soil and water.[50] Abolishing them without creating alternatives was doomed to failure. Tomb visits persisted as long as people had no alternative sources of social security and social services, and still today, tombs even in urban areas continue to draw huge crowds.

Concluding Remarks

The secularizing reforms of Turkey undoubtedly comprised one of the most comprehensive cultural reconstruction processes in world history. Both nationalist-secularist and critical accounts portray them as uncontested, uncompromising and top-down imposition. The role of Atatürk and republican intellectuals cannot be denied. Partially for this reason, the literature about this period abounds with studies focusing primarily on the republican rulers, their ideological and political agenda and legal and administrative changes they introduced. Owing to the splendor of the republic's reforms, the implementation of the policies and people's complex daily interactions with them have been generally underestimated. The projection of the later political rivalry between the RPP and the conservative-right parties in the historiography has reduced everything that happened during the early republic to a clash between secularism and religion. Works on opposition and protest tend to consider a few open uprisings and intellectual opposition as essential forms of resistance motivated solely by religious sentiments. Political Islamism especially enjoyed amplifying how Muslims and Islam were suppressed in this period. Ironically, nostalgia for the Atatürk era led the upholders of the republican tenets to depict the early republic as full of uncompromising revolutionary zeal, which unintentionally supported the Islamists' portrayal of Atatürk's rule. In other words, these two overlapped and justified each other.

This part has shown that the secular reforms were not contested merely through a handful of subdued riots or by conservative politicians and intellectuals for the sake of religion. A remarkable number and forms of resistance, opposition and adaptation strategies occurred in daily life, changing according to several variables. Many criticized the reforms in daily conversations or resisted them in covert ways. None of the changes severed the people from their religious and traditional identity. Those who insisted on maintaining their established way of life, beliefs and practices formed the

282

overwhelming majority of the population. On the other hand, some people, inventing middle ways and combining old and new, selectively adapted the reforms into their life by making little concessions. Hence religious and traditional culture, which ostensibly lost its predominance in the public lifestyles of the elite, remained strong among the ordinary people. Neither the secular reforms nor their implementation by the RPP brought the palpable suppression of Islam into people's mundane lives.

Among the opponents of the regime, government and secular reforms first impacted preachers, sheikhs and their disciples and old imperial officials who lost their former statuses and sources of income. They were the most fervent and vocal dissenters. Low-income groups like artisans, workers and peasants, who suffered a heavy blow due to the state's economic impositions and the Great Depression, also did not enthusiastically embrace the cultural reforms. In other words, popular dislike of the secular reforms and the resulting resistance were fueled by socioeconomic discontent rather than conservatism. Among these groups were also communist activists who criticized the secular reforms as a symbol of elite extravagance.

Despite the government's ambitious efforts to secularize and control public spaces by establishing People's Houses and People's Rooms, traditional places of socialization like mosques, coffeehouses, houses and tombs prevailed as the primary sites of non-elite socialization. Mosque sermons and conversations held in homes and coffeehouses came first in generating and disseminating oppositional views. Rumors, as presented by the informal news media in the absence of free information channels, served to express and disseminate alternative views about the secular reforms, thereby creating a counter voice. Critical letters to authorities and placards attached to walls, trees and doors provided another way to share dissenting opinions. Religious education persisted in homes and in underground Quran courses. Many parents refused to send their children, especially girls, to the new coeducational schools. Clothing reforms also met resistance in various ways. Peer pressure and local habits outweighed the state's directives and propaganda. Many people, caught between the traditional social milieu and the secularist state, created new forms of dress combining the traditional and modern styles. More for practical reasons than out of religious fanaticism, people insisted on wearing the clothes they were accustomed to.

There is no doubt the republic's novelties were fascinatingly extensive and radical, but their practice proved that old habits did not wane
easily. The secularizing reforms did not sweep aside the age-old religious and traditional daily way of life. A huge number of families
avoided official civil marriage, discouraged by the long and costly
official procedures. The Civil Code, legally disestablishing polygamy
and early marriage and introducing gender equality, elicited opposition
from men who feared the new laws would reduce their authority over
women. Gender stereotypes were perpetuated. Women's disadvan-
taged status changed slightly in practice, even among educated middle-
class families. Religious marriages without official marriages, marriage
of young girls earlier than legal age limits and even polygamy, albeit in
low profile as in the pre-republic period, continued. Therefore the
government had to modify the Civil Code several times to accommodate religious and early marriages and the resulting unregistered births.

Replacing strong devotion to spiritualism and mysticism with trust
in rationalism and science was as difficult as transforming established
gender relations. Rather than the secular laws and principles advocat-
ing Enlightenment philosophy, deep-rooted religious and pagan beliefs
and practices continued to dominate republican society. Faith healing
to elicit divine intervention in spiritual and physical healing or to
exorcise evil spirits kept its popularity. The dervish tombs, closed by
the government, did not lose visitors or clients. Due to the weakness of
modern social assistance and medical care, these mystical institutions
provided a kind of social, psychological and even so-called health
service for the poor. They were also a source of income for their staffs.

How did the people's response affect the state and politics?
Undoubtedly, the reforms changed society gradually in the long run,
albeit not very deeply. The first reason for this was the people's insistence on maintaining their lifestyles. Second, contrary to what is widely
believed, the state responded in a flexible and tolerant manner to
nonviolent and individual resistance and nonconformity on many
occasions unless it evolved into organized political challenge. Perhaps
the only exception was the abolition of the fez. Yet men, encouraged to
wear Western hats, actually had room to maneuver and could choose
from among their local traditional headgear. As for women's dress,
Atatürk, aware of the potential danger of forceful intervention in
gender relations, which had triggered backlashes in Iran and
Afghanistan, personally admitted the modernization of women and

the family should be left to time or social evolution (*içtimaî tekâmül*). Republican bureaucrats often shut their eyes to nonconformity and avoided coercive measures against women. Moreover, the people continued to perform their prayers in Arabic and preachers continued to chant the call to prayer in Arabic in many places. Although the ruling elite did not permit the reopening of the tombs, they condoned the ongoing tomb visits. Atatürk and his republic neither assaulted the religion nor prevented the people from fulfilling their religious obligations.

All of this proves that the Republic of Turkey was by no means as strictly secularist as the Third Republic of France, which has been assumed that the republican elite took as a model. The RPP did not contest Islam in itself, but Islam as a political ideology and source of political power – that is, political Islam. Moreover, the republic claimed to inculcate the population with "correct" Islam and tried to purge certain beliefs and practices, dismissing them as superstitious. Nevertheless, religion with its popular pagan characteristics deeply embedded in the fabric of everyday life, survived and even became increasingly intertwined with politics in the multiparty period. Both urban and rural dwellers clung to their beliefs and counted themselves believers. Religious orders also preserved themselves by camouflaging their activities. Aware of the strength of religiosity, the state avoided promoting an anti-religion image, even prosecuting those who offended religious sensibilities.[1] All of this indicates that Turkish secularism, as its concrete practice in daily life rather than its reflection in the elites' ideology, did not develop from top-down decrees. Rather, the people reshaped it to fit their everyday lives.

Epilogue

Infrastructure of Turkey's Modernization

Today's Turkey was designed in the first two decades of the republic by a coterie of bureaucratic and mercantile elites via unparalleled modernization projects. Nonetheless, ordinary people also left their mark on this process, contrary to what is often thought. This book has offered the untold story of ordinary people's quiet but deep and behind the scene role in the emergence of modern Turkey. Neither Turkey's history nor Turkey's politics can be fully understood without casting a searchlight onto the lower and unknown depths of this process, in which not only state policies but also those exposed to them took part.

My aim has been to do precisely this by disclosing the unknown actors and multifaceted dynamics at the grassroots, thereby moving beyond simplistic depictions of Turkish modernization under Atatürk as a top-down and state-dominant phenomenon. I have provided an alternative to the framework that currently underlies both modernist-nationalist and critical narratives of the early republican Turkey. These narratives argue that a strong and uncompromising state and elites, be they good or bad, forcibly imposed modernization projects on society. They imply that people lapsed into inactivity as intimidated opponents or passive ignorant masses, except for a few harshly repressed uprisings. Both modernization narratives or critical accounts, underestimating complex mutual interactions between the republican elite and society, depicted the period as dominated by a cultural clash. The only difference has been whereas modernization literature eulogized the state and elite as enlightened vanguards and merciless struggle against backwardness, the critical studies criticized them for being solely coercive, alienated and isolated from society.

This dominant framework matters not just for historiography but also for current politics. It has become a linchpin of Islamist and conservative anti-elitist and anti-secular rhetoric. When I was putting my final touches on this book, the Justice and Development Party (JDP) government, annulling the 1935 decree that converted the Hagia Sophia into a museum, reconverted it into a mosque. The president of religious affairs, giving the first Friday sermon there in the presence of the president of the republic, referred again "the single-party regime's assault on Muslims' religious values."

Another hegemonic discourse authoritarian Islamist or ultranationalist politicians often employ, in a manner that contradicts their anti-elitist rhetoric, is that politics is the job of politicians acting within a legal and institutional framework. This definition is also unintentionally supported by the state- and elite-centered histories of modern Turkey. Historical accounts confined politics exclusively to organizational, programmatic and formal movements and to the institutional framework. However, it is authoritarian politics that actually hinders the working of the legal institutional platforms on which formal political action and representation rest. This pushes underrepresented groups and those who have been discriminated against to seek different avenues, seemingly apolitical ones, through which to fight injustice and discrimination.

As this book has propounded a broader conception of politics includes all these different avenues. Politics in this sense may be understood as people's ongoing micro and daily struggles for rights, survival and representation. Ordinary people's small actions directly or indirectly influence formal politics. Again, a deliberate foot-dragging has potential to thwart the state's schemes and its hegemony. Indeed, as Hobsbawm wrote, "Passivity is not an ineffective strategy because it exploits the impossibility of making it do some things by force for any length of time. This strategy, reinforced by a functionally useful slowness, imperviousness and stupidity, apparent or real, is a formidable force. The refusal to understand is a form of class struggle." On the other hand, as he also stated, even the most submissive people may use the system to its advantage and, where appropriate, resist and counterattack.[1]

Drawing on such an understanding of politics, substantiated by the untapped historical evidence about the intersections between Atatürk's policies and the people's response, this book has presented an infra-history of the early republic. In other words, it has explored *infrapolitics* in the sense of the social and political fault lines underlying the high politics. It has shown that long-ignored *infrapolitics*, more specifically, daily and micro struggles resistances, people's voices and opinions, have in fact deeply influenced the bigger social and political processes on which historians often focus.

***

The Republic of Turkey was founded in the Ottoman Empire's Muslim heartland, Anatolia, after wrenching wars had devastated the empire. The republic sought to mold the Anatolian population into a modern secular nation through a series of profound economic and cultural renewal projects. As the government's intervention in society increased, occasions for conflict between state and society multiplied. Economic and cultural upheaval accompanied by social inequalities aggravated by the Great Depression also heightened social unrest and struggles. Under an authoritarian single-party system, widespread forms of struggle and resistance mostly took the form of what James C. Scott has called *weapons of the weak*. People took a stand against the challenges they faced through daily and mostly informal coping strategies.

These methods were among the main components of the people's everyday politics, along with cooperation tactics that are beyond the scope of this book, though they deserve close examination. Everyday politics was not isolated from high politics. Rather it formed a layer that brought state and society into contact. Although the state closed the door of politics to the people's organized and legal participation, people's everyday politics intentionally or unintentionally opened smaller doors through which to influence the system. Surely this politics was not capable of altering state policies or the regime itself. Much of the people's everyday politics was for short-term, immediate benefits or even mere survival. Yet thousands of similar actions engendered incrementally cumulative macro effects. People's grievances, demands, noncompliance and resistance, along with the infrastructural weakness of the state administration, further crippled the state's transformative capacity and compelled the rulers to modify their policies. Social discontent also motivated the rulers to monitor state and party administrations and public opinion in order to eliminate bureaucratic malfeasance and redress people's grievances, thereby mending the regime's fragile hegemony. Petitions, politicians' reports and wish lists of provincial party congresses served as conduits conveying public opinion to the state's decision makers and compelling them to respond to public opinion.[2] Hence, contrary to the literature labeling the early republican state as rigid and isolated from society, all these factors made it flexible and responsive to society. Most probably the smooth retreat to a multiparty regime in 1945, thanks to Atatürk's successor President İnönü's decision to liberate the system without any bloodshed, owes something to, among diplomatic factors, the republican rulers' flexibility and awareness of their unpopularity among the masses.[3]

Moreover, the people's everyday struggles for survival delayed the dissolution of the social, economic and cultural structures the republic sought to get rid of. Peasants and artisans survived somehow and did not succumb to being reduced to wage labor. In the cultural sphere, rather than the positivism and secularism propagated by the state, religion, mysticism and tradition continued to be major components of most people's lives. People's resistance also stunted the state's ability to extract the necessary resources to finance state-building and modernization schemes.

Hence, just as much as people were under pressure to adapt to the changes, the republic too had to adapt to the people. The long-term consequences of ordinary people's everyday politics varied from inspiring later generations with the legacy of resistance and protest to preserving some social, economic and cultural traits, which would pave the way for the social and political developments of the following decades. The early republic's slow socioeconomic transformation, survival of rural society untouched by the republican reforms and people's economic woes and discontent marred and even swallowed daring cultural renewal process.

***

In this book I have examined this everyday politics of the ordinary people and its repercussion for high politics on three thematic levels. The first was poor and smallholding peasants' discontent with economic conditions and policies and their resistance to rural exploiters, abusive state agents, extortionate taxes and monopolies. Under the authoritarian system, the mostly illiterate rural poor's struggle for survival took the form of self-protective and loss-minimizing acts. They made use of a variety of stratagems drawn from everyday life to manifest their dissatisfaction and resist both the state and the local notables. Along with other factors at work, the everyday politics of the peasants compelled the state to make some concessions by adopting a peasantist rhetoric and even softening the heavy economic demands. Tax reductions, tax and debt relief programs, wheat purchases at prices slightly above market levels, discounts in monopoly goods and land distribution, although in small amounts, stemmed from the people's resistance, among other factors. Sometimes without any government action the daily acts of resistance yielded small advantages that were nevertheless significant to survival. The peasants' everyday politics also constituted a great obstacle to the state's access to rural surpluses. Not only the state's infrastructural weakness, but also peasants' struggles, which disabled the state's extractive capacity, played a role in delaying Turkey's transformation from a rural to an urban society until the 1990s. In this regard, "weapons of the weak" blunted the force of the burdens imposed by the state and allowed the peasantry to survive.

The prevalence of a rural society with its religious culture would create a fertile ground for the gradual rise of conservative religious politics after the transition to a multiparty system and eventually its ascendance to political power in the 2000s.[4] Even after the rush of rural immigrants to urban areas from the 1950s to the 2000s, urban masses of peasant origin kept close ties with their village communities and agriculture. They brought the urban areas not only foodstuffs but also customs and religious bonds that right-wing populist and Islamist politicians would usurp and politicize. The migrants did not arrive in the urban areas with blank minds. They did not come from calm backwaters, but from areas enmeshed in social, political and cultural struggles. This strengthened the social, cultural and political cleavages that would feed the right-wing and Islamist parties. From the beginning of the multiparty era, the right-wing parties indulged in far-reaching promises on religion. Islamist parties, going further, combined a more radical version of religious discourse with harsh criticisms of big business, social injustice and of the regime's indifference to the material and moral urgencies of provincial society and the urban poor, most of whom were of peasant origin. The Islamist Welfare Party, and then its more opportunistic successor JDP skillfully carried all these cleavages and the economic and cultural baggage of the provincial population and rural migrants in the urban areas to the ballot.[5]

What is more, industrial and housing facilities in the cities did not have the capacity to integrate these masses into urban life. Therefore, these people worked in casual jobs and lived in newly erected squatter houses called *gecekondu*, taking unofficial possession of public lands, using electric and water facilities illegally and engaging in untaxed informal economic activities. High-level jobs in both the public and private sectors were out of their reach. The hierarchy of jobs and status caused widespread resentment against the educated middle-class urbanites and their secular lifestyle. The insufficiency of social policies again led the poor and low-income masses to rely on religious and clientelistic networks that maintained their rural identity. This produced hybrid suburban cultures that combined rural and urban features. *Tariqa*s especially provided them with mutual solidarity and nepotistic networks. Political Islam, conservatism and sectarian politics gained a foothold in these suburban spaces as well as in rural areas. As the welfare state diminished due to the neoliberal recipes of the 1980s, religious networks grew in importance and exerted informal influence over institutional politics. Consequently, political Islam has risen steadily as the rural population barely touched by the secular reforms was moving to and transforming not only the space but also culture of the urban centers.[6]

The second level of the people's politics was urban, low-income wage earners' struggles under unfavorable economic policies. Here I have examined the uncharted terrain of the working-class history of the early republic by focusing on covert forms of working-class struggle. Working people generally avoided open confrontation, which could run the risk of police repression. Under an authoritarian regime not conducive to social movements, people took everyday actions when particular policies or circumstances posed a threat to them. Therefore, their actions varied from petitioning, suing and changing jobs to theft, violence and spontaneous walkouts. The widespread way to ease the burden of workload, poor wages and heavy working conditions was to slow down or ignore duties at work. These practices prompted the government to espouse a populist discourse and enact a series of social policy measures. Their everyday struggles also enabled these laborers to yield small advantages for survival or to win some concessions from their employers, albeit limited. These factors contributed to the development of the wage earners' awareness of their own socioeconomic status as well as the experience of making demands and undertaking action even under the authoritarian system. Labor movements bolstered by the unions, political parties and social policy legislations, which sprang up with the transition to the multiparty regime, emerged against this backdrop. On the other hand, the overwhelming number of peasants within the labor force would bring their own culture, work habits and attitudes to working-class politics such as individualistic tendencies, reluctance to work permanently and lack of labor discipline in a structured environment. The increasing rural-origin casual workers, along with sectoral distribution of workers, were to increase ideological cleavages within labor movement.[7] However, along with working people's everyday struggles, the peasant-origin workers' such inclinations, which can be seen as foot dragging to utter proletarianization, forced the state to act by designing social policies and a labor law to create a stable labor force.

The third level I have focused on here is the most ignored aspect of the people's response to the secular reforms. Resistance, foot dragging and selective adaptation in everyday life proved more impregnable than the few well-known open protests. Indeed, although the conservative political and intellectual oppositions had been easily suppressed, the cultural hegemony of the young republic was far from all-embracing. It failed to extinguish an autonomous current of popular opinion about the secular reforms. Competing and dissonant views remained in circulation in daily life. A system of critical unofficial communication operated through daily conversations, rumors, jokes and disgruntled petitions and letters to bureaucrats and newspapers. Despite censorship, the official discourse was not uncontestable or without alternative. These views were produced and consumed especially in non-elite public places by those who had lost economic or social status with the republic. The secular reforms coinciding with the state's increasing economic impositions and the world's most catastrophic economic disaster thus became equated with worsening life conditions. This further intensified the people's distrust of the state-led cultural changes. However, contrary to widely held views shared by both modernist narratives and Islamist criticisms, the main reason was not a clash of secularism and religion. Rather, complex socioeconomic, gender and psychological factors played a more significant role in spurring social discontent, opposition or indifference to reforms.

Both the people's reserved approach and the state's avoidance of religious backlash, along with the persistence of rural society, restrained secularism in practice, despite the assertive secular official discourse. Undeniably the republic eventually considerably refashioned Turkish politics and society. The sultanate and caliphate were toppled, the fez was discarded and the Latin alphabet, secular education and women's legal and political rights were major changes. Nonetheless, synchronously, the people also refashioned the realization of what the republic's founders had imagined. Many reforms did not find acceptance or found only partial acceptance, which created hybrid practices. Even those who seemed to have adhered to the regime's principles actually utilized them to affirm the validity of their arguments. Some changes were reversed. The call to prayer reverted to Arabic just after the first free elections in 1950. Islamic education in the İmam Hatip Schools restarted in 1949 and then burgeoned steadily from the 1950s on. Men gave up the fez, but hardly wore the Western hat; most opted for smaller-brimmed or brimless headgear. On the other hand, gender relations did not undergo a swift revolution. The downtrodden status of women changed little despite the Civil Code and the political rights granted to them. Early and unregistered religious marriages were still common. Polygamy, albeit at a low rate as in Ottoman society, survived. The already declining use of the face veil decreased still further, but most women did not give up covering their heads. In the following decades, the growing migration from rural to urban areas further increased the salience of the veil. This created a vicious cycle, in which gradually the fear of religious fundamentalism grew among educated urbanite middle classes, whereas veiled women newly arrived to the squatter areas and their conservative male relatives faced not only cultural but also economic hardships and pinned their hopes on the Islamist movement, which made a style of veil its flag. *Tariqa*s, Quran courses and religious indoctrination continued to operate so prevalently that one of these *tariqa*s somehow meddled in a coup attempt in July 2016. Age-old spiritual and pagan beliefs and practices, such as visits to sacred tombs and faith healing, were the most impervious to change in the short term, even though they proved the least resistant to increasing urbanization, education levels and material advances in the long term.

What the people's politics did by disabling the republic's economic and cultural development process was to elicit conservative and then Islamist opposition during the multiparty era. Future conservative and Islamist politics would reap the harvest of the seeds sown by popular politics, which weakened the state's transformative capacity and hence the republican project. Islamist movements grew among rural Anatolian population and the squatter areas inhabited by the newly arrived peasants or townspeople. Political Islamism cannot be explained only with the provincial merchants' competition with the urbanite large conglomerates or with their lending a helping hand to the needy and to those who resented the secular urbanite middle classes by providing social aid. There was also a sociocultural ground marked by rurality, which was ready to embrace those politicians appropriating religious discourse and symbols. Their struggles for survival and to keep their own lifestyles under the republic, along with other socioeconomic developments, gave rise to Islamism. Ultimately, the Islamist JDP has been ruling Turkey for almost two decades by gradually increasing the government intervention to aggrandize the influence of Islam over not only society but also all state institutions.

In later decades, the staunchly nostalgic upholders of Atatürk's legacy would have to give much more public recognition to religion and even political Islamism. Perhaps, from a different angle, this feature of the Turkey's modernization may have been conducive to its longevity in its restricted form by blunting the sharpness of modernization and cushioning the shock of reforms. But at the same time, it resulted in the preservation of a traditional rural Islamic society dragging Turkey into today's authoritarian Islamist rule. Recent developments in Turkey lay bare the frailty of the republic's balanced and moderate approach and the persistence of social and cultural ground on which conservative-authoritarian Islamist politics can easily mobilize and politicize.

Another manifestation of popular politics under the authoritarian regime was the actions labeled crimes. Low-income rural and urban masses' resistance to social injustice manifested itself in social crimes such as tax delinquency, smuggling, theft, arson, robbery, assault, murder and banditry. I have proposed considering the bulk of such crimes as an extension of the politics of poor people, performed with different means devised to resist their oppressors and exploiters. Social inequalities and the state's intrusion into people's livelihoods under an authoritarian system in thrall to the propertied classes left the poor with little choice but to defend themselves by illegal means. Rural violence, even in the form of banditry, was also part of this popular politics. Rural violence and banditry were by no means peculiar to the Kurdish provinces, nor were they much related to pastoralism, tribalism or Kurdish nationalism. The rural poor across Anatolia fled to the mountains to avoid reprisal after challenging the local notables or oppressive state officials. The survival and legacy of banditry in the Kurdish uplands was far more palpable. Banditry would not fade away unless the oppression by the state and local dominants diminished. Social banditry strongly influenced the strategies the Kurdish political movement led by the Kurdistan Workers' Party (PKK) would embrace from the late 1970s on. The state's intrusion into the daily affairs of locals and the resulting peasant resistance would create a tumultuous sociopolitical geography that would in later decades allow the Kurdish political movement to gain mass support. The growing discrimination, inequality and poverty created a bulge in the number of unemployed, poor and frustrated people prone to induction into the Kurdish armed movement. The social bandits of the 1920s and 1930s, even though most had no ideological agenda, served as models of armed resistance for later generations who saw no other way out in the face of Ankara's militarist policies.

Accordingly, another conclusion to be drawn is that people under conditions of political disfranchisement and economic exploitation can adopt "dangerous" politics. This is evident also from the recurrent waves of violence that have engulfed Turkey and the Middle East. Poverty and social injustice exacerbated by political discrimination that befalls the urban poor, minorities and migrants make them feel they have no way to survive other than by violating the law. Not only these groups but also secular and educated middle classes who are underrepresented in politics may tend to extralegal means. Just as republican authoritarianism generated covert opposition during the early republic by excluding religious culture at least in legal sphere, and by putting the burden of modernization on the masses, today's government, undermining the republic's legacy of institutionalism, the rule of law and the secular sensibilities, has put Turkey in a similar framework to the interwar authoritarianism. Therefore, it also spawns widespread dissent and resistance in indirect fashion as the early republic did. However, the early republican rulers had prevented the escalation of social discontent to a mass-scale rebellion by making concessions and allowing a peaceful change of government. This distinguished Turkey from other unstable countries like Egypt, Syria, Iraq and Iran. Today Turkey's stability as well as flawed democracy, at stake more than ever before, depends on how flexibly the ruling party would respond the social discontent, as the RPP did once by leaving the single-party system and peacefully handing over the government to the Democratic Party.

I hope this book will enhance our understanding of the dynamics of Turkey's politics through an historical analysis. The main point I make here is that not only Atatürk, İnönü, the RPP and their spectacular reforms but also the ordinary people shaped Turkey's political, cultural and economic landscape beneath the surface and left a deep mark on the foundation of the republic. The people's everyday politics jolted politicians into adopting more flexible and compromising policies. This shows us that even under an authoritarian system – which is on the rise in Turkey once again – excluded people can raise their voices via different means. Despite authoritarian politicians' attempts to restrict the realm of politics to loyal supporters and cronies, indirect forms of opposition or the people's insistence on keeping their own alternative views and lifestyles can restructure state schemes or create a social ground on which greater opposition and perhaps turmoil may arise if the rulers choose to be uncompromising. Undoubtedly, the political implications of what I have written so far do not downplay the significance of organized and formal opposition. However, I underline that infrastructure of strong oppositions lay in social fabric, where people's everyday and informal discontent and resistance occur. Moreover, regardless of whether bringing up an organized opposition that has clout with the rulers, the accumulation and pervasiveness of daily dissent and resistance empower the people by compelling the state to take the society into account or to thwart its policies. Authoritarianism can weaken organized opposition, but not the long-term persistence of the daily cultures, practices and views that are deeply rooted in daily life. The power of the people lay in just here.

Notes

Introduction

1 Hobsbawm, *Age of Extremes*, 291.
2 Scott, *Weapons of the Weak*.
3 Ginzburg, *The Cheese and the Worms*, xiii–xxvi; Guha, *Elementary Aspects of Peasant Insurgency*, 1–17; Chatterjee, *Nation and Its Fragments*, 170.
4 For the totalitarianism model regarding the Soviet Union, see Pipes, *Russia under the Old Regime*; Friedrich and Brzezinski, *Totalitarian Dictatorship*.
5 Guha, *Elementary Aspects of Peasant Insurgency*; Chatterjee, *Nation and Its Fragments*; Ludden, ed., *Reading Subaltern Studies*; Kershaw, *The Nazi Dictatorship*, 193–205, and *Popular Opinion and Political Dissent in the Third Reich*; Peukert, *Inside Nazi Germany*; Lüdtke, "What Happened to the 'Fiery Red Glow'?" 199.
6 Metinsoy, "Blat Stalin'den Büyüktür." For a few primary examples of this literature, see Fitzpatrick, *Stalin's Peasants*; Davies, *Popular Opinion in Stalin's Russia*; Viola, *Peasant Rebels under Stalin*; Cronin, "Resisting the New State." For a comprehensive account of popular politics in revolutionary Iran in the late 1970s and 1980s, see Bayat, *Street Politics* and *Life As Politics*.
7 Metinsoy, *İkinci Dünya Savaşı'nda Türkiye*; Akın, "Politics of Petitioning"; Akçetin, "Anatolian Peasants in the Great Depression."
8 For the modernization narratives, see Lewis, *The Emergence of Modern Turkey*; Berkes, *The Development of Secularism in Turkey*; Shaw and Kural Shaw, *History of the Ottoman Empire and Modern Turkey*; Tunaya, *Türkiye'nin Siyasi Hayatında Batılılaşma Hareketleri* and *İslamcılık Akımı*. For the critical accounts, see Mardin, *Türkiye'de Toplum ve Siyaset*, 24, 59; Heper, *The State Tradition in Turkey*; Keyder, *State and Class*; Tunçay, *Türkiye Cumhuriyeti'nde Tek Parti*; Köker, *Modernleşme, Kemalizm ve Demokrasi*, 68.
9 Berkes, *Bazı Ankara Köyleri Üzerine*; Stirling, *Culture and Economy*; Yasa's two monographs, *Hasanoğlan Köyü* and *Sindel Köyü*; Szyliowicz,

Political Change in Rural Turkey; Şevki, *Kurna Köyü*. Studies by folklorists such as Pertev Naili Boratav, Mehmet Enver Beşe, Mehmet Halit Bayrı and İlhan Başgöz, published in *Halk Bilgisi Haberleri*, have also contributed to the understanding of popular culture. However, in the past forty years, scholars have published academic articles that examine peasants' everyday experiences during the early republic. See Pamuk, "War, State Economic Policies"; Akçetin, "Anatolian Peasants in the Great Depression."

10 Bell, *Peasants in Power*; Perry, *Challenging the Mandate of Heaven*; Wolf, *Peasant Wars of the Twentieth Century*; Viola, *Peasant Rebels under Stalin*. For the arguments for the passivity of Turkish peasants, see Keyder, "Türk Demokrasisinin Ekonomi Politiği," 50.

11 Birtek and Keyder, "Agriculture and the State"; Keyder, "Türk Tarımında Küçük Meta Üretiminin Yerleşmesi"; Önder, "Cumhuriyet Döneminde Tarım Kesimine Uygulanan Vergi Politikası." For a criticism of this approach, see Köymen, *Kapitalizm ve Köylülük*, 162–4.

12 For Turkish nationalist accounts, see Bender, *Genelkurmay Belgelerinde Kürt İsyanları III*, 322–3; Şimşir, *Kürtçülük*, 74–87, 101–12, 152–60, 312–26; Uluğ, *Tunceli*, 116–20. For critical academic accounts, see McDowall, *A Modern History of the Kurds*, 202–11. McDowall reduces Kurdish peasants' politics to tribal movements, politics of notables or nationalist organizations like Azadi and Xhoybun. For similar accounts, see Van Bruinessen, *Agha, Shaikh and State*, 265–305; Bozarslan, "Kurdish Nationalism in Turkey"; Olson, *The Emergence of Kurdish Nationalism and the Sheikh Said Rebellion*; Jwaideh, *Kürt Milliyetçiliğinin Tarihi*, 403–33; Strohmeier and Yalçın-Heckmann, *Kürtler*, 67–70; Vali, *Kürt Milliyetçiliğinin Kökenleri*, 30–54; Özoğlu, *Kurdish Notables*, 121–30.

13 For a similar approach to seventeenth-century Ottoman banditry, see Barkey, *Bandits and Bureaucrats*, 12–13. Barkey argues that the bandits served local dominants and the state.

14 Geertz, *The Interpretation of Cultures*, 5, 12; see Shanin, ed., *Peasants and Peasant Societies*, 227–74.

15 For the complex process of class formation, see Katznelson, "Working Class Formation," 21–2. Even in critical studies on the Middle East working class, Turkish workers are treated without taking the complex formation of the working class into account. See Lockman, *Workers and Working Classes in the Middle East*; Beinin, *Workers and Peasants in the Modern Middle East*.

16 Koç, *100 Soruda*, 34–7; Yavuz, "Sanayideki İşgücünün Durumu," 171–5; Makal, *Türkiye'de Çok Partili Dönemde Çalışma İlişkileri*, 47–50;

Ahmad, "The Development of Working-Class Consciousness in Turkey," 133–41.

17 Berik and Bilginsoy, "The Labor Movement in Turkey," 38, 57–8; Çalışkan, "Organism and Triangle"; Koç, "Türkiye'de 1923–1946 Döneminde Mülksüzleşme"; Akkaya, "İşçi Sınıfı ve Sendikacılık," 144–5; Yavuz, "Sanayideki İşgücünün Durumu," 176.

18 Koç, *100 Soruda*, 34–7; Güzel, "1940'larda İşgücünün Özellikleri"; Varlık, "İzmir İşçi-Esnaf Kurumlar Birliği" and "İzmir Sanayi İşçileri Birliği-1932"; Uyar, "CHP İzmir İşçi ve Esnaf"; Koç, "1923–1950 Döneminde CHP'nin İşçi Sınıfı Korkusu."

19 For example, see Makal, *Türkiye'de Tek Parti Döneminde Çalışma İlişkileri*; Güzel, *Türkiye'de İşçi Hareketleri*; Koç, *100 Soruda*; Yavuz, "Sanayideki İşgücünün Durumu," 176.

20 One important recent exception is a book by Hale Yılmaz, *Becoming Turkish*. Yılmaz examines both social support for and opposition to the anti-veiling campaigns, hat law and language reform, mostly in urban areas.

21 Lewis, Berkes, Tunaya and many other scholars have produced modernization narratives emphasizing the republican elites' struggle against religious fundamentalism. For liberal accounts that criticize the authoritarian motivations behind the secular reforms, see Tunçay, *Türkiye Cumhuriyeti'nde Tek-Parti*, 80. See also Zürcher, *Turkey*, 167–79. For Islamist critiques, see Kısakürek, *Son Devrin Din Mazlumları*; Albayrak, *İrtica'ın Tarihçesi* and *Türkiye'de Din Kavgası*; Karatepe, *Tek Parti Dönemi*; Ceylan, *Cumhuriyet Dönemi Din-Devlet İlişkileri*.

22 Küçük, "Sufi Reactions against the Reforms"; Toprak, "Dinci Sağ," 246–7; Albayrak, *İrtica'ın Tarihçesi*, 4.

23 For works overemphasizing the impact of the secular reforms, see Berkes, *The Development of Secularism in Turkey*; Lewis, *The Emergence of Modern Turkey*. For critical literature overrating the effects of the secular reforms, see Tapper, *Islam in Modern Turkey*, 189–221; Kuru, *Secularism and State Policies toward Religion*; Albayrak, *İrtica'ın Tarihçesi*, 5.

24 Thompson, *Customs in Common*, 460.

25 Migdal's approach provides insight into everyday interactions between state and society. See *State in Society*, *Strong Societies and Weak States* and "Finding the Meeting Ground."

26 Scott, *Domination and the Arts of Resistance*, 190–200.

27 Lasswell, *Politics*.

28 Scott, *Domination and the Arts of Resistance*, 190–200, and *Weapons of the Weak*, chapter 7; Kerkvliet, *Power of Everyday Politics*, 21–2.

29   Habermas, *The Structural Transformation*, 30.
30   Fraser, "Rethinking the Public Sphere."
31   Mah, "Phantasies of the Public Sphere"; Darnton, "An Early Information Society"; Thompson, *Customs in Common*; Guha, *Elementary Aspects of Peasant Insurgency*; Brophy, *Popular Culture and the Public Sphere in the Rhineland*.
32   Benhabib, "Models of Public Space," 89–90; McGowen, "Power and Humanity," 98–9.
33   Kaye, *The British Marxist Historians*, 7–8; Thompson, *Customs in Common* and *The Making of the English Working Class*. See also Eley and Nield, "Why Does Social History Ignore Politics?" 267.
34   Guha, *Elementary Aspects of Peasant Insurgency*; Chatterjee, *Nation and Its Fragments*.
35   Lüdtke, "What Is the History of Everyday Life?" 7, 24–9; Dehne, "Have We Come Any Closer to *Alltag*?" 128; Guha, *Elementary Aspects of Peasant Insurgency*, 1–17.
36   Weber, *Peasants into Frenchmen*, xvi; Gluckman, "Gossip and Scandal"; Paine, "What Is Gossip About?"
37   Kumar, "Beyond Muffled Murmurs of Dissent?" 95–106; Farge and Revel, *The Vanishing Children of Paris*; Darnton, "An Early Information Society."
38   Bakhtin, *The Dialogic Imagination*, 285, 401, and *Speech Genres*, 143; Evans, "Language and Political Agency," 515.
39   Thompson, "Eighteenth-Century English Society," 158; Steinberg, *Fighting Words*, 17; Hunt, "Rights and Social Movements," 314; Mouffe, "Hegemony and Ideology in Gramsci," 192.
40   Bayat, *Life As Politics*, 15–25; Hirschman, *Exit, Voice, and Loyalty*, 1–43.
41   Akın, "Politics of Petitioning."
42   For the manipulative content of the petitions, see Fitzpatrick, *Everyday Stalinism*, 175; Davies, *Popular Opinion in Stalin's Russia*, 10.
43   Metinsoy, "Fragile Hegemony."
44   For the use of such sources in European history, see Rudé, *The Crowd in History*, 3–16; for the advantages of the secret public opinion reports, see Unger, "Public Opinion Reports," 578.
45   For a study on the local newspapers of the 1950s, see Brockett, *How Happy to Call Oneself a Turk*. Prominent journalist Zekeriya Sertel's memoirs abound with grim instances of state control over journalists during this period. Sertel, *Hatırladıklarım*. About censorship of the press, see Yılmaz and Doğaner, *Sansür*, 12–20, 116–34.
46   Hobsbawm, "History from Below," 17.

47 Fox-Genovese and Genovese, "The Political Crisis of Social History," 211; Unger, "Public Opinion Reports in Nazi Germany," 572; Tauger, "Soviet Peasants and Collectivization," 429.

48 Kershaw, *Popular Opinion and Political Dissent in the Third Reich*, 6.

Chapter 1 The Price of the Republic for the Peasants

1 Boratav, "Anadolu Köyünde." For the social impact of the war on civilians, particularly women, see Mahir-Metinsoy, *Ottoman Women during World War I*.

2 Owen and Pamuk, *A History of Middle East Economies*, 11; Tezel, *Cumhuriyet Döneminin İktisadi Tarihi*, 112–13.

3 The influence of provincial notables increased between the eighteenth and nineteenth centuries. See Toledano, "The Emergence of Ottoman-Local Elites"; Barbir, *Ottoman Rule in Damascus*; Marcus, *The Middle East on the Eve of Modernity*; Hathaway, *Politics of Household*; Khoury, *State and Provincial Society*. The nineteenth century especially witnessed fast commercialization in agriculture, which gave rise to large landowning and capitalist farms. see Quataert, "The Commercialization of Agriculture in Ottoman Turkey."

4 About the wartime economic developments, see Ahmed Emin [Yalman], *Turkey in the World War*; Toprak, *İttihat Terakki ve Cihan Harbi*. About the tragic events falling upon Anatolia's Armenians and Greeks, see Kévorkian, *Armenian Genocide*; Göçek et al., eds., *A Question of Genocide*; Akçam, *Young Turks' Crime*; Aktar, *Türk Milliyetçiliği, Gayrımüslimler*.

5 Aksoy, *Türkiye'de Toprak Meselesi*, 56; Falih Rıfkı [Atay], *Bizim Akdeniz*, 37; Silier, *Türkiye'de Tarımsal Yapının Gelişimi*, 56–60.

6 İsmail Hüsrev [Tökin], *Türkiye Köy İktisadiyatı*, 176–87; Zhukovski, *Türkiye'nin Zirai Bünyesi*, 359.

7 Hâmit Sadi, *İktisadi Türkiye*, 68; Barkan, "Çiftçiyi Topraklandırma Kanunu," 478; Tezel, *Cumhuriyet Döneminin İktisadi Tarihi*, 344–8.

8 Atasagun, *Türkiye'de İçtimai Siyaset*, 5, 14.

9 Esenel, *1940'lı Yıllarda*, 109; Uran, *Hatıralarım*, 216–24; BCA-CHP [490.1/724.477.1], February 7, 1931; [490.1/729.478.1], March 16, 1931.

10 Brautigam, "Taxation and State-Building," 1; Önder, "Cumhuriyet Döneminde Tarım Kesimine Uygulanan Vergi Politikası"; Effimianidis, *Cihan İktisad Buhranı Önünde Türkiye*, 278. By 1929, the land tax constituted 13.7 percent of the government's annual revenue. Hershlag, *Turkey*, 51.

11 *Bütçe Gider ve Gelir Gerçekleşmeleri (1924–1995)*, 74.

12 Hatipoğlu, *Türkiye'de Ziraî Buhran*, 77; BCA-CHP [490.1/729.478.1];
    Berkes, *Bazı Ankara Köyleri Üzerine*, 43; Kıvılcımlı, *İhtiyat Kuvvet*, 29,
    126–7.

13 Emiroğlu, *Vasıtasız Vergiler*, 110–11; Hatipoğlu, *Türkiye'de Ziraî
    Buhran*, 77–9. Önder, "Cumhuriyet Döneminde Tarım Kesimine
    Uygulanan Vergi Politikası," 125–6.

14 Eldem, *Osmanlı İmparatorluğu'nun İktisadi Şartları*, 95; Afet İnan, *Yurt
    Bilgisi Notlarımdan: Vergi Bilgisi*, 95–8; Turan, *Yeni Vergi
    Kanunları'nın*, 97.

15 "Halk Sütunu," *Köroğlu*, July 10, 1929; BCA-MGM [30.10/79.520.3];
    Kıvılcımlı, *İhtiyat Kuvvet*, 126–7; "Haksızlık Olur mu Ya!" *Köroğlu*,
    March 28, 1936.

16 *Buğday Koruma Karşılığı Vergisi*.

17 Eşref, "Haymana Halkı Neler Yapılmasını İstiyor?" *Vakit*, October 10,
    1934; "Fakir Kasaba Halkı Yemeklik Undan Vergi Alınmaması İçin
    Hükümetten Rica Ediyorlar," *Köroğlu*, August 4, 1934; "Un Vergisi,"
    Köroğlu, December 8, 1934.

18 Kıvılcımlı, *İhtiyat Kuvvet*, 29, 86, 126–7, and *Yol*, 383–4.

19 Hill, *The Century of Revolution*, 27–35, 103; Dobb, *Studies in the
    Development of Capitalism*, 114–22.

20 Yılmaz, *Türkiye'de Tütün Eksperliği*, 11; Doğruel and Doğruel, *Tekel*,
    130, 144; Emiroğlu, *İnhisarlar ve Devlet Emlâki*, 64; Kuruç, *Belgelerle
    Türkiye İktisat Politikası 1*, 417.

21 Sadullah, "Orman Teşkilatı," 469.

22 Kuruç, *Belgelerle Türkiye İktisat Politikası 1*, 251; Doğruel and Doğruel,
    Tekel, 150–2.

23 "Kaçakçılığın Men-i ve Takibi Hakkında Kanun," 1126/June 23, 1927,
    Resmi Gazete, no. 629, July 10, 1927, 2827; "Kaçakçılığın Men ve
    Takibi Hakkında Kanun," 1510/June 2, 1929, *Resmi Gazete*, no.
    1216, June 15, 1929, 7539–46; "Kaçakçılığın Men ve Takibine Dair
    Kanun," 1918/January 7, 1932, *Resmi Gazete*, no. 2000, January 12,
    1932, 1141–51.

24 Doğruel and Doğruel, *Tekel*, 133.

25 Ibid., 289–93.

26 Şevket Süreyya [Aydemir], *Ege Günü I*, 54.

27 Tunçay, ed., *Arif Oruç'un Yarını*, 145; Hatipoğlu, *Türkiye'de Ziraî
    Buhran*, 33–5; Taşpınar et al., *The Tobacco Affairs*, 42.

28 See BCA-CHP [490.01/729.478.1.], February 9, 1931; also see İsmail
    Hüsrev [Tökin], *Türkiye Köy İktisadiyatı*, 149–50; *Adliye Encümeni
    Ruznamesi*, 907; CHP *28/12/936 Tarihinde Toplanan Vilâyet Kongresi
    Zabıtnamesi*, 25, 30, 47; Tekeli and İlkin, *Türkiye'de Devletçiliğin
    Oluşumu*, 12; *DİE İstatistik Yıllığı*, 250–1.

29 Beşe, "Safranbolu'da Bir Köylünün Hayatı II," 146; Karacık, *İnhisarlar Mevzuatı*, 39; Doğruel and Doğruel, *Tekel*, 144; *TBMM ZC*, April 29, 1933, 133–4.

30 Demirel, "Osmanlı Devleti'nde Tuz Gelirlerinin."

31 Emiroğlu, *İnhisarlar ve Devlet Emlâki*, 64; Kıvılcımlı, *Emperyalizm*, 82–3; Kuruç, *Belgelerle Türkiye İktisat Politikası*, vol. 2, 231–2; Doğruel and Doğruel, *Tekel*, 143.

32 Veldet, *30. Yılında Türkiye Şeker Sanayi*, 577.

33 Tekeli and İlkin, *Türkiye'de Devletçiliğin Oluşumu*, 127–8; Akıltepe et al., *Türkiye'de Şeker Sanayi*, 30–44.

34 BCA-CHP [490.1/651.165.1], August 5, 1936; *CHP 1936 İl Kongreleri*, 119; Hatipoğlu, *Türkiye'de Ziraî Buhran*, 55–7; Akıltepe et al., *Türkiye'de Şeker Sanayi*, 117; Günay, "Şeker," 79.

35 Koç et al., *Osmanlı Ormancılığı*; Koç, "Osmanlı Devletindeki Orman," 158.

36 Sadullah, "Orman Teşkilatı," 469; Kutluk, *Türkiye Ormancılığı*, 396, 414, 421; Ayanoğlu and Güneş, *Orman Suçları*, 35; Acun, *Ormanlarımız*.

37 Shah, *Kamal*, 274; Oksal, "Ormancılığın Ulusal Ekonomideki Vazifeleri I" and "Ormancılığın Ulusal Ekonomideki Vazifeleri II"; Schöpfer, "Ormanların Medeniyete Hizmetleri."

38 BCA-CHP [490.1/618.27.1]; December 3, 1936 [490.1/618.28.1].

39 BCA-CHP [490.1/500.2008.1]; Ayanoğlu and Güneş, *Orman Suçları*, 35.

40 Kıvılcımlı, *Yol 2*, 202; Ayanoğlu-Güneş, *Orman Suçları*, 35. Election district reports of 1939 include several complaints about the Forest Law and the resulting wood scarcity. BCA-CHP [490.1/515.2062.1]. Newspapers also reported similar complaints. "Odun Yok," *Köroğlu*, October 16, 1937.

41 Boratav, *Türkiye İktisat Tarihi*, 55; Owen and Pamuk, *A History of Middle East Economies*, 15–16; Başar, *Atatürk'le Üç Ay*.

42 Şevket Süreyya [Aydemir], *Cihan İktisadiyatında Türkiye*, 14; *Türk Ekonomisinin 50. Yılı*, 38.

43 Owen and Pamuk, *A History of Middle East Economies*, 16; Tezel, *Cumhuriyet Döneminin İktisadi Tarihi*, 426; Hatipoğlu, *Türkiye'de Ziraî Buhran*, 49, 66.

44 "Kemalpaşa Köylülerinin Çalışkanlığı," *Cumhuriyet*, June 10, 1930. See the memoirs of those who lived in the villages during this period, Karslı, *Köy Öğretmeninin Anıları*, 60; Kudar, *Tahtakuşlar'dan Paris'e*, 21; Yavuz, *Anılarım*, 12–16; Baykurt, *Özüm Çocuktur*, 124.

45 *Ziraat Kongresi [1931]*, 848; İsmail Hüsrev [Tökin], *Türkiye'de Köy İktisadiyatı*, 150; Tezel, *Cumhuriyet Döneminin İktisadi Tarihi*, 127;

Sarç, *Ziraat ve Sanayi Siyaseti*, 254; Hazar, *Ziraat Bankası*, 240; Emrence, *99 Günlük Muhalefet*, 58.

46 See BCA-MGM [30.10/79.520.3], January 5, 1931; BCA-CHP [490.1/ 475.1941.1], February 4, 1933; [490.1/655.182.1], August 21, 1935; [490.1/836.367.1], November 28, 1935.

47 *Gezi Notları*, 27, 31; *Ziraat Kongresi [1931]*, 36, 565, 694; see Us, *Hatıra Notları*, 191; İsmail Hüsrev [Tökin], *Türkiye'de Köy İktisadiyatı*, 147.

48 Kıvılcımlı, *Yol* 2, 126–7; İsmail Hüsrev [Tökin], *Türkiye'de Köy İktisadiyatı*, 147.

49 İsmail Hüsrev [Tökin], *Türkiye'de Köy İktisadiyatı*, 150.

50 Öztürk, *Türk Parlamento Tarihi (1927–1931)*, 207–8; BCA-MGM [030.10/128.923.12.1.].

51 İsmail Hüsrev [Tökin], *Türkiye'de Köy İktisadiyatı*, 146–8. For examples of court notices that appeared in the press from the first half of August 1934 in Aydın alone, see "Aydın Defterdarlığından," *Aydın*, August 1, 1934; "Türkiye Ziraat Bankası Nazilli Şubesinden," *Aydın*, August 4, 1934; "Türkiye Ziraat Bankası Nazilli Şubesinden," *Aydın*, August 5, 1934; "Ziraat Bankası Aydın Şubesinden," *Aydın*, August 16, 1934. Likewise for the announcements for May 1935 in Erzurum, see "Erzurum Ziraat Bankasından," *Erzurum*, May 9, 1935; "Ziraat Bankasından," *Erzurum*, May 18, 1935; "Ziraat Bankasından," *Erzurum*, May 20, 1935; Keyder, *State and Class*, 141.

52 İsmail Hüsrev [Tökin], *Türkiye'de Köy İktisadiyatı*, 141; BCA-MGM [30.10/120.858.5.], May 27, 1930; [30.10/64.432.2], July 26, 1930.

53 BCA-CHP [490.1/725.481.1], January 16, 1936.

54 Kıray, *Toplumsal Yapı*, 111; "Köyde Ağalık Meselesi," 164; Mehmet Zeki, *Mıntıkamızın Kitabı*, 135.

55 BCA-CHP [490.1/836.367.1], November 28, 1935; Metinsoy, "Kemalizmin Taşrası," 124–64.

56 Kıray, *Toplumsal Yapı*, 273–94; Ali Galip, "Köylü," 329; Kıvılcımlı, *Yol* 2, 118–23; Falih Rıfkı [Atay], *Bizim Akdeniz*, 37; Aksoy, *Türkiye'de Toprak Meselesi*, 56; Pamuk, "Intervention during the Great Depression," 334; "Zorbalık Ortadan Kalkmalı !" *Cumhuriyet*, October 19, 1931; Hatipoğlu, "Ziraatimizde Kâhyalar İdaresi."

57 Ali Kemalî, *Erzincan*, 197–202.

58 Kıvılcımlı, *İhtiyat Kuvvet*, 82–4; Uluğ, *Tunceli*, 95–8; Ali Kemalî, *Erzincan*, 196–7; İsmail Hüsrev [Tökin], *Türkiye Köy İktisadiyatı*, 178; Uluğ, *Tunceli*, 113–14.

59 Bardakçı, *Toprak Dâvasından*, 11–15, 33, 41–5; Uluğ, *Tunceli*, 117. See Bilbaşar, *Cemo* (1966) and *Memo* (1970). These novels conveyed in

Turkish literature for the first time the Kurdish peasants' struggle for survival.

60 Scott, *The Village Headman*, 11–14; Szyliowicz, *Political Change in Rural Turkey*, 43–7.

61 Makal, *A Village in Anatolia*, 64; Kıray, *Toplumsal Yapı*, 113; Scott, *The Village Headman*, 20; Boran, "Köyde Sosyal Tabakalanma,"124; Szyliowicz, *Political Change in Rural Turkey*, 45–7; Yasa, *Hasanoğlan Köyü*, 195–6.

62 Boran, "Köyde Sosyal Tabakalanma," 124; Kıvılcımlı, *İhtiyat Kuvvet*, 80; Scott, *The Village Headman*, 19.

63 See Articles 36 and 37 of "Köy Kanunu," 442/March 18, 1924, *Düstur* III, vol. 5, 339–47. For a recent account that examines the headmen as the agents of the government, see Massicard, "The Incomplete Civil Servant?"

64 Tuğal, "Yine Köy Kanunu Tasarısı," 21–2; Artukmaç, *Köylerimizi Nasıl Kalkındırabiliriz?* 75; Yasa, *Hasanoğlan Köyü*, 204; Emiroğlu, *Vasıtasız Vergiler*, 113; *Düstur* III, vol. 10, 1827.

65 Sertel, *Ardımdaki Yıllar*, 118; Nadi, "Gene O Mesele," *Cumhuriyet*, September 17, 1931.

66 Newman, *Turkish Crossroads*, 187; Sertel, *Ardımdaki Yıllar*, 118; Baykurt, *Üzüm Çocuktur*, 232.

67 See "Akköy Halkının Derdi," *Vakit*, April 10, 1934; İmamoğlu, "Ödeşmek."

68 BCA-MGM [30.10/79.520.3], January 5, 1931; BCA-CHP [490.01/655.182.1], September 14, 1931; [490.1/620.36.1], December 1, 1935.

69 Enis, *Toprak Kokusu*, 257–8; Hançerlioğlu, *Karanlık Dünya*, 105–7.

70 Kemal, *Sarı Defterdekiler*, 138.

71 Szyliowicz, *Political Change in Rural Turkey*, 48; Işıksoluğu, *Aydoğdu Köyü*, 74.

72 Nar, *Anadolu Günlüğü*, 58; Belli, *Boşuna mı Çiğnedik?* 76.

73 BCA-CHP [490.1/655.182.1], September 14, 1931; BCA-CHP [490.01/684.317.1], January 17, 1931.

74 BCA-CHP [490.1/475.1941.1], May 18, 1931; July 20, 1931; March 9, 1933.

75 BCA-CHP [490.1/475.1941.1], June 6, 1934.

76 Madaralı, *Ekmekli Dönemeç*, 7. A peasant pressured by gendarmes for payment of the road tax had hanged himself. "960 Kuruş İçin," *Köroğlu*, December 16, 1929. For similar tragic news, see "Vur Abalıya" and "Yol Parasını Vermiyen Borçlulara Dair," *Köroğlu*, February 28, 1934; "Bu Ne Rezalettir?" *Orak Çekiç*, June 1, 1936; "Yol Kesmek," *Orak Çekiç*, August 10, 1936; Sertel, *Ardımdaki Yıllar*, 120.

77 Kıvılcımlı, *İhtiyat Kuvvet*, 99; Bayrak, *Kürtlere Vurulan Kelepçe*, 94–104, 204–20; Madanoğlu, *Anılar*, 81, 136.

78 Bilbaşar, *Cemo*, 71–5, 81–4, 198; Bulut, *Dersim Raporları*, 288; Kıvılcımlı, *İhtiyat Kuvvet*, 177; Bayrak, *Kürtlere Vurulan Kelepçe*, 157; Ekinci, *Lice'den Paris'e*, 90.

Chapter 2 Raising Voice and Rural Discontent

1 Özsoy, *İki Vatan Yorgunları*, 55, 59, 89; BCA-CHP [490.1/1454.34.3].

2 Bayır, *Köyün Gücü*, 165; *Türk Akdeniz* (July 1939), 12; *TBMM Yıllık 1930*, 340, 362, 370, 378, 382, 405, 411.

3 Yalman, *Cenupta Türkmen Oymakları*, 215–22.

4 *TBMM Yıllık 1928*, 321, 325; *TBMM Yıllık 1930*, 355–8, 363, 369, 390–1,397, 401, 412, 418; *TBMM Yıllık 1931*, 371, 375; *TBMM Yıllık 1939*, 334, 336–37, 342, 345, 381, 391, 420, 432, 436; *TBMM Yıllık 1935*, 300; *TBMM Yıllık 1939*, 346, 417, 405–6, 435, 438. See also BCA-MGM [30.10/81.531.19], July 25, 1939.

5 "Toprak İstedik, Fakat Vermediler," *Son Posta*, June 29, 1935; "Akçaabatta Hakkı Kaybolan Bir Köylü Vatandaşımız," *Son Posta*, July 16, 1935; "Toprak İsteyen Köylü," *Köroğlu*, September 26, 1936.

6 *CHP 1936 İl Kongreleri*, 51–2, 63–4, 354, 378–9, 292–3; *CHP 28/12/936 Tarihinde Toplanan Vilâyet Kongresi Zabıtnamesi*, 35, 43, 51, 58.

7 BCA-CHP [490.1/515.2062.1]; [490.01/538.2156.1], 1938.

8 Koraltürk, *Ahmet Hamdi Başar'ın Hatıraları*, 371, 382; Öztürk, *İsmet Paşa'nın Kürt Raporu*, 45, 61.

9 BCA-MGM [30.10/123.879.10], March 5, 1938; Bardakçı, *Toprak Dâvasından Siyasî Partilere*, 24, 37.

10 Koraltürk, *Ahmet Hamdi Başar'ın Hatıraları*, 326, 349–51, 421.

11 Esenel, *1940'lı Yıllarda*, 109; Uran, *Hatıralarım*, 216–24; BCA-CHP [490.1/724.477.1], February 7, 1931; [490.1/729.478.1], March 16, 1931.

12 BCA-CHP [490.1/1454.34.3].

13 "Vergiler Hakkında Anket: Arazi Vergisi Aşar Vergisine Rahmet Okutacak Kadar Ağırdır," *Cumhuriyet*, December 27, 1930; see also the lists of the petitions in the National Assembly yearbooks. *TBMM Yıllık 1939*, 373, 439–41, 444–5.

14 "Hangi Vergilerden, Niçin Şikâyet Ediliyor?" *Cumhuriyet*, January 11, 1931; "Vergiler Hakkında Anket," *Cumhuriyet*, December 27, 1930; "Anketten Neticeler: Arazi Vergisi Çiftçiye Aşarı Arattırmaktadır," *Cumhuriyet*, November 27, 1930; "Arazi Vergisi de İndirilse Köylü Sevinir," *Köroğlu*, October 30, 1935.

15 *TBMM Yıllık* 1929, 367; *TBMM Yıllık* 1931, 260, 370; BCA-CHP [490.01/724.477.1], February 7, 1931; *TBMM Yıllık* 1934, 289; *TBMM Yıllık* 1935, 271, 290; *CHP* 28/12/936 *Tarihinde Toplanan Vilâyet Kongresi Zabıtnamesi*, 25, 40; *CHP* 1936 *İl Kongreleri*, 63–4, 151–3, 281, 383–4.

16 Turan, *Yeni Vergi Kanunları'nın Tatbiki*, 84. See also 1931 Provincial Congresses' Wish Lists, BCA-CHP [490.1/500.2008.1]; *CHP* 1936 *İl Kongreleri*, 16, 17, 42, 43, 70, 77–8, 85, 117, 165, 175, 202, 251–6, 264, 271, 281, 292–3, 316–17, 340, 349, 354, 383–7. See also BCA-CHP [490.1/729.478.1], March 16, 1931; [490.1/651.165.1], November 29, 1934; BCA-CHP [490.1/726.485.1], February 10, 1936.

17 *TBMM Yıllık* 1931, 225, 266, 269, 275, 277, 280, 306; "Sayım Vergisi ve Köylünün Temennisi," *Son Posta*, October 9, 1932; *TBMM Yıllık* 1935, 288, 324–6; Çem, *Qurzeli Usiv'in 70 Yılı*, 64.

18 Baykurt, *Özüm Çocuktur*, 206.

19 See inspection reports, BCA-CHP [490.1/729.478.1], January 20, 1931; [490.01/724.477.1], February 7, 1931; [490.1/651.165.1], November 20, 1934; [490.1/684.317.1], August 2, 1937.

20 BCA-CHP [490.1/1454.34.3]; BCA-MGM [30.10/79.520.3], January 5, 1931; BCA-CHP [490.1/724.477.1], February 7, 1931; [490.1/729.478.1], March 16, 1931.

21 "Köylünün Şikâyet Ettiği Vergiler-Tahsildar Meselesi-Yol Vergisi," *Cumhuriyet*, November 22, 1930; *CHP* 1936 *İl Kongreleri*, 251–6, 413–14; "Milletin Belini Büken Vergilerin Fazlalığı Değil, Yanlış Tahakkuklardır," *Cumhuriyet*, November 24, 1930.

22 "Halk Sütunu," *Köroğlu*, July 10, 1929; BCA-CHP [490.01/724.477.1], February 7, 1931; "Haksızlık Olur mu Ya!" *Köroğlu*, March 28, 1936.

23 "Safranbolu Köylülerinden Bir Çok Mühür ve İmzalı Bir Mektup Aldık," *Köroğlu*, August 29, 1934.

24 Eşref, "Haymana Halkı Neler Yapılmasını İstiyor?" *Vakit*, October 10, 1934; "Fakir Kasaba Halkı Yemeklik Undan Vergi Alınmaması İçin Hükümetten Rica Ediyorlar," *Köroğlu*, August 4, 1934.

25 *CHP* 1936 *İl Kongreleri*, 16, 17, 114, 121, 165, 251–6, 395; "Köy Değirmenlerinden Alınacak Muamele Vergisi," *Vakit*, July 31, 1934.

26 "Halk Sütunu: Tütün İnhisarının Nazarı Dikkatine," *Cumhuriyet*, November 27, 1930; "Tütüncülerimizi Koruyacak Kimse Yok mu?" *Cumhuriyet*, December 5, 1930; *CHP* 1936 *İl Kongreleri*, 158, 413–14.

27 *TBMM ZC*, April 29, 1933, 138; BCA-CHP [490.1/35.146.1], January 26, 1931.

28 Karaalioğlu, *Türk Romanları*, 319; Cumalı, *Tütün Zamanı*, *Zeliş* and *Acı Tütün*; Apaydın, *Tütün Yorgunu*.

29 BCA-CHP [490.01/651.165.1], December 25, 1935; *CHP 1936 İl Kongreleri*, 298, 271, 151–3, 165. See also *TBMM Yıllık 1928*, 330; *TBMM Yıllık 1929*, 344; *TBMM Yıllık 1931*, 273, 291, 303; *TBMM Yıllık 1935*, 330. BCA-CHP [490.1/725.481.1].

30 *TBMM ZC*, April 29, 1933, 131; Turgut, *Kılıç Ali'nin Anıları*, 601. For demands and complaints about Köylü cigarettes and cut rugs, see *CHP 1936 İl Kongreleri*, 16–17, 63–4, 121, 152–3, 165, 202, 251–6, 281, 285–6, 292–3, 316–17, 395, 413–14.

31 Doğruel and Doğruel, *Tekel*, 143; Kuruç, *Belgelerle Türkiye İktisat Politikası 1*, 231.

32 BCA-CHP [490.01/651.165.1], December 25, 1935; *CHP 1936 İl Kongreleri*, 16–17, 20, 77–8, 158, 175, 198, 275, 285–6, 298, 387. "Pancar Eken Köylü," *Köroğlu*, March 18, 1936.

33 Günay, "Şeker," 79; Veldet, *30. Yılında Türkiye Şeker Sanayi*, 235, 401.

34 Veldet, *30. Yılında Türkiye Şeker Sanayi*, 180–2.

35 Eski, *İsmet İnönü'nün Kastamonu Gezileri*, 63.

36 The Summaries of the 1935 Reports, BCA-CHP [490.1/725.481.1]; The Summaries of the 1939 Reports, BCA-CHP [490.1/515.2062.1].

37 For the elite perception of the peasantry as "killer of trees," see Demir, "Adana'da Orman Kaçakçılığı," 7. For the peasants' demands, see *TBMM Yıllık 1929*, 316, 330, 344, 351, 361; *TBMM Yıllık 1935*, 276; *TBMM Yıllık 1936*, 282; *TBMM Yıllık 1939*, 418–20.

38 A. Fuat, "Memlekette," *Cumhuriyet*, November 27, 1930; "Bir Orman İşi," *Cumhuriyet*, October 19, 1930.

39 1931 RPP Provincial Congresses' Wish Lists, BCA-CHP [490.1/500.2008.1]; *CHP 1936 İl Kongreleri*, 63–4, 85, 165, 245, 260, 275, 383–4; BCA-CHP [490.1/502.2016.2], September 26, 1936; *CHP 28/12/936 Tarihinde Toplanan Vilâyet Kongresi Zabıtnamesi*, 27, 51.

40 BCA-CHP [490.1/631.79.1], November 11, 1935; The Summaries of the 1935 Reports, [490.01/725.481.1.]; [490.1/502.2016.2], September 26, 1936; [490.1/684.317.1], August 2, 1937; The Summaries of the 1939 Reports, [490.1/515.2062.1].

41 "Anketimize Cevaplar," *Cumhuriyet*, March 15, 1931; "Çiftçi Sakat Usullerden ve Kırtasiyecilikten Müşteki," *Cumhuriyet*, March 19, 1931.

42 Hazar, *Ziraat Bankası*, 240; "Ziraat Bankası ve Halk," *Yeşilgireson*, July 12, 1934; "Anketimize Cevaplar," *Cumhuriyet*, March 31, 1931; BCA-CHP [490.1/500.2008.1]; [490.1/651.165.1], November 20, 1934; [490.1/724.477.1], February 7, 1931; [490.1/500.2008.1]; *CHP 1936 İl Kongreleri*, 198, 260, 317. There were many other petitions to the National Assembly asking for agricultural loans; see *TBMM Yıllık 1930*, 332, 416; *TBMM Yıllık 1935*, 320, 327.

43 BCA-CHP [490.1/500.2008.1]; [490.1/724.477.1], February 7, 1931; "Bankanın Parası Zürradan Ziyade Tüccarların Elinde Tedavül Etmektedir," *Cumhuriyet*, March 12, 1931; "Anketimize Cevaplar," *Cumhuriyet*, March 15, 1931.

44 BCA-CHP [490.1/500.2008.1]; "Kısa Vadeli İstikraz Muameleleri Köylüyü Muzdarip Ediyor," *Cumhuriyet*, March 9, 1931; "Ziraat Bankası Münhasıran Çiftçilerin Bankası Olmalıdır," *Cumhuriyet*, March 10, 1931; "Ziraat Bankası'ndan Para Almağı Zorlaştıran Sebepler Nelerdir?" *Cumhuriyet*, March 16, 1931; "Çiftçilerin Belini Büken Faiz Miktarile İkrazat Vadelerinin Kısalığıdır," *Cumhuriyet*, March 20, 1931; "Zürraın Belini Büken En Ağır Şey Faizdir," *Cumhuriyet*, March 25, 1931; "Vade Az, Faiz Çoktur," *Cumhuriyet*, April 11, 1931; BCA-CHP [490.1/724.477.1], February 7, 1931.

45 Kıvılcımlı, *Yol 2*, 149; "Bir Zat," *Cumhuriyet*, June 14, 1931.

46 Peasants, sometimes collectively, demanded the suspension of their agricultural loan debts. *TBMM Yıllık 1929*, 316, 326, 331; *TBMM Yılllık 1930*, 339, 343–5, 352, 363, 373, 386, 402, 408, 413–18, 420–1; *TBMM Yıllık 1931*, 224–6, 228, 230, 237, 244, 252, 255, 267, 271, 380–3; *TBMM Yıllık 1935*, 273, 277–9, 290, 300, 308, 322, 325; BCA-CHP [490.1/500.2008.1]; [490.1/500.2010.1]; "Ne İstemişler?" *Köroğlu*, September 24, 1932; "İnek Haczedilir mi?" *Köroğlu*, October 22, 1932; Ragıp Kemal, "İslamköy ve Atabey Halkı Ne İstiyor?" *Vakit*, October, 25, 1934.

47 "Köylü Ziraat Bankasına Buğday Vermiyor," *Köroğlu*, September 12, 1931; Atasagun, *Türkiye Cumhuriyeti Ziraat Bankası*, 306; BCA-CHP [490.1/648.151.1], November 27, 1934; [490.1/684.317.1], August 2, 1937; *CHP 1936 İl Kongreleri*, 16–17, 42–3, 175, 198, 202, 292–3, 316–17. The wheat purchases at fixed prices did not benefit smallholders. See Özbek, "Kemalist Rejim ve Popülizmin Sınırları."

48 BCA-CHP [490.01/60.231.3], March 10, 1937.

49 *TBMM Yıllık 1930*, 349, 361–5, 381, 401, 421; *TBMM Yıllık 1931*, 230, 245, 287, 304; *TBMM Yıllık 1934*, 222, 230, 245, 304; *TBMM Yıllık 1935*, 270, 273.

50 EGMA [13216–7]; BCA-CHP [490.1/612.125.2], July 11, 1940.

51 Soyak, *Atatürk'ten Hatıralar*, 467; BCA-CHP [490.1/729.478.1], March 16, 1931; "Köy Kanunundan Doğan Bir Mesele," *Son Posta*, December 5, 1936; "Halkın ve Göçmenlerin Derdi," *Köroğlu*, January 25, 1936; "Bu Muhtar Ceza Görmeli," *Orak Çekiç*, November 7, 1936.

52 Szyliowicz, *Political Change in Rural Turkey*, 48; Nar, *Anadolu Günlüğü*, 58, 66; BCA-CHP [490.1/729.478.1], March 16, 1931.

53 *TBMM Yıllık 1929*, 350, 362, 363, 364; *TBMM Yıllık 1930*, 336, 344, 355, 361, 414; *TBMM Yıllık 1935*, 284, 333, 335; BCA-CHP [490.1/ 475.1941.1].

54 "Savur Kadınlarının Fevzi Paşa'ya Şikâyetleri," *Cumhuriyet*, October 18, 1930; "Şark Vilayetlerinde Milis Teşkilatı," *Cumhuriyet*, October 24, 1930; Yıldız, *Dersim Dile Geldi*, 68.

55 Bayır, *Köyün Gücü*, 165; BCA-CHP [490.1/729.478.1], March 16, 1931; [490.1/724.477.1], February 7, 1931; [490.1/ 725.481.1]; [490.1/35.146.1], 26.01.1931; Uran, *Hatıralarım*, 216–24.

56 Karaömerlioğlu, "Bir Tepeden Reform Denemesi," 32–3; Afet İnan, *Devletçilik İlkesi*, 108; Kuruç, *Belgelerle Türkiye İktisat Politikası 2*, 369–70; *Atatürk'ün Söylev ve Demeçleri I*, 374–9; Türkeş, *Kadro Hareketi*, 186–92; *Düstur III*, vol. 10, 1793; BCA-BKK [30.18.1/ 02.78.76], August 27, 1937; [30.18.1/02.84.85], September 26, 1938.

57 *CHP Dördüncü Büyük Kongre Zabıtları*, 81; *CHP Programı*, 14; Barkan, "Çiftçiyi Topraklandırma Kanunu," 456–7.

58 Barkan, "Çiftçiyi Topraklandırma Kanunu," 455; Aksoy, *Türkiye'de Toprak Meselesi*, 58–9; Rıza, *Türkiye Ziraati*, 4; *DİE Türkiye İstatistik Yıllığı, 1968*, 164.

59 BCA-CHP [490.1/502.2016.2], September 26, 1936.

60 "Tuz Fiyatı Hakkında Kanun," 2752/June 5, 1935, *Düstur III*, vol. 16, 1281; *CHP 1936 İl Kongreleri*, 85, 158, 260, 264, 271, 281. See also summaries of the deputies' inspection reports in 1935: BCA-CHP [490.1/725.481.1].

61 See BCA-CHP [490.1/502.2016.2]; Atasagun, *Türkiye Cumhuriyeti Ziraat Bankası*, 290–6. Those debtors who could not pay back their debts in İstanbul alone filled a book of 270 pages. See *TC Ziraat Bankası'nın İpotekli ve Zincirleme Kefaletli Tarımsal Alacaklarının Taksitlendirilmesine Dair*. Ankara: ZB, 1935; "Hayvanlarına ve Mahsullerine Haciz Konmayacak," *Son Posta*, July 6, 1935; BCA-CHP [490.1/502.2016.2]; BCA-CHP [490.1/3.12.11], February 8, 1936.

Chapter 3 Resisting Agricultural Taxes

1 Işık Kansu, "Vergiler," *Cumhuriyet*, September 10, 2007.

2 Burg, *A World History of Tax Rebellions*, ix.

3 "Vergi Bakayasının Tasfiyesi ve Mükelleflere Bazı Kolaylıklar Gösterilmesi Hakkında Kanun Lâyihası Görüşmeleri," Kuruç, *Belgelerle Türkiye İktisat Politikası 2*, 218.

4 Egesoy, *Cumhuriyet Devrinde Vasıtasız Vergiler*, xii–xiv.

5 BCA-MGM [30.10/69.457.11], October 20, 1932; Öztürk, *İsmet Paşa'nın Kürt Raporu*, 55, 61; BCA-MGM [30.10/65.433.1], July 15, 1935; *CHP 28/12/936 Tarihinde Toplanan Vilâyet Kongresi Zabıtnamesi*, 25, 40.

6 BCA-MGM [30.10/69.455.11]; [30.10/69.457.11], October 20, 1932; [30.10/65.433.1], July 15, 1935.

7 Bulut, *Dersim Raporları*, 253; *Jandarma Umum Komutanlığı Raporu*, 100.

8 "Bugünden İtibaren Yedi Bin Köylü Yollarda Çalışacak," *Son Posta*, April 1, 1932; "Yol Parasını Vermiyen Borçlulara Dair," *Köroğlu*, February 28, 1934; *CHP 28/12/936 Tarihinde Toplanan Vilâyet Kongresi Zabıtnamesi*, 25; *CHP 1936 İl Kongreleri*, 63–4.

9 Aksoy, *Köylülerimizle Başbaşa*, 54; Ali Kemâlî, *Erzincan*, 423.

10 Esenel, *1940'lı Yıllarda*, 107–10; Sertel, *Ardımdaki Yıllar*, 118.

11 Barkan, "Çiftçiyi Topraklandırma Kanunu," 509.

12 Nar, *Anadolu Günlüğü*, 45; Baykurt, *Özüm Çocuktur*, 234–6; Aksoy, *Köylülerimizle Başbaşa*, 81; *Hayvanlar İstatistiği*, 2.

13 "Devlet Vergisinden Kaçanlar," *Yeşilgireson*, May 22, 1937; Akekmekçi and Pervan, eds., *Necmeddin Sahir Sılan Raporları*, 74; BCA-MGM [30.10/69.457.11], October 20, 1932; Aksoy, *Köylülerimizle Başbaşa*, 81; Tahir, *Sağırdere*, 77, 86–7.

14 Akekmekçi and Pervan, eds., *Necmeddin Sahir Sılan Raporları*, 74; Mimaroğlu, *Gördüklerim ve Geçirdiklerim'den*, 105–14; Bulut, *Dersim Raporları*, 254.

15 Akçetin, "Anatolian Peasants in the Great Depression," 84; *Hayvanlar İstatistiği 1929–35*, 6, 16, 20; "Ağnam Resminin Ağırlığı Koyunculuğumuzu Baltalıyor," *Cumhuriyet*, December 6, 1930; "Sayım Vergisi," *Son Posta*, May 27, 1936.

16 *Nüfus Sayımı Propagandası İçin Muhtelif Gazetelerde İntişar Eden Yazılar ve Radyoda Verilen Konferanslar*. Ankara: DİE Yayınları, 1941; Özer, *Toprağın Sancısı*, 11; İmamoğlu, "Ödeşmek."

17 Türkoğlu, *Genç Cumhuriyet'te Köy Çocuğu Olmak*, 111–14.

18 Linke, *Allah Dethroned*, 130; İmamoğlu, "Ödeşmek."

19 Miroğlu, *Canip Yıldırım'la Söyleşi*, 53; Ekinci, *Lice'den Paris'e*, 69.

20 "Gözcüler," *Orak Çekiç*, August 10, 1936; Baykurt, *Özüm Çocuktur*, 235.

21 Kıvılcımlı, *İhtiyat Kuvvet*, 128; Tahir, *Sağırdere*, 77–87. See also politicians' reports, BCA-MGM [30.10/69.457.11], October 20, 1932; BCA-CHP [490.1/696.365.1], February 19, 1935.

22 Esenel, *1940'lı Yıllarda*, 109.

23 *1937 Temyiz Kararları*, 80.

24 BCA-MGM [30.10/104.676.24], June 14, 1934; [30.10/104.676.24], July 8, 1934; "Köy Değirmenlerinden Alınacak Muamele Vergisi," *Vakit*, July 31, 1934.
25 BCA-MGM [30.10/127.914.14], May 26, 1929; [30.10/105.684.13], April 8, 1930.
26 BCA-MGM [30.10/128.923.7], March 21, 1935; [30.10/105.686.2], June 14, 1937.
27 "Tahsildarı Öldürdü," *Köroğlu*, January 24, 1931; BCA-BKK [30.18.1.2/21.43.5.], June 17, 1931; "Tahsildarı Vuran Asıldı," *Köroğlu*, May 23, 1936; BCA-BKK [30.18.1.2/62.17.17], March 2, 1936; Seçkin, *Bir Hâkime Yakışanı Yazdım*, 23.
28 For the role of the kinship ties as well as nationalism in the Kurdish people's rebellions, see Belge, "Seeing the State."
29 The majority of the Kurdish peasant communities resembled societies that were avoiding organization in the form of state, as Scott examines in the case of South Asian upland communities free from any state intervention. Scott, *The Art of Not Being Governed*.
30 Gürbüz, *Mondros'tan Milenyuma*, 92.
31 Gürbüz, *Mondros'tan Milenyuma*, 93; Madanoğlu, *Anılar*, 289–90.
32 "Sason Kaymakamı Nasıl Vuruldu?" *Köroğlu*, June 12, 1935; Hallı, *Türkiye Cumhuriyeti'nde Ayaklanmalar*, 156.
33 İBA [12212–4], January 24, 1939.
34 İBA [12212–4], January 11, 1939; [12212–4], February 16, 1939.
35 Koraltürk, *Ahmet Hamdi Başar'ın Hatıraları*, 391. For the tax revisions, see "Hayvanlar Vergisi Kanunu," 1839/06.07.1931, *Resmi Gazete*, no. 1849, July 15, 1931, 617–20; "Hayvanlar Vergisi Kanunu," 2897/ 20.01.1936, *Resmi Gazete*, no. 3218, January 29, 1936, 6005–8; "Hayvanlar Vergisinin Bazı Hükümlerinin Değiştirilmesine ve Bazı Hükümler Eklenmesine Dair Kanun," 3343/23.03.1938, *Resmi Gazete*, no. 3869, March 30, 1938, 9557–8; Turan, *Yeni Vergi Kanunları'nın Tatbiki*, 79–84; "İnen Hayvan Vergileri," *Köroğlu*, November 13, 1935; "Hayvan Vergisi Kanunu Kabul Edildi," *Son Posta*, January 14, 1936.
36 Kuruç, *Belgelerle Türkiye İktisat Politikası* 2, 369–70; Us, *Hatıra Notları*, 247.
37 Turan, *Yeni Vergi Kanunlarının Tatbiki*, 82.
38 *CHP 1936 İl Kongreleri*, 12; "Vergi Bakayasının Tasfiyesine Dair Kanun," 2566/04.07.1934, *Resmi Gazete*, no. 2750, July 12, 1934, 4126–28; "Vergi Bakayasının Tasfiyesinde Dair 12/7/1934 Tarihli 2566 Sayılı Kanunun Sureti Tatbikine Dair İzahname," *Resmi Gazete*, no. 2916, January 29, 1935, 4795–4804; "Arazi ve Bina Vergilerile Binalardan Alınan İktisadi Buhran Vergisinin Vilayet Hususi İdarelerine Devri Hakkında Kanun," 2871/23.12.1935, *Resmi Gazete*,

no. 3193, January 30, 1935, 5879–80; "Arazi Vergisinin 1935 Mali Yılı Sonuna Kadar Olan Bakayasının Terkinine Dair Kanun," 3586/ 26.01.1939, *Resmi Gazete*, no. 4126, February 7, 11251. See also Çetin, "Vergi Aflarının," 177.

39 Kuruç, *Belgelerle Türkiye İktisat Politikası* 2, 327.

Chapter 4 Social Smuggling: Resisting Monopolies

1 Doğruel and Doğruel, *Tekel*, 150–1; Kuruç, *Belgelerle Türkiye İktisat Politikası*, vol. 1, 251.

2 Karras, *Smuggling*; May, *Smugglers and Smuggling*; Coxe, *Smuggling in the West Country*; Philipson, *Smuggling*.

3 Quataert, *Social Disintegration*, 13–40; Salih Zeki, *Türkiye'de Tütün*, 16–17; Hüseyin Avni [Şanda], *1908'de Ecnebi Sermayesine Karşı İlk Kalkınmalar*, 40.

4 Ruff, *Violence in Early Modern Europe*, 239–40.

5 "Adliye İstatistiklerine Göre Memleketimizde Cürümler ve Mücrimler," 43; Karabuda, *Goodbye to the Fez*, 79; "Kaçak," *Köroğlu*, April 13, 1932.

6 "Ağır Bir Duruşma," *Son Posta*, April 10, 1935 ; BCA-MGM [30.10/ 65.433.4], July 24, 1935.

7 See Hirschman, *Exit, Voice, and Loyalty*, 21–30.

8 Tobacco Smuggling in Afyon, BCA-MGM [30.10/180.242.15], January 20, 1927; The Sale of Smuggled Tobacco in the Shops in the Gaziantep City Center [30.10/180.242.19]; Report of the Interior Ministry about the Contraband Items Captured during the Last Three Months in Various Provinces [30.10/180.242.23], November 29, 1928; The Smuggling Activities That Took Place in 60 Provinces in October, November and December of 1929 [30.10/ 180.243.1], February 1, 1930. See also the press news, "Sigara Kağıdı Kaçakçıları," *İkdam*, January 24, 1926; "Bursa'da Yakalanan Kaçakçılar," *İkdam*, November 13, 1927.

9 "Muğla'da Mahkum Olan Kaçakçılar," *Son Posta*, June 2, 1932 ; "Yalnız 1 Ayda Neler Yakalandı," *Köroğlu*, August 30, 1933; "Kim Kâr Ediyor?" *Köroğlu*, October 17, 1934; "Bir Haftada 53 Kaçakçı," *Köroğlu*, July 29, 1936.

10 "Kaçakçılık," *Son Posta*, April 1, 1932; "Kaçakçılara Hiç Aman Yok," *Son Posta*, January 30, 1935; "Adliye İstatistiklerine Göre Memleketimizde Cürümler ve Mücrimler," 43.

11 Cillov, *Denizli El Dokumacılığı*, 147; Kıvılcımlı, *İhtiyat Kuvvet*, 47.

12 Toksoy, "Cenup Hudutlarımızda Kaçakçılık," 21; Beşikçi, *Doğu Anadolu'nun Düzeni*, 283–4; Kıvılcımlı, *İhtiyat Kuvvet*, 47–52, 71.

13 Berkes, *Bazı Ankara Köyleri Üzerine*, 55; Koca, *Umumi Müfettişlikten*, 474.

14 Toksoy, "Cenup Hudutlarımızda Kaçakçılık," 20; Kıvılcımlı, *İhtiyat Kuvvet*, 51.

15 "Kaçakçılığın Men-i ve Takibi Hakkında Kanun," 1126/23.06.1927, *Resmi Gazete*, no. 629, July 10, 1927, 2827; "Kaçakçılığın Men ve Takibi Hakkında Kanun," 1510/June 2, 1929, *Resmi Gazete*, no. 1216, June 15, 1929, 7539–46; "Gümrük Muhafaza Memurlarının Askeri Teşkilata Göre Tensiki Hakkında Kanun," 1841/19.07.1931, *Resmi Gazete*, no. 1858, July 27, 1931, 667–8.

16 *Akbaba*, October 23, 1931; Çoker, *Türk Parlamento Tarihi*, 334; Kuruç, *Belgelerle Türkiye İktisat Politikası*, vol. 1, 398–9; Toksoy, "Cenup Hudutlarımızda Kaçakçılık," 21; "Kaçakçılığın Men ve Takibine Dair Kanun," 1918/07.01.1932, *Resmi Gazete*, no. 2000, January 12, 1932, 1141–51. For the decree about the smuggling courts, see *Resmi Gazete*, no. 2012, January 26, 1932, 1183.

17 Çoker, *Türk Parlamento Tarihi*, 337; "Kaçakçıların Takibi ve Muhafaza Hususlarında Büyük Yararlılıkları Görülenlere Verilecek İkramiye Hakkında Kararname," *Resmi Gazete*, no. 2937, February 23, 1935; 4869–70; "Kaçakçılığı İhbar Edenler Gizlenecek," *Cumhuriyet*, January 16, 1937.

18 "Kaçakçılık ve Mektep Müdürleri, Muallimleri," *İkdam*, November 10, 1927.

19 Aksoy, *Köylülerimizle Başbaşa*, 62; "Kaçakçılar Vatan Hainidir," *Yeni Adana*, December 5, 1936.

20 Naşit Hakkı, "Kaçakçılar," *Milliyet*, February 24, 1931.

21 Türkoğlu, *Genç Cumhuriyet'te Köy Çocuğu Olmak*, 501.

22 "Tütün İnhisarı Kanunu," 1701/09.06.1930, *Resmi Gazete*, no. 1531, June 28, 1930, 9158–60; "Kaçakçılar," *Köroğlu*, December 10, 1931; "İşe Bakın!" *Köroğlu*, December 12, 1931; *TBMM ZC*, May 4, 1935, 43.

23 Emiroğlu, *İnhisarlar ve Devlet Emlaki*, 49; Işıksoluğu, *Aydoğdu Köyü*, 74; "Sigara Kağıdı Kaçakçıları," *İkdam*, January 24, 1926; Ökten, "Cumhuriyet'in İlk Yıllarında Tütün," 174.

24 *TBMM ZC*, April 20, 1933, 134; *TBMM ZC*, May 4, 1935, 43.

25 "Tesadüfen Yakalanan Kaçakçı," *Son Posta*, March 16, 1932; "İstanbul'da Bu Sigaradan İçenler Takip Ediliyor," *Son Posta*, December 7, 1932; "İstanbul'da Köylü Cigarası İçilmez," *Son Posta*, December 15, 1932; "Halkın Köşesi," *Köroğlu*, August 8, 1934.

26 Ökten, "Cumhuriyet'in İlk Yıllarında Tütün," 175; "Tütününü Ateşe Verip Yakan Çiftçi," *Son Posta*, February 1, 1932; Yesari, *Çulluk*, see

especially the second chapter; "Köylü Rahmi Ne Kaçakçı Ne de Kundakçı"; *Orak Çekiç*, March 15, 1936.

27 Ragıp Kemal, "İslamköy ve Atabey Halkı Ne İstiyor?" *Vakit*, October 25, 1934; *1937 Temyiz Kararları*, 139.

28 Tülay Bilginer, "Kelepçeli Günler." *Hürriyet*, July 28, 1987.

29 Gürbüz, *Mondros'tan*, 93; "Bitlis Civarında 460 Bin Kaçak Cigara Kağıdı Ele Geçirildi," *Son Posta*, April 9, 1932.

30 "Kaçakçılık Yapan Üç Muhtar," *Son Posta*, May 14, 1932; "Tokat'ta Kaçakçılarla Mücadele," *Son Posta*, June 3, 1935.

31 Toksoy, "Cenup Hudutlarımızda Kaçakçılık," 22; Erk, *Kaçakçılık İşleri*, 172.

32 Erk, *Kaçakçılık İşleri*, 134–8, 172; Göksu, *İzmir ve Suç Coğrafyası*, 199; "Çorum'da Kaçakçılar," *Köroğlu*, July 24, 1929; "İzmaritçiler Arasında," *Son Posta*, August 5, 1932.

33 "Tabur Tabur Kaçakçılar," *Köroğlu*, March 14, 1931; "Kaçakçılığın Sonu," *Son Posta*, June 6, 1932; "Kızılbaş Bekir Dede!" *Köroğlu*, April 25, 1934; "Merzifon'da Bir Kaçakçılık Vakası," *Son Posta*, January 8, 1935; "Dur! Ateş!" *Köroğlu*, June 24, 1936; "Bir Haftada 53 Kaçakçı," *Köroğlu*, July 29, 1936. See also BCA-MGM [30.10/105.684.33], October 16, 1933; [30.10/105.685.9], April 15, 1936.

34 Madanoğlu, *Anılar*, 135–6; Gürbüz, *Mondros'tan*, 93.

35 Doğruel and Doğruel, *Tekel*, 144–6; "Gizli," *Köroğlu*, January 12, 1929.

36 *TBMM ZC*, April 29, 133–4.

37 Emiroğlu, *İnhisarlar ve Devlet Emlâki*, 89; "Her Gün Bir Kaçak Rakı Fabrikası Yakalanıyor," *Köroğlu*, January 12, 1929; "Gizli Bir İçki Fabrikası Daha Bulundu," *Son Posta*, March 23, 1932; "Rakı Çok Pahalı," *Köroğlu*, January 31, 1934; Göksu, *İzmir ve Suç Coğrafyası*, 198–9.

38 Güler, ed., *Açıklamalı Yönetim Zamandizini*, 296; "Kaçakçının Sonu," *Köroğlu*, May 26, 1934; "Tokat'ta Kaçakçılarla Mücadele," *Son Posta*, June 3, 1935; "Kaçakçılar Tutuldu," *Yeşilgireson*, January 12, 1936.

39 Kuruç, *Belgelerle Türkiye İktisat Politikası*, vol. 1, 231–2 ; Doğruel and Doğruel, *Tekel*, 152; BCA-MGM [30.10/65.433.4], July 24, 1935; [30.10/180.245.4], July 10, 1936; Öztürk, *İsmet Paşa'nın Kürt Raporu*, 25.

40 Yağcı, "Tuz, Tahta Kaşık Kaçakçılığı ve Yol Parası"; Türkoğlu, *Genç Cumhuriyet'te Köy Çocuğu Olmak*, 108; Kutay, "Halil Menteşe'nin Tuz Hikâyesi."

41 Gürbüz, *Mondros'tan Milenyuma*, 89.

42 Hatipoğlu, *Türkiye'de Ziraî Buhran*, 54–8; "Bitlis Civarında Bir Çok Kaçak Eşya Yakalandı," *Son Posta*, March 19, 1932 ; "Kim Kâr Ediyor?" *Köroğlu*, October 17, 1934.

43 Alpay, *Köy Dâvamız*, 75; Ali Nihat, "Elbistan'da Vaziyet-i İktisadiye," *Cumhuriyet*, November 22, 1930; Berkes, *Bazı Ankara Köyleri Üzerine*, 55; Eski, *İsmet İnönü'nün Kastamonu Gezileri*, 30.

44 Hatipoğlu, *Türkiye'de Ziraî Buhran*, 63–4.

45 Toksoy, "Cenup Hudutlarımızda Kaçakçılık," 22; Öztürk, *İsmet Paşa'nın Kürt Raporu*, 25, 29; Ekinci, *Lice'den Paris'e*, 64, 83; Kıvılcımlı, *İhtiyat Kuvvet*, 49.

46 Karacan, "Ağaç"; BCA-BATDB/ÜK [30.11.1/101.1.3], January 4, 1936; [30.11.1/116.32.12], September 18, 1937; [30.11.1/123.30.14], September 1, 1938; [30.11.1/135.39.18], October 19, 1939; [30.11.1/ 135.43.6], December 3, 1939; [30.11.1/133.29.16], August 2, 1939; Falih Rıfkı [Atay], *Bizim Akdeniz*, 36; Us, *Hatıra Notları*, 225; Eyriboz, "Plansız Köycülük," 102.

47 İsmail Hüsrev [Tökin], *Türkiye Köy İktisadiyatı*, 49; BCA-CHP [490.1/ 35.146.1], January 26, 1931.

48 Şevket Raşit [Hatipoğlu], "Meşelerin Cenaze Alayı," 10; "1 Köylünün Başına Gelenler," *Köroğlu*, February 1, 1936.

49 Baykurt, *Özüm Çocuktur*, 124, 150.

50 Yund, "Ermenâk Ceviz Ağaçları," 8–10; Erkal, "Pozantı-Toros Ormanlarında Gördüklerim."

51 Demir, "Adana'da Orman Kaçakçılığı"; "Adana'da Kaçakçılık," *Verim* 5 (1935), 12. For complaints about the forest administration, see the Summaries of the 1935 Reports of the Deputies, BCA-CHP [490.1/ 515.2062.1].

52 Toygar, "Kaçak Mes'elesi"; Yund, "Ermenâk Ceviz Ağaçları," 9; Eski, *İsmet İnönü'nün Kastamonu Gezileri*, 63.

53 "Orman Kaçakçıları," *Yeşilgireson*, January 9, 1937; Yağcı, "Tuz, Tahta Kaşık Kaçakçılığı ve Yol Parası."

54 Kutluk, "Tahtacılar," 6–8; Demir, "Adana'da Orman Kaçakçılığı," 7.

55 Öztürk, *İsmet Paşa'nın Kürt Raporu*, 43–5; Bayar, *Şark Raporu*, 40–1.

56 Compare "Tütün İnhisarı Kanunu," 1701/09.06.1930, *Resmi Gazete*, no. 1531, June 28, 1930, 9158–9, and "Tütün ve Tütün İnhisarı Kanunu," 3437/10.06.1938, *Resmi Gazete*, no. 3943, June 25, 1938, 10090; Tekeli and İlkin, *Türkiye'de Devletçiliğin Oluşumu*, 119; *Adliye Encümeni Ruznamesi*, TBMM Encümenler Ruznamesi, 1 Teşrinisani 1934, 906.

57 Compare the prices in 1927 given in Salih Zeki, *Türkiye'de Tütün*, 337– 9, and the prices in 1932 listed in Emiroğlu, *İnhisarlar ve Devlet Emlâki*, 53–5; "Sigara Fiyatlarında Tenzilat," *Yeşilgireson*, January 18, 1936.

58 The Summaries of the 1935 Reports of the Deputies, BCA-CHP [490.1/ 725.481.1]; Toksoy, "Cenup Hudutlarımızda Kaçakçılık," 22.

59 Günay, "Şeker," 79; see also "Şeker İstihlak ve Gümrük Resmi Hakkındaki 2785 Sayılı Kanuna Müzeyyel Kanun," 3101/25.01.1037, *Resmi Gazete*, no 3517, January 26, 1937, 7581; "Hariçten İhraç Edilecek Şekerlerin Gümrük Resmi Hakkında Kararname," *Resmi Gazete*, no. 3788, December 21, 1937, 9105; Hatipoğlu, *Türkiye'de Ziraî Buhran*, 57; The Summaries of the 1935 Reports of the Deputies, BCA-CHP [490.1/725.481.1].

60 Tuz Fiyatı Hakkında Kanun, 2752/05.06.1935, *Düstur* III, vol. 16, 1281; "Tuz İstihsal ve Satışında İnkişaf," *İnhisarlar İstihbarat Bülteni*, vol. 6, no. 102 (1938), 1322.

61 BCA-CHP [490.1/ 725.481.1]; Öztürk, *İsmet Paşa'nın Kürt Raporu*, 26; "Kaçakçılığa Karşı Ancak Ucuzlukla Karşı Konulabilir," *Son Posta*, December 29, 1936.

62 Effimianidis, *Cihan İktisad Buhranı Önünde Türkiye*, 275.

63 Evaluation of the 1933 Provincial RPP Congresses' Wish Lists about Agriculture and Forests, BCA-CHP [490.1/502.2016.2], September 26, 1936; Gümüş, *Türk Orman Devrimi*, 165; Ayaz, "Türkiye'de Orman Mülkiyetinde," 190.

Chapter 5 Theft, Violence and Banditry

1 "Köylü Hareketi," *Kızıl İstanbul*, April 1934.

2 BCA-MGM [30.10/64.432.2], July 26, 1930.

3 Barkan, "Çiftçiyi Topraklandırma Kanunu," 513.

4 "Adliye İstatistiklerine Göre Memleketimizde Cürümler ve Mücrimler," 31–9.

5 *Emniyet İşleri Umum Müdürlüğü: Geçen Dört Yılda Yapılan ve Gelecek Dört Yılda Yapılacak İşler*, 13; Abdülkadir, "Köy ve Köylüler," 383.

6 Ecevid, "Suçluluk Bakımından Köylümüzün Ruhi Yapılışı," 49–50; Atasagun, *Türkiye'de İçtimai Siyaset Meseleleri*, 5.

7 "Köylü Hareketi," *Kızıl İstanbul*, April 1934; "Ya Kadın Dalgası, Ya Toprak Davası," *Köroğlu*, February 8, 1936; Ali Galip, "Köylü," 330.

8 Kıvılcımlı, *Yol 2*, 145–7, 290; Eski, *İsmet İnönü'nün Kastamonu Gezileri*, 48.

9 Boran, "Köyde Sosyal Tabakalanma," 126.

10 "360 Köylü Mahkemeye Verildi," *Cumhuriyet*, August 18, 1931.

11 "Toprak Yüzünden Bir Facia," *Son Posta*, September 8, 1932; "Kabahat Köylülerde Mi?" *Son Posta*, September 9, 1932; "Deli mi idi?" *Köroğlu*,

August 1, 1934; "İzmitte," *Orak Çekiç*, July 20, 1936; BCA-MGM [30.10/65.433.5], August 19, 1939.

12 Bardakçı, *Toprak Dâvasından Siyasî Partilere*, 30–7.

13 Aksoy, *Köylülerimizle Başbaşa*, 36; "Aydın'da Hayvan Hırsızları," *Son Posta*, April 3, 1932; "Yakalanan At Hırsızları," *Son Posta*, September 10, 1932; "Karaman'da Hırsızlar," *Köroğlu*, October 24, 1936.

14 Ali Galip, "Köylü," 327–8; Kuruç, *Belgelerle Türkiye İktisat Politikası*, vol. 2, 99–101; Yunus Nadi, "Hayvan Hırsızlığı Hakkındaki Kanunun Bir Maddesi," *Cumhuriyet*, December 8, 1933.

15 BCA-MGM [30.10/65.433.5], August 1, 1935; CHP 28/12/936 *Tarihinde Toplanan Vilâyet Kongresi Zabıtnamesi*, 31, 50; "Gediz'de Hayvan Hırsızları," *Köroğlu*, October 31, 1936; BCA-MGM [30.10/123.879.10], February 16, 1938.

16 For such violence of the peasantry, see Fitzpatrick, *Stalin's Peasants*, 235.

17 "Muhtarı Vurdu," *Köroğlu*, June 20, 1934; "Köy Sandığı Parası İçin Muhtarı Vurmuşlar," *Köroğlu*, October 7, 1936; "Muhtarı Vurdular," *Köroğlu*, October 17, 1936; "Muhtarı Niçin Vurdular," *Köroğlu*, April 24, 1937; Erhan, *Ermeniler, Eşkıyalar, İnsanlar*, 17–24.

18 "Bir Jandarma Askeri Görevi Başında Şehit Edildi," *Son Posta*, August 29, 1932; BCA-MGM [30.10/105.684.13], April 8, 1930; Kıvılcımlı, *Yol 2*, 290–2.

19 BCA-MGM [30.10/127.914.14], May 26, 1929; BCA-BKK [30.18.1.2/21.43.5], July 17, 1931; [30.18.1.2/62.17.17], March 2, 1936; "Tahsildara Karşı Gelinmez," *Yeşilgireson*, February 8, 1936; "Tahsildarı Öldürdü," *Köroğlu*, January 24, 1931; "Tahsildar Uyumaz!" *Köroğlu*, May 20, 1936.

20 "Seferihisar Cinayetinin Ayrıntıları," *Cumhuriyet*, November 8, 1931; "Seferihisar Cinayeti," *Cumhuriyet*, November 9, 1931.

21 See Shanin, *Peasants and Peasant Societies*, 259.

22 On banditry during the Ottoman era, see Barkey, *Bandits and Bureaucrats*; Yetkin, *Ege'de Eşkıyalar*; Dural, *Bize Derler Çakırca*. For a recent analytical account of banditry in the Middle East, see Cronin, "Noble Robbers."

23 BCA-CHP [490.1/227.898.3], February 15, 1938; for a long list of bandits in all regions, see "On Beş Yıl Zarfında Cumhuriyet Zabıtasının Çalışmaları Hakkında Rapor," 15, 57–63.

24 "Candarma Bekir Eşkıya Peşinde," *Köroğlu*, January 30, 1932; Kemal, *İnce Memed*; Bilbaşar, *Memo* and *Cemo*; Tahir, *Rahmet Yolları Kesti*; Ali Galip, "Köylü," 328.

25 Hobsbawm, *Bandits*. Hobsbawm's notion of "social banditry" has been criticized by scholars who have argued that very few cases fit the model. However, some scholars have contended that because the social and economic conditions created banditry, many bandits – whether or not they had all the features delineated by Hobsbawm – can be labeled social bandits. I agree with the latter. For the discussion, see White, "Outlaw Gangs"; O'Malley, "Social Bandits"; Blok, "The Peasant and the Brigand."

26 For relations of power, patronage and economic exploitation in the Kurdish villages, see İsmail Hüsrev [Tökin], *Türkiye Köy İktisadiyatı*, 177–9; Beşikçi, *Doğu Anadolu'nun Düzeni*, 266, 297; Seçkin, *Bir Hâkime Yakışanı Yazdım*, 25.

27 Yetkin, *Ege'de Eşkıyalar*, 144.

28 Hobsbawm, *Bandits*, 22, 67; Scott, *Moral Economy*, 120.

29 *TBMM Yıllık 1928*, 339; *TBMM Yıllık 1934*, 251, 287, 297, 370, 381; *TBMM Yıllık 1936*, 315.

30 Yurtsever, *Kadirli Tarihi*, 259–61.

31 Avcı, "Eşkiya Çöllo." The date of his death was recorded in the security reports as 1936; "On Beş Yıl Zarfında Cumhuriyet Zabıtasının Çalışmaları Hakkında Rapor," 63. Bayrak, *Öyküleriyle Halk Anlatı Türküleri*, 527, 548, 558.

32 Madanoğlu, *Anılar*, 153–6.

33 Bayrak, *Öyküleriyle Halk Anlatı Türküleri*, 565, 616.

34 Ali Galip, "Köylü," 328; Bayrak, *Öyküleriyle Halk Anlatı Türküleri*, 123.

35 BCA-MGM [30.10/128.923.6], December 29, 1936.

36 BCA-MGM [30.10/127.914.14], May 8, 1929.

37 BCA-MGM [30.10/128.923.2], November 9, 1932. In this file, especially see the security report on the incidents during October 1932.

38 BCA-MGM [30.10/128.923.6], December 29, 1936; Övünç, "Zilân Asilerinden Reşo," 17–18; BCA-MGM [30.10/128.923.19].

39 "İdo ve İbo," *Köroğlu*, August 18, 1934; "Başbelası Bir Çete Reisi Gebertildi," *Son Posta*, December 1, 1935.

40 BCA-MGM [30.10/128.923.6], December 29, 1936. In this file are security reports about the incidents that occurred in 1933 and 1934; "Kemah Ovalarında Can Yakan Haydut," *Köroğlu*, October 2, 1937.

41 BCA-BKK [30.18.1.2/16.84.5.], December 31, 1930; [30.18.1.2/21.41.19.], June 10, 1931; [30.10/128.923.6.], December 29, 1936; Gökdemir, *Annemin Anlattıkları*, 109–13; Övünç, "Zilân Asilerinden Reşo," 17–18; BCA-MGM [30.10/128.923.2], November 9, 1932.

42 Alakom, *Bir Türk Subayının Ağrı İsyanı Anıları*, 26; "9 Otomobil Soyanlar," *Köroğlu*, July 24, 1929; "Cinayet ve Soygun Yapan Haydutlar

Yakalandı," *Son Posta*, August 21, 1932; "15 Yıllık Eşkıya," *Köroğlu*, May 8, 1935.

43 "Mağaradaki Çete," *Köroğlu*, June 24, 1936.

44 "Yolcular Hakkınızı Helal Edin!" *Köroğlu*, July 21, 1937.

45 Alakom, *Bir Türk Subayının Ağrı İsyanı Anıları*, 21–2.

46 Linke, *Allah Dethroned*, 52; Alakom, *Bir Türk Subayının Ağrı İsyanı Anıları*, 32; BCA-CHP [490.1/648.151.1], November 28, 1934; BCA-MGM [30.10/128.923.6], December 29, 1936; [30.10/128.923.19]; Kayra, *Sümbül Dağı'nın Karları*, 104.

47 BCA-MGM [30.10/ 128.923.19].

48 BCA-BKK [30.18.1.1/13.28.6], May 10, 1925; [30.18.1.1/14.23.1], May 27, 1925; BCA-MGM [30.10/105.683.6], December 14, 1926; BCA-BKK [30.18.1.1/19.36.5], May 25, 1926; BCA-BKK [30.18.1.1/ 22.74.9], December 15, 1926; [30.18.1.1/20.53.15], August 11, 1926; BCA-MGM [30.10/105.683.13], September 10, 1927; BCA-CHP [490.1/475.1941.1], March 6, 1934; BCA-MGM [30.10/ 128.923.6], December 29, 1936; see also "On Beş Yıl Zarfında Cumhuriyet Zabıtasının Çalışmaları Hakkında Rapor," 57–63.

49 "Müthiş Bir Çarpışma," *Köroğlu*, May 8, 1929; "Bu Ne Vahşet İş," *Köroğlu*, January 31, 1931; "Baskın: 12 Haydut," *Köroğlu*, April 11, 1931; "Adana Köylerini Soyan Bir Çete Yakalandı," *Son Posta*, October 20, 1932.

50 "Amma İş Ha!" *Köroğlu*, January 30, 1929; "Amma İş!" *Köroğlu*, March 2, 1929; BCA-MGM [30.10/105.685.25], August 6, 1937.

51 "Eşkıya," *Köroğlu*, July 29, 1929; "Jandarma Eşkiyaya Aman Vermesin!" *Köroğlu*, June 6, 1931.

52 Bayrak, *Eşkıyalık ve Eşkıya Türküleri*, 188–90.

53 "Bir Çete Türedi," *Köroğlu*, June 24, 1931; "Eşkıya Yatağı," *Köroğlu*, July 26, 1933.

54 BCA-CHP [490.1/475.1941.1], March 6, 1934.

55 "Konya'nın 4 Haydutu," *Köroğlu*, July 10, 1929; "Çorum Yolunda," *Köroğlu*, June 3, 1931; *Cumhuriyet*, August 16, 1931; "Urla Yolunda Yol Kesenler," *Köroğlu*, February 6, 1932; "Bir Çete Nasıl Yakalandı?" *Köroğlu*, February 18, 1933.

56 For an analytical account of the Menemen incident, see Azak, "A Reaction to Authoritarian Modernization."

57 "Köy Baskını: Maskeli Haydutlar," *Köroğlu*, May 10, 1933; "Aferin Şoföre," *Köroğlu*, March 7, 1934; "Haydutlar," *Köroğlu*, April 25, 1934; "Bursa Eskişehir Yolunda 5 Silahlı Ne Yaptı?" *Köroğlu*, September 21, 1935; "Muradoğlu Geberdi," *Köroğlu*, May 8, 1935.

58 "Bir Yıldan Beri Ünye Taraflarını Kasıp Kavuran Eşkıyadan Şakirle Arif," *Köroğlu*, December 26, 1928; "Posta," *Köroğlu*, June 8,

1929; BCA-MGM [30.10/105.683.29], July 30, 1929; Grew, *Atatürk ve Yeni Türkiye*, 148; "Eşkıya Reisi Kara Mustafa Nasıl Vuruldu?" *Köroğlu*, June 13, 1931; "Dostunu Dağdan Dağa Taşıyan Eşkıya," *Köroğlu*, October 14, 1931. See also Erhan, *Ermeniler, Eşkıyalar, İnsanlar*, 17–24.

59 For such discursive analysis, see Üngör, "Rethinking the Violence of Pacification," 767; Ergut, *Modern Devlet ve Polis*, 307.

PART I Concluding Remarks

1 Karaömerlioğlu, *Orada Bir Köy Var Uzakta*; about the fact that even peasantists were strangers to village realities, see Berkes, *Unutulan Yıllar*, 88.

Chapter 6 The Price of the Republic for the Working Class

1 Beinin, *Workers and Peasants in the Modern Middle East*, 77; Karakışla, "The 1908 Strike Wave," 154–9.

2 Quataert, "Workers and the State," 27–8, and *Social Disintegration*, 113–45; Toprak, *İttihat Terakki ve Cihan Harbi*, 153–68; Gülmez, *Türkiye'de 1936 Öncesinde İşçi Hakları*, 54; Erişçi, *Sosyal Tarih Çalışmaları*, 97–101.

3 Quataert, "Workers and the State," 30; Türkoğlu, "Hüseyin Sami Bey'in Hayatı ve Ankara'daki Ajanlık Yılları," 215–22. See also Serim, *Siyasi Polis Hizmeti*; Ergut, *Modern Devlet ve Polis*, 192.

4 Bulutay et al., *Türkiye Milli Geliri*, table 8.6.A, and see Boratav, *Türkiye İktisat Tarihi*, 71; Pamuk, *Uneven Centuries*, 178; Akkaya, "Cumhuriyetin Kuruluş Yıllarında," 246–7; Makal, *Ameleden İşçiye*, 70–2; Kesler, "Türk İş İstatistikleri," 249; Kıvılcımlı, *Türkiye İşçi Sınıfının Sosyal Varlığı*, 29–33.

5 Kazgan, "Türk Ekonomisinde 1927–1935 Depresyonu," 273; Hines et al., *Türkiye'nin İktisadi Bakımdan Umumi Bir Tetkiki*, 233–8; Suad Derviş, "Günü Gününe Geçinenler," *Cumhuriyet*, April 13, 1936; Makal, *Tek Partili Dönemde Çalışma İlişkileri*, 310.

6 Makal, *Çok Partili Dönemde Çalışma İlişkileri*, 437; Erişçi, *Sosyal Tarih Çalışmaları*, 113; Korniyenko, *The Labor Movement in Turkey*, 47; "Fethiye'de," *Orak Çekiç*, July 20, 1936; Grew, *Atatürk ve Yeni Türkiye*, 144; Kosova, *Ben İşçiyim*, 59, 71; Özçelik, *Tütüncülerin Tarihi*, 75–8; Tunçay, *Arif Oruç'un Yarın'ı*, 56.

7 BCA-CHP [490.1/670.258.01], April 15, 1942; Bayrı, "Balıkesir'de Saraçlık," 237–8, and "Balıkesir'de Pabuçculuk," 295.

8 Egesoy, *Cumhuriyet Devrinde Vasıtasız Vergiler*, 187; Tezel, *Cumhuriyet Döneminin İktisadi Tarihi*, 437; Saraçoğlu, "1930–1939 Döneminde Vergi Politikası," 142; Keleş, *100 Soruda Türkiye'de Şehirleşme*, 183; "İstanbul'da Bir Aile Nasıl Geçinir?" *Köroğlu*, June 7, 1933.

9 See Makal, *Çok Partili Dönemde Çalışma İlişkileri*, 437–74; Soyak, *Atatürk'ten Hatıralar*, 18; "Günah Be Yahu!" *Köroğlu*, April 22, 1931; "Muallim Aylıkları," *Köroğlu*, August 12, 1931; "Konya Muallimlerinin Maaşı," *Son Posta*, May 24, 1932; "İşten Çekilen Memurlar," *Köroğlu*, December 10, 1932. See also BCA-CHP [490.1/1444.26.1], June 17, 1933.

10 Linke, *Allah Dethroned*, 265; Özçelik, *Tütüncülerin Tarihi*, 25. "8 Saat İş Günü," *Orak Çekiç*, December 20, 1935; "İş Kanunu ve Esnafımız," *Esnaf Meslek Mecmuası*, vol. 3 (1934), 2; Beşe, "Safranbolu'da ve Köylerinde Aile," 189. See also BCA-CHP [490.1/1444.26.1], June 17, 1933; Cillov, *Denizli El Dokumacılığı*, 129.

11 Talas, *İçtimaî İktisat*, 103; "İşçilere Yazık Oluyor," *Tan*, June 22, 1935.

12 Linke, *Allah Dethroned*, 189, 267.

13 BCA-CHP [490.1/655.182.1], September 14, 1931; BCA-BKK [30.18.1.1/15.58.1]; "Fethiye'de," *Orak Çekiç*, July 20, 1936; Çıladır, *Zonguldak Havzasının Tarihi Gelişimi*, 118–19; Ahmet Naim, *Zonguldak Havzası*, 153; BCA-CHP [490.1/1444.26.1], June 17, 1933; Özçelik, *Tütüncülerin Tarihi*, 71–89.

14 Armstrong, *Turkey and Syria Reborn*, 176–7; Newman, *Turkish Crossroads*, 172; Cillov, *Denizli El Dokumacılığı*, 36.

15 BCA-CHP [490.1/726.485.1], January 1, 1936; [490.1/662.215.1], November 23, 1943; Cillov, *Denizli El Dokumacılığı*, 132–3; Linke, *Allah Dethroned*, 268; "8 Saat İşgünü," *Orak Çekiç*, December 20, 1935.

16 Hines et al., *Türkiye'nin İktisadi Bakımdan Umumi Bir Tetkiki*, 242–4; Patton, "US Advisory Aid to Turkey," 46; BCA-CHP [490.1/1444.26.1], June 17, 1933; Ege, *Türkiye'nin Sağlık Hizmetleri*, 26.

17 For the development of social security from the Ottoman Empire to the early republic, see Saymen, *Türkiye'de Sosyal Sigortaların Gelişme Hareketleri*; Tuna, "İş İstatistikleri," 344; "Tazminat Verilmiyor," *Son Posta*, March 11, 1932; BCA-CHP [490.1/1444.26.1], June 17, 1933; [490.1/1444.22.1], February 7, 1936. The memoirs of contemporary workers include many cases of abuses by foremen; see Kosova, *Ben İşçiyim*, 66–78; Akgül, *Şoför İdris*, 47–53, 64, 99; Özçelik, *Tütüncülerin Tarihi*, 10–17, 86, 101.

18 Akkaya, "Cumhuriyetin Kuruluş Yıllarında," 254–5. For the role of corporatist ideology, see Parla and Davison, *Corporatist Ideology in Kemalist Turkey*.

19 Uran, *Adana Ziraat Amelesi*, 7–35; Bayar, *Şark Raporu*, 89.

20 Başgöz, *Hayat Hikâyem*, 79–80.

21 Tezel, *Cumhuriyet Döneminin İktisadi Tarihi*, 115; "Küçük Sanayicilerin Temennileri: Büyük Sanayi Erbabının Rekabetinden Şikayet Ediyorlar," *Son Posta*, May 26, 1936.

22 Armstrong, *Turkey and Syria Reborn*, 176; Cillov, *Denizli El Dokumacılığı*, 152; Baykurt, *Özüm Çocuktur*, 149.

23 Şevket Süreyya [Aydemir], *Ege Günü I*, 39, 64.

24 BCA-CHP [490.1/726.481.1], January 21, 1936.

25 Şevket Süreyya [Aydemir], *Ege Günü I*, 64; BCA-CHP [490.1/684.317.1], December 15, 1935; Küçükerman, *Batı Anadolu'daki Türk Halıcılık Geleneği*, 21; "Uşak'ta," *Son Posta*, October 21, 1932.

26 Enç, *Selamlık Sohbetleri*, 221; "Samsun Tacirleri Japon Dampingi Karşısında Şaşırdılar," *Son Posta*, April 2, 1932.

27 Vahdi, "Lastik Ayakkapların Yerli Sanayiye Verdiği Zararlar," 14; Küçükerman, *Beykoz Fabrikası*, 150–87; "Halkın Sesi," *Son Posta*, May 2, 1932; Bayrı, "Balıkesir'de Pabuçculuk," 289–97; Hüseyin Avni, "Harp Senesi İçinde Fabrikalarımızın Faaliyeti," 11, and "Kauçuk ve Deri Meselesi."

28 Uğurlu, *Kahramanmaraş Şehrengizi*, 287; for the power of the *debbağ şeyhi*, see İnalcık, *Osmanlı Tarihi'nde İslâmiyet ve Devlet*, 47–8; Bayrı, "Balıkesir'de Dabaklık," 65; "Rekabet: Dericiler Geçimsizliğe Başladı," *Son Posta*, June 6, 1932; Yelmen, *Kazlıçeşme'de 50 Yıl*, 245.

29 Bayrı, "Balıkesir'de Keçecilik," 120–6.

30 "Atlı Arabalar ve Otomobil," *Tan*, February 5, 1935; "15 Bin Kişinin Derdi," *Son Posta*, February 7, 1935; Bayrı, "Balıkesir'de Saraçlık," 237.

Chapter 7 Labor Discontent

1 BCA-CHP [490.1/721.464.2], August 8, 1937.

2 "Bir İşçi Kadın Diyor ki!" *Cumhuriyet*, March 9, 1929; "Amele Gündeliğini Alamıyormuş," *Cumhuriyet*, January 24, 1930; *Kızıl İstanbul*, July 1930; "Seyrisefain İşçileri İdareden Şikayetçidir," *Son Posta*, March 13, 1932; "Yevmiyeler," *Köroğlu*, February 7, 1934; "Süreyyapaşa Dokuma Fabrikası Grevi," 109; "İstanbul'da," *Orak Çekiç*, July 20, 1936.

3 Osman, "Muallimlerin Mesken Bedelleri"; "Islahiye Muallimleri Maaş Alamıyorlarmış," *Son Posta*, June 11, 1932; "Muallim Aylıkları," *Köroğlu*, August 12, 1931; "Konya Muallimlerinin Maaşı," *Son Posta*, May 24, 1932; "Kemaliye ve Urfa'da Muallimler 5 Aydır Maaş

Alamıyorlar," *Cumhuriyet*, September 14, 1929; "Bir Muallimin Şikayeti," *Cumhuriyet*, January 14, 1930; "Muallim Aylıkları," *Cumhuriyet*, January 29, 1939; "Öğretmenlerin Ev Paraları Ne Bu Yıl Ne Gelecek Yıl Verilmeyecek," *Son Posta*, August 4, 1935; BCA-MGM [30.10/ 142.16.19], August 19, 1932.

4 "Günah Be Yahu!" *Köroğlu*, April 22, 1931; "Halkın Köşesi," *Köroğlu*, August 4, 1934; "Tütün Depolarında Biz Amelelere Karşı Yapılan Haksızlık ve Hakaretler Feci Şekilde Devam Ediyor," *Bolşevik*, vol. 38 (1932).

5 "Ekmek Fiyatı Pahalıdır," *Son Posta*, June 4, 1932; "Yine Ekmek Meselesine Dair," *Son Posta*, February 4, 1933; "Ekmek 9 Buçuk," *Köroğlu*, June 6, 1934; "Gündelik Ekmeğin Pahalılığı," *Son Posta*, June 28, 1935; "Karaman'da Fırıncılar Ekmeğe Narh Konduğu İçin Fırınlarını Kapadılar," *Son Posta*, July 21, 1935; "Samsunda Ekmek 12 Kuruş," *Köroğlu*, October 12, 1935; "Ekmek Pahalanıyor, Bir Çare Bulalım," *Köroğlu*, November 2, 1935; "Ekmek Her Yerde Biraz Pahalandı," *Köroğlu*, January 30, 1937.

6 "Halkın Dilekleri," *Cumhuriyet*, September 7, 1929; "Hayat Pahalılığı: Harpten Evveline Nazaran Hayat 15 Misli Pahalılanmıştır," *Cumhuriyet*, January 5, 1930; "Şekerde Yine İhtikâr Var," *Son Posta*, April 9, 1932; "Tuz Fiyatları Pahalı," *Son Posta*, December 14, 1932; "Fatih'ten Mehmet Bey Yazıyor: Tuzun Kilosu 12.5 Kuruş Pahalıdır," *Son Posta*, December 14, 1932.

7 "Ayıp Şey," *Köroğlu*, January 20, 1932 ; "Yerli Malların Satışında İhtikâr Vardır," *Son Posta*, February 18, 1932; Turgut, *Kılıç Ali'nin Anıları*, 601; "Cigaralar Çok Pahalıdır!" *Köroğlu*, December 12, 1931; "Cigara Fiyatı Ucuzlamalıdır," *Köroğlu*, November 4, 1933.

8 "Adana Ziraat Bankası Mensucat Fabrikası Amelesi A.'nın Mektubu," *Kommunist*, 1929, 3; "Tütün İnhisar İdaresi Amelesinden Bir Grup," *Kızıl İstanbul*, November 1930; "Tütün Amelesi," *Köroğlu*, August 4, 1932; *Bolşevik*, vol. 38 (1932); "11 Saat İş Başı," *Köroğlu*, November 21, 1934; "Amele 10 Saat Çalışmaz," *Köroğlu*, May 27, 1936; "Yerli Fabrika Sahiplerimizden Rica Ediyoruz 13 Saat Çalışılmaz," *Köroğlu*, August 30, 1933; "İş Kanunu ve Esnafımız," *Esnaf Meslek Mecmuası*, vol. 3 (1934), 2. See also Derviş, "İzmir İşçileri Nasıl Çalışır, Nasıl Yaşarlar," *Son Posta*, October 20, 1936.

9 BCA-CHP [490.1/500.2008.1], January 11, 1931; "İşçi Hakkı," *Köroğlu*, May 15, 1934.

10 TTKA SSJ [47, 25.11.1340/1924].

11 "Cumartesi Tatili Sözde mi Kalıyor?" *Son Posta*, June 17, 1935; "Tütün İşçileri," *Köroğlu*, June 22, 1935; "Hafta Tatili Şikâyetleri," *Son Posta*, June 15, 1935; "İşçilere Yazık Oluyor," *Tan*, June 22, 1935 ; "Halk Ne

Diyor, Ne İstiyor?" *Köroğlu*, December 21, 1935; "Vur Abalıya!" *Köroğlu*, April 15, 1936; "Halkın Köşesi," *Köroğlu*, May 9, 1936.

12 *TBMM Yıllık 1930*, 339, 342–4, 371; *TBMM Yıllık 1935*, 268, 280–4; Akgül, *Şoför İdris*, 106; "Halkın Sesi: İşçilerin Hakları ve Halk," *Son Posta*, January 26, 1935.

13 *TBMM Yıllık 1930*, 337, 344, 357, 391; *TBMM Yıllık 1934*, 235, 237–9, 251–2, 266; *TBMM Yıllık 1935*, 269, 282, 284, 301; "Amelenin Hakkı Neden Verilmiyor?" *Cumhuriyet*, November 19, 1930.

14 For these social security funds, see Makal, *Türkiye'de Tek Parti Döneminde Çalışma İlişkileri*, 427; "Müstahdimler ve Memurlar," *Son Posta*, February 2, 1932; *TBMM Zabıt Ceridesi*, April 29, 1933, 132.

15 "İşten Çekilen Memurlar," *Köroğlu*, December 10, 1932 ; *TBMM Yıllık 1930*, 336, 339–41, 347, 371, 390; *TBMM Yıllık 1934*, 267; BCA-CHP [490.1/475.1941.1], December 24, 1935; [490.1/47.189.2.], January 24, 1939.

16 *TBMM Yıllık 1930*, 345; *TBMM Yıllık 1934*, 280, 282; *TBMM Yıllık 1935*, 268–9, 278; *TBMM Yıllık 1936*, 269, 276, 279–81, 293, 298; "Soruyoruz!" *Cumhuriyet*, December 8, 1930; "Sekiz Senedir Maaşımı Alamıyorum," *Son Posta*, March 25, 1932; "Okuyucu Mektupları," *Son Posta*, June 7, 1936.

17 "Yetimler, Dullar ve Mütekaidlere Maaş Tahsisi," *Cumhuriyet*, February 2, 1930; "36 Seneden Sonra Sefalet," *Cumhuriyet*, July 11, 1930; "Dert Bir, Feryat İki," *Cumhuriyet*, September 18, 1930; *TBMM Yıllık 1930*, 336–7, 351, 388; *TBMM Yıllık 1934*, 235; *TBMM Yıllık 1934*, 254; *TBMM Yıllık 1935*, 282.

18 "İki Senede Bir Maaş Bağlanamaz mı?" *Cumhuriyet*, January 29, 1930; "Bir Maaş Tahsisi İçin Yıllar mı Geçmeli," *Cumhuriyet*, April 6, 1930; "Vatandaşı Aç Bırakmak Hakkı Selahiyeti Kime Verilmiştir," *Cumhuriyet*, November 21, 1930.

19 TTKA SSJ [35–2, 1341/1925]; [26–2, 1341/1925]. About the PRP opposition, see Zürcher, *Political Opposition*.

20 "İş Kanunu Hakkında Anketimize Gelen İlk Cevap," *İkdam*, April 20, 1927; "Anketimize Dün Gelen Cevaplar," *İkdam*, April 24, 1927; "İş Kanunu: Anketimize Gelen Cevaplar," *İkdam*, April 25, 1927; "Amelemizin Anketimize Gönderdiği Cevaplar," *İkdam*, April 26, 1927; "Amelemizin Anketimize Gönderdiği Cevaplar," *İkdam*, April 27, 1927; "Amelemizin Anketimize Gönderdiği Cevaplar," *İkdam*, April 28, 1927; "Amelemizin Anketimize Gönderdiği Cevaplar," *İkdam*, April 29, 1927; Korniyenko, *The Labor Movement in Turkey*, 57.

21 İlkin, "1932 İş Kanunu Tasarısı," 252. About the 1927 Labor Law draft, see Gülmez, "Amele Teali Cemiyetinin"; Emrence, *99 Günlük*

Muhalefet, 93–105; Yetkin, *Serbest Cumhuriyet Fırkası Olayı*, 244–5; Makal, *Türkiye'de Tek Parti Döneminde Çalışma İlişkileri*, 342.

22 BCA-CHP [490.1/500.2008.1], January 11, 1931; İlkin, "1932 İş Kanunu Tasarısı," 267–77.

23 BCA-CHP [490.1/1438.3.2], March 21, 1933; "İş Kanunu ve Esnafımız," *Esnaf Meslek Mecmuası*, vol. 3 (1934), 1–2; "Halkın Köşesi," *Köroğlu*, October 13, 1934.

24 "Halkın Sesi: Yeni İş Kanunu Layihasına Ne Dersiniz?" *Son Posta*, November 8, 1935.

25 "Halkın Fikri: İş Kanunu Çıktı," *Son Posta*, June 9, 1936.

26 BCA-CHP [490.1/728.495.5], December 30, 1947; Toydemir, "Türkiye'de İş İhtilaflarının Tarihçesi," 12.

27 For such an approach, see Güzel, *Türkiye'de İşçi Hareketleri*, 133; Sülker, *100 Soruda Türkiye'de İşçi Hareketleri*, 160.

28 BCA-CHP [490.01/655.182.1], September 14, 1931; "Çok Şükür," *Köroğlu*, June 3, 1936; "Deniz Tahmil ve Tahliye Amelesi Şikâyet Ediyor," *Cumhuriyet*, February 23, 1935.

29 "Kari Mektupları," *Son Posta*, May 10, 1932; "Bir Dokun Bin Ah Dinle Bizim Şoförlerden," *Son Posta*, July 17, 1935; "Şoförlerin Şikayetleri Neymiş?" *Son Posta*, September 19, 1935; "Şoförlerin Durumu Fena," *Son Posta*, December 12, 1935; "Şoförler Cemiyeti," *Son Posta*, December 14, 1935.

30 "Bir İşçimizin Dilekleri," *Esnaf Meslek Mecmuası*, vol. 3 (1934), 9–10; Yelmen, *Kazlıçeşme'de 50 Yıl*, 154; Özçelik, *Tütüncülerin Tarihi*, 86; "Esnaf Cemiyetlerinde," *Orak Çekiç*, November 7, 1936; "Ayıp Günah!" *Köroğlu*, May 13, 1931; "Zorla Olmaz: Esnaf, Cemiyetlerden Usandı," *Köroğlu*, May 23, 1931.

31 "Küçük Sanayicilerin Temennileri: Büyük Sanayi Erbabının Rekabetinden Şikâyet Ediyorlar," *Son Posta*, May 25, 1936; Muhittin Birgen, "İplik Derdi ve Dokumacılık Tezgahları," *Son Posta*, November 29, 1936; "Samsun Tacirleri Japon Dampingi Karşısında Şaşırdılar," *Son Posta*, April 2, 1932.

32 Cillov, *Denizli El Dokumacılığı*, 145–6; "Türk Terzilerinden Türk Sanayicilerine," *Son Posta*, February 28, 1935.

33 "Halkın Sesi," *Son Posta*, May 2, 1932; Bayrı, "Balıkesir'de Pabuçculuk," 289–97; Hüseyin Avni, "Kauçuk ve Deri Meselesi" and "Harp Senesi İçinde"; Bayrı, "Balıkesir'de Dabaklık," 65; "Rekabet: Dericiler Geçimsizliğe Başladı," *Son Posta*, June 6, 1932; "Diyarbakır Debbağları Lastik Ayakkabıların Rekabetinden Müteessir," *Son Posta*, May 29, 1935.

34 "15 Bin Kişinin Derdi," *Son Posta*, February 7, 1935; "Arabacılık Tarihe mi Karışıyor?" *Son Posta*, May 26, 1935; "Arabacılık ve Arabacı

Vatandaşlar Buhran İçinde," *Tan*, November 26, 1935; "Atlı Arabalar ve Otomobil," *Tan*, February 5, 1935.

35 Bayrı, "Balıkesir'de Saraçlık," 237, and "Balıkesir'de Keçecilik," 125–6.

Chapter 8 Survival Struggles and Everyday Resistance

1 Özçelik, *Tütüncülerin Tarihi*, 97; Doğruel and Doğruel, *Tekel*, 223; "Bey, Hanım!" *Köroğlu*, September 27, 1929; "Ayıp," *Köroğlu*, September 28, 1929.

2 Kemal, *Avare Yıllar*, 14; "Sümerbank İşçilerinin Bir Temennisi," *Son Posta*, January 18, 1936.

3 Dölen and Koraltürk, *İlk Çimento Fabrikamızın Öyküsü*, 110, 123–6.

4 "Adliye İstatistiklerine Göre Memleketimizde Cürümler ve Mücrimler," 38–43; "Mahkumlar Yüzde Yüz Fazlalaştı," *Son Posta*, February 16, 1932; "Adana'da Hırsızlıklar Son Günlerde Çoğaldı," *Son Posta*, May 3, 1932; "1 Yılda 2500 Hırsızlık," *Köroğlu*, August 20, 1932; "Adana'da Hapishanede Mahkum Miktarı Artıyor," *Son Posta*, February 9, 1933; "Hapishaneler Dolu!" *Köroğlu*, April 8, 1936; "İzmir Hapishanesi Dolu," *Köroğlu*, May 16, 1936.

5 Göksu, *1929 Dünya Ekonomik Buhranı Yıllarında İzmir ve Suç Coğrafyası*; "Adliye İstatistiklerine Göre Memleketimizde Cürümler ve Mücrimler," 39, 43.

6 Linke, *Allah Dethroned*, 304.

7 Dölen and Koraltürk, *İlk Çimento Fabrikamızın Öyküsü*, 123–6; "Fabrikadan İpek Çalan İki İşçi Kadın," *Tan*, July 21, 1936; *1937 Temyiz Kararları*, 303; "Bir İşçi Yeni Paraları Aşırarak Kaçmış," *Son Posta*, May 20, 1935; "Anason ve İspirto Fıçılarına Su Dolduranlar," *Son Posta*, August 31, 1936; "Bir Fabrika Ambarcısı Yakalandı," *Son Posta*, February 1, 1936; "Çalıştığı Mağazayı Soymuş," *Son Posta*, January 24, 1935; "Yaman Bekçi," *Son Posta*, February 18, 1932.

8 "Bayram Harçlığı," *Köroğlu*, December 8, 1937; "Hayırlı Çırak," *Son Posta*, June 30, 1932; "Ekmek Kapısı," *Köroğlu*, August 7, 1937. According to a study on child delinquency between 1938 and 1955, the apprentices were one of the primary groups who committed thievery and pilfering. See Nirun, "Suç Hadisesinin Sosyal Sebepleri Üzerine Bir Araştırma," 156; "Bir Kadın Hırsız," *Son Posta*, May 3, 1932; "Hayırlı Hizmetçi!" *Son Posta*, May 27, 1932; "Hırsızlık Suçlusu Bir Hizmetçi Adliyede," *Son Posta*, May 6, 1934.

9 "Kolay Değil," *Köroğlu*, January 30, 1929; "Para Almadan İş Gören Var mı?" *Köroğlu*, December 2, 1933. According to the press, the bribery was an epidemic. "Şıp Diye Enselendi," *Köroğlu*, April 1, 1936;

Grew, *Atatürk ve Yeni Türkiye*, 127; Tesal, *Selânik'ten İstanbul'a*, 203; "Ah, Ah," *Köroğlu*, January 16, 1929; "Hırsızlık Resmi Dairelerde," *Köroğlu*, May 30, 1931.

10 "16,000 Lira Çalan Bir Veznedar Mahkûm Oldu," *Son Posta*, May 4, 1932; "Eski Paralar Ne Olacak," *Köroğlu*, April 8, 1933; "Çaldı Kaçtı Ama!" *Köroğlu*, February 17, 1934; "Şeytana Uymuş," *Köroğlu*, June 13, 1936; "Tahsildar Efendi Sandıkta," *Köroğlu*, July 1, 1933; "Gün Geçtikçe Kabarıyor," *Köroğlu*, May 30, 1936; "6 Yıl Hapis," *Köroğlu*, June 3, 1936; "5 Yıl Yatacak," *Köroğlu*, August 1, 1936; "17 Lira İçin," *Köroğlu*, October 3, 1936; "Hokkabazlık," *Köroğlu*, April 20, 1938; "Şimdi Ne Olacak?" *Köroğlu*, December 28, 1938.

11 Şahingiray, *Celal Bayar'ın Söylev ve Demeçleri*, 295–96.

12 Metinsoy, *İkinci Dünya Savaşı'nda Türkiye*, 251–6.

13 Hatipoğlu, *Türkiye'de Ziraî Buhran*, 86–7; Atasagun, *Türkiye'de İçtimaî Siyaset*, 8; H. Z., "Arazi ve Müsakkafat Vergilerinin Tahrir Usulleri Niçin Tadile Muhtaçtır?" *Cumhuriyet*, June 19, 1931; Hines et al., *Türkiye'nin İktisadi Bakımdan Umumî Bir Tetkiki*, 238; "Köylü İş Bulmak İçin Şehirlere Geliyor," *Köroğlu*, May 9, 1931; Linke, *Allah Dethroned*, 189.

14 Mümtaz Faik, "Kayseri Kombinaları ve İşçi Buhranı," *Tan*, October 2, 1936; Çalgüner, *Türkiye'de Ziraat İşçileri*, 19; Newman, *Turkish Crossroads*, 79, 179.

15 *Labour Problems in Turkey*, 216; Metinsoy, "İkinci Dünya Savaşı Yıllarında Zonguldak Kömür Ocaklarında," 93–112; *Sümerbank: Cumhuriyet'in 25'inci Yılı*, 54.

16 Mümtaz Faik, "Kayseri Kombinaları ve İşçi Buhranı," *Tan*, October 2, 1936; Linke, *Allah Dethroned*, 268–70; Webster, *The Turkey of Atatürk*, 250; Cillov, *Denizli El Dokumacılığı*, 149.

17 BCA-CHP, [490.1/726.481.1], 1936; Dölen and Koraltürk, *İlk Çimento Fabrikamızın Öyküsü*, 110, 126.

18 Ekin, "Memleketimizde İşçi Devri Mevzuunda Yapılan Araştırmalar," 136–41.

19 Tekeli and İlkin, *Türkiye'de Devletçiliğin Oluşumu*, 189; "İş Arayanlar İçin," *Köroğlu*, September 18, 1935; Mümtaz Faik, "Kayseri Kombinaları ve İşçi Buhranı" *Tan*, October 2, 1936; Dölen and Koraltürk, *İlk Çimento Fabrikamızın Öyküsü*, 110.

20 Şahingiray, *Celal Bayar'ın Söylev ve Demeçleri*, 295–6; Metinsoy, *İkinci Dünya Savaşı'nda Türkiye*, 306–17.

21 Mehmed Halid, "Balıkesir'de Saraçlık," 237; Osman Cemal, "Esnaf Arasında Köşe Kapmaca," 16; "Beş, Altı Sene Evvel 400 Olan Lokantacı Dükkanları Tam 2200'ü Bulmuştur," *Son Posta*, May 26, 1932.

22 Karslı, *Köy Öğretmeninin Anıları*, 21–4, 50; Çerkezyan, *Dünya Hepimize Yeter*, 97; "Doğru mu?" *Köroğlu*, October 16, 1929;

"Kitapçılar Şikayet Ediyorlar," *Köroğlu*, October 23, 1929; "Halk Ne Diyor, Ne İstiyor?" *Köroğlu*, November 23, 1935; Allen, *The Turkish Transformation*, 181; EGMA [13211-11], July 22, 1934; [13211-16], 1938; Kara, *Kutuz Hoca*, 33–42; "Ezan Sesi," *Köroğlu*, May 25, 1932; "Üfürükçü Yakalandı," *Köroğlu*, January 31, 1931; "Üfürük!" *Köroğlu*, December 21, 1932; "Hala mı Yahu," *Köroğlu*, January 31, 1934; "Muska 6 Papel," *Köroğlu*, April 13, 1935; "15 Liraya Muska," *Köroğlu*, October 23, 1935; "Büyücü," *Köroğlu*, January 11, 1936; "Hacı Baba: Üfürükçü Nasıl Enselendi," *Köroğlu*, October 17, 1936.

23 "Peki Ama Ne İle Geçinsinler?" *Son Posta*, April 29, 1931; "50 Bin Satıcı," *Köroğlu*, December 12, 1934; Belli, *Esas Hadise*, 85; "Bit Pazarında," *Köroğlu*, April 6, 1929; Kosova, *Ben İşçiyim*, 60–3, 117; TTKA SSJ [22, 1340/1924].

24 Akgül, *Şoför İdris*, 103–5.

25 "Bunlar da Hazirandan Beri Maaş Alamıyorlarmış," *Cumhuriyet*, September 14, 1929; "Konya Muallimlerinin Maaşı," *Son Posta*, May 24, 1932 ; "Islahiye Muallimleri Maaş Alamıyorlarmış," *Son Posta*, June 11, 1932; "Halkın Köşesi," *Köroğlu*, July 6, 1929; "Halkın Köşesi," *Köroğlu*, August 4, 1934 ; "Beş Ay Maaş Bekliyenler," *Köroğlu*, August 11, 1934.

26 "Amele Gündeliğini Alamıyormuş," *Cumhuriyet*, January 24, 1930; "Yevmiyelerimizi Niçin Alamadık?" *Son Posta*, May 14, 1932; "Yevmiyeler," *Köroğlu*, February 7, 1934; "Balya Madeninde İşçiler," *Köroğlu*, June 30, 1937.

27 "Bir İkramiye Meselesi," *Son Posta*, February 17, 1932; "Ayda Dört Lira İle Geçinilir mi?" *Köroğlu*, February 4, 1931; "Sekiz Senedir Maaşımı Alamıyorum," *Son Posta*, March 25, 1932; "Kaç Yıllık İş?" *Köroğlu*, September 25, 1935.

28 "İşçi Kaç Saat Çalışır?" *Köroğlu*, June 30, 1937; "Tütün Amelesi," *Köroğlu*, August 3, 1932; "11 Saat İş Başı," *Köroğlu*, November 21, 1934; "Amele 10 Saat Çalışmaz," *Köroğlu*, May 27, 1936; "Alpullu Şeker Fabrikasından Bir Grup Amelenin Şikâyeti," *Köroğlu*, December 21, 1935.

29 "Halkın Köşesi," *Köroğlu*, July 25, 1934.

30 "İşçi Hakkı," *Köroğlu*, May 16, 1934; "Taksim'den Çıkarılan Garsonların Şikâyeti," *Tan*, July 3, 1935.

31 "Seyrisefain İşçileri İdareden Şikâyetçidir," *Son Posta*, March 13, 1932; "Haliç Şirketinde Bir İhtilaf," *Son Posta*, September 2, 1935; "Haliç Şirketi ve Memurları," *Son Posta*, November 21, 1935.

32 "Müzelerde Bekçilik Yapanların Maaşları," *Tan*, November 11, 1935.

33 Dölen and Koraltürk, *İlk Çimento Fabrikamızın Öyküsü*, 111.

34 "225 Kuruş Yevmiye Yerine 40 Kuruş," *Tan*, August 10, 1935; "İşçilerin İstediği Olabilecek mi?" *Tan*, August 11, 1935; "Liman İşçilerini Yeni Bir Haber Endişeye Düşürdü," *Tan*, August 16, 1935.

35 Turgut, *Kılıç Ali'nin Hatıraları*, 603.

36 BCA-CHP [490.1/538.2156.2], May 21, 1935; [490.1/538.2156.2], July 11, 1935.

37 BCA-CHP [490.1/1443.19.1], September 7, 1936; BCA-CHP [490.10/726.481.1].

38 BCA-CHP [490.1/475.1941.1], April 16, 1936.

39 BCA-CHP [490.1/1452.16.1], July 6, 1939.

40 "Amelelerin Yevmiyelerini Vermemişler," *Son Posta*, June 26, 1932.

41 "Tütün Depolarındaki Amelenin Vaziyeti," *Kızıl İstanbul*, 1932; "İzmir'de Bir Sanayi Meselesi," *Son Posta*, January 25, 1935.

42 "Tütün Depolarında Ne Rezaletler Oluyor?" *Orak Çekiç*, October 1, 1936.

43 "Sarı Kart Nedir?" *Köroğlu*, April 25, 1936.

44 "İkramiye Marşı," *Köroğlu*, February 13, 1934.

45 EGMA [22552-39], April 14, 1937.

46 EGMA [22552-39], December 27, 1936; CHP-BCA [490.1/532.2132.2], December 30, 1934; BCA-CHP [490.1/34.143.1]; BCA-NV [230.0/91.25.1], November 8, 1928.

47 *Temyiz Kararları: Hukuk Hey'eti Umumiyesi, 1930–1934*, 265–6.

48 "Zonguldak İşçileri Cemiyetleri Aleyhine Bir Dava Açtılar; Fakat Reddedildi," *Son Posta*, April 5, 1935; "Zonguldak'ta 200,000 Liralık Bir Dava," *Son Posta*, August 10, 1935. BCA-MGM [30.10/166.158.14], March 25, 1936; BCA-CHP [490.1/721.464.2], September 29, 1936. For a summary of the court decisions, see "Kömür Ameleleri İle Birlik Arasındaki İhtilaf," *Son Posta*, May 14, 1936.

49 For a contemporaneous jurist's analysis of legal cases of coal miners, see Yiğiter, *Kömür Havzasında Amele Hukuku*, 25–56; "Bir İşçi 10 Bin Lira İstiyor," *Son Posta*, June 18, 1935; "Bir Amelenin Davası," *Son Posta*, August 18, 1932.

50 *1937 Temyiz Kararları*, 89.

51 Acun, "Yeni İş Kanunu Tatbik Sahasına Girerken," 20; see the articles from 78 to 83 of "İş Kanunu," 3008/08.06.1936, Articles 78–83, *Resmi Gazete*, no. 3330, June 15, 1936, 6631–2.

52 Hüseyin Avni, "İş Kanunu Nasıl Tatbik Ediliyor?"; Toydemir, "Türkiye'de İş İhtilaflarının Tarihçesi," 12.

53 Erişçi, *Sosyal Tarih Çalışmaları*, 104; Esen, *Türk İş Hukuku*, 157.

54 Hüseyin Avni, "İş Kanunu Nasıl Tatbik Ediliyor?"

55 Kosova, *Ben İşçiyim*, 115.

56 See Quataert, *Ottoman Manufacturing* and *Social Disintegration*; Vatter, "Militant Journeymen"; Faroqhi, *Artisans of Empire*, 188–207; Cole, *Colonialism and Revolution*, 164, 188; Chalcraft, *Striking Cabbies*, 67–104. For the contexts of Great Britain and France, see respectively Thompson, *The Making of the English Working Class*, especially chapter 8, "Artisans and Others," and Johnson, "Economic Change and Artisan Discontent"; Longuenesse, "Labor in Syria," 105.

57 "Halkın Sesi," *Son Posta*, May 2, 1932; Vahdi, "Lastik Ayakkapların Yerli Sanayiye Verdiği Zararlar," 15.

58 "Kunduracılar Hariçten Gelen Mukavva Eşya İçin İtiraz Ettiler," *Son Posta*, June 24, 1932; "Türk Kunduracıları Himaye Etmeli," *Köroğlu*, June 27, 1934; "Kunduracılar ve Municialer Toplandılar," *Esnaf Meslek Mecmuası*, vol. 9 (1934), 16–17; "Kunduracıların İsteği," *Son Posta*, April 14, 1935.

59 "Fabrika ile El İşçiliğinin Mücadelesi," *Esnaf Meslek Mecmuası*, vol. 3 (1934), 18–19; "El Emeği," *Köroğlu*, January 13, 1934.

60 "15 Bin Kişinin Derdi," *Son Posta*, February 7, 1935.

61 "Bir Dokun Bin Ah Dinle Bizim Şoförlerden," *Son Posta*, July 17, 1935; "Şoförlerin Durumu Fena," *Son Posta*, December 12, 1935; "Şoförler Meselesi," *Tan*, December 26, 1935.

62 "Rekabet: Municialer Geçimsizliğe Başladı," *Son Posta*, June 1, 1932.

63 "Garsonlarla Lokanta ve Gazino Sahipleri Arasında Bir Anlaşmazlık," *Son Posta*, June 11, 1935; "Garsonların Yüzde 10 Hakkı," *Son Posta*, June 19, 1936.

64 Mehmet Enver Beşe, "Safranbolu'da ve Köylerinde Aile," 188–9; "Fırıncılardan Şikâyetler," *Son Posta*, November 11, 1935 ; BCA-CHP [490.1/1444.26.1], June 17, 1933.

Chapter 9 Violence, Protests and Walkouts

1 Kosova, *Ben İşçiyim*, 66–78; Akgül, *Şoför İdris*, 47–64, 99; Özçelik, *Tütüncülerin Tarihi*, 10, 17, 29, 43, 86, 101.

2 Akgül, *Şoför İdris*, 32–48, 98; Özçelik, *Tütüncülerin Tarihi*, 10.

3 "Tütün Depolarında Kadın İşçinin Vaziyeti," *Bolşevik*, vol. 40 (1932).

4 Linke, *Allah Dethroned*, 305; Binyazar, *Masalını Yitiren Dev*, 103.

5 Akgül, *Şoför İdris*, 43; "Bir Amelenin Marifeti," *Cumhuriyet*, December 16, 1929; "İki Amele Patronlarını Yaraladılar," *Cumhuriyet*, September 8, 1930; "Bir Hamalın Cinayeti," *Cumhuriyet*, February 12, 1930; "Böyle Olmaz," *Köroğlu*, May 30, 1931; "Bir Cinayet," *Son Posta*, May 31, 1932; "Yüzlerce İnsanı Öldürecekti," *Son Posta*, May 7, 1935;

"Bir Fabrikada Cinayet," *Son Posta*, December 15, 1935; "Akıllan Bakalım," *Köroğlu*, December 21, 1935.

6 For examples of the institutionalist approach, see Yavuz, "Sanayideki İşgücünün Durumu," 172; Koç, *Türkiye'de İşçi Sınıfı ve Sendikacılık Tarihi*, 37.

7 Tunçay, *Türkiye'de Sol Akımlar*, 21, 52; "Feshane Fabrikasında Grevci Arkadaşlara," *Kızıl İstanbul*, January 1932; BCA-MGM [30.10/ 88.579.27], January 15, 1927.

8 Güzel, *Türkiye'de İşçi Hareketleri*, 110.

9 Korniyenko, *The Labor Movement in Turkey*, 48–51; Akkaya and Altıok, "Çukurova'da İşçi Hareketi ve Sendikacılık," 249; Yükselen, "1924 İstanbul Tramvay İşçileri Grevleri," 69; Yavuz, "Sanayideki İşgücünün Durumu," 170; Makal, *Tek Partili Dönemde Çalışma İlişkileri*, 333.

10 Tunçay, *Türkiye'de Sol Akımlar*, 21; Korniyenko, *The Labor Movement in Turkey*, 52; Akkaya and Altıok, "Çukurova'da İşçi Hareketi ve Sendikacılık," 249; Keskinoğlu, "Türkiye'de Grevler," 492–3; Toprak, "Şirketi Hayriye Amele Cemiyeti ve 1925 Grevi"; Yavuz, "Sanayideki İşgücünün Durumu," 170; Kosova, *Ben İşçiyim*, 17.

11 Korniyenko, *The Labor Movement in Turkey*, 54.

12 "İstanbul Liman İşçileri Grevi 1927," *Türkiye Sendikacılık Ansiklopedisi*, vol. 2, 61; Koraltürk, *Ahmet Hamdi Başar'ın Hatıraları*, 240–5.

13 Korniyenko, *The Labor Movement in Turkey*, 54; Oğuz, *1927 Adana Demiryolu Grevi*, 43–68; Darendelioğlu, *Türkiye'de Komünist Hareketleri*, 48.

14 Korniyenko, *The Labor Movement in Turkey*, 56; BCA-NV [230.0/ 91.25.1], November 6, 1928; Sadi, *Türkiye'de Sosyalizmin Tarihine Katkı*, 709–15; Akgül, *Şoför İdris*, 35.

15 Topçuoğlu, *Anılar ve Hikâyeler*, 19–21. See also Ağaoğlu, *Serbest Fırka Hatıraları*, 29–64; Emrence, *99 Günlük Muhalefet*, 93–105; Akgül, *Şoför İdris*, 40.

16 "Hak Yenmesin," *Köroğlu*, December 23, 1931; Yavuz, "Sanayideki İşgücünün Durumu," 173; "Seyrisefain İşçileri İdareden Şikâyetçidir," *Son Posta*, March 13, 1932; "Seyrisefain'in Bazı Ateşçileri İşlerini Terketti," *Son Posta*, April 12, 1932; "Yevmiyemizi Niçin Alamadık?" *Son Posta*, May 14, 1932.

17 Kemal, *Avare Yıllar*, 19; Kosova, *Ben İşçiyim*, 70.

18 "İzmir Şayak Fabrikası Grevi, 1934," *Türkiye Sendikacılık Ansiklopedisi*, vol. 2, 178.

19 Korniyenko, *The Labor Movement in Turkey*, 71; "Bu İşçiler Niçin İşten Çıkarıldı?" *Son Posta*, March 29, 1935; Akgül, *Şoför İdris*, 66.

20 BCA-CHP [490.1/1444.22.1]. In this file, see the documents dated January 18 and 25, 1936, February 5 and 7, 1936, June 29, 1936, November 28, 1936. Özçelik estimates the number of strikers at 1,500; see Özçelik, *Tütüncülerin Tarihi*, 92.
21 "Trikotaj İşçilerinin Grevi," *Orak Çekiç*, February 25, 1936.
22 "Süreyyapaşa Dokuma Fabrikası Grevi," 109.
23 "İşsiz Kalan Tütün Amelesi," *Cumhuriyet*, April 3, 1936; "Patron ve İşçi İhtilafları," *Son Posta*, April 1, 1936; "İstanbul'da," *Orak Çekiç*, July 20, 1936.
24 "Bir Tütün Deposu 800 İşçisine Yol Verdi," *Son Posta*, November 6, 1936; "İşsiz Kalan 800 Tütün Amelesi Neticeyi Bekliyor," *Tan*, November 8, 1936; "Ameleden Bir Kısmı İşe Başladı," *Tan*, November 13, 1936.
25 *Orak Çekiç*, April 1, 1936; "Kömür Ameleleri İle Birlik Arasındaki İhtilaf," *Son Posta*, May 14, 1936.
26 Akgül, *Şoför İdris*, 93–9.
27 Hüseyin Avni, "İş Kanunu Nasıl Tatbik Ediliyor?" 4; Kosova, *Ben İşçiyim*, 115–16.

Part II Concluding Remarks

1 About the 1927 Draft of Labor Law, see Gülmez, "Amele Teali Cemiyetinin"; İlkin, "1932 İş Kanunu Tasarısı," 252; Makal, *Türkiye'de Tek Parti Döneminde Çalışma İlişkileri*, 342.
2 "Çiftçi ve Amele Mebuslar," *Cumhuriyet*, April 18, 1931; "Gazinin Beyannamesi," *Cumhuriyet*, April 21, 1931. About one of these deputies' efforts to assure workers' rights, see Varlık, *Ali Tunalı*, 189–95; *CHF Nizamnamesi ve Programı*. Ankara: n.p., 1931, 32.
3 Saymen, *Türkiye'de Sosyal Sigortaların Gelişme Hareketleri*, 13–23; Makal, *Türkiye'de Tek Partili Dönemde Çalışma İlişkileri*, 419–29; Koraltürk, "Şirket-i Hayriye Tekaüd Sandığı," 127; "Kazanç Vergisi'nde Değişiklik," *Son Posta*, April 20, 1936.

Chapter 10 Hotbeds of Opposition to Secularism: Mosques, Coffeehouses and Homes

1 Koraltürk, *Ahmet Hamdi Başar'ın Hatıraları*, 375.
2 Allen, *The Turkish Transformation*, 178–83. About the political mobilization capacity of the *tariqa*s, see Vett, *Dervişler Arasında*, 15, 132. For the Kemalist perception of *tariqa*s, see Soyak, *Atatürk'ten Hatıralar*, 322–3.

3 About the politics of symbols in the revolutionary moments, see Hunt, *Politics, Culture and Class in the French Revolution*, 58; Figes and Kolonitskii, *Interpreting the Russian Revolution*; Connerton, *How Societies Remember*, 10–11. For the symbolic politics of Turkish hat reform, see Metinsoy, "Everyday Resistance and Selective Adaptation to the Hat Reform," 12.

4 Bertaux, *Projecting the Nation*, 274; Üstel, *"Makbul Vatandaş"ın Peşinde*, 130–54; Karaömerlioğlu, "The People's Houses"; Türkoğlu, "Hüseyin Sami Bey'in Hayatı ve Ankara'daki Ajanlık Yılları."

5 Davison, *Türkiye'de Sekülarizm*, 234; Bozkurt, "Halkevlerine Dair"; Ahmad, *The Making of Modern Turkey*, 91–2; Albayrak, *İrtica'ın Tarihçesi*, 139; Lewis, *The Emergence of Modern Turkey*, 410, 427; Jäeschke, *Yeni Türkiye'de İslamcılık*, 66; Esen, "Tek Parti Dönemi Cami Satma/Kapatma."

6 Albayrak, *Türkiye'de Din Kavgası*, 223–37; Section 9, Articles 83–6 of "Köy Kanunu," 442/18.03.1924, *Düstur III*, vol. 5, 336; BCA-BKK [30. 18.1.1/15.61.9], September 16, 1925; BCA-DİR [51.0/ 3.16.5], April 1, 1926; [51.0/12.101.18], November 27, 1934; [51.0/4.36.10], April 21, 1939.

7 "Günah Be Yahu!" *Köroğlu*, April 22, 1931; "Halkın Köşesi," *Köroğlu*, August 4, 1934.

8 Yusuf Ziya, *İslam Dini*, 139; Profesör Abdülbaki, *Cumhuriyet Çocuğunun Din Dersleri*, 6; Albayrak, *İrtica'ın Tarihçesi*, 130–43.

9 Garnett, *Mysticism and Magic in Turkey*, 66–78; Us, *Hatıra Notları*, 91.

10 Ayverdi, *Ne İdik*, 104; for the functions of religious lodges, see Kara, *Tekkeler*; Sarıkoyuncu, *Millî Mücadelede Din Adamları*, 19; Kutay, *Kurtuluşun ve Cumhuriyetin Manevî Mimarları*, 76; Nesin, *Böyle Gelmiş Böyle Gitmez 1*, 108–34.

11 Gözaydın, *Diyanet*, 24.

12 Armstrong, *Turkey and Syria Reborn*, 203; Allen, *The Turkish Transformation*, 181; "Halk Ne Diyor, Ne İstiyor?" *Köroğlu*, November 23, 1935; Esenel, *1940'lı Yıllarda*, 134; Uyguner, "Zuhuri ve Şiirleri." Zuhuri composed this poem in the 1930s.

13 Kara, *Tasavvuf Hareketleri*, 46, 171; Gölpınarlı, *Melâmîlik*; Küçük, "Sufi Reactions against the Reforms," 133–5.

14 Vett, *Dervişler Arasında*, 132; Albayrak, *Türkiye'de Din Kavgası*, 234–8.

15 Yorulmaz, *Celal Hoca*, 104–8.

16 BCA-DİR [51.0/2.14.24], December 13, 1928; BCA-CHP [490.01/ 500.2010.2].

17 Albayrak, *Türkiye'de Din Kavgası*, 227.

18 Sadi, *Türkiye'de Sosyalizmin Tarihine Katkı*, 746, 790.

19 TTKA SSJ [19, 22.11.1340/1924]; [10, 1341/1925].

20 Ahmed Emin, *The Development of Modern Turkey As Measured by Its Press*, 19.

21 Duben and Behar, *Istanbul Households*, 29; Peters, "The Battered Dervishes of Bab Zuwayla"; Vett, *Dervişler Arasında*, 15; Özköse, "Kurtuluş Savaşı'na Katılan Din Bilginleri," 18; Kahraman, *Millî Mücadele*, 72; Küçük, *Kurtuluş Savaşında Bektaşiler*, 95.

22 Ahmad, *The Making of Modern Turkey*, 113; BCA-DİR [51.0/3.19.5], April 17, 1926; [51.0/4.30.12]; [51.0/4.30.12]. See also "Regulation about the Duties of the Presidency of Religious Affairs, 2–7647/11.11.1937." Karakoç, *Sicilli Kavanini*, 868–71; Albayrak, *İrtica'ın Tarihçesi 5*, 147–8, 160–6.

23 Vett, *Dervişler Arasında*, 135–6; Pekolcay, *Geçtim Dünya Üzerinden*, 63; Yasa, *Hasanoğlan Köyü*, 189.

24 Alpay, *Köy Dâvamız*, 28, 94; Gürbüz, *Mondros'tan Milenyuma*, 202; İslamoğlu, *İslami Hareketler*, 269; Seal, *A Fez of the Heart*, 107; "Bursa Hadisesi," *Son Posta*, February 6, 1933.

25 Selim Tevfik, "Ramazanın İkinci Günü İstanbul'da Bir Dolaşma," *Son Posta*, November 18, 1936; Armstrong, *Turkey and Syria Reborn*, 179; Albayrak, *Türkiye'de Din Kavgası*, 239–41.

26 BCA-MGM [30.10/102.668.9.], February 28, 1928; [30.10/102.668.8.], February 25, 1929.

27 "Vay Yobaz Vay!" *Köroğlu*, February 14, 1931; "Bir Ahund Tutuldu," *Son Posta*, May 23, 1935; "Vay Yobaz!" *Köroğlu*, January 8, 1936.

28 BCA-CHP [490.01/677.288.1.], April 19, 1933; Baykurt, *Özüm Çocuktur*, 262.

29 BCA-MGM [30.10/104.679.24.], March 5, 1929; [30.10/102.668.12.], March 7, 1929; [30.10/102.668.13.], March 7, 1929; BCA-CHP [490.01/677.288.1.], April 19, 1933; Szyliowicz, *Political Change in Rural Turkey*, 56.

30 See Cündioğlu, *Meşrutiyetten Cumhuriyete Din ve Siyaset*. See also the same author's *Türkçe Kur'an*.

31 Tan et al., *Cumhuriyet'te Çocuktular*, 82; Başgöz, *Hayat Hikâyem*, 49; Kara, *Kutuz Hoca'nın Hatıraları*, 92; "Yapma Hoca Yeter," *Köroğlu*, June 18, 1935; EGMA [13211–16]; İBA [12212–4], February 16, 1939.

32 "Biga'da Üç Kişi Tevkif Olundu," *Son Posta*, February 16, 1933; "İzmir'de de İki Kişi Tevkif Edildi," *Son Posta*, February 15, 1933; BCA-CHP [490.1/3.12.9], February 8, 1936.

33 BCA-DİR [051.V33/12.102.12.]; EGMA [13211–4], November 5, 1938; Atasoy, *Tahiri Mutlu*, 49, 298.

34 Nar, *Anadolu Günlüğü*, 57; "Tarihe 1000 Canlı Tanık," An Interview with Ahmet Kaya, *Milliyet Pazar*, August 15, 2004; Toroslar, *Sürgün*, 84.

35 EGMA [13211-4], November 5, 1938; Kara, *Kutuz Hoca'nın Hatıraları*, 92; Özcan, *İnönü Dönemi Dini Hayat*, 192–5; Linke, *Allah Dethroned*, 21.

36 *Yargıtay İçtihadı Birleştirme Karar Özetleri*, 100; see also Bozdağ, *Celal Bayar*, 108; "Türk Ceza Kanununun Bazı Maddelerini Değiştiren Kanun," 4055/02.06.1941, *Resmi Gazete*, no. 4827, June 6, 1941, 1126.

37 Koca, *Umumi Müfettişlikten*, 271.

38 BCA-CHP [490.1/831.28.1]; [490.1/825.265.1], June 17, 1938; BCA-CHP [490.01/725.481.1].

39 Uğurlu, *Kahramanmaraş Şehrengizi*, 311; Kıray, *Toplumsal Yapı*, 294–7; Öztürk, *Cumhuriyet Türkiye'sinde Kahvehane*, 162–83.

40 Özeke, *Neyzenler Kahvesi*, 29; Akgül, *Şoför İdris*, 33; Kosova, *Ben İşçiyim*, 17; Aydemir, *Suyu Arayan Adam*, 362–3. Politicians recorded the contents of workers' conversations in coffeehouses. See BCA-CHP [490.1/721.464.2.], November 8, 1937; Uran, *Adana Ziraat Amelesi*, 4.

41 Teymur, *Kahvede Konuştular Camide Buluştular*.

42 Öztürk, *Cumhuriyet Türkiye'sinde Kahvehane*, 364.

43 TTKA SSJ [22, 1340/1924]; [23, 19.11.1340–01.12.1340/1924]; [18, 24.02.1341/1925]; [26–2, 14.01.1341/1925].

44 Öztürk, *Cumhuriyet Türkiye'sinde Kahvehane*, 434–6.

45 EGMA [22552–33], October 25, 1937; [13211–16], December 7, 1938; İBA [12213–20], March 14, 1940. For coffeehouse owners who were prosecuted due to swearing at the regime, the government, President Atatürk or Turkishness, see İBA [12273–40], May 6, 1938; BCA-MGM [30.10/34.194.19], September 25, 1927; [30.10/34.196.16], November 6, 1927; [30.10/35.207.20], October 18, 1929; [30.10/36.213.16], December 19, 1927; [30.10/36.214.12], December 29, 1929; [30.10/37.220.11], September 25, 1930. These are only a few examples among many.

46 BCA-CHP [490.01/684.317.1], November 28, 1935.

47 BCA-MGM [030.10/8.46.24.]; Ergut, *Modern Devlet ve Polis*, 321; Öztürk, *Cumhuriyet Türkiye'sinde Kahvehane*, 185–92, 300.

48 Metinsoy, "Kemalizmin Taşrası."

49 Alpay, *Köy Dâvamız*, 76.

50 Enç, *Selamlık Sohbetleri*, 25–49, 203; Ayverdi, *Ne İdik*, 170; Yasa, *Hasanoğlan Köyü*, 186; Barbarosoğlu, *Cumhuriyetin Dindar Kadınları*, 83.

51 Aswad, "Visiting Patterns," 20.

52 Güntekin, *Anadolu Notları*, 123; İBA [12212–4], November 28, 1938; Uluğ, *Tunceli*, 118.

53 Lindisfarne, *Elhamdülillah Laikiz*, 228–38.
54 BCA-CHP [490.1/677.288.1], 1933. "Bunlar Yola Gelmez," *Köroğlu*, January 17, 1931; "Manisa'daki Bektaşiler," *Son Posta*, June 19, 1932; "Hay Huy," *Köroğlu*, August 18, 1934; "Gizli Tarikatçılar," *Son Posta*, January 25, 1936.
55 BCA-CHP [490.1/587.24.5.]; EGMA [13211–8]; [13211–9]; Barbarosoğlu, *Cumhuriyetin Dindar Kadınları*, 71. Along with homes, the disciples of some sheikhs turned shops into meeting places. Rifaî sheikh Ali Haydar Efendi's *attar* shop in Üsküdar was one of them. Varol, *Tekkede Zaman*, 122.
56 Nar, *Anadolu Günlüğü*, 14; Berkes, *Bazı Ankara Köyleri Üzerine*, 32; Karslı, *Köy Öğretmeninin Anıları*, 24, 55; Balkır, *Eski Bir Öğretmenin Anıları*, 181–90.
57 Yasa, *Hasanoğlan Köyü*, 174–90; BCA-MGM [30.10/65.433.1]; [30.10/65.433.4.], July 24, 1935.
58 BCA-MGM [30.10/79.520.3], January 5, 1931; see also Allen, *The Turkish Transformation*, 120; Balkır, *Eski Bir Öğretmenin Anıları*, 65, 281; Nesin, *Böyle Gelmiş Böyle Gitmez 1*, 46; İBA [12273–25]; Yasa, *Hasanoğlan Köyü*, 214.
59 EGMA [12253–11], April 20, 1932; "Şimdi de Yamyam Masalı," *Son Posta*, May 16, 1935.
60 Selamoğlu and Selamoğlu, *Tayinlerle Anadolu*, 20.
61 Enç, *Selamlık Sohbetleri*, 205.
62 Kara, *Kutuz Hoca'nın Hatıraları*, 36–46; Neyzi, *Kızıltoprak Anıları*, 261; Barbarosoğlu, *Cumhuriyet'in Dindar Kadınları*, 46; Uğurlu, *Kahramanmaraş Şehrengizi*, 69–71.
63 Beşe, "Safranbolu'da Bir Köylünün Hayatı I," 104; Ekinci, *Lice'den Paris'e*, 73; Türkoğlu, *Genç Cumhuriyet'te Köy Çocuğu Olmak*, 131; Toroslar, *Sürgün*, 85; Subaşı, *Kayseri'nin Manevi Mimarları*, 296–301.
64 Vakkasoğlu, *Maneviyat Dünyamızda İz Bırakanlar*, 65–6; Saran, *Omuzumda Hemençe*, 34, 99; Özcan, *İnönü Dönemi Dini Hayat*, 234.
65 BCA-MGM [30.10/79.520.3.], January 5, 1931; EGMA [13211–11], July 22, 1934.
66 EGMA [13211–16], 1938; [12273–60], March 21, 1938; [13211–7], April 5, 1938; BCA-CHP [490.1/587.25.1].
67 *Başbakanlık İstatistik Genel Müdürlüğü, Milli Eğitim, Meslek, Teknik ve Yükseköğretim İstatistikleri 1945–1946*, 34; EGMA [13211–11/2], July 7, 1938. See also Ayhan, *Türkiye'de Din Eğitimi*, 457.

Chapter 11 Informal Media vs. Official Discourse: Word of Mouth, Rumors and Placards

1 Vett, *Dervişler Arasında*, 102; Armstrong, *Turkey and Syria Reborn*, 224.
2 EGMA [22552–33], October 25, 1937; İBA [12212–8], January 17, 1940; [12213–20], February 1, 1940; Nar, *Anadolu Günlüğü*, 50, 144.
3 Nar, *Anadolu Günlüğü*, 77.
4 Newman, *Turkish Crossroads*, 177; EGMA [12253–7]; [12253–4], August 5, 1938.
5 About the power of rumor as informal media, see Darnton, "An Early Information Society"; Kumar, "Beyond Muffled Murmurs of Dissent?" and Farge and Revel, *The Vanishing Children of Paris*.
6 İBA [12212–8], November 19, 1938.
7 BCA-BKK [30.18.1.1/16. 71.14.], 23.10.1341/1925; BCA-DİR [51. V05/2.2.3.], March 11, 1926; Bali, *US Diplomatic Documents on Turkey IV*, 115.
8 BCA-CHP [490.1/1.2.9.], December 2, 1928; Kudar, *Tahtakuşlar'dan Paris'e*, 17.
9 BCA-MGM [30.10/88. 580.6.], May 2, 1928.
10 BCA-MGM [30.10/102.668.7.], February 14, 1929; [30.10/102.668.10.], February 28, 1929; Serdengeçti, *Bir Nesli Nasıl Mahvettiler*, 27.
11 BCA-MGM [30.10/104.679.19.], January 14, 1929; [30.10/104.679.24.], March 5, 1929; [30.10/104.679.25.], February 12, 1929; [30.10/102.668.15.], March 16, 1929; [30.10/104.679.29.], April 22, 1929; [30.10/104.679.30.], June 22, 1929. Memoirs and the representatives of the foreign states also recorded such rumors; see Tanju, *Doludizgin*, 94; Bali, *US Diplomatic Documents on Turkey IV*, 127.
12 For a few rumors in this period, see Koçak, *Muhalif Sesler*, 41, 102. Unfortunately, Koçak replicates the RPP's view by arguing rumors were propaganda of the opponent elite.
13 BCA-MGM [30.10/102.667.18.], November 10, 1927; BCA-CHP [490.01/ 1.4.8 and 9]; Soyak, *Atatürk'ten Hatıralar*, 432.
14 İBA [12253–6], November 8, 1938; [12212–4], February 24, 1939.
15 İBA [12212–4].
16 İBA [12212–4], February 24, 1939.
17 İBA [13211–10], November 7, 1938; İBA [12212–4], January 23, 1939; [12212–4], February 11, 1939; [12212–4], February 16, 1939.
18 İBA [12212–8], November 22, 1938; İBA [12212–4].
19 BCA-MGM [030.10/102.668.1], January 9, 1939.
20 İBA [12213–20], February 1, 1940; [12213–20], January 17, 1940; [12213–20], November 12, 1940.
21 Farge, *Subversive Words*, 62.

22 BCA-MGM [30.10/101.654.15.], November 16, 1925; Seal, *A Fez of the Heart*, 107; BCA-MGM [30.10/102.668.3.], January 14, 1929.

23 "Yapma Hoca Yeter Artık," *Köroğlu*, June 18, 1932; "Yapma Hocam," *Köroğlu*, December 21, 1932; "Mürteci Tahrikçiler," *Son Posta*, November 14, 1936; "Aklım Ermedi," *Köroğlu*, November 18, 1936.

24 BCA-CHP [490.1/586.23.1.], March 14, 1937.

25 Sadi, *Türkiye'de Sosyalizmin*, 790.

26 Boratav, *Halk Hikâyeleri*, 169–81; BCA-CHP [490.10/ 587.25.1].

Chapter 12 Neither Fez Nor Hat: Contesting Hat Reform

1 Linke, *Allah Dethroned*, 180.

2 About the politics of dress during revolutionary epochs, see Baumqarten, *What Clothes Reveal*; Wrigley, *The Politics of Appearances*.

3 Mango, *Atatürk*, 433.

4 Aydemir, *Suyu Arayan Adam*, 369–74.

5 Metinsoy, "Everyday Resistance and Selective Adaptation to the Hat Reform," 12. For the same purpose, Atatürk supported anthropological research. Toprak, *Darwin'den Dersim'e*. For a critical analysis of the concept of the "Muslim world," see Aydın, *The Idea of the Muslim World*.

6 Baydar, *Geçidi Bekleyen Şehir*, 86.

7 Norton, "Faith and Fashion in Turkey," 149–57.

8 Baykara, *Osmanlılarda Medeniyet Kavramı*, 60–3, 101–8; Timur, *Osmanlı Çalışmaları*, 119–80.

9 Metinsoy, "Everyday Resistance and Selective Adaptation to the Hat Reform."

10 Hobsbawm, *Uncommon People*, 150; Gençosman, *Altın Yıllar*, 116; Newman, *Turkish Crossroads*, 65.

11 Armstrong, *Turkey and Syria Reborn*, 123; Baydar, *Geçidi Bekleyen Şehir*, 86; Kılıç, *Erzurum Fıkraları*, 78.

12 İBA [12212–4], November 28, 1938; EGMA [13211–16], December 7, 1938; BCA-MGM [30.10/101.654.15.], November 16, 1925; Sadi, *Türkiye'de Sosyalizmin Tarihine Katkı*, 790.

13 Orga, *Bir Türk Ailesinin Öyküsü*, 219; Tan et al., *Cumhuriyet'te Çocuktular*, 92.

14 Çerkezyan, *Dünya Hepimize Yeter*, 76.

15 Orga, *Bir Türk Ailesinin Öyküsü*, 219; Nesin, *Böyle Gelmiş Böyle Gitmez 1*, 157.

16 Enç, *Selamlık Sohbetleri*, 196.

17 Armstrong, *Turkey and Syria Reborn*, 122; Kara, *Kutuz Hoca'nın Hatıraları*, 174–8; Rıza Nur, *Hayat ve Hatıratım*, IV, 1316; Linke, *Allah Dethroned*, 22.

18 Van Millingen and Shah, *Turkey*, 13; Nar, *Anadolu Günlüğü*, 105–12; BCA-CHP [490.1/729.478.1].

19 EGMA [13211–16], March 30, 1930; [13211–16], April 11, 1933; [13211–16], August 2, 1935.

20 EGMA [13211–16], February 7, 1940.

21 EGMA [13211–16], May 8, 1935; [13211–4], March 19, 1939; Orga, *Bir Türk Ailesinin Öyküsü*, 220; Ekinci, *Lice'den Paris'e*, 78.

22 EGMA [13211–16], March 7, 1939; BCA-MGM [30.10/128.923.10], April 1, 1936.

23 EGMA [13211–16], March 21, 1939; Gemalmaz, *Türk Kıyafet Hukuku ve Türban*, 682–3.

24 Turhan, *Kültür Değişmeleri*, 73.

25 EGMA [13211–10], November 7, 1938.

Chapter 13 Negotiating Anti-veiling Campaigns

1 Esenel, *1940'lı Yıllarda*, 135.

2 Davis, *Osmanlı Hanımı*, 207; Georgeon, *Abdülhamid II*; Mahir-Metinsoy, *Moda ve Kadın*, 17–32; Toprak, "Tesettürden Telebbüse."

3 Armstrong, *Turkey and Syria Reborn*, 121, 176, 220–1.

4 Grew, *Atatürk ve Yeni Türkiye*, 159; Alvaro, *Türkiye'ye Yolculuk*, 66–7.

5 Linke, *Allah Dethroned*, 5–8, 18, 267.

6 Balkan, *Anılar*, 53; Mahir-Metinsoy, *Moda ve Kadın*, 18–19; Türkoğlu, *Genç Cumhuriyet'te Köy Çocuğu Olmak*, 480; Nihal, *Domaniç Dağlarının Yolcusu*, 59; Tanman, *Batnas Tepelerinde Zaman*, 31; Beşe, "Safranbolu'da Bir Köylünün Hayatı I," 104.

7 Turhan, *Kültür Değişmeleri*, 73; Ekinci, *Lice'den Paris'e*, 78; Gökdemir, *Annemin Anlattıkları*, 108.

8 EGMA [13216–7]; [13211–16]; [13216–7], November 7, 1939; [13211–16], March 18, 1939; BCA-MGM [30.10/65.433.5].

9 "Kütahya Hanımları," *Köroğlu*, January 27, 1934; "Peçeli, Peştemallı Kadınlar," *Köroğlu*, April 25, 1934; "Çarşaf-Peçe!" *Köroğlu*, June 23, 1934; "Çarşaf, Peçe ve Yabancı Dil," *Son Posta*, April 21, 1935.

10 Peirce, *The Imperial Harem*, 267–72.

11 BCA-MGM [30.10/102.668.9.], February 28, 1928; BCA-MGM [30.10/102.668.8.], February 25, 1929; "Bir Ahund Tutuldu," *Son Posta*, May 23, 1935; "Vay Yobaz!" *Köroğlu*, January 8, 1936; BCA-

CHP [490.01/677.288.1.], April 19, 1933. For such sermons in later years, see İsvan, *Köprüler, Gelip Geçmeye*, 122.

12 Ekrem, *Turkey, Old and New*, 81; Enç, *Selamlık Sohbetleri*, 204; Yasa, *Hasanoğlan Köyü*, 165.

13 For shortage of labor in the industry during the period, see Ekin, "Memleketimizde İşçi Devri," 123–92.

14 Kıvılcımlı, *Türkiye İşçi Sınıfının Sosyal Varlığı*, 57; Yavuz, "Sanayideki İşgücünün Durumu," 190; "Erkek İşçiler Kadınlardan Şikâyetçi," *Köroğlu*, October 23, 1935.

15 *Orak Çekiç*, October 1, 1936; BCA-CHP [490.1/1446.26.1.], June 17, 1933; Cantek, "Kabadayıların ve Futbolun Mahallesi Hacettepe," 187; Linke, *Allah Dethroned*, 312.

16 "Manto mu Ekmek mi?" *Köroğlu*, October 14, 1935; "Çarşaf, Peçe," *Köroğlu*, January 9, 1935; "Çarşaf ve Peçe," *Köroğlu*, August 10, 1935; Newman, *Turkish Crossroads*, 88; Türkoğlu, *Genç Cumhuriyet'te Köy Çocuğu Olmak*, 173; Zorlutuna, *Bir Devrin Romanı*, 247.

17 EGMA [13216–7], August 22, 1935; BCA-CHP [490.1/17.88.1], January 14, 1936.

18 Regarding the community pressure in Muslim neighborhoods, see Mardin, "Religion and Secularism in Turkey," 214; Hegland, "The Power Paradox in Muslim Women's Majales," 117–19.

19 EGMA [13211–16], March 18, 1939.

20 Yasa, *Hasanoğlan Köyü*, 214; Türkoğlu, *Genç Cumhuriyet'te Köy Çocuğu Olmak*, 5; Toroslar, *Sürgün*, 65.

21 Binyazar, *Masalını Yitiren Dev*, 124–8.

22 EGMA [13216–7], February 7, 1936; [22552–33], October 25, 1937; BCA-CHP [490.1/677.289.1], February 16, 1936.

23 EGMA [13216–7], 1935; [13216–7], 1937; Enç, *Selamlık Sohbetleri*, 200.

24 About the symbolic violence, see Darnton, *The Great Cat Massacre*. Darnton underlines the social protests through symbolic acts by describing how poor apprentices protested by killing their masters' beloved cats in eighteenth-century France.

25 Turgut, *Kılıç Ali'nin Anıları*, 391.

26 BCA-MGM [30.10/104.679.4], February 16, 1926; EGMA [13216–7], November 13, 1935.

27 Karabuda, *Goodbye to the Fez*, 74; Korle, *Kızıltoprak Günlerim*, 42; Neyzi, *Kızıltoprak Anıları*, 279; Nesin, *Böyle Gelmiş Böyle Gitmez 1*, 157; BCA-MGM [30.10/101.654.15], November 16, 1925; Binyazar, *Masalını Yitiren Dev*, 124–8.

28 "Kodese," *Köroğlu*, September 14, 1929; "1 Lafa 15 Gün," *Köroğlu*, October 31, 1936.

29 BCA-DİR [51.V05/2.2.3.], March 11, 1926; BCA-BKK [30.18.1.1/16. 71.14.], October 23, 1925; BCA-MGM [30.10/88.580.6], May 2, 1928; EGMA [13216–7].

30 Enç, *Selamlık Sohbetleri*, 199; İBA [12213–69], 1939; [12212–8], November 22, 1938; [12212–4], November 28, 1938; [12212–4], January 27, 1939; [12212–4], February 16, 1939; EGMA [12212–4], January 23, 1939.

31 *Yeşilgireson*, January 6, 1926; *Yeşilgireson*, October 29, 1926; Diken, *İsyan Sürgünleri*, 52.

32 EGMA [13216–7], January 8, 1938.

33 EGMA [13216–7], January 6, 1936; [13216–7], 1940.

34 EGMA [13216–4].

35 EGMA [13211–16], March 20, 1939.

36 "Alâiye'de Şemsiyesiz Gezen Kadın Göremezsiniz," *Son Posta*, May 3, 1932; "Hala Eski Kafa!" *Köroğlu*, December 21, 1935; Örik, *Anadolu'da*, 92.

37 Pekolcay, *Geçtim Dünya Üzerinden*, 163; *Ayın Tarihi* 42 (June 1937), quoted from Vâlâ Nurettin, *Haber*, May 1, 1937.

38 İnan, *Cumhuriyet'in Kurucu Kuşağı İle Söyleşiler*, 361; Soyak, *Atatürk'ten Hatıralar*, 270.

39 EGMA [13216–7-1], November 17, 1934; [13216–7-1], 14.12.1934; Uyar, "Çarşaf, Peçe ve Kafes," 6–11.

40 EGMA [13211–10], November 14, 1938; [13216–7], November 22, 1939.

41 Zahedi, "Concealing and Revealing Female Hair," 254–5; Chehabi, "Dress Codes for Men in Turkey and Iran," 221–3, and "The Banning of the Veil and Its Consequences"; Katouzian, "State and Society under Reza Shah," 34; Nawid, *Religious Response to Social Change in Afghanistan*, 88–102; Poullada, *Reform and Rebellion in Afghanistan*, 74. For an analytical interpretation of the Republic's approach to women and gender, see Kandiyoti, "Women, Islam, and the State," 187.

Chapter 14 Old Habits Die Hard: Tenacity of Old Lifestyles in New Times

1 Taşkıran, *Türk Kadın Hakları*, 170.

2 Duben and Behar, *İstanbul Households*, 213–14.

3 BCA-CHP [490.1/212.840.1].

4 Berkes, *Bazı Ankara Köyleri Üzerine*, 86; Yasa, *Hasanoğlan Köyü*, 163; Szyliowicz, *Political Change in Rural Turkey*, 50–1; Koşay, *Türk Düğünleri Üzerine*; *Adliye Vekâleti Hukuk İşleri Umum Müdürlüğü Raporu. Adliye Ceridesi*, vol. 12 (1942), 1336.

5 BCA-CHP [490.1/500.2010.1], July 26, 1933.
6 Timur, "Civil Marriage in Turkey," 34; "Türk Ceza Kanununun Bazı Maddelerini Değiştiren Kanun, 3038/11.06.1936," *TBMM Kavanin Mecmuası*, vol. 16, 971; Jäeschke, "Türk Hukukunda Evlenme Aktinin Şekli," 1151.
7 BCA-CHP [490.1/212.840.1]; Berkes, "Nesebi Sahih Olmayan Çocuklar," 1401.
8 Alpay, *Köy Dâvamız*, 83; Güriz, "Evlilik Dışı Birleşmeler," 127–31; see Civil Code, Article 95.
9 Ekrem, *Turkey Old and New*, 60; Montagu, *The Complete Letters*, 329; Turan, "Ta'addüd-i Zevcat," 119–23; Magnarella, *Anatolia's Loom*, 266; Toledano, "The Imperial Eunuchs of İstanbul."
10 Allen, *The Turkish Transformation*, 139.
11 For the statistics regarding polygamous marriages from the 1960s on, see Van Os "Polygamy"; *Adliye Vekâleti Hukuk İşleri Umum Müdürlüğü Raporu. Adliye Ceridesi*, 12, (1942), 1336; Kıray, *Toplumsal Yapı*, 249; Berkes, *Bazı Ankara Köyleri Üzerine*, 161–4; Şahinkaya, *Orta Anadolu Köylerinde Aile Strüktürü*; Tütengil, "Keçiller Köyü İncelemesi."
12 Berkes, *Bazı Ankara Köyleri Üzerine*, 162–3; Yalman, *Cenupta Türkmen Oymakları*, 208–19; *Gezi Notları*, 30; Yasa, *Hasanoğlan Köyü*, 237; Turhan, *Kültür Değişmeleri*, 73; Varlık, *Ali Tunalı*, 199. See also Tanman, *Ilgaz Dağlarından Batnas Tepelerine*, 39–42. Her memoirs show that even in the villages of a big western province like Aydın, there were men with two wives.
13 BCA-CHP [490.1/500.2010.1], July 26, 1933; Jäeschke, "Türk Hukukunda Evlenme Aktinin Şekli," 51.
14 Beşe, "Safranbolu'da Bir Köylünün Hayatı I," 105; Yasa, *Hasanoğlan Köyü*, 60, 139–40, 181.
15 "Af Kanunu," 2330/26.10.1933, *Resmi Gazete*, no. 2540, October 28, 1933, 3184; "Gizli Nüfusların Yazımı Hakkında Kanun," 2576/5.7.1934, *Resmi Gazete*, no. 2752, July 15, 1934, 4146; "Evlenmek Bedava," *Köroğlu*, February 10, 1937; TBMM *Kavanin Mecmuası*, 20/3686 (July 7, 1939), 852.
16 Us, *Hatıra Notları*, 260; "Evlenme Kanunu Dün Mecliste Kabul Edildi," *Cumhuriyet*, June 16, 1938; Velidedeoğlu, "The Reception of the Swiss Civil Code in Turkey."
17 Evlenmeye İzin Verme-Yargıtay İçtihadı Birleştirme Kararı 1935–15/June 7, 1935. *Yargıtay İçtihadı Birleştirme Karar Özetleri: Hukuk-Ceza, 1926–1998*, 35; Güriz, "Evlilik Dışı Birleşmeler," 140–1.
18 Tan et al., *Cumhuriyet'te Çocuktular*, 93.
19 Tan et al., *Cumhuriyet'te Çocuktular*, 93.

20 Kayra, '38 Kuşağı, 108; Taşkıran, Türk Kadın Hakları, 173; Diken, İsyan Sürgünleri, 85–6; Yasa, Hasanoğlan Köyü, 128.

21 Ekrem, Turkey Old and New, 81; Esenel, 1940'lı Yıllarda, 135.

22 Linke, Allah Dethroned, 31; Cantek, "Kabadayıların ve Futbolun Mahallesi Hacettepe," 187; Enç, Selamlık Sohbetleri; Diken, İsyan Sürgünleri, 88; "Harem Selamlık Kalkmalıdır," Yeşilgireson, December 26, 1936; Güntekin, Anadolu Notları, 104.

23 "Beylerbeyi İskelesindeki Tahta Perde," Vakit, May 17, 1929, and "Kadın Erkek Birlikte Sinemaya Gidemiyorlar," Milliyet, July 28, 1931, both were quoted by Dinç, Aydınlığa Mektuplar, 153, 161; "Amma İş Ha!" Köroğlu, March 22, 1933; "Gebze Hanımları," Köroğlu, April 7, 1934; "Hala Harem-Selamlık Zihniyet Var!" Son Posta, January 3, 1936.

24 Pamuk, "Son 200 Yılda Türkiye'de ve Dünyada Sağlık ve Eğitim," 18.

25 Akşit, "Ankara'nın Kılıkları," 150; Yasa, Hasanoğlan Köyü, 191; Esenel, 1940'lı Yıllarda, 167; Işıksoluğu, Aydoğdu Köyü, 72, 198; Ekinci, Lice'den Paris'e, 59; Seçkin, Bir Hâkime Yakışanı Yazdım, 31; Gökdemir, Annemin Anlattıkları, 59.

26 Enç, Selamlık Sohbetleri, 205; Ekinci, Lice'den Paris'e, 99; Başgöz, Hayat Hikâyem, 49, 58; Tan et al., Cumhuriyet'te Çocuktular, 137; Gökdemir, Annemin Anlattıkları, 61.

27 Durakbaşa and İlyasoğlu, "Formation of Gender Identities in Republican Turkey"; Belli, Boşuna mı Çiğnedik?, 69; Duman, "Cumhuriyet Baloları," 47; Cantek, "'Yaban'lar ve 'Yerli'ler," 267; Kinross, Mustafa Kemal, 720.

28 Zorlutuna, Bir Devrin Romanı, 223; Ağaoğlu, Bir Ömür Böyle Geçti, 46–7; Cantek, " 'Yaban'lar ve 'Yerli'ler," 266; Tanç, Bir Cumhuriyet Askerinin Anıları, 67.

29 BCA-CHP [490.1/540.2160.2].

30 Berkes, Bazı Ankara Köyleri Üzerine, 130; Szyliowicz, Political Change in Rural Turkey, 50; Hurşit Sait, "Gaziantep'te Halk İnanmaları," 127; Özbay, Aile, Kent ve Nüfus, 118.

31 Grew, Atatürk ve Yeni Türkiye, 227.

32 See Bozdoğan, Modernism and Nation Building, 300–1. Karabuda, Goodbye to the Fez, 67; Linke, Allah Dethroned, 34; Kâzım, "Anadolu Hurafeleri," 315; see also Nesin, Böyle Gelmiş Böyle Gitmez 1, 289–90.

33 Van Millingen and Shah, Turkey, 44; Bayrı, İstanbul Folkloru, 86–110; Baykurt, Özüm Çocuktur, 30; Nesin, Böyle Gelmiş Böyle Gitmez 2, 52.

34 "Üfürükçü Yakalandı," Köroğlu, January 31, 1931; "Üfürük!" Köroğlu, December 21, 1932; "Hala mı Yahu!" Köroğlu, January 31, 1934; "1 Muska 6 Papel," Köroğlu, April 13, 1935; "15 Liraya Muska," Köroğlu, October 23, 1935; "Bir Üfürükçü Yakalandı," Son Posta,

January 6, 1936; "Büyücü," *Köroğlu*, January 11, 1936; "Hacı Baba: Üfürükçü Nasıl Enselendi," *Köroğlu*, October 17, 1936.

35 Newman, *Turkish Crossroads*, 241; Van Millingen and Shah, *Turkey*, 48; Yasa, *Hasanoğlan Köyü*, 219; Szyliowicz, *Political Change in Rural Turkey*, 52; Berkes, "Üfürükçülük"; Kâzım, "Anadolu Hurafeleri," 316.

36 Ekinci, *Lice'den Paris'e*, 85–6; Fahri, *Doğu Köylerinde*, 11; Baykurt, *Özüm Çocuktur*, 189–92; Vett, *Dervişler Arasında*, 42; Kâzım, "Anadolu Hurafeleri," 314.

37 Belli, *Boşuna mı Çiğnedik?*, 16, 44; Kâzım, "Anadolu Hurafeleri," 314–15.

38 For the verdicts by the Supreme Court, see Zoga and Muradoğlu, *Yargıtay'ın Hususi Kanun ve Nizamnamelere Ait Yaşayan Bütün İçtihat ve Kararları*, 926–7; Taşçıoğlu et al., *İçtihatlı ve İzahatlı Ceza*, 264; Akdoğan et al., *Ceza Hükümleri Taşıyan*, 377.

39 Van Millingen and Shah, *Turkey*, 48.

40 Ali Vahit, "Kemal Ümmi Hakkında," 214.

41 Esenel, *1940'lı Yıllarda*, 140.

42 Kâzım, "Anadolu Hurafeleri," 317; Neyzi, *Kızıltoprak Anıları*, 291; Seçkin, *Bir Hâkime Yakışanı Yazdım*, 27.

43 Kâzım, "Anadolu Hurafeleri," 316–17. A contemporary field survey on popular culture in northern Anatolia, including Sinop, Gümüşhane, Trabzon, Bayburt, Rize and Erzincan provinces, includes several holy shrine and places frequented by the people. Abdülkadir, *Birinci İlmi Seyahate Dair Rapor*, 38–42.

44 Hurşit Sait, "Gaziantep'te Halk İnanmaları," 129–30.

45 Hasan Fehmi, "Tanrıya Arzuhâl," 105.

46 İnan, "Urfa'da Ziyaret Yerleri II."

47 Önus, "İstanbul'da Bazı Ziyaret Yerleri."

48 Nesin, *Böyle Gelmiş Böyle Gitmez 2*, 418.

49 Yasa, *Hasanoğlan Köyü*, 219; Tevfik, *İnsan ve Mekân Yüzüyle Mübadele*, 118.

50 For material advantages that tombs provided for dervishes or tomb keepers, see Önus, "İstanbul'da Bazı Ziyaret Yerleri"; İnan, "Urfa'da Ziyaret Yerleri II"; Hasan Fehmi, "Tanrıya Arzuhâl"; Hurşit Sait, "Gaziantep'te Halk İnanmaları."

Part III Concluding Remarks

1 Bayar, "The Dynamic Nature of Educational Policies," 29; Çınar, *Modernity, Islam, and Secularism*, 17; Yılmaz and Doğaner, *Cumhuriyet Döneminde Sansür*, 81–3.

Epilogue

1 Hobsbawm, *Uncommon People*, 157.
2 For the role of reports and petitions in bridging state and society, see Metinsoy, "Fragile Hegemony and Governing from Below;" Akın, "Politics of Petitioning."
3 For the social dynamics that forced the state to undertake political liberalization and social policy reforms, see Metinsoy, *İkinci Dünya Savaşı'nda Türkiye*.
4 In the 1950s, the Islamic ideology of provincial society reared its head via the local press with the transition to democracy; see Brockett, *How Happy to Call Oneself a Turk*.
5 For how the rural background of the migrants who flowed into the cities affected their political culture, and why it was unwise to neglect the past experiences of the peasantry to understand current politics, see Hobsbawm, *Uncommon People*, 165; see also Lloyd, *Slums of Hope*, 92–108. For conservative and religious political culture among peasant-origin squatter dwellers, see Karpat, *Türkiye'de Toplumsal Dönüşüm*, 308. Nobel laureate novelist Orhan Pamuk notes in his memoirs that Turkey's urbanite middle classes supported military intervention in Turkish politics not because they feared the leftist revolution, but rather because they feared the rural-origin migrants' Islamist culture. Pamuk, *Istanbul*, 166. Until the rise of authoritarian Islamism in the past decade, many intellectuals, including Pamuk, stigmatized this fear as paranoia, but in fact these concerns had a sociological ground.
6 For how rural society, peasantry and rural migrants in urban areas played a role in the rise of conservative and Islamist politics, see Margulies and Yıldızoğlu, "The Resurgence of Islam," 145–7; Arat and Pamuk, *Turkey between Authoritarianism and Democracy*, 45–7, 152–3, 263, 290–312.
7 For the peasant characteristics of the working class in the 1950s and 1960s, see İçduygu, Sirkeci and Aydıngün, "Türkiye'de İçgöç," 211.

Bibliography

Archival Sources

Başbakanlık Cumhuriyet Arşivi (Prime Ministry Republic Archive) (BCA), Ankara
  Bakanlar Kurulu Kararnameleri (Cabinet Decrees) (BKK)
  Bakanlıklar Arası Tayin Daire Başkanlığı/Üçlü Kararnameler (Interministries Appointment Office/Tripple Decrees)(BATDB/ÜK)
  Başbakanlık Muamelat Genel Müdürlüğü (Prime Ministry, General Directorate of Transactions) (MGM)
  Cumhuriyet Halk Partisi (Republican People's Party) (CHP)
  Diyanet İşleri Reisliği (Presidency of Religious Affairs) (DİR)
  Nafia Vekâleti (Public Works Ministry) (NV)
Emniyet Genel Müdürlüğü Arşivi (Police Archive) (EGMA), Ankara
İçişleri Bakanlığı Arşivi (Interior Ministry Archive) (İBA), Ankara
Tarih Vakfı Arşivi (History Foundation of Turkey Archive, Pertev Naili Boratav Catalogue) (TVA PNB), İstanbul
Türk Tarih Kurumu Arşivi (Turkish Historical Society Archive, Saadet Sevencan Jurnalleri/Secret Reports) (TTKA SSJ), Ankara
Türkiye Büyük Millet Meclisi Kütüphane ve Arşivi (Grand National Assembly of Turkey Library and Archive), Ankara

Official and Semiofficial Publications

1930 Sanayi Kongresi: Raporlar, Kararlar, Zabıtlar. Ankara: Millî İktisat ve Tasarruf Cemiyeti Umum Merkezi, Ankara Sanayi Odası, 2008.
1937 Temyiz Kararları. Ankara: T. C. Adliye Vekâleti Neşriyat Müdürlüğü, 1938.
Adliye Encümeni Ruznamesi, TBMM Encümenler Ruznamesi, 1 Teşrinisani 1934. Ankara: TBMM, [1934].
Adliye Vekâleti Hukuk İşleri Umum Müdürlüğü Raporu. Adliye Ceridesi, 12 (1942): 1327–53.

Başbakanlık İstatistik Genel Müdürlüğü, Milli Eğitim, Meslek, Teknik ve Yükseköğretim İstatistikleri 1945–1946. İstanbul: Pulhan Matbaası, 1947.

CHF Büyük Kongre Zabıtları. İstanbul: Devlet Matbaası, 1931.

CHF Nizamnamesi ve Programı. Ankara, 1931.

CHP 28/12/936 Tarihinde Toplanan Vilâyet Kongresi Zabıtnamesi. İzmir: Anadolu Matbaası, 1937.

CHP 1936 İl Kongreleri. Ankara: n.p., 1937.

CHP Programı. Ankara: Ulus Basımevi, 1935.

CHP Teftiş Bölgeleri ve Teftiş İşlerini Yürütme Planı. Ankara: CHP Genel Sekreterliği, 1935.

Dersim: Jandarma Umum Komutanlığı Raporu (1932). İstanbul: Kaynak Yayınları, 2010 (First edition, Jandarma Umum Komutanlığı, 1932).

DİE İstatistik Yıllığı. Ankara: Devlet İstatistik Enstitüsü Yayını, 1948.

DİE Türkiye İstatistik Yıllığı 1968. Ankara: Devlet İstatistik Enstitüsü Matbaası, 1969.

Düstur, 3. Tertip, vol. 5. İstanbul: Necmi İstikbal Matbaası, 1931.

Düstur, 3. Tertip, vol. 10. Ankara: Başvekâlet Matbaası, 1934.

Düstur, 3. Tertip, vol. 16. Ankara: Başvekâlet Matbaası, 1935.

Emniyet İşleri Umum Müdürlüğü: Geçen Dört Yılda Yapılan ve Gelecek Dört Yılda Yapılacak İşler Hülasası. Ankara: T. C. Dâhiliye Vekâleti, Başvekâlet Matbaası, 1935.

Labour Problems in Turkey: A Report of a Mission of the International Labor Office (March–May 1949). Geneva: International Labour Organization, 1950.

Nüfus Sayımı Propagandası İçin Muhtelif Gazetelerde İntişar Eden Yazılar ve Radyoda Verilen Konferanslar. Ankara: Başvekâlet İstatistik Umum Müdürlüğü, 1941.

Resmi Gazete.

TBMM Encümenler Ruznamesi.

TBMM Kavanin Mecmuası.

TBMM Yıllıkları – 1928, 1929, 1930, 1931, 1932, 1933, 1934, 1935, 1936, 1937, 1938, 1939. Ankara. TBMM Matbaası.

TBMM Zabıt Ceridesi. Dönem 4, Cilt 14. Ankara: TBMM Matbaası, 1933.

TBMM Zabıt Ceridesi. Dönem 5, Cilt 3. Ankara: TBMM Matbaası, 1935.

T. C. Başbakanlık İstatistik Genel Müdürlüğü. Hayvanlar İstatistiği 1944. [İstanbul]: Hüsnütabiat Basımevi, 1946.

T. C. Maliye Bakanlığı Bütçe ve Mali Kontrol Genel Müdürlüğü Sayı: 1995/ 5. Bütçe Gider ve Gelir Gerçekleşmeleri (1924–1995). Ankara, 1995.

Temyiz Kararları: Hukuk Hey'eti Umumiyesi, 1930–1934. İstanbul: Halk Basımevi, 1935.

Türkiye Cumhuriyeti Ziraat Bankası'nın İpotekli ve Zincirleme Kefaletli Tarımsal Alacaklarının Taksitlendirilmesine Dair Olan 2814 Nolu Kanun Mucibince İstanbul İline Bağlı İlçe, Kamun ve Köylerdeki Borçluların İsimlerini Gösterir Kitaptır. Ankara: Ziraat Bankası, 1935.

Yargıtay İçtihadı Birleştirme Karar Özetleri: Hukuk-Ceza, 1926–1998. Ankara: Yargıtay Birinci Başkanlığı Yayın İşleri Müdürlüğü, 1999.

Ziraat Kongresi [Birinci Ziraat Kongresi, 1931]. Ankara: Millî İktisat ve Tasarruf Cemiyeti, 1931.

Journals

Adliye Ceridesi
Akbaba
Aydınlık
Bolşevik
Çalışma Dergisi
Dönüm
Esnaf Meslek Mecmuası
Halk Bilgisi Haberleri
Hep Bu Topraktan
İktisadi Yürüyüş
İnhisarlar İstihbarat Bülteni
İ.Ü. Hukuk Fakültesi Mecmuası
İ.Ü. İktisat Fakültesi Mecmuası
Jandarma Karakol Mecmuası
Kızıl İstanbul
Köye Doğru
Muallimler Mecmuası
Mülkiyeliler Birliği Dergisi
Orak Çekiç
Polis Dergisi
Resimli Ay
Siyasi İlimler Mecmuası
Sosyoloji Dergisi
Tarih Sohbetleri
Türk Akdeniz
Türk Folklor Araştırmaları
Türk İdare Dergisi
Ülkü
Verim
Yarım Ay
Yeni Adam
Yurt ve Dünya
Ziraat Gazetesi

Newspapers

Aydın
Cumhuriyet
Erzurum
İkdam
Kayseri
Kommunist
Köroğlu
Milliyet
Son Posta
Tan
Vakit
Yeni Adana
Yeşilgireson

Memoirs, Diaries, Interviews, Speeches, Letters, Literary Works and Contemporary Surveys

Acun, Niyazi. *Ormanlarımız ve Cumhuriyet Hükümeti'nin Orman Davası.* Ankara: Recep Ulusoğlu Basımevi, 1945.

"Yeni İş Kanunu Tatbik Sahasına Girerken." *Yarım Ay* 49 (1937): 20–1.

"Adliye İstatistiklerine Göre Memleketimizde Cürümler ve Mücrimler." *Polis Dergisi* 10 (1940): 31–45.

Afet, İnan. *Devletçilik İlkesi ve Türkiye Cumhuriyetinin Birinci Sanayi Planı, 1933.* Ankara: Türk Tarih Kurumu Yayınları, 1972.

Yurt Bilgisi Notlarımdan: Vergi Bilgisi. İstanbul: Devlet Matbaası, 1930.

Ağaoğlu, Ahmet. *Serbest Fırka Hatıraları.* İstanbul: İletişim Yayınları, 1994.

Ağaoğlu, Samed. "Polis İstatistiklerine Göre Memleketimizde Cürümler ve Mücrimler." *Polis Dergisi* 11 (1940): 42–8.

Ağaoğlu, Süreyya. *Bir Ömür Böyle Geçti.* İstanbul: İshak Basımevi, 1975.

Ahmet, Naim. *Zonguldak Havzası: Uzun Mehmetten Bugüne Kadar.* İstanbul: Hüsnütabiat Matbaası, 1934.

Akar, Nejat. *Bozkır Çocuklarına Bir Umut. Dr. Albert Eckstein.* İstanbul: Gürer Yayınları, 2008.

Akar, Nejat, and Alp Can. *Fifteen Years of Anatolia with Professor Albert Eckstein, 1935–1950.* Ankara: Ankara University Culture and Art Publications, 2005.

Akdoğan, Kazım, Fahrettin Kıyak, Niyazi Gencer, Cebbar Şenel and Sadık Perinçek. *Ceza Hükümleri Taşıyan Kanun ve Nizamnameler.* Vol. 3. Ankara: Balkanoğlu Matbaacılık, 1964.

Akekmekçi, Tuba, and Muazzez Pervan, eds. *Doğu Sorunu: Necmeddin Sahir Sılan Raporları, 1939-1953.* İstanbul: Tarih Vakfı Yurt Yayınları, 2010.

Akgül, Hikmet, ed. *Şoför İdris: Anılar.* İstanbul: Yar Yayınları, 2004.

Aksoy, Refet. *Köylülerimizle Başbaşa.* Yozgat: Yozgat İlbaylik Basımevi, 1936.

Aksüt, Ali Kemalî. *Erzincan: Tarihî, Coğrafî, İçtimaî, Etnografî, İdarî, İhsaî Tetkikat Tecrübesi.* İstanbul: Resimli Ay Matbaası, 1932.

Alakom, Rohat, ed. *Bir Türk Subayının Ağrı İsyanı Anıları.* İstanbul: Avesta, 2011.

Allen, Henry Elisha. *The Turkish Transformation: A Study in Social and Religious Development.* Chicago: University of Chicago Press, 1935.

Alpay, Mehmet Nuri. *Köy Dâvamız ve Köyün İç Yüzü.* Ankara: Örnek Matbaası, 1953.

Alvaro, Corrado. *Türkiye'ye Yolculuk.* İstanbul: Literatür, 2003 (First publication in 1932).

Apaydın, Talip. *Tütün Yorgunu.* İstanbul: Cem Yayınevi, 1975.

Arat, Yeşim, and Şevket Pamuk. *Turkey between Democracy and Authoritarianism.* Cambridge: Cambridge University Press, 2019.

Armstrong, Harold C. *Turkey and Syria Reborn: A Record of Two Years of Travel.* London: J. Lane, 1930.

Artukmaç, Sadık. *Köylerimizi Nasıl Kalkındırabiliriz?* Ankara: Güney Matbaacılık ve Gazetecilik, TAO, 1955.

Atasagun, Yusuf Zaim. *Türkiye Cumhuriyeti Ziraat Bankası, 1888-1939.* İstanbul: Kenan Basımevi ve Klişe Fabrikası, 1939.

Türkiye'de İçtimai Siyaset Meseleleri/Sozialpolitische Probleme der Turkei: İktisat Fakültesi Mecmuasından Ayrı Bası. İstanbul: Güven Basımevi, 1941.

Türkiye'de Zirai Borçlanma ve Zirai Kredi Politikası. İstanbul: Kenan Matbaası, 1943.

Atasoy, İhsan. *Kulluğu İçinde Bir Sultan: Tahiri Mutlu.* İstanbul: Nesil Yayınları, 2007.

Atatürk'ün Söylev ve Demeçleri I. İstanbul: Maarif Matbaası, 1945.

[Atay], Falih Rıfkı. *Bizim Akdeniz.* Ankara: Hakimiyet-i Milliye Matbaası, 1934.

Aydemir, Şevket Süreyya. *Cihan İktisadiyatında Türkiye.* Ankara: Ticaret Mektebi, 1931.

Suyu Arayan Adam. İstanbul: Remzi Kitabevi, 2003.

Aydemir, Şevket Süreyya, ed. *Ege Günü I.* Ankara: Milli İktisat ve Tasarruf Cemiyeti, 1934.

Ayverdi, Sâmiha. *Ne İdik, Ne Olduk: Hatıralar.* İstanbul: Hülbe Basım ve Yayın, 1985.

Bali, Rıfat N. *US Diplomatic Documents on Turkey IV: New Documents on Atatürk. Atatürk As Viewed through the Eyes of American Diplomats.* İstanbul: ISIS Press, 2007.

Balkan, Arif. *Cumhuriyet Türkiye'sinin İnşası: Anılar.* İstanbul: Papirüs Yayınları, 1996.

Balkır, S. Edip. *Eski Bir Öğretmenin Anıları, 1908–1940.* İstanbul: Arı Kitabevi, 1968.

Barbarosoğlu, Fatma K. *Cumhuriyetin Dindar Kadınları.* İstanbul: Profil Yayıncılık, 2009.

Bardakçı, Cemal. *Toprak Dâvasından Siyasî Partilere.* İstanbul: Işıl Matbaası, 1945.

Başar, Ahmet Hamdi. *Atatürk'le Üç Ay ve 1930'dan Sonraki Türkiye.* İstanbul: Tan Matbaası, 1945.

Başgöz, İlhan. *Gemerek Nire Bloomington Nire: Hayat Hikâyem.* İstanbul: İş Bankası Kültür Yayınları, 2017.

Bayar, Celal. *Şark Raporu.* İstanbul: Kaynak Yayınları, 2006.

Bayır, Ferit Oğuz. *Köyün Gücü.* Ankara: Ulusal Basımevi, 1971.

Baykurt, Fakir. *Özüm Çocuktur: Özyaşam 1.* İstanbul: Literatür, 1998.

Bayrı, Mehmet Halid. "Balıkesir'de Dabaklık." *Halk Bilgisi Haberleri* 27 (1933): 58–66.

"Balıkesir'de Keçecilik." *Halk Bilgisi Haberleri* 29 (1933): 120–7.

"Balıkesir'de Pabuçculuk." *Halk Bilgisi Haberleri* 48 (1935): 289–98.

"Balıkesir'de Saraçlık." *Halk Bilgisi Haberleri* 32 (1934): 233–8.

İstanbul Folkloru. İstanbul, Türk Yayınevi, 1947.

Belli, Mihri. *Esas Hadise O Kiraz Ağaçları.* İstanbul: Çiviyazıları, 2002.

Belli, Sevim. *Boşuna mı Çiğnedik? Anılar.* İstanbul: Belge Yayınları, 1994.

Berkes, Mediha. "Köyde Kadının Durumu." *Yurt ve Dünya* 21 (1942): 327–32.

"Üfürükçülük." *Yurt ve Dünya* 9 (1941): 155–63.

Berkes, Niyazi. *Bazı Ankara Köyleri Üzerine Bir Araştırma.* Ankara: Uzluk Basımevi, 1942.

The Development of Secularism in Turkey. Montreal: McGill University Press, 1964.

"Nesebi Sahih Olmayan Çocuklar." *Adliye Ceridesi* 12 (1942): 1396–1404.

Unutulan Yıllar. İstanbul: İletişim Yayınları, 1997.

Beşe, Mehmet Enver. "Safranbolu'da ve Köylerinde Aile." *Halk Bilgisi Haberleri* 44 (1935): 177–92.

"Safranbolu'da Bir Köylünün Hayatı I." *Halk Bilgisi Haberleri* 89–90 (1939): 102–11.

"Safranbolu'da Bir Köylünün Hayatı II." *Halk Bilgisi Haberleri* 91 (1939): 144–51.

Bilbaşar, Kemal. *Cemo*. İstanbul: Tekin Yayınevi, 1966.

Memo. İstanbul: Tekin Yayınevi, 1970.

Binyazar, Adnan. *Masalını Yitiren Dev*. İstanbul: Can Yayınları, 2003.

Boran, Behice. "Köyde Sosyal Tabakalanma." *Yurt ve Dünya* 15–16 (1942): 123–8.

Boratav, Pertev Naili. *Halk Hikâyeleri ve Halk Hikâyeciliği*. İstanbul: MEB, 1946.

"Mudurnu'nun Abant-Dibi Köyleri Üzerine 1940 Yılında Yapılmış Bir İncelemeden Notlar." *Sosyoloji Konferansları, On Yedinci Kitap*, 94–122. İstanbul: İstanbul Ünversitesi İktisat Fakültesi Yayını, 1979.

Bozdağ, İsmet. *Zaferlerle ve Şereflerle Dolu Bir Hayat: Celal Bayar*. İstanbul: Tercüman Yayınları, 1986.

Bozkurt, Kamuran. "Halkevlerine Dair." *Ülkü* 6/36 (1936): 450.

Buğday Koruma Karşılığı Vergisi. İstanbul: T. C. Maliye Vekâleti Varidat Umum Müdürlüğü, 1938.

Cillov, Halûk. *Denizli El Dokumacılığı Sanayii*. İstanbul: İÜ İktisat Fakültesi İktisat ve İçtimaiyat Enstitüsü Neşriyatından-İsmail Akgün Matbaası, 1949.

Cumalı, Necati. *Acı Tütün*. İstanbul: E Yayınları, 1975.

Tütün Zamanı. İstanbul: Remzi Kitabevi, 1959.

Zeliş. İstanbul: Cem Yayınevi, 1971.

Çalgüner, Cemil. *Türkiye'de Ziraat İşçileri*. Ankara: Ankara Yüksek Ziraat Enstitüsü Rektörlüğü Yayını, 1943.

Çem, Munzur. *Qurzeli Usiv'in 70 Yılı*. İstanbul: İletişim Yayınları, 2014.

Çerkezyan, Sarkis. *Dünya Hepimize Yeter*. Ed. Yasemin Gedik. 2nd ed. İstanbul: Belge Yayınları, 2003.

Demir, Azmi. "Adana'da Orman Kaçakçılığı." *Verim* 7–8 (1935): 5–7.

Diken, Şeyhmus. *İsyan Sürgünleri*. İstanbul: İletişim, 2005.

Dinç, Güney. *Aydınlığa Mektuplar (1928–1937)*. İstanbul: Yapı Kredi Yayınları, 2010.

Ecevid, Fahri. "Suçluluk Bakımından Köylümüzün Ruhi Yapılışı." *Polis Dergisi* 3/4 (1938): 43–51.

Effimianidis, Yorğaki. *Cihan İktisad Buhranı Önünde Türkiye*. İstanbul: Kaadçılık ve Matbaacılık Anonim Şirketi, 1935–6.

[Ekinci], Salih Zeki. *Türkiye'de Tütün*. İstanbul, 1928.

Ekinci, Tarık Ziya. *Lice'den Paris'e Anılarım*. İstanbul: İletişim Yayınları, 2013.

Ekrem, Selma. *Turkey, Old and New*. New York: C. Scribner's Sons, 1947.

Emiroğlu, Cezmi. *Türkiye'de Vergi Sistemi: İnhisarlar ve Devlet Emlaki*. Ankara: Damga Matbaası, 1933.

Türkiye'de Vergi Sistemi: Vasıtasız Vergiler. Ankara: Damga Matbaası, 1932.

Enç, Mitat. *Selamlık Sohbetleri.* İstanbul: Ötüken Neşriyat, 2007.

Erhan, Halil. *1915'ten 1980'e Karadeniz: Ermeniler, Eşkıyalar, İnsanlar, Yaşamlar.* İstanbul: İletişim Yayınları, 2016.

Erk, Hasan Basri. *Kaçakçılık İşleri.* İstanbul: Cumhuriyet Matbaası, 1946.

Erkal, Pertev. "Pozantı-Toros Ormanlarında Gördüklerim." *Verim* 3 (1935): 10.

Esen, Bülent Nuri. *Türk İş Hukuku.* Ankara: Maarif Matbaası for Ankara Üniversitesi Hukuk Fakültesi, 1944.

Esenel, Mediha. *Geç Kalmış Kitap: 1940'lı Yıllarda Anadolu Köylerinde Araştırmalar ve Yaşadığım Çevreden İzlenimler.* İstanbul: Sistem Yayıncılık, 1999.

Eyriboz, Nihat. "Plansız Köycülük Yerine Planlı Köycülük." *Hep Bu Topraktan 5* (1944): 102–4.

Fahri, Rükneddin. *Doğu Köylerinde Tetkikler.* İstanbul: Çığır Kitabevi, 1938.

Gençosman, Kemal Zeki. *Altın Yıllar.* İstanbul: Hür Yayınları, 1981.

Gezi Notları: Çanakkale-Bolayır, İzmir Köyleri ve Orta Anadolu. İstanbul: Asri Basımevi, 1935.

Gökdemir, Oryal. *Annemin Anlattıkları.* İstanbul: Arkın Kitabevi, 1998.

[Gölpınarlı], Abdülbaki. *Cumhuriyet Çocuğunun Din Dersleri, 3. Sınıf.* İstanbul: Teyeffüz Kütüphanesi, 1929.

Melâmîlik ve Melâmîer. İstanbul: Gri Yayın, 1992.

Grew, Joseph C. *Atatürk ve Yeni Türkiye (1927–1932).* Trans. Gülşen Ulutekin and Kamil Yüceoral. İstanbul: Gündoğan Yayınları, 2002.

Günay, Behçet. "Şeker." *Ülkü* 31 (1935): 79–80.

Güntekin, Reşat Nuri. *Anadolu Notları.* İstanbul: İnkılâp Kitabevi, 1998. (First publication in 1936).

Hançerlioğlu, Orhan. *Karanlık Dünya – Ekilmemiş Topraklar.* İstanbul: Varlık Yayınevi, 1954.

Hasan Fehmi. "Tanrıya Arzuhâl." *Halk Bilgisi Haberleri* 28 (1933): 104–5.

[Hatipoğlu], Şevket Raşit. "Meşelerin Cenaze Alayı." *Verim* 5 (1935): 10.

Türkiye'de Ziraî Buhran. Ankara: Yüksek Ziraat Enstitüsü, 1936.

"Ziraatimizde Kâhyalar İdaresi." *Dönüm* 42 (1936): 235–9.

Hines, Walker D., ed. *Türkiye'nin İktisadi Bakımdan Umumi Bir Tetkiki (1933–1934).* Vols. 5–7. Ankara: Mehmet İhsan Matbaası, 1936.

Hurşit, Sait. "Gaziantep'te Halk İnanmaları." *Halk Bilgisi Haberleri* 29 (1933): 127–33.

Işıksoluğu, Mehmet Ali. *Geçmişten Günümüze Aydoğdu Köyü ve Söz Dağarcığı.* Ankara: Payda Yayıncılık, 2013.

[İnan], Abdülkadir. *Birinci İlmi Seyahate Dair Rapor-Türk Halk Bilgisine Ait Maddeler IV.* İstanbul: İktisat Matbaası, 1930.

"Köy ve Köylüler." *Ülkü* 35 (1936): 375–85.

İnan, Arı. *Tarihe Tanıklık Edenler: Cumhuriyet'in Kurucu Kuşağıyla Söyleşiler.* İstanbul: İş Bankası Kültür Yayınları, 2017.

İnan, Müşfika. "Urfa'da Ziyaret Yerleri II." *Halk Bilgisi Haberleri* 100 (1940): 77–9.

İsvan, Ahmet. *Köprüler, Gelip Geçmeye: Tarımda Bir Modernleşme Öyküsü.* İstanbul: İş Bankası Kültür Yayınları, 2015.

Kara, İsmail, ed. *Kutuz Hoca'nın Hatıraları: Cumhuriyet Devrinde Bir Köy Hocası.* İstanbul: Dergâh Yayınları, 2000.

Karabuda, Barbro. *Goodbye to the Fez: A Portrait of Modern Turkey.* Trans. Maurice Michael. London: Denis Dobson, 1959.

Karacan, Ali Naci. "Ağaç." *Verim* 3 (1935): 11.

Karacık, Münir, ed. *İnhisarlar Mevzuatı.* İstanbul: İnhisarlar Umum Müdürlüğü, 1944.

Karakoç, Sarkis, ed. *Sicilli Kavanini.* Vol. 18. İstanbul: Cihan Kitaphanesi, 1938.

Karslı, M. Ferid. *Köy Öğretmeninin Anıları.* Ankara: Köyhocası Basımevi, 1935.

[Kaygılı], Osman Cemal. "Esnaf Arasında Köşe Kapmaca." *Esnaf Meslek Mecmuası* 10 (1934): 16–17.

Kayra, Cahit. *'38 Kuşağı: Cumhuriyet'le Yetişenler.* İstanbul: İş Bankası Kültür Yayınları, 2002.

——. *Sümbül Dağı'nın Karları: 1946 Yılında Bir Hakkâri Seyahati.* İstanbul: Tarihçi Kitabevi, 2014.

Kâzım, Musa. "Anadolu Hurafeleri." *Halk Bilgisi Haberleri* 48 (1935): 314–20.

Kemal, Orhan. *Avare Yıllar.* 13th ed. İstanbul: Epsilon Yayınevi, 2005 (First publication in 1950).

——. *Bereketli Topraklar Üzerinde.* İstanbul: Remzi Kitabevi, 1954.

Kemal, Yaşar. *İnce Memed.* Vol. 1. İstanbul: Çağlayan, 1955.

——. *Sarı Defterdekiler: Folklor Denemeleri.* Ed. Alpay Kabacalı. İstanbul: Türkiye İş Bankası Kültür Yayınları, 2002.

Kessler, Gerhard. "Türk İş İstatistikleri." *İstanbul Üniversitesi İktisat Fakültesi Dergisi* 4/1 (1942): 236–54.

Koç, Bekir, İsmail Çetinkaya and Eftal Şükrü Batmaz. *Osmanlı Ormancılığı İle İlgili Belgeler I.* Ankara: Orman Bakanlığı Yayınları, 1999.

Koraltürk, Murat, ed. *Ahmet Hamdi Başar'ın Hatıraları: "Gazi Bana Çok Kızmış!"* İstanbul: İstanbul Bilgi Üniversitesi Yayınları, 2007.

Korle, Sinan. *Kızıltoprak Günlerim.* İstanbul: İletişim Yayınları, 1997.

Koşay, Hâmit Zübeyr. *Türkiye Türk Düğünleri Üzerine Mukayeseli Malzeme.* Ankara: T. C. Maarif Vekilliği, Eski Eserler ve Müzeler Umum Müdürlüğü Yayınları, 1944.

Kosova, Zehra. *Ben İşçiyim.* İstanbul: İletişim Yayınları, 1996.

"Köyde Ağalık Meselesi," *Yurt ve Dünya*, 17 (1942): 164.

[Köylü], Kâzım Rıza. *Türkiye Ziraati ve Türkiye Ziraatinin Mühim Şubeleri.* Ankara: T. C. Yüksek Ziraat Enstitüsü Yayını, 1935.

Kudar, Hasan. *Tahtakuşlar'dan Paris'e.* İstanbul: İletişim Yayınları, 2001.

Kutluk, H. N. "Tahtacılar." *Verim* 4 (1935): 6–9.

Linke, Lilo. *Allah Dethroned.* London: Constable, 1937.

Madanoğlu, Cemal. *Anılar (1911–1938).* İstanbul: Çağdaş Yayınları, 1982.

Madaralı, Fikret. *Ekmekli Dönemeç.* İstanbul: Hür Yayınevi, 1965.

Makal, Mahmut. *A Village in Anatolia.* Ed. Paul Stirling. Trans. Sir Wyndham Deedes. London: Valentine, Mitchell and Company, 1954.

[Malkoç], Sadullah. "Orman Teşkilatı." *Ziraat Gazetesi* 9–10/47 (1933): 468–72.

Mango, Andrew. *Atatürk.* London: John Murray, 1999.

Mehmet, Zeki. *Mıntıkamızın Kitabı: Güzel İzmir ve İzmir İktisadi Mıntıkasının Tabii Hazineleri, Ticari, Sınai ve Mali Vaziyeti.* İzmir: İzmir Ticaret ve Sanayi Odası Yayını, 1930.

Mimaroğlu, M. Reşat. *Gördüklerim ve Geçirdiklerim'den: Memurluk Hayatımın Hatıraları.* Ankara: T. C. Ziraat Bankası Matbaası, 1946.

Miroğlu, Orhan. *Hevsel Bahçesinde Bir Dut Ağacı: Canip Yıldırım'la Söyleşi.* İstanbul: İletişim Yayınları, 2005.

Montagu, Lady Mary Wortley. *The Complete Letters of Lady Mary Wortley Montagu.* Vol. 1. Ed. Robert Halsband. Oxford: Clarendon Press, 1965–7.

Nar, Ali. *Anadolu Günlüğü.* İstanbul: Beyan Yayınları, 1998.

Nesin, Aziz. *Böyle Gelmiş Böyle Gitmez 1: Yol.* İstanbul: Adam Yayınları, 1998 (First publication in 1966).

   Böyle Gelmiş Böyle Gitmez 2: Yokuşun Başı. İstanbul: Adam Yayınları, 1998 (First publication in 1976).

Newman, Bernard. *Turkish Crossroads.* London: Robert Hale, 1951.

Neyzi, Nezih H. *Osmanlı'dan Cumhuriyet'e Kızıltoprak Anıları.* İstanbul: İş Bankası Kültür Yayınları, 2009.

Nihal, Şukûfe. *Domaniç Dağlarının Yolcusu.* İstanbul: L&M Yayınları, 2007.

Nur, Rıza. *Hayat ve Hatıratım.* Vol. 4. İstanbul: Altındağ Yayınevi, 1967–8.

Oksal, Esad Muhlis. "Ormancılığın Ulusal Ekonomideki Vazifeleri I." *Verim* 1 (1935): 2–3.

   "Ormancılığın Ulusal Ekonomideki Vazifeleri II." *Verim* 4 (1935): 4–5.

"On Beş Yıl Zarfında Cumhuriyet Zabıtasının Çalışmaları Hakkında Rapor – Emniyet İşleri." *İdare – Dâhiliye Vekâletinin Aylık Mecmuası-Cumhuriyetin On Beşinci Yıl Dönümü Münasebetile Fevkalâde Nüsha* 127 (1938): 11–63.

Orga, İrfan. *Bir Türk Ailesinin Öyküsü*. İstanbul: Ana Yayıncılık, 2002. (First Publication is *Portrait of a Turkish Family*, London, 1950).

Osman, F. "Muallimlerin Mesken Bedelleri." *Muallimler Mecmuası* 12/38–9 (1935): 208.

Önus, Muammer. "İstanbul'da Bazı Ziyaret Yerleri." *Halk Bilgisi Haberleri* 105 (1940): 218–25.

Örik, Nahid Sırrı. *Anadolu'da: Yol Notları – Kayseri, Kırşehir, Kastamonu – Bir Edirne Seyahatnamesi*. İstanbul: Arma Yayınları, 2000 (First publication İstanbul, Kanaat Kitabevi, 1939).

Övünç, F. "Zilân Asilerinden Reşo Çetesinin Takip ve Tenkilinde Hangi Usuller Tatbik Olundu ve Nasıl Yapıldı." *Jandarma Karakol Mecmuası* 15 (1939): 5–20.

Özeke, Ahmet Doğan. *Bir Neyzenin Hatıraları: Neyzenler Kahvesi*. İstanbul: Pan Yayıncılık, 2000.

Özer, Sabri. *Toprağın Sancısı*. İstanbul: Logos Yayınları, 2008.

Özsoy, İskender. *İki Vatan Yorgunları: Mübadele Acısını Yaşayanlar Anlatıyor*. İstanbul: Bağlam Yayınları, 2003.

Patton, Marcie J. "US Advisory Aid to Turkey: The Hines-Kemmerer Mission, 1933–1934." *The United States and the Middle East: Diplomatic and Economic Relations in Perspective*. Ed. Abbas Amanat, 69–86. New Haven: Yale Center for International and Area Studies, 2000.

[Pekel] Ali Galip. "Köylü." *Ülkü* 10 (1933): 327–32.

Pekolcay, Necla. *Geçtim Dünya Üzerinden*. İstanbul: L&M Yayınları, 2005.

Reşat, Enis. *Toprak Kokusu*. İstanbul: Örgün Yayınevi, 2002 (First publication İstanbul, Semih Lûtfi Kitabevi, 1944).

Saran, Ali Kemal. *Omuzumda Hemençe: Cumhuriyet Devrinde Bir Medrese Talebesinin Hatıraları*. Ankara: Kurtuba Yayınları, 2010.

Sarç, Celal Ömer. *Ziraat ve Sanayi Siyaseti*. İstanbul: İstanbul Yüksek İktisat ve Ticaret Mektebi, 1934.

Schöpfer, Walter (Professor Schöpfer). "Ormanların Medeniyete Hizmetleri." *Verim* 5 (1935): 9.

Seal, Jeremy. *A Fez of the Heart: Travels around Turkey in Search of a Hat*. London: Picador, 1996.

Seçkin, A. Hilmi. *Bir Hâkime Yakışanı Yazdım*. İstanbul: Literatür Yayınları, 2018.

Selamoğlu, Ayten, and Esra Üstündağ Selamoğlu. *Tayinlerle Anadolu*. İstanbul: Ceres Yayınları, 2017.

[Selen], Hâmit Sadi. *İktisadi Türkiye: Tabii, Beşeri ve Mevzii Coğrafya Tetkikleri*. İstanbul: Yüksek İktisat ve Ticaret Mektebi Yayınları, 1932.

Serdengeçti, O. Yüksel. *Bir Nesli Nasıl Mahvettiler*. İstanbul: TEDEV Yayınları, 2018.

Serim, Nazmi. *Siyasi Polis Hizmeti, İstihbarat II: İç İstihbarat.* Ankara: Alâeddin Kıral Basımevi, 1941.

Sertel, Yıldız. *Ardımdaki Yıllar.* İstanbul: İletişim Yayınları, 2001.

Sertel, Zekeriya. *Hatırladıklarım.* İstanbul: Gözlem Yayınları, 1977.

Shah, Sirdar Ikbal Ali. *Kamal: Maker of Modern Turkey.* London: H. Joseph, 1934.

Soyak, Hasan Rıza. *Atatürk'ten Hatıralar.* İstanbul: Yapı Kredi Yayınları, 2004.

Subaşı, Muhsin İlyas. *Kayseri'nin Manevi Mimarları.* Ankara: Türkiye Diyanet Vakfı, 1995.

Sümerbank. *Cumhuriyet'in 25'inci Yılı.* İstanbul: Kulen Basımevi, 1948.

Şahingiray, Özel. *Celal Bayar'ın Söylev ve Demeçleri, 1920–1953.* İstanbul: Türkiye İş Bankası Yayınları, 1954.

Şahinkaya, Rezan. *Orta Anadolu Köylerinde Aile Strüktürü.* Ankara: AÜ Ziraat Fakültesi Yayınları, 1966.

[Şanda], Hüseyin Avni. *1908'de Ecnebi Sermayesine Karşı İlk Kalkınmalar.* İstanbul: Akşam Matbaası, 1935.

"Harp Senesi İçinde Fabrikalarımızın Faaliyeti Arttı mı Azaldı mı?" *İktisadi Yürüyüş* 27 (1941): 11.

"İş Kanunu Nasıl Tatbik Ediliyor?" *Yeni Adam* 201 (1937): 4.

"Kauçuk ve Deri Meselesi." *Yeni Adam* 24 (1934): 9.

Şevki, Mehmet Ali. *Kurna Köyü (Kocaeli Yarımadası) Monografisinden Üç Makale.* Siyasi İlimler Mecmuası 77–9 and 90 (1936–9).

Tahir, Kemal. *Rahmet Yolları Kesti.* İstanbul: Düşün, 1957.

Sağırdere. Ankara: Bilgi Yayınevi, 1971.

Tanç, Salahattin. *Bir Cumhuriyet Askerinin Anıları.* İstanbul: Doğan Kitap, 2017.

Tanju, Sadun. *Doludizgin: Milliyet'in Kurucusu Naci Karacan-Bir Gazetecinin Hayatı.* İstanbul. İş Bankası Kültür Yayınları, 2018.

Tanman, Saffet. *Batnas Tepelerinde Zaman.* İstanbul: YKY, 2005.

Ilgaz Dağlarından Batnas Tepelerine. İstanbul: YKY, 2008.

Taşçıoğlu, Sabiha, Fahrettin Kıyak, Sadi Kazancı and Ömer Faik Güven. *İçtihatlı ve İzahlı Ceza Hükümlerini Muhtevi Kanun ve Nizamnameler.* Vol. 2. Ankara: Yıldız Matbaası, 1955.

Taşpınar, Adnan Halet, ed. *The Tobacco Affairs.* Ankara: State Monopolies of Turkey, 1939.

Tesal, Reşat Dürri. *Selânik'ten İstanbul'a Bir Ömrün Hikâyesi.* İstanbul: İletişim Yayınları, 1998.

Tevfik, İhsan. *İnsan ve Mekân Yüzüyle Mübadele: 1923'ten Bugüne Zorunlu Göç.* İstanbul: İnkılap Kitabevi, 2017.

Toksoy, Ali Enver. "Cenup Hudutlarımızda Kaçakçılık." *Resimli Ay* 28 (1938): 20–2.

Topçuoğlu, İbrahim Sırrı. *Savaş Yarası: Anılar ve Hikâyeler.* İstanbul: Güryay Matbaası, 1977.

Toroslar, Ferman. *Sürgün: İsyan Ateşinden Geçen Mutkili Bir Ermeni Aile.* İstanbul: Aras, 2013.

Toygar, Süreyya. "Kaçak Mes'elesi." *Verim* 7–8 (1935): 16.

"Kaçakçılık İşleri II." *Verim* 11 (1936): 4–5.

[Tökin] İsmail Hüsrev. *Türkiye Köy İktisadiyatı.* İstanbul: Matbaacılık ve Neşriyat Türk Anonim Şirketi, 1934.

Tuğal, B. Sıtkı. "Yine Köy Kanunu Tasarısı Hakkında." *Türk İdare Dergisi* 22/212 (1951): 14–30.

Tuna, Orhan. "İş İstatistikleri." İstanbul Üniversitesi İktisat Fakültesi Mecmuası 6/1–2 (1944–5): 325–48.

Turan, Kemal. *Yeni Vergi Kanunları'nın Tatbiki Mahiyeti ve Tediye Kabiliyeti Hakkında Tahliller.* İzmir: Hafız Ali Matbaası, 1931.

Turgut, Hulûsi, ed. *Atatürk'ün Sırdaşı Kılıç Ali'nin Anıları.* İstanbul: İş Bankası Kültür Yayınları, 2005.

Türkoğlu, Ömer. "Hüseyin Sami Bey'in Hayatı ve Ankara'daki Ajanlık Yılları." *Kebikeç* 4 (1996): 215–22.

Türkoğlu, Pakize. *Kızlar da Yanmaz. Genç Cumhuriyet'te Köy Çocuğu Olmak.* İstanbul: İş Bankası Kültür Yayınları, 2011.

Tütengil, Cavit Orhan. "Keçiller Köyü İncelemesi." *Sosyoloji Dergisi* 10–11 (1955): 36–43.

Uğurlu, Kâmil. *Kahramanmaraş Şehrengizi: Bir Maraş Güzellemesi.* İstanbul: TEDEV, 2018.

Uluğ, Naşit Hakkı. *Tunceli Medeniyete Açılıyor.* İstanbul: Kaynak Yayınları, 2007 (First edition, Cumhuriyet Matbaası, 1939).

Uluğer, A. Nazi. *Polisin İdari, Siyasi, Adli Görevleri ve Tatbikatı.* Ankara: Doğuş Matbaası, 1950.

Uran, Hilmi. *Adana Ziraat Amelesi.* İstanbul: Vakit Kitabevi, 1939.

Hatıralarım. Ankara: Ayyıldız Matbaası, 1959.

[Uryani], Ali Vahit. "Kemal Ümmi Hakkında." *Halk Bilgisi Haberleri,* 31 (1933): 212–17.

Us, Asım. *Asım Us'un Hatıra Notları: 1930'dan 1950 Yılına Kadar Atatürk ve İsmet İnönü Devirlerine Ait Seçme Fıkralar.* İstanbul: Vakit Matbaası, 1966.

Uyguner, Muzaffer. "Zuhuri ve Şiirleri." *Türk Folklor Araştırmaları* 69 (1955): 1093–4.

Vahdi, A. "Lastik Ayakkapların Yerli Sanayiye Verdiği Zararlar." *Esnaf Meslek Mecmuası* 7 (1934): 14–16.

Varlık, Bülent, ed. *Ali Tunalı: Vatana Hizmette 70 Yıl.* İstanbul: Tarih Vakfı Yurt Yayınları, 2005.

Varol, Muharrem. *Tekkede Zaman: Üsküdar'da Rifâi Sandıkçı Dergâhı ve Vukuât-ı Tekâyâ.* İstanbul: Dergâh Yayınları, 2017.

Velidedeoğlu, H. Veldet. "The Reception of the Swiss Civil Code in Turkey." *UNESCO International Social Science Bulletin* 9/1 (1957): 60–5.

Vett, Carl. *Dervişler Arasında İki Hafta: Danimarkalı Parapsikoloğun 1925 Yılında İstanbul'daki Kelâmî Dergâhı'nda Başından Geçen Son Derece İlginç Olaylar.* Trans. Ethem Cebecioğlu. İstanbul: Kaknüs Yayınları, 2004 (The first publication is in 1925 in Danish).

[Yalman], Ahmed Emin. *The Development of Modern Turkey As Measured by Its Press.* New York: Columbia University, AMS Press, 1914.

Turkey in the World War. New Haven, CT: Yale University Press, 1930.

Yasa, İbrahim. *Hasanoğlan Köyü'nün İçtimaî-İktisadî Yapısı.* Ankara: Doğuş Ltd. O. Matbaası for Türkiye ve Orta Doğu Amme İdaresi Enstitüsü, 1955.

Sindel Köyü'nün Toplumsal ve Ekonomik Yapısı. Ankara: Türkiye ve Orta Doğu Amme İdaresi Enstitüsü, 1960.

Yavuz, Fehmi. *Anılarım.* Ankara: Mülkiyeliler Birliği Vakfı Yayınları, [n.d.].

Yelmen, Hasan. *Kazlıçeşme'de 50 Yıl.* İstanbul: Ezgi Ajans, 1998.

Yesari, Mahmut. *Çulluk.* İstanbul: Sühulet Kitaphanesi, 1927.

Yiğiter, Ümran Nazif [Zonguldak Milli Korunma Mahkemesi C.M.U. Muavini]. *Kömür Havzasında Amele Hukuku.* Zonguldak: n.p. 1943.

Yıldız, Celal. *Dersim Dile Geldi: 1938'in Çocukları Konuştu.* 2nd ed. İstanbul: Su Yayınları, 2008.

Yorulmaz, Hüseyin. *Bir Neslin Öncüsü: Celal Hoca.* İstanbul: Hat Yayınevi, 2011.

Yund, Kerim. "Ermenâk Ceviz Ağaçları." *Verim* 7–8 (1935): 8–11.

Zhukovski, Peter Mihailovich. *Türkiye'nin Zirai Bünyesi.* Ankara: Türkiye Şeker Fabrikaları, 1951.

Zoga, F. Ziya, and Hikmet Muradoğlu. *Yargıtay'ın Hususi Kanun ve Nizamnamelere Ait Yaşayan Bütün İçtihat ve Kararları.* Vol. 2. Ankara: Yeni Cezaevi Matbaası, 1949.

Zorlutuna, Halide Nusret. *Bir Devrin Romanı.* Ankara: Kültür Bakanlığı Yayınları, 1978.

Other Sources

Ahmad, Feroz. "The Development of Working-Class Consciousness in Turkey." *Workers and Working Classes in the Middle East: Struggles, Histories, Historiographies.* Ed. Zachary Lockman, 133–64. New York: State University of New York Press, 1993.

The Making of Modern Turkey. London and New York: Routledge, 1993.

Ahmida, Ali Abdullatif, ed. *Beyond Colonialism and Nationalism in the Maghrib: History, Culture and Politics.* New York: Palgrave, 2000.

Akçam, Taner. *The Young Turks' Crime against Humanity: The Armenian Genocide and Ethnic Cleansing in the Ottoman Empire.* Princeton, NJ: Princeton University Press, 2012.

Akçetin, Elif. "Anatolian Peasants in the Great Depression, 1929–1933." *New Perspectives on Turkey* 23 (2000): 79–102.

Akıltepe, Habil, Sabri Malkoç and İhsan Molbay. *Türkiye'de Şeker Sanayi ve Şeker Pancarı Ziraati.* Ankara: Mars Matbaası, 1964.

Akın, Yiğit. "Reconsidering State, Party, and Society in Early Republican Turkey: Politics of Petitioning." *International Journal of Middle East Studies* 39/3 (2007): 435–57.

Akkaya, Yüksel. "İşçi Sınıfı ve Sendikacılık." *Praksis* 5 (2002): 131–76.

"Cumhuriyetin Kuruluş Yıllarında Düzen ve Kalkınma Kıskacında Emek." *Cumhuriyet Tarihinin Tartışmalı Konuları.* Ed. Bülent Bilmez, 245–76. İstanbul: Tarih Vakfı Yurt Yayınları, 2013.

Akkaya, Yüksel, and Metin Altıok. "Çukurova'da İşçi Hareketi ve Sendikacılık." *Türkiye Sendikacılık Ansiklopedisi.* Vol. 1. 249–53. Ankara: Kültür Bakanlığı, and İstanbul: Türkiye Ekonomik ve Toplumsal Tarih Vakfı, 1996–8.

Aksoy, Suat. *100 Soruda Türkiye'de Toprak Meselesi.* İstanbul: Gerçek Yayınevi, 1971.

Akşit, Elif Ekin. "Ankara'nın Kılıkları, 1930: Boydan Boya Bir Karşı Koyma." *Sanki Viran Ankara.* Ed. Funda Şenol Cantek, 149–74. İstanbul: İletişim Yayınları, 2006.

Aktar, Ayhan. *Türk Milliyetçiliği, Gayrimüslimler ve Ekonomik Dönüşüm.* İstanbul: İletişim Yayınları, 2006.

Albayrak, Sadık. *İrtica'ın Tarihçesi.* Vols. 4–5. İstanbul: Araştırma Yayınları, 1990.

Türkiye'de Din Kavgası. İstanbul: Sebil Matbaacılık, 1975.

Aswad, Barbara C. "Visiting Patterns among Women of the Elite in a Small Turkish City." *Anthropological Quarterly* 47/1 (1974): 9–27.

Avcı, Ali Haydar, "Bir Sosyal İsyancı: Ekıya Çöllo. Yaşamı ve Destanı." *Folklor/Edebiyat* 11/2 (1997): 31–8.

Ayanoğlu, Sedat, and Yusuf Güneş. *Orman Suçları Ders Kitabı.* İstanbul: İstanbul Üniversitesi, 2003.

Ayaz, Hüseyin. "Türkiye'de Orman Mülkiyetinde Tarihi Süreç ve Avrupa İnsan Hakları Mahkemesi Kararları III." *Ulusal Karadeniz Ormancılık Kongresi* 1, 189–98 (Artvin, May 20–22, 2010).

Aydın, Cemil. *The Idea of the Muslim World: A Global Intellectual History.* Cambridge, MA: Harvard University Press, 2017.

Ayhan, Halis. *Türkiye'de Din Eğitimi.* İstanbul: Dem Yayınları, 2014.

Azak, Umut. "A Reaction to Authoritarian Modernization in Turkey: The Menemen Incident and the Creation and Contestation of a Myth, 1930–31." *The State and the Subaltern: Modernization, Society and the State in Turkey and Iran*. Ed. Touraj Atabaki, 143–58. New York: I. B. Tauris, 2007.

Bakhtin, Mikhail. *The Dialogic Imagination: Four Essays*. Ed. Michael Holquist. Trans. Caryl Emerson and Michael Holquist. Austin: University of Texas Press, 1981.
Speech Genres and Other Late Essays. Trans. Vern W. McGee. Austin: University of Texas Press, 1986.

Barbir, Karl. *Ottoman Rule in Damascus, 1708–1758*. Princeton, NJ: Princeton University Press, 1980.

Barkan, Ömer Lütfi. "'Çiftçiyi Topraklandırma Kanunu' ve Türkiye'de Zirai Bir Reformun Ana Meseleleri." *Türkiye'de Toprak Meselesi: Toplu Eserler 1*, 449–521. İstanbul: Gözlem Yayınları, 1980 (Original version in *İktisat Fakültesi Mecmuası*, 6/1–2, 1946: 54–145).

Barkey, Karen. *Bandits and Bureaucrats: The Ottoman Route to State Centralization*. Ithaca, NY, and London: Cornell University Press, 1994.

Baumqarten, Linda. *What Clothes Reveal: The Language of Clothing in Colonial and Federal America*. New Haven, CT: Yale University Press, 2012.

Bayar, Yeşim. "The Dynamic Nature of Educational Policies and Turkish Nation-Building: Where Does Religion Fit In?" *Secular State and Religious Society*. Ed. Berna Turam, 19–38. New York: Palgrave Macmillan, 2012.

Bayat, Asef. *Life As Politics: How Ordinary People Change the Middle East*. Stanford, CA: Stanford University Press, 2013.
Street Politics: Poor People's Movements in Iran. New York: Columbia University Press, 1997.

Baydar, Mustafa Çetin. *Geçidi Bekleyen Şehir, Erzurum*. Ankara: Akçağ, 1997.

Baykara, Tuncer. *Osmanlılarda Medeniyet Kavramı*. İstanbul. IQ Kültür Sanat Yayınları, 2007.

Bayrak, Mehmet. *Eşkiyalık ve Eşkiya Türküleri: İnceleme, Antoloji*. Ankara: Yorum Yayınevi, 1985.
Kürtlere Vurulan Kelepçe: Şark Islahat Planı. Ankara: Özge Yayınları, 2009.
Öykülerle Halk Anlatı Türküleri: İnceleme, Antoloji. Ankara: M. Bayrak, 1996.

Beinin, Joel. *Workers and Peasants in the Modern Middle East*. Cambridge and New York: Cambridge University Press, 2001.

Beinin, Joel, and Frédérich Vairel. "Introduction: The Middle East and North Africa: Beyond Classical Social Movement Theory." *Social Movements, Mobilization, and Contestation in the Middle East and North Africa*. Ed. Joel Benin and Frédérich Vairel, 1–23. Stanford, CA: Stanford University Press, 2011.

Belge, Ceren. "Seeing the State: Kinship Networks and Kurdish Resistance in Early Republican Turkey." *The Everyday Life of the State: A State in Society Approach*. Ed. Adam White, 14–29. Seattle: University of Washington Press, 2013.

Bell, John D. *Peasants in Power: Alexander Stamboliski and the Bulgarian Agrarian National Union, 1899–1923*. Princeton, NJ: Princeton University Press, 1977.

Bender, Cemşid. *Genelkurmay Belgelerinde Kürt İsyanları III*. İstanbul: Kaynak Yayınları, 1992.

Benhabib, Seyla. "Models of Public Space: Hannah Arendt, the Liberal Tradition, and Jurgen Habermas." *Habermas and the Public Sphere*. Ed. Craig Calhoun, 73–98. Cambridge, MA: MIT Press, 1992.

Berik, Günseli, and Cihan Bilginsoy. "The Labor Movement in Turkey: Labor Pains, Maturity, Metamorphosis." *The Social History of Labor in the Middle East*. Ed. Ellis Jay Goldberg, 37–64. Boulder, CO: Westview Press, 1996.

Bertaux, Sandrine. *Ulusu Tasarlamak: 1920'ler ve 1930'larda Avrupa Devletleri / Projecting the Nation: European States in the 1920s and 1930s*. İstanbul: Osmanlı Bankası Arşiv ve Araştırma Merkezi, 2006.

Beşikçi, İsmail. *Doğu Anadolu'nun Düzeni: Sosyoekonomik ve Etnik Temeller*. İstanbul: İsmail Beşikçi Vakfı Yayınları, 2014.

Birtek, Faruk, and Çağlar, Keyder. "Agriculture and the State: An Inquiry into Agricultural Differentiation and Political Alliances: The Case of Turkey." *Journal of Peasant Studies* 2/4 (1975): 447–63.

"Türkiye'de Devlet Tarım İlişkileri (1923–1950)." *Toplumsal Tarih Çalışmaları*. Ed. Çağlar Keyder, 191–220. Ankara: Dost Yayınevi, 1983.

Blok, Anton. "The Peasant and the Brigand: Social Banditry Reconsidered." *Comparative Studies in Society and History* 14/4 (1972): 495–503.

Boratav, Korkut. "Anadolu Köyünde Savaş ve Yıkım: Bekir Eliçin'in Romanının Öğrettikleri ve Düşündürdükleri." *Toplum ve Bilim* 15–16 (1982): 61–75.

Türkiye İktisat Tarihi, 1908–2002. 9th ed. Ankara: İmge Kitabevi, 2005.

Bozarslan, Hamit. "Kurdish Nationalism in Turkey: From Tacit Contract to Rebellion (1919–1925)." *Essays on the Origins of Kurdish Nationalism*. Ed. Abbas Vali. 163–90. Costa Mesa, CA: Mazda, 2003.

Bozdoğan, Sibel. *Modernism and Nation Building: Turkish Architectural Culture in the Early Republic*. Washington, DC: University of Washington Press, 2001.

Brautigam, Deborah A. "Introduction: Taxation and State-Building in Developing Countries." *Taxation and State-Building in Developing Countries: Capacity and Consent*. Ed. Deborah A. Brautigam, Odd-Helge Fjeldstad and Mick Moore, 1–33. New York: Cambridge University Press, 2008.

Brockett, Gavin D. *How Happy to Call Oneself a Turk: Provincial Newspapers and the Negotiation of a Muslim Identity*. Austin: University of Texas Press, 2012.

——— "Revisiting the Turkish Revolution, 1923–1938: Secular Reform and Religious 'Reaction.'" *History Compass* 4/6 (2006): 160–72.

Brophy, James. *Popular Culture and the Public Sphere in the Rhineland 1800–1850*. London: Cambridge University Press, 2007.

Bulut, Faik. *Dersim Raporları*. İstanbul: Evrensel Basım Yayın, 1992.

Bulutay, Tuncer, Yahya Sezai Tezel and Nuri Yıldırım. *Türkiye Milli Geliri: 1923–1948*. Ankara: Ankara Üniversitesi Siyasal Bilgiler Fakültesi Yayını, 1974.

Burg, David F. *A World History of Tax Rebellions: An Encyclopedia of Tax Rebels, Revolts, and Riots from Antiquity to the Present*. New York: Routledge, 2004.

Cantek, Funda Şenol. *"Yaban"lar "Yerli"ler: Başkent Olma Sürecinde Ankara*. İstanbul: İletişim Yayınları, 2003.

Cantek, Levent. "Kabadayıların ve Futbolun Mahallesi Hacettepe." *Sanki Viran Ankara*. Ed. Funda Şenol Cantek, 175–210. İstanbul: İletişim Yayınları, 2006.

Ceylan, Hasan Hüseyin. *Cumhuriyet Dönemi Din-Devlet İlişkileri I*. İstanbul: Risale Yayınları, 1991.

Chalcraft, John T. *Striking Cabbies of Cairo and Other Stories: Crafts and Guilds in Egypt, 1863–1914*. New York: State University of New York Press, 2004.

Chatterjee, Partha. *Nation and Its Fragments: Colonial and Post-colonial Histories*. Princeton, NJ: Princeton University Press, 1993.

Chehabi, Houchang. "The Banning of the Veil and Its Consequences." *The Making of Modern Iran: State and Society under Riza Shah, 1921–1941*. Ed. Stephanie Cronin, 193–210. London: Routledge, 2003.

——— "Dress Codes for Men in Turkey and Iran." *Men of Order, Authoritarian Modernization under Atatürk and Reza Shah*. Ed. Touraj Atabaki and Erik J. Zürcher, 209–37. London and New York: I. B. Tauris, 2004.

Cole, Juan. *Colonialism and Revolution in the Middle East: Social and Cultural Origins of Egypt's 'Urabi Movement.* Princeton, NJ: Princeton University Press, 1993.

Connerton, Paul. *How Societies Remember.* Cambridge and New York: Cambridge University Press, 1989.

Coxe, Anthony D. Hippisley. *Smuggling in the West Country, 1700–1850.* Exeter: A. Wheaton and Company, 1984.

Cronin, Stephanie. "Noble Robbers, Avengers and Entrepreneurs: Eric Hobsbawm and Banditry in Iran, the Middle East and the North Africa." *Middle Eastern Studies* 52/5 (2016): 845–70.

"Resisting the New State: The Rural Poor, Land and Modernity in Iran, 1921–1941." *Subalterns and Social Protest: History from Below in the Middle East and North Africa.* Ed. Stephanie Cronin, 141–70. New York: Routledge, 2008.

Cronin, Stephanie, ed. *Anti-veiling Campaigns in the Muslim World: Gender, Modernism, and the Politics of Dress.* New York: Routledge, 2014.

Cündioğlu, Dücane. *Meşrutiyetten Cumhuriyete Din ve Siyaset.* İstanbul: Kaknüs Yayınları, 2005.

Türkçe Kur'an ve Cumhuriyet İdeolojisi. İstanbul: Kitabevi, 1998.

Çalışkan, Koray. "'Organism and Triangle': A Short History of Labor Law in Turkey (1920–1950)." *New Perspectives on Turkey* 15 (1996): 95–118.

Çetin, Güneş, "Vergi Aflarının Vergi Mükelleflerinin Tutum ve Davranışları Üzerindeki Etkisi." *Yönetim ve Ekonomi* 14/2 (2007): 171–87.

Çıladır, Sina. *Zonguldak Havzasının Tarihi Gelişimi.* Zonguldak: Genel Maden-İş Yayınları, 1994.

Çınar, Alev. *Modernity, Islam, and Secularism in Turkey.* Minneapolis: University of Minnesota Press, 2005.

Çoker, Fahri. *Türk Parlamento Tarihi: TBMM IV. Dönem (1931–1935).* Vol. 1. Ankara: Türkiye Büyük Millet Meclisi Vakfı, 1996.

Darendelioğlu, İlhan E. *Türkiye'de Komünist Hareketleri.* İstanbul: Toprak Yayınları, 1961.

Darnton, Robert. "An Early Information Society: News and the Media in Eighteenth-Century Paris." *American Historical Review* 105/1 (2000): 1–35.

The Great Cat Massacre and Other Episodes of French Cultural History. New York: Vintage Books, 1985.

Davies, Sarah. *Popular Opinion in Stalin's Russia: Terror, Propaganda and Dissent, 1934–1941.* Cambridge: Cambridge University Press, 1997.

Davis, Fanny. *Osmanlı Hanımı: 1718'den 1918'e Bir Toplumsal Tarih.* İstanbul: Yapı Kredi Yayınları, 2006.

Davison, Andrew. *Türkiye'de Sekülarizm ve Modernlik: Hermenötik Bir Yeniden Değerlendirme*. Trans. Tuncay Birkan. İstanbul: İletişim Yayınları, 2002.

Dehne, Harald. "Have We Come Any Closer to *Alltag*? Everyday Reality and Workers' Lives as an Object of Historical Research in the German Democratic Republic." *The History of Everyday Life: Reconstructing Historical Experiences and Ways of Life*. Ed. Alf Lüdtke. Trans. William Templer, 116–49. Princeton, NJ: Princeton University Press, 1995.

Demirel, Fatmagül. "Osmanlı Devleti'nde Tuz Gelirlerinin Düyûn-ı Umumiye'ye Devredilmesinden Sonra Tuz Kaçakçılığı." *İstanbul Üniversitesi Yakın Dönem Türkiye Araştırmaları Dergisi* 1 (2002): 147–57.

Dobb, Maurice. *Studies in the Development of Capitalism*. London: George Routledge & Sons, 1946.

Doğruel, Fatma, and A. Suut Doğruel. *Osmanlı'dan Günümüze Tekel*. İstanbul: Tarih Vakfı Yurt Yayınları, 2000.

Dölen, Emre, and Murat Koraltürk. *İlk Çimento Fabrikamızın Öyküsü, 1910–2004*. İstanbul: Lafarge Aslan Çimento, 2004.

Duben, Alan, and Cem Behar. *İstanbul Households: Marriage, Family and Fertility (1880–1940)*. New York: Cambridge University Press, 1991.

Duman, Doğan. "Cumhuriyet Baloları." *Toplumsal Tarih* 37 (1997): 44–8.

Durakbaşa, Ayşe, and Aynur İlyasoğlu. "Formation of Gender Identities in Republican Turkey and Women's Narratives as Transmitters of 'Herstory' of Modernization." *Journal of Social History* 35/1 (2001): 195–203.

Dural, Halil. *Bize Derler Çakırca: 19. ve 20. Yüzyılda Ege'de Eşkıyalar*. İstanbul: Tarih Vakfı Yurt Yayınları, 1999.

Ege, Rıdvan. *Türkiye'nin Sağlık Hizmetleri ve İsmet Paşa*. Ankara: Türk Hava Kurumu Basımevi, 1992.

Egesoy, Muzaffer. *Cumhuriyet Devrinde Vasıtasız Vergiler*. Ankara: Siyasal Bilgiler Fakültesi Maliye Enstitüsü, 1962.

Ekin, Nusret. "Memleketimizde İşçi Devri Mevzuunda Yapılan Araştırmalar ve Ortaya Koydukları Neticeler." *Sosyal Siyaset Konferansları, 9–10-11. Kitap*, 123–92. İstanbul: İstanbul Üniversitesi İktisat Fakültesi, 1960.

Eldem, Vedat. *Osmanlı İmparatorluğu'nun İktisadi Şartları Hakkında Bir Tetkik*. Ankara: Türk Tarih Kurumu Yayınları, 1994.

Eley, Geoff, and Keith Nield. "Why Does Social History Ignore Politics?" *Social History* 5/2 (1980): 249–71.

Emrence, Cem. *Serbest Cumhuriyet Fırkası: 99 Günlük Muhalefet*. İstanbul: İletişim Yayınları, 2006.

Ergut, Ferdan. *Modern Devlet ve Polis: Osmanlı'dan Cumhuriyet'e Toplumsal Denetimin Diyalektiği*. İstanbul: İletişim Yayınları, 2004.

Erişçi, Lütfi. *Sosyal Tarih Çalışmaları*. İstanbul: Tüstav Yayınları, 2003.

Esen, A. Kıvanç. "Tek Parti Dönemi Cami Kapatma/Satma Uygulamaları." *Tarih ve Toplum* 13 (2011): 91–158.

Eski, Mustafa. *İsmet İnönü'nün Kastamonu Gezileri*. İstanbul: Çağdaş Yayınları, 1995.

Evans, Fred. "Language and Political Agency: Derrida, Marx, and Bakhtin." *Southern Journal of Philosophy* 27/4 (1990): 505–23.

Farge, Arlette. *Subversive Words: Public Opinion in Eighteenth-Century France*. Trans. Rosemary Morris. Malden: Polity Press, 2005.

Farge, Arlette, and Jacques Revel. *The Vanishing Children of Paris: Rumor and Politics before the French Revolution*. Cambridge, MA: Harvard University Press, 1991.

Faroqhi, Suraiya. *Artisans of Empire: Crafts and Craftspeople under Ottomans*. London and New York: I. B. Tauris, 2011.

Figes, Orlando, and Boris Kolonitskii. *Interpreting the Russian Revolution: The Language and Symbols of 1917*. New Haven, CT: Yale University Press, 1999.

Fitzpatrick, Sheila. *Everyday Stalinism: Ordinary Life in Extraordinary Times: Soviet Russia in the 1930s*. New York: Oxford University Press, 2000.

Stalin's Peasants: Resistance and Survival in the Russian Village after Collectivization. New York: Oxford University Press, 1996.

Fox-Genovese, Elizabeth, and Eugene D. Genovese. "The Political Crisis of Social History: A Marxian Perspective." *Journal of Social History* 10/2 (1976): 205–20.

Fraser, Nancy. "Rethinking the Public Sphere: A Contribution to the Critique of Actually Existing Democracy." *Habermas and the Public Sphere*. Ed. Craig Calhoun, 109–42. Cambridge, MA: MIT Press, 1992.

Friedrich, Carl J., and Zbigniew Brzezinski. *Totalitarian Dictatorship and Autocracy*. Cambridge, MA: Harvard University Press, 1965.

Garnett, Lucy M. J. *Mysticism and Magic in Turkey: An Account of the Religious Doctrines, Monastic Organisation, and Ecstatic Powers of the Dervish Orders*. London: Sir Isaac Pitman & Sons, 1912.

Geertz, Clifford. *The Interpretation of Cultures*. New York: Basic Books, 1973.

Gemalmaz, Mehmet Semih. *Türk Kıyafet Hukuku ve Türban (Tarihçe, İdeoloji, Mevzuat, İçtihat, Siyaset)*. İstanbul: Legal, 2005.

Georgeon, François. *Sultan Abdülhamid*. Translated by Ali Berktay. İstanbul: Homer Kitabevi, 2006.

Ginzburg, Carlo. *The Cheese and the Worms: The Cosmos of A Sixteenth Century Miller*. Baltimore, MD: Johns Hopkins University Press, 1992.

Gluckman, Max. "Gossip and Scandal." *Current Anthropology* 4/3 (1963): 307–15.

Göksu, Emel. *1929 Dünya Ekonomik Buhranı Yıllarında İzmir ve Suç Coğrafyası.* İzmir: İzmir Büyükşehir Belediyesi Kültür Yayını, 2003.

Gözaydın, İştar. *Diyanet: Türkiye Cumhuriyetinde Dinin Tanzimi.* İstanbul: İletişim Yayınları, 2009.

Guha, Ranajit. *Elementary Aspects of Peasant Insurgency in Colonial India.* Durham, NC: Duke University Press, 1999.

Güler, Birgün Ayman, ed. *Açıklamalı Yönetim Zamandizini, 1929–1939.* Ankara: Ankara Üniversitesi Basımevi, 2007.

Gülmez, Mesut. "1932 İş Yasası Tasarısı Konusuna Amele Birliği'nin ve Madencilerin Görüşleri." *Amme İdaresi Dergisi* 17/4 (1984): 135–72.

"Amele Teali Cemiyetinin 1927 İş Yasası Tasarısına Karşı Hazırladığı 'İşçi Layihası.'" *Amme İdaresi Dergisi* 16/2 (1983): 70–86.

Türkiye'de 1936 Öncesinde İşçi Hakları. Ankara: Türkiye Yol-İş Sendikası'nın Türkiye İşçi Hakları Kitabından Ayrı Basım, 1986.

Gümüş, Cantürk. *Türk Orman Devrimi.* Ankara: Türkiye Ormancılar Derneği, 2018.

Gürbüz, A. Cenani. *Mondros'tan Milenyuma Türkiye'de İsyanlar, Olaylar ve Bölücü Faaliyetler.* İstanbul: Bilge Karınca Yayınları, 2006.

Güriz, Adnan. "Evlilik Dışı Birleşmeler ve Bu Birleşmelerden Doğan Çocuklar." *Türk Hukuku ve Toplumu Üzerine İncelemeler.* Ed. Adnan Güriz and Peter Benedict, 93–162. Ankara: Türkiye Kalkınma Vakfı Yayınları, 1974.

Güzel, M. Şehmus. "1940'larda İşgücünün (İşçilerin) Özellikleri." *Mülkiyeliler Birliği Dergisi* 119 (1990): 18–22.

Türkiye'de İşçi Hareketleri (1908–1984). İstanbul: Kaynak Yayınları, 1996.

Habermas, Jürgen. *The Structural Transformation of the Public Sphere: An Inquiry into a Category of Bourgeois Society.* Cambridge, MA: MIT Press, 1991.

Hallı, Reşat. *Türkiye Cumhuriyeti'nde Ayaklanmalar (1924–1938).* Ankara: Genelkurmay Harb Tarihi Başkanlığı, 1972.

Hathaway, Jane. *Politics of Household in Ottoman Egypt: The Rise of Qazdağlıs.* Cambridge: Cambridge University Press, 1997.

Hazar, Nurettin. *T. C. Ziraat Bankası, 1863–1983.* Ankara: T. C. Ziraat Bankası, 1986.

Hegland, Mary E. "The Power Paradox in Muslim Women's *Majales*: North West Pakistani Mourning Rituals As Sites of Contestation over Religious Politics, Ethnicity and Gender." *Gender, Politics and Islam.* Ed. Therese Saliba, Carolyn Allen and Judith A. Hovard, 95–132. Chicago: Univerity of Chicago Press, 2002.

Heper, Metin. *The State Tradition in Turkey.* Walkington: Eothen Press, 1985.

Hershlag, Z. Yehuda. *Turkey: The Challenge of Growth.* Leiden: E. J. Brill, 1968.

Hill, Christopher. *The Century of Revolution, 1603–1714.* New York and London: Norton, 1982.

Hirschman, Albert O. *Exit, Voice, and Loyalty: Responses to Decline in Firms, Organizations and States.* Cambridge, MA: Harvard University Press, 1970.

Hobsbawm, Eric. *Age of Extremes: A History of the World, 1914–1991.* New York: Vintage Books, 1994.

Bandits. New York: Pantheon Books, 1981.

"History from Below: Some Reflections." *History from Below: Studies in Popular Protest and Popular Ideology.* Ed. Frederick Krants, 13–27. Oxford and New York: Basil Blackwell, 1998.

Uncommon People: Resistance, Rebellion and Jazz. New York: New Press, 1998.

Hunt, Alan. "Rights and Social Movements: Counter-Hegemonic Strategies." *Journal of Law and Society* 17/3 (1990): 309–28.

Hunt, Lynn. *Politics, Culture and Class in the French Revolution.* Berkeley: University of California Press, 1984.

Issawi, Charles, ed. *The Economic History of the Middle East, 1800–1914: A Book of Readings.* Chicago: University of Chicago Press, 1966.

İçduygu, Ahmet, İbrahim Sirkeci and İsmail Aydıngün. "Türkiye'de İçgöç ve İçgöçün İşçi Hareketine Etkisi." *Türkiye'de İçgöç: Sorunsal Alanları ve Araştırma Yöntemleri Konferansı 6–8 Haziran 1997,* 207–44. İstanbul: Tarih Vakfı Yurt Yayınları, 1998.

İlkin, Selim. "Devletçilik Döneminin İlk Yıllarında İşçi Sorununa Yaklaşım ve 1932 İş Kanunu Tasarısı." *ODTÜ Gelişme Dergisi,* Special Issue (1978): 251–348.

İmamoğlu, Memedali. "Ödeşmek." http://nihatakkaraca.blogspot.com, May 6, 2007.

İnalcık, Halil. *Osmanlı Tarihi'nde İslâmiyet ve Devlet.* İstanbul: İş Bankası Kültür Yayınları, 2016.

İslamoğlu, Mustafa. *İslami Hareketler ve Kıyamlar Tarihi.* İstanbul: Denge Yayınları, 2003.

İslamoğlu-İnan, Huri, ed. *The Ottoman Empire and the World Economy.* Cambridge and New York: Cambridge University Press, 1987.

Jäeschke, Gotthard. "Türk Hukukunda Evlenme Aktinin Şekli." *İstanbul Üniversitesi Hukuk Fakültesi Mecmuası* 18/3–4 (1952): 1128–54.

Yeni Türkiye'de İslamcılık. Trans. H. Örs. Ankara: Bilgi Yayınevi, 1972.

Johnson, Christopher. "Economic Change and Artisan Discontent: The Tailors' History, 1800–1848." *Revolution and Reaction: 1848 and the Second French Republic*. Ed. Roger Price, 87–114. London: Croom Helm, 1975.

Jwaideh, Wadie. *Kürt Milliyetçiliğinin Tarihi: Kökenleri ve Gelişimi.* Introduction by Martin van Bruinessen. 5th ed. İstanbul: İletişim Yayınları, 2008.

Kahraman, Kemal. *Millî Mücadele.* İstanbul: Ağaç Yayıncılık, 1992.

Kandiyoti, Deniz. "Women, Islam, and the State." *Political Islam.* Ed. Joel Beinin and Joe Stork, 185–93. Berkeley and Los Angeles: University of California Press, 1997.

Kara, İsmail. *Cumhuriyet Türkiyesi'nde Bir Mesele Olarak İslâm.* Vol. 1. İstanbul: Dergâh Yayınları, 2014.

Kara, Mustafa. *Din, Hayat ve Sanat Açısından Tekkeler ve Zaviyeler.* İstanbul: Dergâh Yayınları, 1999.

Metinlerle Günümüz Tasavvuf Hareketleri, 1839–2000. İstanbul: Dergâh Yayınevi, 2010.

Karaalioğlu, Seyit Kemal. *Türk Romanları.* İstanbul: İnkılap Kitabevi, 1989.

Karakışla, Yavuz Selim. "The 1908 Strike Wave in the Ottoman Empire." *Turkish Studies Association Bulletin* 16/2 (1992): 153–77.

Karaömerlioğlu, M. Asım. "Bir Tepeden Reform Denemesi: Çiftçiyi Topraklandırma Kanunun Hikayesi." *Birikim* 107 (1998): 31–7.

Orada Bir Köy Var Uzakta: Erken Cumhuriyet Döneminde Köycü Söylem. İstanbul: İletişim Yayınları, 2006.

"The People's Houses and the Cult of the Peasant in Turkey." *Middle Eastern Studies* 34/4 (1998): 67–91.

Karatepe, Şükrü. *Türkiye'de Tek Parti Dönemi.* İstanbul: İz Yayıncılık, 1997.

Karpat, Kemal. *Türkiye'de Toplumsal Dönüşüm.* Ankara: İmge Kitabevi, 2003.

Karras, Alan L. *Smuggling: Contraband and Corruption in World History.* New York: Rowman & Littlefield, 2012.

Katouzian, Homa. "State and Society under Reza Shah." *Men of Order, Authoritarian Modernization under Atatürk and Reza Shah.* Ed. Touraj Atabaki and Erik J. Zürcher, 13–43. London and New York: I. B. Tauris, 2004.

Katznelson, Ira. "Working Class Formation: Constructing Class and Comparisons." *Working-Class Formation: Nineteenth-Century Patterns in Western Europe and the United States.* Ed. I. Katznelson and A. R. Zolberg, 3–41. Princeton, NJ: Princeton University Press, 1986.

Kaye, Harvey J. *The British Marxist Historians: An Introductory Analysis.* New York: St. Martin's Press, 1984.

Kazgan, Gülten. "Türk Ekonomisinde 1927–1935 Depresyonu, Kapital Birikimi ve Örgütleşmeler." *Atatürk Döneminin Ekonomik ve Toplumsal Sorunları Sempozyumu,* 231–74. İstanbul: İktisadi ve Ticari İlimler Akademisi Mezunları Derneği, 1977.

Keleş, Ruşen. *100 Soruda Türkiye'de Şehirleşme, Konut ve Gecekondu.* İstanbul: Gerçek Yayınevi, 1972.

Kerkvliet, Benedict J. Tria. *Power of Everyday Politics: How Vietnamese Peasants Transformed National Policy.* Ithaca, NY: Cornell University Press, 2005.

Kershaw, Ian. *The Nazi Dictatorship Problems and Perspectives of Interpretation.* London: Arnold Press, 2000.

Popular Opinion and Political Dissent in the Third Reich: Bavaria 1933–1945. Oxford: Oxford University Press, 2002.

Keskinoğlu, İvrem. "Türkiye'de Grevler." *Türkiye Sendikacılık Ansiklopedisi.* Vol 1, 492–6. İstanbul: Kültür Bakanlığı & Türkiye Ekonomik ve Toplumsal Tarih Vakfı, 1996–8.

Kévorkian, Raymond. *Armenian Genocide: A Complete History.* London: I. B. Tauris, 2011.

Keyder, Çağlar. *State and Class in Turkey: A Study in Capitalist Development.* London; New York: Verso, 1987.

"Türk Demokrasisinin Ekonomi Politiği." *Geçiş Sürecinde Türkiye.* Ed. Irvin C. Shick and Ertuğrul A. Tonak, 38–75. İstanbul: Belge Yayınları, 1998.

"Türk Tarımında Küçük Meta Üretiminin Yerleşmesi (1946–1960)." *Türkiye'de Tarımsal Yapılar.* Ed. Şevket Pamuk and Zafer Toprak, 163–75. Ankara: Yurt Yayınevi, 1988.

Khoury, Dina Rizk. *State and Provincial Society in the Ottoman Empire, 1540–1834.* Cambridge: Cambridge University Press, 1997.

Kılıç, M. Zeki. *Erzurum Fıkraları.* İstanbul: Erzurum Kitaplığı, 2001.

Kıray, Mübeccel B. *Toplumsal Yapı ve Toplumsal Değişme,* İstanbul: Bağlam Yayınları, 1999.

Kısakürek, Necip Fazıl. *Son Devrin Din Mazlumları.* İstanbul: BD Yayınları, 1974.

Kıvılcımlı, Hikmet. *İhtiyat Kuvvet Milliyet (Şark),* İstanbul: Yol Yayınları, 1979.

Türkiye İşçi Sınıfının Sosyal Varlığı. İstanbul: Sosyal İnsan Yayınları, 2008.

Yol 2. İstanbul: Bibliotek Yayınları, 1992.

Kinross, Lord. *Mustafa Kemal: Bir Milletin Yeniden Doğuşu.* Trans. N. Yeğinobalı and A. Tezel. İstanbul: Sander Yayınevi, 1966.

Koca, Hüseyin. *Yakın Tarihten Günümüze Hükümetlerin Doğu-Güneydoğu Anadolu Politikaları: Umumi Müfettişlikten Olağanüstü Hal Bölge Valiliğine.* Konya: Mikro Basım Yayım, 1998.

Koç, Bekir. "Osmanlı Devletindeki Orman ve Koruların Tasarruf Yöntemleri ve İdarelerine İlişkin Bir Araştırma." *OTAM* 10 (2000): 139–58.

Koç, Yıldırım. *100 Soruda Türkiye'de İşçi Sınıfı ve Sendikacılık Hareketi Tarihi.* İstanbul: Gerçek Yayınevi, 1998.

"1923–1950 Döneminde CHP'nin İşçi Sınıfı Korkusu." *Mülkiyeliler Birliği Dergisi* 170 (1994): 43–4.

"Türkiye'de 1923–1946 Döneminde Mülksüzleşme ve İşçi Sınıfının Oluşumu." *Mülkiyeliler Birliği Dergisi* 174 (1994): 14–28.

Türkiye İşçi Sınıfı ve Sendikacılık Tarihi, Olaylar- Değerlendirmeler. Ankara: Yol-iş Sendikası Yayınları, 1996.

Koçak, Cemil. *Tek Parti Döneminde Muhalif Sesler.* İstanbul: İletişim Yayınları, 2011.

Koraltürk, Murat. "İşçi Sicil Dosyalarının Dili: Aslan ve Eskihisar Çimento Fabrikaları İşçi Sicil Dosyalarından Notlar." *Bilanço '98, 75 Yılda Çarkları Döndürenler.* Ed. Oya Baydar and Gülay Dinçel, 221–7. İstanbul: Tarih Vakfı Yayınları, 1999.

"Şirket-i Hayriye Tekaüd Sandığı." *Türkiye Sendikacılık Ansiklopedisi.* Vol. 3, 126–7. İstanbul: Kültür Bakanlığı and İstanbul: Türkiye Ekonomik ve Toplumsal Tarih Vakfı, 1996–8.

Korniyenko, Radmir Platonovich. *The Labor Movement in Turkey (1918–1963).* Washington, DC: US Department of Commerce, Clearinghouse for Federal Scientific and Technical Information, Joint Publications Research Service, 1967.

Köker, Levent. *Modernleşme, Kemalizm ve Demokrasi.* İstanbul: İletişim Yayınları, 1990.

Köymen, Oya. *Kapitalizm ve Köylülük: Ağalar, Üretenler, Patronlar.* İstanbul: Yordam Kitap, 2008.

Kumar, Arun. "Beyond Muffled Murmurs of Dissent? Kisan Rumour in Colonial Bihar." *Journal of Peasant Studies* 28/1 (2000): 95–125.

Kuru, Ahmet T. *Secularism and State Policies toward Religion: The United States, France, and Turkey.* Cambridge: Cambridge University Press, 2009.

Kuruç, Bilsay. *Belgelerle Türkiye İktisat Politikası.* Vol. 1. Ankara: Ankara Üniversitesi Basımevi, 1988.

Belgelerle Türkiye İktisat Politikası. Vol. 2. Ankara: Ankara Üniversitesi Siyasal Bilgiler Fakültesi Yayınları, 1993.

Kutay, Cemal. "Halil Menteşe'nin Tuz Hikâyesi." *Tarih Sohbetleri* 5, 1967: 16–18.

Kurtuluşun ve Cumhuriyetin Manevî Mimarları. Ankara: Diyanet İşleri Başkanlığı Yayınları, 1973.

Kutluk, Halil. *Türkiye Ormancılığı İle İlgili Tarihi Vesikalar.* Vol. 2. Ankara: Ongun Kardeşler Matbaası, 1967.

Küçük, Hülya. *Kurtuluş Savaşında Bektaşiler.* İstanbul: Kitap Yayınevi, 2003.

"Sufi Reactions against the Reforms after Turkey's National Struggle: How a Nightingale Turned into a Crow." *The State and the Subaltern: Modernization, Society and the State in Turkey and Iran.* Ed. Touraj Atabaki, 123–42. London and New York: I. B. Tauris, 2007.

Küçükerman, Önder. *Batı Anadolu'daki Türk Halıcılık Geleneği İçinde İzmir Limanı ve Isparta Halı Fabrikası.* Ankara: Sümerbank/ Sümerhalı, 1990.

Geleneksel Türk Sanayii ve Beykoz Fabrikası. Ankara: Sümerbank, 1988.

Lasswell, Harold D. *Politics: Who Gets What, When, How?* Cleveland, OH: World, 1958.

Lewis, Bernard. *The Emergence of Modern Turkey.* London and New York: Oxford University Press, 1961.

Lindisfarne, Nancy. *Elhamdülillah Laikiz: Cinsiyet, İslâm ve Türk Cumhuriyetçiliği.* Trans. Selda Somuncuoğlu. İstanbul: İletişim Yayınları, 2002.

Lloyd, Peter. *Slums of Hope: Shanty Towns of the Third World.* Middlesex: Penguin, 1979.

Lockman, Zachary, ed. *Workers and Working Classes in the Middle East: Struggles, Histories, Historiographies.* New York: State University of New York Press, 1993.

Longuenesse, Elisabeth. "Labor in Syria: The Emergence of New Identities." *The Social History of Labor in the Middle East.* Ed. E. Jay Goldberg, 99–129. Boulder, CO: Westview Press, 1996.

Ludden, David, ed. *Reading Subaltern Studies: Critical History, Contested Meaning and the Globalization of South Asia.* London: Anthem, 2002.

Lüdtke, Alf. "What Happened to the 'Fiery Red Glow'? Workers' Experiences and German Fascism." *The History of Everyday Life: Reconstructing Historical Experiences and Ways of Life.* Ed. Alf Lüdtke. Trans. William Templer, 198–251. Princeton, NJ: Princeton University Press, 1995.

"What Is the History of Everyday Life and Who Are Its Practitioners?" *The History of Everyday Life: Reconstructing Historical Experiences and Ways of Life.* Ed. Alf Lüdtke. Trans. William Templer, 3–40. Princeton, NJ: Princeton University Press, 1995.

Magnarella, Paul J. *Anatolia's Loom: Studies in Turkish Culture, Society, Politics and Law.* İstanbul: ISIS Press, 1998.

Mah, Harold. "Phantasies of the Public Sphere: Rethinking the Habermas of Historians." *Journal of Modern History* 72 (2000): 153–82.

Mahir-Metinsoy, Elif. *Mütareke Dönemi İstanbulu'nda Moda ve Kadın, 1918–1923.* İstanbul: Libra Books, 2014.

Ottoman Women during World War I: Everyday Experiences, Politics and Conflict. Cambridge: Cambridge University Press, 2017.

Makal, Ahmet. *Ameleden İşçiye: Erken Cumhuriyet Dönemi Emek Tarihi Çalışmaları.* İstanbul: İletişim Yayınları, 2007.

Türkiye'de Çok Partili Dönemde Çalışma İlişkileri: 1946–1963. Ankara: İmge Kitabevi, 2002.

Türkiye'de Tek Partili Dönemde Çalışma İlişkileri: 1920–1946. Ankara: İmge Kitabevi, 1999.

Marcus, Abraham. *The Middle East on the Eve of Modernity: Aleppo in the Eighteenth Century.* New York: Columbia University Press, 1989.

Mardin, Şerif. "Religion and Secularism in Turkey." *Atatürk: The Founder of a Modern State.* Eds. Ergun Özbudun and Ali Kazancıgil, 191–218. London. C. Hurst and Company, 1981.

Türkiye'de Toplum ve Siyaset, Makaleler. Vol. 1. İstanbul: İletişim Yayınları, 2002.

Margulies, Roni, and Ergin Yıldızoğlu. "The Resurgence of Islam and the Welfare Party in Turkey." *Political Islam.* Eds. Joel Beinin and Joe Stork, 144–53. Berkeley: University of California Press, 1997.

Massicard, Elise. "The Incomplete Civil Servant? The Figure of the Neighbourhood Headman (Muhtar)." *Order and Compromise: Government Practices in Turkey from the Late Ottoman Empire to the Early 21st Century.* Ed. Marc Aymes, Benjamin Gourisse and Elise Massicard, 256–90. Leiden and Boston: Brill, 2015.

May, Trevor. *Smugglers and Smuggling.* Oxford: Shire, 2014.

McDowall, David. *A Modern History of the Kurds.* London: I. B. Tauris, 2004.

McGowen, Randal. "Power and Humanity, or Foucault among Historians." *Reassessing Foucault: Power, Medicine, and the Body.* Ed. Colin Jones and Roy Porter, 91–112. New York: Routledge, 1998.

Metinsoy, Murat. "'Blat, Stalin'den Büyüktür': Erken Dönem Sovyet Sosyal Tarihçiliğinde Revizyonizm." *Tarih ve Toplum* 7 (2008): 181–244.

"Everyday Resistance and Selective Adaptation to the Hat Reform in Early Republican Turkey." *International Journal of Turcologia* 8/16 (2013): 7–49.

"Everyday Resistance to Unveiling and Flexible Secularism in Early Republican Turkey." *Anti-veiling Campaigns in the Muslim World:*

Gender, Modernism, and the Politics of Dress. Ed. Stephanie Cronin, 86–117. New York: Routledge, 2014.

"Fragile Hegemony, Flexible Authoritarianism and Governing from Below: Politicians' Report in Early Republican Turkey." *International Journal of Middle East Studies* 43/4 (2011): 699–719.

"İkinci Dünya Savaşı Yıllarında Zonguldak Kömür Ocaklarında Ücretli İşçi Mükellefiyeti ve İşçi Direnişi." *Zonguldak Kent Tarihi Bienali'nden Seçmeler,* 93–112. Zonguldak: ZOKEV & TMMOB, 2005.

İkinci Dünya Savaşı'nda Türkiye: Gündelik Yaşamda Devlet ve Toplum. İstanbul: Homer Kitabevi, 2007 (Revised 3rd ed. İş Bankası Kültür Yayınları, 2020).

"Kemalizmin Taşrası: Erken Cumhuriyet Taşrasında Parti, Devlet ve Toplum." *Toplum ve Bilim* 118 (2010): 124–64.

Migdal, Joel S. "Finding the Meeting Ground of Fact and Fiction: Some Reflections on Turkish Modernization." *Rethinking Modernity and National Identity.* Ed. Sibel Bozdoğan and Reşat Kasaba, 252–60. Washington, DC: University of Washington Press, 1997.

State in Society: Studying How States and Societies Transform and Constitute One Another. Cambridge: Cambridge University Press, 2001.

Strong Societies and Weak States: State-Society Relations and State Capabilities in the Third World. Princeton, NJ: Princeton University Press, 1988.

Mouffe, Chantal. "Hegemony and Ideology in Gramsci." *Gramsci and Marxist Theory.* Ed. Chantal Mouffe, 168–204. London and Boston: Routledge & Kegan Paul, 1979.

Nawid, Senzil K. *Religious Response to Social Change in Afghanistan, 1919–1929: King Amanallah and the Afghan Ulama.* Costa Mesa, CA: Mazda, 2000.

Nirun, Nihat. "Suç Hadisesinin Sosyal Sebepleri Üzerine Bir Araştırma." *Suut Kemal Yetkin'e Armağan,* 121–88. Ankara: Hacettepe Üniversitesi Yayınları, 1968.

Norton, John. "Faith and Fashion in Turkey." *Languages of Dress in the Middle East.* Ed. Nancy Lindisfarne-Tapper and Bruce Ingham, 149–77. London: Curzon and the Centre of Near and Middle Eastern Studies, SOAS, 1997.

Oğuz, Şeyda. *1927 Adana Demiryolu Grevi.* İstanbul: TÜSTAV, 2005.

Olson, Robert W. *The Emergence of Kurdish Nationalism and the Sheikh Said Rebellion, 1880–1925.* Austin: University of Texas Press, 1989.

O'Malley, Pat. "Social Bandits, Modern Capitalism and the Traditional Peasantry: A Critique of Hobsbawm." *Journal of Peasant Studies* 6/4 (1979): 489–501.

Owen, Roger, and Şevket Pamuk. *A History of Middle East Economies in the Twentieth Century*. London: I. B. Tauris, 1998.

Ökten, Ertuğrul. "Cumhuriyet'in İlk Yıllarında Tütün." *Tütün Kitabı*. Ed. Emine Gürsoy Naskali, 155–90. İstanbul: Kitabevi, 2003.

Önder, İzzettin. "Cumhuriyet Döneminde Tarım Kesimine Uygulanan Vergi Politikası." *Türkiye'de Tarımsal Yapılar: [Bildiriler]*. Ed. Şevket Pamuk and Zafer Toprak, 113–33. Ankara: Yurt Yayınları, 1988.

Öz, Esat. *Tek Parti Yönetimi ve Siyasal Katılım*. Ankara: Gündoğan Yayınları, 1992.

Özbay, Ferhunde. *Aile, Kent ve Nüfus*. İstanbul: İletişim Yayınları, 2015.

Özbek, Nadir. "Kemalist Rejim ve Popülizmin Sınırları: Büyük Buhran ve Buğday Alım Politikaları." *Toplum ve Bilim*, 96 (2003): 219–40.

Özcan, Zeynep. *İnönü Dönemi Dini Hayat*. İstanbul: Dem Yayınları, 2015.

Özçelik, Mustafa. *1830–1950 Arasında Tütüncülerin Tarihi*. İstanbul: Tüstav Yayınları, 2003.

Özköse, Kadir. "Kurtuluş Savaşı'na Katılan Din Bilginleri ve Tekkeler." *Somuncu Baba* 77 (2007): 18–21.

Özoğlu, Hakan. *Kurdish Notables and the Ottoman State: Evolving Identities, Competing Loyalties, and Shifting Boundaries*. New York: State University of New York Press, 2004.

Öztürk, Kazım. *Türk Parlamento Tarihi (1927–1931)*. Vol. 1. Ankara: Türkiye Büyük Millet Meclisi Vakfı Yayınları, 1995.

Öztürk, Saygı. *İsmet Paşa'nın Kürt Raporu*. 5th ed. İstanbul: Doğan Kitap, 2008.

Öztürk, Serdar. *Cumhuriyet Türkiye'sinde Kahvehane ve İktidar, 1930–1945*. İstanbul: Kırmızı Yayınları, 2005.

Paine, Robert. "What Is Gossip About? An Alternative Hypothesis." *Man 2/2* (1967): 278–85.

Pamuk, Orhan. *Istanbul: Memories and the City*. London: Faber & Faber, 2006.

Pamuk, Şevket. "Intervention during the Great Depression: Another Look at Turkish Experience." *The Mediterranean Response to Globalization before 1950*. Ed. Şevket Pamuk and Jeffrey G. Williamson, 321–39. New York: Routledge, 2000.

"Son 200 Yılda Türkiye'de ve Dünyada Sağlık ve Eğitim." *Kalkınma İktisadının Penceresinden Türkiye'ye Bakmak*. Ed. Hasan Cömert, Emre Özçelik and Ebru Voyvoda, 11–26. İstanbul: İletişim Yayınları, 2017.

Uneven Centuries: Economic Development of Turkey since 1800. Princeton, NJ: Princeton University Press, 2018.

"War, State Economic Policies and Resistance by Agricultural Producers in Turkey, 1939–1945." *Peasants and Politics in the Middle East*. Ed.

Farhad Kazemi and John Waterbury, 125–42. Miami: Florida International University Press, 1991.

Parla, Taha, and Andrew Davison. *Corporatist Ideology in Kemalist Turkey: Progress or Order?* Syracuse, NY: Syracuse University Press, 2004.

Peirce, Leslie. *The Imperial Harem: Women and Sovereignty in the Ottoman Empire.* New York and Oxford: Oxford University Press, 1993.

Perry, Elizabeth J. *Challenging the Mandate of Heaven: Social Protests and State Power in China.* New York: M. E. Sharpe, 2002.

Peters, Rudolph. "The Battered Dervishes of Bab Zuwayla: A Religious Riot in Eighteenth-Century Cairo." *Eighteenth-Century Renewal and Reform in Islam.* Ed. Nehemia Levtzion and John O. Voll, 93–115. Syracuse, NY: Syracuse University Press, 1987.

Peukert, Detlev J. K. *Inside Nazi Germany: Conformity, Opposition, and Racism in Everyday Life.* Trans. Richard Deveson. New Haven, CT: Yale University Press, 1987.

Philipson, David. *Smuggling: A History 1700–1970.* Newton Abbot: David & Charles, 1973.

Pipes, Richard. *Russia under the Old Regime.* New York: Scribner, 1974.

Poullada, Leon P. *Reform and Rebellion in Afghanistan, 1919–1929: King Amanullah's Failure to Modernize a Tribal Society.* New York: Cornell University Press, 1973.

Quataert, Donald. "The Commercialization of Agriculture in Ottoman Turkey." *International Journal of Turkish Studies* 1 (1980): 38–55.

Ottoman Manufacturing in the Age of the Industrial Revolution. Cambridge: Cambridge University Press, 1993.

Social Disintegration and Popular Resistance in the Ottoman Empire, 1881–1908: Reactions to European Economic Penetration. New York: New York University Press, 1983.

"Workers and the State during the Late Ottoman Empire." *The State and the Subaltern: Modernization, Society and the State in Turkey and Iran.* Ed. Touraj Atabaki, 17–30. New York: I. B. Tauris, 2007.

Quataert, Donald, and E. J. Zürcher, eds. *Osmanlı'dan Cumhuriyet Türkiye'sine İşçiler, 1839–1950.* Trans. Cahide Ekiz, 155–95. İstanbul: İletişim Yayınları, 1998.

Rudé, George F. E. *The Crowd in History: A Study of Popular Disturbances in France and England.* New York: Wiley, 1964.

Ruff, Julius R. *Violence in Early Modern Europe, 1500–1800.* Cambridge: Cambridge University Press, 2001.

Sadi, Kerim. *Türkiye'de Sosyalizmin Tarihine Katkı.* İstanbul: İletişim Yayınları, 1994.

Saraçoğlu, Fatih. "1930–1939 Döneminde Vergi Politikası." *Maliye Dergisi* 157 (2009): 131–49.

Sarıkoyuncu, Ali. *Millî Mücadelede Din Adamları*. Vol. 2. Ankara: Diyanet İşleri Başkanlığı, 1997.

Saymen, Ferit Hakkı. *Türkiye'de Sosyal Sigortaların Gelişme Hareketleri ve Yeni Temayülleri*. İstanbul: İsmail Akgün Matbaası, 1953.

Scott, James C. *The Art of Not Being Governed: An Anarchist History of the Upland Southeast Asia*. New Haven, CT: Yale University Press, 2010.

——. *Domination and the Arts of Resistance: Hidden Transcripts*. New Haven, CT: Yale University Press, 1990.

——. *The Moral Economy of the Peasant: Rebellion and Subsistence in South-East Asia*. New Haven, CT: Yale University Press, 1976.

——. *Weapons of the Weak: Everyday Forms of Peasant Resistance*. New Haven, CT: Yale University Press, 1985.

Scott, Richard B. *The Village Headman in Turkey: A Case Study*. Ankara: Institute of Public Administration for Turkey and the Middle East, 1968.

Shanin, Teodor, ed. *Peasants and Peasant Societies*. Middlesex: Penguin, 1971.

Shaw, Stanford, and Ezel Kural Shaw. *History of the Ottoman Empire and Modern Turkey*. Cambridge: Cambridge University Press, 1977.

Silier, Oya. *Türkiye'de Tarımsal Yapının Gelişimi (1923–1938)*. İstanbul: Boğaziçi Üniversitesi İdari Bilimler Fakültesi, 1981.

Steinberg, Marc W. *Fighting Words: Working-Class Formation, Collective Action, and Discourse in Early Nineteenth-Century England*. Ithaca, NY: Cornell University Press, 1999.

Stirling, Paul. *Culture and Economy: Changes in Turkish Villages*. Huntingdon: Eothen, 1993.

Strohmeier, Martin, and Lale Yalçın-Heckmann. *Kürtler: Tarih, Siyaset, Kültür*. İstanbul: Tarih Vakfı Yurt Yayınları, 2013.

Suny, Ronald Grigor, Fatma Müge Göçek and Norman M. Naimark. *A Question of Genocide: Armenians and Turks at the End of the Ottoman Empire*. Oxford: Oxford University Press, 2011.

Sülker, Kemal. *100 Soruda Türkiye'de İşçi Hareketleri*. İstanbul: Gerçek Yayınevi, 1973.

"Süreyyapaşa Dokuma Fabrikası Grevi." *Türkiye Sendikacılık Ansiklopedisi*. Vol. 3. Ankara: Kültür Bakanlığı & İstanbul: Türkiye Ekonomik ve Toplumsal Tarih Vakfı, 1996–8.

Szyliowicz, Joseph S. *Political Change in Rural Turkey: Erdemli*. The Hague: Mouton, 1966.

Şimşir, Bilâl N. *Kürtçülük II, 1924–1999*. Ankara: Bilgi Yayınevi, 2009.

Talas, Cahit. *İçtimai İktisat*. Ankara: A. Ü. Siyasal Bilgiler Fakültesi Yayınları, 1961.

Tan, Mine Göğüş, Özlem Şahin, Mustafa Sever and Aksu Bora. *Cumhuriyet'te Çocuktular*. İstanbul: Boğaziçi Üniversitesi Yayınları, 2007.

Tapper, Richard. *Islam in Modern Turkey*. London: I. B. Tauris, 1991.

Taşkıran, Tezer. *Cumhuriyetin 50. Yılında Türk Kadın Hakları*. Ankara: Başbakanlık Basımevi, 1973.

Tauger, Mark B. "Soviet Peasants and Collectivization, 1930–1939, Resistance and Adaptation." *Journal of Peasant Studies* 31/3–4 (2004): 427–56.

Tekeli, İlhan, and Selim İlkin. *Uygulamaya Geçerken Türkiye'de Devletçiliğin Oluşumu*. Ankara: Ortadoğu Teknik Üniversitesi, 1982.

Teymur, Atanur. *Kahvede Konuştular Camide Buluştular*. İstanbul: Fatih Yayınevi, 1970.

Tezel, Yahya Sezai. *Cumhuriyet Döneminin İktisadi Tarihi (1923–1950)*. 5th ed. İstanbul: Tarih Vakfı Yurt Yayınları, 2002.

Thompson, E. P. *Customs in Common*. New York: New Press, 1991.

"Eighteenth-Century English Society: Class Struggle without Class?" *Journal of Social History* 3/2 (1978): 133–65.

The Making of the English Working Class. New York: Vintage Books, 1966.

Timur, Hıfzı. "Civil Marriage in Turkey, Difficulties, Causes, and Remedies." *UNESCO International Social Science Bulletin* 9/1 (1957): 34–6.

Timur, Tamer. *Osmanlı Çalışmaları*. Ankara: İmge Yayınları, 2010.

Toledano, Ehud R. "The Emergence of Ottoman-Local Elites in the Middle East and North Africa (1700–1900)." *Middle Eastern Politics and Ideas: A History from Within*. Ed. Illan Pappe and Moshe Ma'oz, 145–62. New York: I. B. Tauris, 1997.

"The Imperial Eunuchs of İstanbul: From Africa to the Heart of Islam." *Middle Eastern Studies* 20/3 (1984): 379–90.

Toprak, Binnaz. "Dinci Sağ." *Geçiş Sürecinde Türkiye*. Ed. Irvin C. Schick and E. Ahmet Tonak, 237–54. İstanbul: Belge Yayınları, 1998.

Toprak, Zafer. *Darwin'den Dersim'e: Cumhuriyet ve Antropoloji*. İstanbul: Doğan Kitap, 2012.

İttihat Terakki ve Cihan Harbi: Savaş Ekonomisi ve Türkiye'de Devletçilik, 1914–1918. İstanbul: Homer Kitabevi, 2003.

"Şirketi Hayriye Amele Cemiyeti ve 1925 Grevi." *Toplumsal Tarih* 30 (1996): 6–14.

"Tesettürden Telebbüse ya da Çarşaf veya Elbise-Milli Moda ve Çarşaf." *Tombak* 19 (1998): 52–63.

Toydemir, Sedat. "Türkiye'de İş İhtilaflarının Tarihçesi ve Bugünkü Durumu." *İktisat ve İçtimaiyat Enstitüsü, İçtimai Siyaset Konferansları Dördüncü Kitaptan Ayrı Basım.* İstanbul: İsmail Akgün Matbaası, 1951.

Tunaya, Tarık Zafer. *İslamcılık Akımı.* İstanbul: İstanbul Bilgi Üniversitesi, 2003.

Türkiye'nin Siyasi Hayatında Batılılaşma Hareketleri. Vols. 1–2. İstanbul: Cumhuriyet, 1999.

Tunçay, Mete, ed. *Arif Oruç'un Yarını (1933).* İstanbul: İletişim Yayınları, 1991.

Türkiye Cumhuriyeti'nde Tek-Parti Yönetimi'nin Kurulması (1923–1931). İstanbul: Tarih Vakfı Yurt Yayınları, 2005.

Türkiye'de Sol Akımlar, 1925–1936. İstanbul: BDS Yayınları, 1991.

Turan, Namık Sinan. "Modernleşme Olgusunun Osmanlı Toplum Yaşamına Yansımaları ve Ta'addüd-i Zevcat (Çokeşlilik) Sorunu." *Yakın Dönem Türkiye Araştırmaları* 4/7 (2004): 117–52.

Turhan, Mümtaz. *Kültür Değişmeleri. Sosyal Psikoloji Bakımından Bir Tetkik.* Ankara: Altınordu Yayınları, 2016.

Türk Ekonomisinin 50. Yılı. İstanbul: İstanbul İktisadi ve Ticari İlimler Akademisi, Fatih Yayınevi, 1973.

Türkeş, Mustafa. *Kadro Hareketi: Ulusçu Sol Bir Akım.* Ankara: İmge Kitabevi, 1999.

Unger, Aryeh L. "The Public Opinion Reports in Nazi Germany." *Public Opinion Quarterly* 29/4 (1965–6): 565–82.

Uyar, Hakkı. "Çarşaf, Peçe ve Kafes Üzerine Bazı Notlar." *Toplumsal Tarih* 33 (1996): 6–11.

"Devletin İşçi Sınıfı ve Örgütlenme Girişimi: CHP İzmir İşçi ve Esnaf Cemiyetleri Birliği (1935)." *Tarih ve Toplum* 160 (1997): 14–20.

Ünder, Hasan. "Atatürk İmgesinin Siyasal Yaşamdaki Rolü." *Modern Türkiye'de Siyasi Düşünce: Kemalizm.* Vol. 2, 138–55. İstanbul: İletişim Yayınları, 2002.

Üngör, Uğur Ümit. "Rethinking the Violence of Pacification: State Formation and Bandits in Turkey, 1914–1937." *Comparative Studies in Society and History* 54/4 (2012): 746–69.

Üstel, Füsun. *"Makbul Vatandaş"ın Peşinde: II. Meşrutiyet'ten Bugüne Vatandaşlık Eğitimi.* 4th ed. İstanbul: İletişim Yayınları, 2009.

Vakkasoğlu, Vehbi. *Maneviyat Dünyamızda İz Bırakanlar.* 19th ed. İstanbul: Nesil Yayınları, 2006.

Vali, Abbas. *Kürt Milliyetçiliğinin Kökenleri.* İstanbul: Avesta, 2005.

Van Bruinessen, Martin. *Agha, Shaikh and State: Social and Political Structures of Kurdistan.* London: Zed Books, 1992.

Kürdistan Üzerine Yazılar. İstanbul: İletişim Yayınları, 2002.

Van Millingen, Julius R. and Sirdar Ikbal Ali Shah. *Turkey*. London: A&C Black, 1932.

Van Os, Nicole. "Polygamy before and after the Introduction of the Swiss Civil Code in Turkey." *The State and Subaltern: Modernization, Society, and the State in Turkey and Iran*. Ed. Touraj Atabaki, 179–98. New York: I. B. Tauris, 2007.

Varlık, M. Bülent. "İzmir İşçi-Esnaf Kurumlar Birliği Yardım Talimatnameleri (1935–1936)." *Kebikeç* 4 (1996): 195–201.

"İzmir Sanayi İşçileri Birliği-1932." *Mülkiyeliler Birliği Dergisi* 155 (1995): 35–40.

Vatter, Sherry. "Militant Journeymen in Nineteenth Century Damascus: Implications for the Middle Eastern Labor History Agenda." *Workers and Working Classes in the Middle East: Struggles, Histories, Historiographies*. Ed. Zachary Lockman, 1–21, New York: State University of New York Press, 1994.

Veldet, Turan. *30. Yılında Türkiye Şeker Sanayi*. Ankara: Doğuş Ltd. Şirketi Matbaası, 1958.

Viola, Lynne. *Peasant Rebels under Stalin: Collectivization and Culture of Peasant Resistance*. New York: Oxford University Press, 1996.

Weber, Eugen. *Peasants into Frenchmen: The Modernization of Rural France, 1870–1914*. Stanford, CA: Stanford University Press, 1976.

Webster, Donald Everett. *The Turkey of Atatürk: Social Process in the Turkish Reformation*. Philadelphia, PA: American Academy of Political and Social Science, 1939.

White, Richard. "Outlaw Gangs of the Middle Border: American Social Bandits." *Western Historical Quarterly* 12 (1981): 387–408.

Wolf, Eric R. *Peasant Wars of the Twentieth Century*. New York: Harper & Row, 1969.

Wrigley, Richard. *The Politics of Appearances: Representations of Dress in Revolutionary France*. New York: Berg, 2002.

Yağcı, İsmail. "Tuz, Tahta Kaşık Kaçakçılığı ve Yol Parası." July 18, 2007. www.turkiyegazetesi.com.tr

Yalman [Yalgın], Ali Rıza. *Cenupta Türkmen Oymakları*. Vol. 1. Ankara: Kültür Bakanlığı Yayınları, 1977.

Yavuz, Erdal. "Sanayideki İşgücünün Durumu, 1923–40." *Osmanlı'dan Cumhuriyet Türkiye'sine İşçiler, 1839–1950*. Ed. Donald Quataert and Erik Jan Zürcher. Trans. Cahide Ekiz, 155–95. İstanbul: İletişim Yayınları, 1998.

Yetkin, Çetin. *Serbest Cumhuriyet Fırkası Olayı*. İstanbul: Karacan Yayınları, 1982.

Yetkin, Sabri. *Ege'de Eşkıyalar*. İstanbul: Tarih Vakfı Yurt Yayınları, 2003.

Yılmaz, Hale. *Becoming Turkish: Nationalist Reforms and Cultural Negotiations in Early Republican Turkey, 1923–1945.* New York: Syracuse University Press, 2013.

Yılmaz, Mustafa, and Yasemin Doğaner. *Cumhuriyet Döneminde Sansür, 1923–1973.* Ankara: Siyasal Kitabevi, 2007.

Yılmaz, Naşit. *Türkiye'de Tütün Eksperliği Mesleği ve Tarihi Gelişimi.* İzmir: Tütün Eksperleri Derneği, 1995.

[Yörükan], Yusuf Ziya. *İslam Dini.* İstanbul: Kanaat Kütüphanesi, 1931.

Yurtsever, Cezmi. *Kadirli Tarihi.* Osmaniye: Kadirli Hizmet Birliği Kültür Yayınları, 1999.

Yükselen, İ. Hakkı. "1924 İstanbul Tramvay İşçileri Grevleri." *Türkiye Sendikacılık Ansiklopedisi.* Vol. 2, 66–9. İstanbul: Kültür Bakanlığı & Türkiye Ekonomik ve Toplumsal Tarih Vakfı, 1996–8.

Zahedi, Ashraf. "Concealing and Revealing Female Hair: Veiling Dynamics in Contemporary Iran." *The Veil: Women Writers on Its History, Lore and Politics.* Ed. Jennifer Heath, 250–65. Berkeley and Los Angeles: University of California Press, 2008.

Zürcher, Erik Jan. *Political Opposition in the Early Turkish Republic: The Progressive Republican Party, 1924–1925.* Leiden: E. J. Brill, 1991.

Turkey: A Modern History. London: I. B. Tauris, 2004.

Index